OUR DAILY BREAD

OUR DAILY BREAD

366 DEVOTIONAL MEDITATIONS

by

M. R. DE HAAN, M.D.

and

HENRY G. BOSCH

Editor and Co-Author

ZondervanPublishingHouse

Grand Rapids, Michigan

A Division of HarperCollinsPublishers

OUR DAILY BREAD
Copyright © 1959, 1988 by Richard DeHaan

Assigned to the Radio Bible Class, 1966

Requests for information should be addressed to:
Zondervan Publishing House
Grand Rapids, Michigan 49530

Library of Congress Cataloging-in-Publication Data

DeHaan, M. R. (Martin Ralph), 1891–1964.
    Our daily bread.

    "Daybreak Books."
    Includes indexes.
    1. Devotional calendars. I. Bosch, Henry Gerard,
1914-   .   II. Title.
BV4810.D38   1988   242'.2   88-20791
ISBN 0-310-23410-7

Printed in the United States of America

96 97 98 99 00 / DH / 45 44 43 42 41

This edition is printed on acid-free paper and meets the American
National Standards Institute Z39.48 standard.

DEDICATION

To the great host of aged, invalids, and shut-ins who find
their strength and encouragement in the promises
of God, this volume is prayerfully dedicated,
in the confidence that God will bless
according to His Word in
Isaiah 55:10, 11

INTRODUCTION

When the Radio Bible Class began publishing the monthly editions of *Our Daily Bread,* we had no idea that it would be so enthusiastically received. The response, however, was almost immediate and the publication has had a rapid and steady growth. It has now become one of our principal ministries, and the reports of blessing have been thrilling, and many of them unusual. Numerous invalids, shut-ins, and aged ones have been especially enthusiastic about *Our Daily Bread,* and great numbers eagerly await its arrival each month. The reports of conversion as a result of these booklets have also cheered our hearts.

Especially helpful has been their ministry of reviving the custom of daily devotions. Unnumbered thousands have written that it has revolutionized their family life. In hundreds of homes where no family altar existed, they now gather at the breakfast table and read *Our Daily Bread.* Many testify that the devotional period has become for parents and children alike a joy eagerly awaited, instead of a dull and tiresome duty.

In response to many requests, this present cloth-bound volume of *Our Daily Bread* brings an entire year of these daily devotionals into permanent form. It contains a carefully selected group of articles taken from the booklets of the past years — those which, according to the information received in our mail, have been the most appreciated and helpful.

We, the editors, send out this volume of devotionals with a prayer that God who blessed them so wonderfully when they were presented in the small booklets, may bless them even more as they appear now in this attractive and more durable form.

M. R. DeHaan, M.D.

Henry G. Bosch

Grand Rapids, Michigan

A BRAND NEW YEAR

SUGGESTED SCRIPTURE READING: II Peter 3:11-14

. . . ye have not passed this way heretofore. Joshua 3:4

We stand on the threshold of a brand new year. We cannot see one step ahead. We know nothing of what lies before us. It is to us a new, a strange, an unknown path. Will we see another year? Will Jesus come this year? Will death strike our home? Will war break out again? From the signs round about us we may ominously expect many unwelcome surprises, for we have not passed this way before. We enter upon a path unknown. We would be filled with fear were it not for the promises of God. What a glorious privilege to be assured that God knows every step of the way and has made provision for us. How wonderful, as we stand at the beginning of this period of time to know that we have a Captain and a Guide who knows the way and has planned it all ahead for us. And so we rest upon His promises. Here are a few of them:

"Known unto God are all His works from the beginning of the world" (Acts 15:18).

"Lo, I am with you alway" (Matt. 28:20).

"As thy days, so shall thy strength be" (Deut. 33:25).

"But he knoweth the way that I take: when he hath tried me, I shall come forth as gold" (Job 23:10).

"He which hath begun a good work in you will perform it until the day of Jesus Christ" (Phil. 1:6).

We have not passed this way before, but HE KNOWS THE WAY. Only follow! Let Him guide, and it will indeed be a HAPPY NEW YEAR!
—M.R.D

I know not whether dark or bright,
This year shall be —
I only know He giveth light,
And I can trust His love and might,
Who leadeth me! —Anon.

"Make use of time if thou lovest eternity; yesterday cannot be recalled and tomorrow cannot be assured; only today is thine." —QUARLES

BE PREPARED!

SUGGESTED SCRIPTURE READING: Psalm 139

> . . . *prepare to meet thy God.*   Amos 4:12

It was said of a certain Scotch minister of some prominence, that he was very eccentric, and had his own peculiar way of doing things to startle men into the realization of their need of Christ. "Just as the year was opening," said one of his parishioners, "I was very busy in my shop, when, right in the midst of my work, in stepped the doctor, without so much as knocking or a word of announcement. 'Did you expect me?' was his abrupt inquiry. 'No, Sir,' was the reply, 'I did not.' He waited a minute and then said grimly, 'What if I had been Death?' Then he turned on his heel and departed as suddenly as he had come, while his solemn warning re-echoed in my ears: 'What if I had been Death?' Although his approach was unusual and startling, it set me to thinking, with the result that I made my 'calling and election sure.'"

How about you, fellow traveler to eternity's shores — pause a moment in life's busy whirl; have you answered God's call of grace? Have you counted the cost if your soul should be lost? There is but one way to reach heaven's sinless and holy bowers: not by your own poor works, not by your impotent and feeble strivings, but only by sovereign grace. Have you asked the Saviour for His blessed, unmerited favor and pardon? Have you asked Him for a new heart? Oh, delay no longer; for "except a man be born again, he cannot see the kingdom" (John 3:3). "Prepare to meet thy God" (Amos 4:12b). . . . "Set thine house in order; for thou shalt die, and not live" (II Kings 20:1).

—H.G.B.

> Should the death angel knock at thy chamber,
>   In the still watch of the night,
> Say . . . would your spirit pass into torment,
>   Or to the land of Delight?
> Many sad spirits now are departing
>   Into a world of despair;
> Ev'ry brief moment brings your doom nearer;
>   Sinner, Oh, sinner, beware!
> Say, are you ready? Oh, are you ready?
>   If the death angel should call;
> Say, are you ready? Oh, are you ready?
>   Mercy stands waiting for all!   —Anon.

"Delay not till tomorrow to be wise; tomorrow's sun to thee may never rise." — CONGREVE

I AM THE WAY

SUGGESTED SCRIPTURE READING: John 14:1-12

. . . I am the way.   John 14:6

Jesus said "I AM." Again and again He used this expression. "I AM" is one of the names for God. When Moses asked the Lord what to answer the children of Israel when they should ask him "Who sent you?" the Lord replied, "Thus shalt thou say unto the children of Israel, 'I AM' hath sent me unto you" (Ex. 3:14). God is the eternal One. He did not say to Moses "I was," or "I will be," but "I AM." God has no past and no future, but He lives in the eternal present. Jesus asserts that He is God by taking upon Himself this name, "I AM." He said, "I AM" the Bread of life, the good Shepherd, the Light of the world, the Door of the sheep, etc.

In John 8:58 He said of Himself, "Before Abraham was, I AM." The Pharisees knew the meaning of that name and accused Jesus of blasphemy and "took up stones to cast at him." Stoning was the penalty for blasphemy. But Jesus proved that He was indeed the "I AM," by going through the midst of them and so passed by.

Jesus was not only God, but the *Way* to God. He is the only Way to Heaven. We do not know much about Heaven. The Bible does not tell us *where* it is, but it does tell us *how* to get there. It is by Him who said, "I AM THE WAY."

A traveler in a strange country asked a native lad where a certain town was, and the lad said, "I don't know 'where' it is, but I can tell you how to get there." The Bible is silent concerning many things about Heaven that we would like to know, but it is very clear on *how* to get there.   —M.R.D.

> Thou art the Way, the Truth, the Life:
> Grant us that Way to know,
> That Truth to keep, that Life to win,
> Whose joys eternal flow.   —Anon.

"It is not talking for display, but rather WALKING in His way that will bring us at last to heaven."—G.W.

"SINGLE-EYED" CHRISTIANS

SUGGESTED SCRIPTURE READING: Luke 11:33-36

> *. . . if therefore thine eye be single, thy whole body
> shall be full of light.* Matthew 6:22

Although Jesus spoke these words long before science and medicine had advanced to a point where much was known about the function and physiology of the human eye, His conclusions are in perfect accord with the considered opinions of modern specialists today. In fact, a noted oculist once had this to say in regard to this very Scripture:

"The seeing power of the body requires two eyes, each receiving its own impressions, slightly different from that of the other, but apprehended by the brain as one impression. Select an individual object to look at. With the right eye you see the center and a little of the right side of the model, and vice versa with the left. By combining the two images, the brain has a comprehensive idea of the total object. The perception may then be said to be 'single,' and, therefore, in regard to that object the whole body is 'full of light'; but if the two eyes look in different directions, two separate images are carried to the brain. There is no true impression. The person having this double impression cannot regard and follow both images without getting into great confusion."

Jesus made a spiritual application of this physical truth by pointing out that "no man can serve two masters." A Christian needs an "undivided heart" (Eph. 6:5b-7; Col. 3:22b-24), if his eye is to be "single" to God's glory!

In South Africa when looking for diamonds, they often find a substance which is half charcoal and half precious stone. It was intended to be a diamond; but it stopped short and, therefore, will never get into the king's diadem. Christian, don't be content to be saved "so as by fire"; don't be part diamond and part slag. Be a jewel for His Crown. —H.G.B.

> Consecrate me now to thy service, Lord,
>   By the pow'r of grace divine;
> Let my soul look up with a steadfast hope,
>   And my will be lost in Thine. —F. Crosby

"The Church is often powerless today, because it has too many confused and undedicated members who are spiritually 'cross-eyed.' "

GOING IN CIRCLES

SUGGESTED SCRIPTURE READING: II Peter 3:15-18

Ye have compassed this mountain long enough.
Deuteronomy 2:3

The word "compassed" is *Cabab* in the Hebrew original. It means to "revolve." It may be translated to "go in circles." Israel had been to the very borders of the promised land of Canaan. They could have gone in immediately. In Deuteronomy 1:21 we read, "Behold the Lord thy God hath set the land before thee: go up and possess it." Then they had sent spies, who, with the exception of Caleb and Joshua, brought in a discouraging report of great walled cities and mighty giants in the land; and Israel believed the spies instead of God. Going to possess the land meant fighting and hard work, and they were afraid. Moses says, "Notwithstanding ye would not go up, but rebelled against the commandment of the Lord your God" (Deut. 1:26). As a result Israel turned back into the wilderness instead of going into Canaan in victory. They found a place of comfort and ease at Mt. Seir. Here were no battles, no toil. All they did was drink from the rock and eat of the manna. There was no progress, no victory. And here they abode many days. "We compassed Mt. Seir *many days.*" They went in circles around and around and around and got nowhere. And then the Lord says, "Ye have compassed this mountain long enough, turn you northward."

Believer, how far have you progressed since you were saved? Have you just gone in circles? Is the Word more precious to you now than a year ago? Do you pray more effectively than a year ago? Is your love for Christ and souls more fervent than a year ago? Are you growing, or just going in circles? Take stock this day and listen to His Word, "Turn you northward," where Canaan and victory lies.　　　　　　　　　—M.R.D.

Sons of God, earth's trifles leaving,
Be not faithless but believing,
To your conquering Captain cleaving,
Forward to the fight!　　　—Anon.

"On the plains of hesitation lie the bones of countless millions who, at the dawn of victory sat down to rest, and resting died!"

FALLING FROM GRACE!

SUGGESTED SCRIPTURE READING: I Peter 1:1-5

Now unto him that is ABLE TO KEEP YOU FROM FALLING!
Jude 1:24

To the evil suggestion of Satan that it will be impossible to hold out on "The Jesus Way," the Word of God comes with its assurances to the weak and fearful saint. While in ourselves we may not have sufficient strength to withstand temptation, yet we need not despair. There is One who is able to keep us from falling! The same grace that empowered us to become the sons of God (John 1:12) is also available to keep us in fellowship!

In regard to our STANDING (Salvation), we can *"never perish"* (John 10:28); and as to our WALK (Sanctification), if we "draw nigh to God" (James 4:8), He will draw nigh to us and bestow upon us the miracle of His *keeping power* for the life of victory! To keep us "not stumbling" (as the original can be translated) is God's purpose for us in *this life,* and some day soon to present us "faultless before the presence of his glory" (Jude 1:24) is His design for our future! The result of this keeping grace will be "peace" here (Phil. 4:7; Rom. 14:17), and "exceeding joy" by and by!

A little girl was once looking at the famous picture which shows a rock in the midst of a stormy sea, bearing on its summit a cross. A woman, just recovered from the angry waves, clings faint and exhausted to this refuge. At her feet a hand, grasping part of the wreckage of a ship, is disappearing into the dark waters. "What does it mean?" asked the child. "It's called 'Rock of Ages,' and means that we must cling to Jesus!" said her mother. The little one thought a moment and then replied, "Oh, but that rock can't be my Jesus; for when I cling to Him, *He reaches down and clings too!"*

Let us be clear on this matter. In SALVATION *God does all the holding on* so that nothing shall separate us from His love! (Rom. 8:35-39). In SANCTIFICATION we first hold on to Him (Jude 1:21), and then He in turn holds on to us! (Mal. 3:7).

—H.G.B.

He holds me fast; I hold Him too,
His keeping grace will see me through!—Anon.

"Salvation is of the Lord (Jonah 2:9), and God always finishes what He begins!" (Phil. 1:6)

DEATH IN THE POT

SUGGESTED SCRIPTURE READING: Ephesians 4:30-32

> *. . . they cried out, and said, O thou man of God, there*
> *is death in the pot.*   II Kings 4:40

The sons of the prophets in Gilgal were entertaining their teacher, the great prophet Elisha. But it was a time of famine and drought, and food was scarce. Elisha instructs them to gather what vegetables they could find and put them in the common pot for a meal of soup. One of the young men came upon a vine laden with gourds and jubilantly brings them in. They are shredded into the boiling pot of vegetables. But when they tried to eat it they became violently ill. They were "poisoned cucumbers," common in Palestine, probably the same as the vine which grew over Jonah's head (Jonah 4:6). One ingredient spoiled the whole meal. All the other ingredients were excellent but the addition of this one mess of gourds made all the rest unpalatable and worthless. How true this is in our Christian experience. One little habit, one unyielded faculty, one unsurrendered sin can undo our entire testimony. How many Christians are hindered and limited in their testimony because of some worldly practice, some pet sin they will not surrender. What is there in your life which you know is the "death in the pot" and which hinders your witness for Him? People will overlook all the other virtues you may have, and judge you only by this one inconsistent fruit of the flesh. Surrender it today and know the joy of victory.

"I beseech you, therefore, brethren, by the mercies of God, that ye present your bodies a living sacrifice, holy, acceptable unto God, which is your reasonable service" (Rom. 12:1).

—M.R.D.

> The dearest idol I have known,
> Whate'er that idol be,
> Help me to tear it from its throne,
> And worship only Thee! —W. Cowper

"The measure of your usefulness is determined by the measure of your consecration!"

NO HARM IN THE POT

SUGGESTED SCRIPTURE READING: Colossians 3:12-17

. . . . And there was no harm in the pot. II Kings 4:41

The sons of the prophets were greatly dismayed when they found that a kettle of soup they had prepared at great labor was unpalatable and unfit to eat. One of the students who could not discern between "edible gourds" and "poisoned cucumbers" had added a lapful of noxious gourds to the pot of soup, and everyone became sick. Had this student been able to discern between the good and the bad this would not have occurred. We too need to have the gift of discernment between good and bad if we are to have our testimony remain potent and be able to show others the way of salvation.

One little inconsistency, one little habit can spoil it all with its "death in the pot." But there is a remedy. Elisha the prophet took "meal" and threw it in the pot. Meal in the Scripture speaks of two things: (1) the perfect humanity of Christ (Lev. 2:1), and (2) the truth of the gospel (Matt. 13:33). We can overcome the deadly habits in our lives as we emulate Jesus (I Peter 2:21), and order our lives in obedience to His Word. Read carefully Ephesians 5:1-7, and then look to Him before you begin the day and claim the victory over that pet sin which you know is the "death in the pot." Surrender it and trust Him for victory and there will be "no harm in the pot."

"He that saith he abideth in him ought himself also so to walk, even as he walked" (I John 2:6).   —M.R.D.

Lord, I long to be like Jesus,
Ever loving, kind and true;
That my life may speak His praises,
Keep me true, Lord, keep me true!—H. W. VomBruch

"To have Christian character means to renounce everything that is inconsistent with the glory of God!" — W. SKIDMORE

A "LOAN" FOR THE LORD!

SUGGESTED SCRIPTURE READING: Matthew 25:34-46

> *He that hath pity upon the poor* LENDETH UNTO THE LORD; *and that which he hath given will he pay him again.* Proverbs 19:17

Has the Lord ever asked you for a "loan"? This statement may shock you, but if it does, it is probably because you have failed to recognize in the needs of others a direct request to you from Heaven for some of your earthly goods. We are to "do good unto all men, especially unto them who are of the household of faith!" (Gal. 6:10). James warns against the sin of passing by the needy with pious words while keeping a tight grip on our purse-strings. "What doth it profit, my brethren, though a man *say* he hath faith, and have not works? Can faith save him? If a brother or sister be naked, and destitute of daily food, and one of you say unto them, depart in peace, be ye warmed and filled; notwithstanding *ye give them not* those things which are needful to the body; what doth it profit? Even so faith, if it hath not *works,* is *dead,* being alone" (James 2:14-17).

A father once gave his little boy a half dollar and told him he might do with it as he pleased. Later when he asked about it, the little fellow told him that he had lent it. "Did you get good security?" he asked. "Yes, sir!" said the boy. "I gave it to a poor beggar who looked hungry!" "Oh, how foolish you are. You will never get it back!" said the father. "But, father, I have the best security; for the Bible says: he that giveth to the poor *lendeth to the Lord!*" The father was so pleased that he gave the boy another half dollar! "There, father," said the son, "you see, *I told you I would get it again,* only I did not think it would come so soon!"

Depend upon it, bread cast upon the waters will be found again, though it may be "after many days" (Eccl. 11:1)! —H.G.B.

Give as you would to the Master,
If you met His searching look;
Give as you would of your substance,
If His hand your offering took! —Anon.

"Charity begins anywhere, and should have no end!"

GOD'S LITTLE MEN

SUGGESTED SCRIPTURE READING: Proverbs 11:23 30

And he brought him to Jesus.   John 1:42

Andrew had met the Lord Jesus Christ, and immediately wanted others to know Him too. And so He "first findeth his own brother Simon . . . and he brought him to Jesus." Andrew was one of the "least" and most obscure of our Lord's disciples. He evidently had few talents and was limited in his abilities to do big things. He never wrote a book like John or Paul or Matthew. He never preached a sermon like Peter, but he knew how to introduce people to Jesus. He was a personal worker and soul winner.

Only three things are mentioned about Andrew. He brought his own brother to Jesus (John 1:42). He brought a lad with a simple lunch to Jesus (John 6:8, 9). He brought the Greeks to Jesus (John 12:22). That is all we know about Andrew. Unnoticed, unappreciated, all but forgotten, but what a ministry was his. Without Andrew there would not have been that great preacher of Pentecost, Peter. Without Andrew the hungry multitude would not have been fed nor the Greeks brought to Christ! Tradition tells us one of these Greeks was Luke, the physician, who wrote the Gospel of Luke and the book of Acts. In heaven, Andrew's name will stand high as the man who knew how to bring souls to Christ. You too can be a little Andrew. You may not be able to preach, sing, write, or do the "flashy" things that people notice, but you can by prayer and witnessing be a little Andrew and wait for your praise till you get to heaven. Then to hear His "well done" will mean everything! We have many Peters and Dr. Lukes, but most important of all is Andrew who led them to Christ.

WILL YOU RECOMMEND CHRIST TO SOMEONE TODAY? —M.R.D.

> No service in itself is small,
>   None great, though earth it fill:
> But that is small that seeks its own,
>   And great that does God's will!—Unknown

"Christ came into the world to 'save sinners' (I Tim. 1:15), and He says, 'As my Father hath sent me, EVEN SO SEND I YOU' (John 20:21)!"
                                                        — H.G.B

THE CONVICTING WORD

Suggested Scripture Reading: Hebrews 4:11-16

For the word of God is quick, and powerful . . . and is a discerner of the thoughts and intents of the heart.

Hebrews 4:12

The Bible is a living instrument of God by which the Holy Spirit reveals to men their sin and the need of salvation. This is well illustrated in the following story.

It seems that a salesman from a New York concern had registered in a Chicago hotel. He had been stealing money from his company for some time; and the thought of the disgrace which might come to him, were he to be discovered, forced him to work long hours in the daytime and then seek places of amusement at night to avoid the qualms of conscience. After many days of such harried existence he was stropping an old-fashioned razor one morning, and finding no piece of paper on which to wipe the blade, he tore a page out of the Gideon Bible. Using it to clean the razor, his eyes caught these words, "The wages of sin is death." Conviction struck his heart, and smoothing out the page, he read, "The wages of sin is death; but the gift of God is eternal life through Jesus Christ our Lord."

The startled salesman read the Bible for two hours, and then on his knees beside the bed he acknowledged himself to be a sinner and in need of a Saviour. Having received Christ, he realized that a new life had been bestowed upon him; and so he wired the firm in New York, and made a full confession. To his surprise he was not prosecuted nor even discharged, but was allowed to pay back something each month out of his salary until the debt was erased. It is said that he is now living in New Jersey and bears a good testimony to the convicting power of the Word of God and the regenerating, soul-satisfying work of the Holy Spirit.

Are you daily consulting and studying your Bible so that the Holy Spirit through its pages may also convict and guide you? Unless you do, you cannot expect to reach higher spiritual ground, for it is the Word that sanctifies (John 17:17). —H.G.B.

> Thy Word is a lamp to my feet,
> A light to my path alway,
> To guide and to save me from sin,
> And show me the heav'nly way.—E. Sellers

"If God is a reality, and the soul a reality, and you are an immortal being, what are you doing with your Bible shut?" — H. JOHNSON

THE GREATER MIRACLE

SUGGESTED SCRIPTURE READING: II Timothy 1:1-7

. . . suffer little children . . . to come unto me.

Matthew 19:14

When an old man or woman is saved in our meetings, we think it wonderful and talk about it to everyone; but when a little child is saved, we scarcely pay attention to it. Yet saving a "child" is a thousand times better. I read a story of a discussion in heaven concerning "who was the greatest monument of grace among the heavenly throng." After a long debate in which each stated his case separately and each claimed to have been by far the most wonderful trophy of God's love in all the multitude of the redeemed, it was finally agreed to settle the matter by a vote. Vote after vote was taken, and the list of competitors was gradually reduced until only two remained. These were allowed to state their case again. The first to speak was a very old man. He began by saying that it was a mere waste of time to go any further; it was absolutely impossible that God's grace could have done more for any man in heaven than for him. He told again how he had led a most wicked and vicious life — a life filled up with every conceivable indulgence and marred with every crime. He had been a thief, a liar, a blasphemer, a drunkard, and a murderer. On his deathbed, at the eleventh hour, Christ came to him and he was forgiven.

The other was an old man who said in a few words, that he was brought to Christ when he was a boy. He had led a quiet and uneventful life and had looked forward to heaven as long as he could remember.

The vote was taken; and, of course, you would say it resulted in favor of the first. But no, the votes were all given to the last. It required great grace, no doubt, to pluck that "brand" from the burning. But it required more grace to save the other, as a boy, *and keep him from sin through a long lifetime.*

When you save an old man, you save a unit; when you save a child, you save the multiplication table. Are your children saved?

—M.R.D.

"Suffer the children!" Oh, hear His voice,
Let every heart leap forth and rejoice,
And let us freely make Him our choice;
Do not delay, but come! —G. F. Root

"Get the boys and girls started right with the Lord, and the devil will have to hang a crepe on his door." — BILLY SUNDAY

"OUT OF SEASON"!

SUGGESTED SCRIPTURE READING: Ecclesiastes 11:1-6

Preach the word; be instant in season, OUT OF SEASON!
II Timothy 4:2

We are admonished in these words to scatter the Living Seed both when conditions are favorable, and when they seem to give little promise of success. We often excuse ourselves for not giving a word of testimony by saying, "It was not an opportune moment!" It is true that we must be "wise as serpents and harmless as doves," but this applies to the *method* of our approach rather than to the *season* of our sowing!

"In the morning sow thy seed, and in the evening withhold not thy hand: for thou knowest not whether shall prosper, either this or that, or whether they both shall be alike good" (Eccl. 11:6).

I heard recently of some Christian men who had been engaged to hold meetings in a community where there was a great need for the Gospel. As they drove to their destination, they saw that, due to the heavy rain storm through which they were passing, they would not have time for their usual season of prayer unless they held it while they were driving along the highway. This they decided to do. At last it was the driver's turn to pray. He slowed down and with his eyes on the traffic began to earnestly beseech the Lord for the souls of them to whom they would soon minister. Between his own tears and the rain that was beating against the windshield, his vision became clouded and he failed to see that the traffic light ahead had turned red! A whistle sounded, and soon a man in uniform put in his appearance. With his face wet with tears, the man of God put his arm around the officer, and pulling him part way into the car out of the rain, explained the situation. The traffic cop saw that these were Spirit-led individuals, and reverently removed his hat. Soon they were dealing with him about his own soul. The Holy Spirit blessed this "out of season" testimony, and the officer was gloriously saved!

Yes, you testify for the Lord "in season," but how are you at scattering precious seed "OUT OF SEASON"? —H.G.B.

"In season, out of season," living for the Lord;
This will bring the blessing and a rich reward!—H.G.B.

"The seed is the WORD; the sowing time is ALWAYS; and the reward is SURE!" (Ps. 126:6)

BARKING AT THE MOON

SUGGESTED SCRIPTURE READING: Mark 15:3-5

Let all . . . evil speaking, be put away . . . Ephesians 4:31

Of all the sins people commit there is none worse than the sin of gossip, whispering and slandering. When we are misrepresented and slandered, the natural reaction is to requite evil for evil in retaliation. Yet, the evidence of real Christlikeness is to be able to reward evil with good and go right on living our life for Christ. Peter says of Jesus that He "did not sin, neither was guile found in his mouth: Who, when he was reviled, reviled not again; when he suffered he threatened not" (I Peter 2:22, 23). And He is our example, for Peter tells us we should follow in His steps.

A certain judge was constantly annoyed by the sneering remarks of a certain "wise cracking," and abusing attorney. Instead of cracking down on the lawyer and silencing him the judge would only smile and chew his pencil until people wondered at his patience. At a dinner someone asked him, "Judge, why don't you slap down that 'wise-guy' lawyer?" The judge laid down his knife and fork and resting his chin on his hands said, "Up in our town there lives a widow who has a dog which, whenever the moon shines, goes out and barks and barks all night at the moon." Then the judge quietly resumed eating. One of the company asked, "But judge, what about the dog and the moon?" And he replied, "Oh, well the moon just kept right on shining!" Oh, for grace today to keep on shining for Him amid all the barking dogs.   —M.R.D.

> Let me no wrong or idle word
>   Unthinking say;
> Set Thou a seal upon my lips,
>   Just for today!   —Anon.

"He who relates the faults of others to you, designs to relate yours to others. Scandal always runs best in the gutter of evil minds."

READY FOR EITHER!

Suggested Scripture Reading: II Corinthians 6:14-18

I beseech you therefore, brethren, by the mercies of God, that ye present your bodies a living sacrifice!
Romans 12:1

On one of the old Roman coins was the figure of an ox, standing between a plow and an altar, with the inscription, "Ready for either." That is the spirit that typifies the true Christian — readiness for service or for sacrifice! Having been bought with a price, the precious blood of Jesus, we are no longer our own but belong, body and soul, to our Lord and Redeemer. Therefore, it is only our "reasonable service" that we offer our physical being upon the altar of consecration. Only the best, unblemished creature was considered a fit sacrifice in the Old Testament dispensation. Today, we too must keep our body healthy, undefiled and holy if it is to be an acceptable offering, fit to be employed for His glory.

A good example of offering the body as a "living sacrifice" is set forth in the following true incident: A Moravian missionary to the West Indies found that he could get no access to the natives, whom he desired to reach for Christ, because they were kept at work all day, and at night they were too weary and exhausted to listen to his preaching. He tried everything he could think of to get them under the sound of the Gospel, all without success. After every other plan had failed, he thought of Romans 12:1 and decided to make a drastic move. *He sold himself as a slave* to one of the plantation owners and was driven with the colored men into the fields to work. Here, at odd moments, he had opportunity to talk to the natives, and it is said that though he "lost his life" for the Gospel's sake, he found it again in the hearts of the many who were led to Christ by his witness!

Have you selfishly let the Lord save your *soul*, but kept back from Him your *body* so that you might consume it upon your lusts? Brethren, this is not "reasonable"! —H.G.B.

This moment, Lord, Thy will I choose,
Nor let me live except for Thee;
My life, my all, I'll gladly lose
To know Thy perfect victory! —Anon.

"You give but little when you give of your possessions. It is when you give of yourself that you truly give!"

WHAT CAN YOU PAY?

SUGGESTED SCRIPTURE READING: Psalm 116

> *What shall I render unto the LORD for all his benefits toward me?*
> Psalm 116:12

After David had recounted the innumerable blessings he had received of the Lord, he seeks for something to show his deep and intense gratitude for all God's benefits to him and cries out, "What shall I render unto the LORD?" No use to bring money for the gold and silver are already His. No use to bring a gift of flowers, for He Himself created them. What can I bring? What can I render unto Him? David's answer is twofold. First, he says, "I will take the cup of salvation and call upon the name of the Lord." Second, "I will pay my vows unto the Lord now." The word "salvation" is plural and should be "salvations." He is determined to praise the Lord. Then he will keep his vows. You will find the vow in Psalm 116:9; "I will walk before the LORD." First, I will *talk* and then I will *walk*. Testimony and service — both are expressions of gratitude.

After a medical missionary had finished a very difficult operation on a poor, penniless native, he was asked, "How much money would you have received in the States for such an operation?" He replied, "At least $600.00." "And how much will you receive for this one?" The reply was immediate, "My fee will be this man's gratitude, and there can be no richer return than that." How much do you show your gratitude to the GREAT PHYSICIAN, who redeemed you, both soul and body?   —M.R.D.

> Let wonder still with love unite,
>   And gratitude, and joy;
> Be Jesus our supreme delight,
>   His praise our best employ.
>
> Dear Lord, while we, adoring, pay
>   Our humble thanks to Thee,
> May every heart with rapture say,
>   The Saviour died for me!—A. Steele

"The praise life wears out the self life."

PRICKED OR SAWN?

SUGGESTED SCRIPTURE READING: Acts 2:37-41

Now when they heard this, they were PRICKED *in their heart.* Acts 2:37

When they heard these things, they were cut (SAWN THROUGH) *to the heart, and they gnashed on him with their teeth.* Acts 7:54

The Word of God is either "a savor of life unto life" or of "death unto death" to those who hear it. When Peter preached, the Holy Spirit "pricked" the hearts of the hearers so that they repented, and were saved. However, when Stephen presented a similar message to certain members of the Jewish council, the Word was not mixed with faith in them. Therefore, instead of "pricking" them it *cut them to the heart* and made them angry, bitter and murderous in their attitude. Their response was not one of repentance and salvation, but rather of hostility. Becoming the instruments of hell itself, they rose up and stoned the messenger of God, making Stephen the first Christian martyr.

The word translated "cut" in our Bible, in the original language actually means to "saw through," to rip or lacerate by means of a sharp jagged instrument! Those who do not properly respond to the Sword of the Spirit, which is the Word of God, are mangled by its sharp blade of truth.

The reaction to the preaching of Peter and Stephen illustrates the two extreme extents of man's response to the Word of God. It either "pricks" with conviction that leads, sooner or later, to conversion; or it cuts, "saws" and rips the unyielding heart and makes it release all its hidden and pent-up flood of unrepentant iniquity! No man can hear the Gospel and remain unmoved.

How does the preached Word affect you? Does it convict, admonish, comfort and bless you through its gentle pricking to a new and holy walk; or does it antagonize, anger, and irritate you beyond measure? Are you *"pricked"* or *"sawn"*? Real preaching is bound to produce one reaction or the other! —H.G.B.

Thy Word doth search the life,
And all the thoughts within,
Oh may my heart's response,
Thy full approval win. —Anon.

"The Word of God is a sword of conviction that divides humanity into two opposing classes." — G. WOODS

THE FEAR OF DEATH

Suggested Scripture Reading: Hebrews 2:14-18

> *. . . through fear of death . . . subject to bondage.*
> Hebrews 2:15

The Christian may fear the "dying," but he need not fear "death." Death to the believer is a release — a going home. Only as we realize this, does death lose its dread and fear. The Rev. John Angell James of Birmingham once said: "I am persuaded from long observation that there is nothing about which a Christian has less need to be anxious than his dying hour."

When Dr. James Hamilton of Regent Square, London, was lying on his deathbed, his brother quoted to him this verse, which he himself had frequently repeated in the pulpit:

> "Jesus, the vision of Thy face,
> Hath overpowering charms;
> I scarce would feel death's cold embrace,
> If Thou wert in mine arms."

The dying saint replied: "There is no cold embrace, William. There is no cold embrace."

As Dr. Samuel Gobat, Bishop of Jerusalem, was nearing the end of his earthly journey, his son reminded him that he had no need to be afraid of any evil in the dark valley of the shadow of death. The Bishop smiled and whispered, "It is not dark."

Dr. Adolph Saphir, in his *Expository Lectures on the Epistle to the Hebrews,* relates the following:

"Are you afraid of death?" said a friend to a German pastor.

"Which death do you mean?" replied the dying man. "Jesus, my Saviour, saith, 'He that believeth in Me shall never die.' Why then should I be afraid of what I shall not even see?"

When Henry Reed of Tasmania was dying, he said: "I find no shadow of death in the valley; it is to me full of light, green pastures, and living water. Never so happy since I was born. Glory, glory, glory to the triune God."　　　　　—M.R.D.

> We speak of the realms of the blest,
> 　That country so bright and so fair,
> And oft are its glories confessed:
> 　But what must it be to be there!—E. Mills

"God in love conceals from us here much of the wonders and blessings of heaven, lest the longing to depart should become so keen that we no longer could endure this life." — G.W.

BURDENS!

For we that are in this tabernacle do groan, being burdened! II Corinthians 5:4

John Newton once wrote, "I compare the troubles which we have to undergo in the course of the year to a great bundle of fagots, far too large for us to lift. But God does not require us to carry the whole at once. He mercifully unties the bundle, and gives us first one stick, which we are to carry today, and then another, which we are to carry tomorrow, and so on. This we might easily manage, if we would only take the burden appointed for us each day; but we choose to increase our troubles by carrying yesterday's stick over again today, and adding tomorrow's burden to our load, before we are required to bear it!"

We are indeed subject to much trouble and many burdens, but we often increase our load by assuming unnecessarily that which God has not laid upon us by refusing to forget "those things which are behind," and by anticipating those for which the promised grace has not yet been provided. Yes, there are certain burdens which must be borne, but these are much more easily endured when we have first taken the inspired advice of the Psalmist and cast ourselves upon the Lord's mercy (Ps. 55: 22). Strengthened by His sustaining hand, we shall find His yoke "easy" and His burden "light"!

Burdens, too, can often be stepping stones to higher ground! A biologist tells how he watched an ant carrying a piece of straw which seemed a big burden for it. The ant came to a crack in the earth which was too wide for it to cross. It stood for a time as though pondering the situation, then it put the straw across the crack and walked over upon it! What a lesson for us! The burden can become a bridge for spiritual progress if we endeavor by God's help to live the overcoming life! —H.G.B

Upon the Lord thy burden cast,
To Him bring all thy care;
He will sustain and hold thee fast,
And give thee strength to bear!—Anon.

"We are always in the forge, or on the anvil; for by trials God is shaping us for higher things!" — H. BEECHER

SINS OF THE TONGUE

SUGGESTED SCRIPTURE READING: Proverbs 16:16-25

. . . a whisperer separateth chief friends. Proverbs 16:28

Whispering! The words conjure up for us the all too familiar scene of a couple of long-tongued gossipers, standing in a corner, casting sly glances at someone else, and whispering some choice garbage of gossip about a friend. Probably no sin is more common among Christians and does more harm and damage than evil speaking. How easy it is to condemn some inconsistency or habit in another's life, little realizing that our gossip is often a greater sin than what we are condemning in someone else. Nothing has wrecked reputations, broken up friendships, ruined churches, and killed preachers more than this spirit of criticism and judging.

John Wesley was once preaching. He was wearing a bow tie with two long ends hanging down. A dear sister in the meeting saw nothing but the tie and never heard a word that Wesley preached. When the service was ended, she went to him and said piously, "Brother Wesley, will you permit a little criticism? Your bow tie is entirely too long, and it is an evidence of worldliness to me." Wesley said, "Have you a pair of shears?" Receiving the shears he gave them to her and said, "Now trim them down to suit yourself." She reached over and clipped off the streamers and said, "Now that is much better." Then Wesley replied, "Do you mind letting me have those scissors? Please stick out your tongue. It is entirely too long and is an offense to me. Stick it out while I cut it down to size." May we learn the lesson. Let our words today be words of kindness — not those of criticism, faultfinding, scolding and backbiting.—M.R.D.

> Only a word of anger,
>   But it wounded one sensitive heart;
> Only a word of sharp reproach,
>   But it made the teardrops start;
> Only a hasty, thoughtless word,
>   Sarcastic and unkind;
> But it darkened the day before so bright
>   And left a sting behind.   —Anon.

"As empty vessels make the loudest sound, so they that have least wisdom are the greatest babblers." — PLATO

SATAN'S WILES

SUGGESTED SCRIPTURE READING: Ephesians 6:10-18

*Put on the whole armour of God, that ye may be able
to stand against the wiles of the devil.* Ephesians 6:11

Satan is a clever and diabolical foe. His tactics are deceitful.
He delights in laying snares for the unlearned and unsuspecting. "Babes in Christ" who have not as yet put on the full armor
of God are his prime targets. These fall easy prey to his half-
truths and pious frauds. The schemes of the archenemy are
many and varied, but they all partake of one Satanic deception. To a greater or lesser degree they attack the supreme and
unique deity of Jesus Christ, mutilating in the process the simple
plan of salvation by which men are to be saved through free
grace apart from human works and effort (see I John 4:1-3;
II John 1:9, 10; and Jude 4).

Duveen, the famous English art critic, once took his little
daughter to the beach but was unable to get her to go into the
chilly water. After persuasion failed, he borrowed a teakettle,
built a fire, heated a little water until it steamed beautifully,
and then with a great flourish, poured it into the ocean. His
greatly impressed daughter then went in without a murmur.
Where can we find a better example of one of Satan's tricks?
He dilutes an ocean of unbelief with a steaming teakettle of
Christian ethics, and people go wading into it self-satisfied, feeling that all is well, but completely unaware that they are bath-
ing in unbelief.

Read the sixth chapter of Ephesians, and then put on the full
armor that God provides. Only thus will you "be able to stand"!

—H.C.B.

To him that o'ercometh, God giveth a crown;
Thro' faith we will conquer, tho' often cast down;
He Who is our Saviour, our strength will renew;
Look ever to Jesus, He will carry you through.—H. Palmer

**"Gross deceptions are easily discerned, but there is not a greater or
more dangerous lie than a half-truth." — H.G.B.**

TAKE YOUR NEIGHBOR'S PLACE

SUGGESTED SCRIPTURE READING: Philippians 2:1-11

> *Look not every man on his own things, but every man also on the things of others.*   Philippians 2:4

Before we pass judgment upon anyone else, it would be well if we put ourselves in his place and see how the problem looks through his eyes. Look on the other side of the question. Until we see both sides we are not fit to pass judgment. Things may look quite different through your neighbor's windows.

A well-known Ohio judge was noted for his defense of slavery. He was converted from the error of his ways by the following conversation with a runaway slave, who had crossed the Ohio River from Kentucky.

Judge: "What did you run away for?"

Fugitive: "Well, judge, I wanted to be free."

"Oh! Wanted to be free did you? Bad master I suppose?" "Oh, no; berry good man, massa." "You had to work too hard then?" "Oh, no; fair day's work." "Well, you hadn't a good home?" "Hadn't I though! You should see my pretty cabin in Kentucky!" "Well, didn't you get enough to eat?" "Oh, yes, sir. Plenty to eat." "You had a good master, plenty to eat, were not overworked, a good home — I don't see what you wanted to run away for." "Well, judge, I left de situation down dar open. You can just go down and git it."

Christians will find it a healthy exercise to place themselves in the position of others before they pass judgment on them. The "one-anothers" of the Epistle to the Romans will help to this end among Christians — to keep from wrong-doing on the one hand (Rom. 14:13), and help them to do right on the other (Rom. 15:5).   —M.R.D.

So easy to say what another should do,
  So easy to settle his cares;
So easy to tell him what road to pursue
  And dispose of the burden he bears.
It is easy to bid him be brave and be strong,
  And to make all his shortcomings known;
But, oh, it's so hard when the care and the wrong
  And the dangers we face are our own!—Anon.

"Faults are thick where love is thin."

THE "FENCED-IN THINGS"

SUGGESTED SCRIPTURE READING: Psalm 91

Call unto me, and I will answer thee, and shew thee great and mighty things, which thou knowest not. Jeremiah 33:3

Some years ago there appeared in a national periodical a story written by a Christian bomber pilot concerning an outstanding answer to prayer. He told how his plane had been hit by anti-aircraft fire, and spinning out of control had headed for the sea beneath. "Immediately I began to pray," he said, "but that was the last I knew until I came to in the water. I was in bad shape. My leg was gone below the knee, and the water was red all around, and I knew I'd bleed to death in a few minutes. Then something nudged me. Believe it or not, it was a piece of plywood with the plane's first-aid kit on it. I got the tourniquet out of it, and my co-pilot helped me to get the thing on and stop the bleeding. Another plane came along and dropped a life raft, and four hours later we were picked up by a rescue launch. If you don't call that a miracle, I would like to know what is. God answered my prayer!"

On a radio program which I conducted, I once requested folk to send me remarkable answers to their petitions. The many startling replies which I received proved to all who listened that God still does unexpected and "mighty things" when we rest with implicit faith upon His promises and claim His aid in prevailing prayer.

The words "great and mighty things" may also be translated "inaccessible," or "difficult things." I like the even more literal rendition which allows for the following phraseology, "Call upon me and I will answer thee, and shew thee great and *fenced-in things* which thou knowest not." When we pray according to His will, God often honors our trust by performing that which the world, with its limited perspective, deems to be hedged in by the "impossible." Yes, many of us have proved that He is able to do "exceeding abundantly above all that we ask or think" (Eph. 3:20).

—H.G.B.

> Got any rivers you think are uncrossable?
> Got any mountains you can't tunnel thro'?
> God specializes in things thought impossible
> And He can do what no other pow'r can do.—O. Eliason

"Faith expects from God what is beyond all expectation."

LIVING UPSTAIRS

SUGGESTED SCRIPTURE READING: Hebrews 13:1-14

Set your affection on things above. Colossians 3:2

Someone asked a Scotsman: "Are you on the way to heaven?" He replied: "Why man, I live there." What he meant was, he was only a pilgrim here. Heaven was his home. Over the door of a joiner's shop, which is on the ground floor, the words are written: "Residence above." We, too, should work below, but live above. "Here we have no continuing city, but we seek one to come" (Heb. 13:14). "Our citizenship is in heaven; from whence also we look for the Saviour, the Lord Jesus Christ" (Phil. 3:20, R.V.).

In Christ, the believer is already in heaven, as a member of His body (Eph. 2:4-7). We are here only to "work" and show others how to get there!

A Christian postman in a Scottish village was going his rounds one day when he was asked by a tramp the way to a certain town seven miles away. The postman replied: "Turn to the left and keep straight on." The tramp was pleasantly surprised by the prompt and clever answer, and he said to the postman: "Can you tell me the way to heaven?" Just as instantly the postman replied: "Yes, turn to the right and keep straight on." He was correct. The way to the "promised land" is the right way: "He led them forth by the right way, that they might go to a city of habitation" (Ps. 107:7). "Enter ye in at the strait gate: for wide is the gate, and broad is the way, that leadeth to destruction, and many there be which go in thereat. Because strait is the gate, and narrow is the way, which leadeth unto life, and few there be that find it" (Matt. 7:13, 14).   —M.R.D.

I'm pressing on the upward way,
New heights I'm gaining ev'ry day;
Still praying as I onward bound,
Lord, plant my feet on higher ground.

Lord, lift me up, and I shall stand
By faith, on heaven's tableland;
A higher plane than I have found,
Lord, plant my feet on higher ground.—J. Oatman, Jr.

"If the way to heaven is narrow, it is not long; and if the gate be strait, it opens into endless life."

WITNESSES!

SUGGESTED SCRIPTURE READING: Acts 1:1-9

. . . ye shall be witnesses unto me.   Acts 1:8

The world called Jesus' disciples "Christians" (meaning—followers of Christ), but our Lord Himself never so designated His own. He called them "WITNESSES"! How important an emphasis He thus placed upon their *testimony.* Many seem to have mistaken the meaning of our Saviour. They proceed as if He had said, "Ye are my *lawyers!*" They are always arguing with unsaved people in an attempt to convince them of the advantages of their particular brand of religion. A lawyer is always debating and reasoning, but *a witness simply tells what he knows!* If we would only quote the Scripture to those whom we seek to win, the Holy Spirit would be able to use the Word as a sharp tool to carve conviction in their soul. One word of Inspired Writ has more impact than a thousand arguments. An ounce of Bible has more weight than a ton of human philosophy. Your personal experiences in connection with your conversion and other definite leadings of the Lord in your life are also worth reciting for "a man with an *experience* is never at a loss with a man who has only an *argument!*" Stop being a lawyer, start being a WITNESS if you want to bring forth "much fruit"!

Many years ago Charles Bradlaugh, an atheist, challenged Hugh P. Hughes, a consecrated man of God, to debate with him concerning the reality of the Christian faith. The challenge was accepted in these words: "I will bring with me to the debate one hundred men and women who have been saved from lives of sin by the Gospel of Christ. They will give their evidence and you will be allowed to cross-examine them. I will ask that you bring with you one hundred men and women who have been similarly helped by the gospel of infidelity which you preach."

The atheist backed down and the debate was never held. The unbeliever had no evidence. The Christian, on the other hand, had all the "witnesses"!   —H.G.B.

> I will tell the wondrous story
> Of the Christ who died for me,
> How He left His home in glory
> For the cross of Calvary!—F. Rowley

"The love of Christ which overflows in every word, action, and thought is the secret of evangelism!" — ELISABETH MITCHELL

THE HEAVENLY BANQUET

SUGGESTED SCRIPTURE READING: John 6:5-14

Thou preparest a table before me.   Psalm 23:5

Two poor boys, who had never been in the country and knew nothing of the sweetness of its air, were sent into the most "country" of country places. There was plenty of food. They found there was meat for breakfast. They were surprised, as they had not been accustomed to such a luxury. They did their duty and went out to play. At dinner time there was hot meat, and what was more astonishing, when they went to supper there was meat again. Meat three times a day was something they had never dreamed of. When they went to bed that night, the little one said to his brother: "Jim, if they set that table again in the middle of the night, don't you forget to call me."

The Lord always meets the need of His people in a most ample and satisfying manner. He gives us:

1. The fatted calf of His provision to satisfy us (Luke 15:23).
2. The whole lamb of His love to bless us (Ex. 12:8).
3. The manna of His grace to strengthen us (Deut. 8:3; John 6:51).
4. The milk of His Word to nourish us (I Peter 2:2).
5. The wine of His joy to gladden us (Ps. 104:15).
6. The honey of His promises to nerve us (Ps. 19:10; Isa. 7:15).
7. The fruit of His blessings to assure us (Num. 6:24; Eph. 1:13, 14).

There are two main feeders to the sustenance of the spiritual life; and these are meditation in the truth, so that we may understand it, and application of the truth, so that we may practice it.
—M.R.D.

Thou spread'st a table in my sight,
Thy boundless grace bestoweth;
And O! what transport of delight
From Thy pure chalice floweth!—H. W. Baker

"Many Christians are anemic and undernourished, because they are content to chew on the husks of worldly pleasure rather than feed upon the bounties of God's well-prepared table." — G.W.

LITTLE MOUND

SUGGESTED SCRIPTURE READING: II Samuel 12:13-23

But now he (David's little child) is dead, wherefore should I fast? can I bring him back again? I shall go to him, but he shall not return to me. II Samuel 12:23

There is nothing like the death of a little child to pluck at the heartstrings and stir the deepest emotions. We expect the old and "bearded grain" to be harvested by the sickle of time, but the untimely crushing of a tiny rosebud of humanity, the sight of a little green mound in the family plot wrings a tear from the most calloused individual. Recently I went to comfort a heartbroken mother and father who had just laid to rest their little darling. Amidst the tears there were the blessed overtones of Christian victory. The same feelings expressed by David in II Samuel 12 were voiced. This was one child that they could be sure they would meet in heaven (Matt. 18:10, 14). They realized that the Lord never makes any mistakes. They yielded their precious baby to God's loving embrace and explained simply to their other little ones that, "God needs some *rosebuds* in His heavenly bouquet, too!" Eternal values were underscored for them as never before; heaven was nearer and more precious. They sorrowed not as those who had no hope. I was reminded forcibly of the following incident:

A shepherd once led his flock to the banks of a swift flowing stream. Now sheep are naturally afraid of rapidly running water, therefore, the shepherd could not induce them to cross. Finally, he picked up a little lamb and stepped with it into the river, bearing it carefully and tenderly to the opposite shore. When the mother sheep saw where her lamb had gone, she forgot her fear and stepped into the rushing current and was soon safely on the other side. All the rest of the flock followed her leadership. So, too, when our children go ahead of us to glory, the "valley" loses much of its terrors for us.

Bereaved parents, lift your eyes from that "little mound" unto the "hills from whence cometh (your) help"! —H.G.B.

Only a baby's life—brief as a perfumed kiss,
So fleet it goes; but our Father knows
We are nearer to Him for this!

"Death is but the voice of Christ saying, 'Come unto Me!'"

SPREAD THE GOOD NEWS

SUGGESTED SCRIPTURE READING: Acts 8:1-8

. . . they . . . went everywhere preaching the word. Acts 8:4

"It was just too good to keep to myself," said a friend to me one day long ago. He had discovered a certain "fishing hole," where the fishing was fantastically good, and he wanted me to enjoy it also. But how loath and slow we are to tell others about the Lord Jesus, which is the best news of all. Truly the joy of salvation is too good to keep to ourselves.

A party of missionaries were sitting at tea one afternoon, when suddenly an ant appeared on the white tablecloth, made its way to one of the tea plates, walked around it, and finding nothing to eat there, made straight for the sugar bowl. After eating some bits of sugar, it went off with a small piece. The party watched it go off the table, down the table leg, along the floor of the room, and disappear underneath the door. Not long afterwards, it returned with several of its relations, climbed up the leg of the table, and marched along the top. Led by the first ant, they all entered the sugar bowl. After they had eaten their fill of sugar, they all departed, each with a piece of sugar in its mouth. But that was not all — presently a swarm of ants arrived to partake of the same sweet food. What a great lesson those ants teach us. The one who came first of all, went and told others the "good news"; they, in turn, went out and told the glad story to many more. Shall we let the ants put us to shame? Surely not. Like Isaiah, the Demoniac, the Woman of Samaria, and others, we must "go and tell" the glad story of God's redeeming love!   —M.R.D.

> Tell it again, tell it again,
>   Salvation's story repeat o'er and o'er;
> Till none can say of the children of men,
>   Nobody ever has told me before. —M. B. Slade

"It is a solemn responsibility to have in one's possession a reprieve for men under condemnation and then not deliver it."

NONE FORGOTTEN

SUGGESTED SCRIPTURE READING: Luke 12:1-7

Are not five sparrows sold for two farthings, and not one of them is forgotten before God? . . . Fear not therefore: ye are of more value than many sparrows. Luke 12:6, 7

Jesus chose a sparrow, a lowly feathered creature, to illustrate the great truth that God cares for us in a tender and wonderful way. Five of these scrawny, unattractive birds could be purchased for a penny in the market place, and yet Jesus said the Father in heaven remembered and thought about each one individually. He then reminded His audience that if God cares for and protects such insignificant creatures certainly He has an infinitely greater regard for us who have an eternal soul and are made in His own image. In God's eyes nothing and no one is insignificant. The cure for all loneliness is found in the thought that He never forgets us and never considers us unimportant. The Psalmist thrilled when he contemplated this comforting truth, and exclaimed, "I am poor and needy; yet the LORD thinketh upon me" (Ps. 40:17a). Though the world may be thoughtless and cruel, though familiar friends may often prove untrue, yet our heavenly Father constantly watches over us in sympathy and love.

It is said that once when Sir Michael Costa was having a rehearsal with a vast array of performers and hundreds of voices, one man who played the piccolo far up in the corner ceased to play, probably thinking that in all the din of the chorus and orchestra his instrument would not be missed. Suddenly the great conductor threw up his hands, and all was still. Then he cried out, "Where is the piccolo?" The quick ear of the master musician had missed it, and the chorus was spoiled because one man had failed in carrying his part. So, too, your contribution as an individual Christian is important. Do not neglect to do your part, small as it may seem in the eyes of man. To God, you and your efforts are always worthwhile. "He careth for you."

—H.G.B.

Oh, now I know my Father cares,
Tho' friendless here, alone.
I know my each and every prayer
Shall reach His blessed throne!—L. Kortz

"Often those of whom we speak least on earth are best known in heaven!"

THE POWERLESS LAW

SUGGESTED SCRIPTURE READING: Galatians 3:1-10

. . . what the law could not do.   Romans 8:3

Some people will be shocked by the assertion that there are some things the law cannot do. The law can only reveal sin, but it is powerless to save from sin. It can show us our weakness, but cannot provide strength. It can only condemn, but cannot justify. The law commands, but does not enable; the law slays, but grace alone can make alive. Grace disposes and gives the needed power. Law is outward; grace is inward.

Sometime ago a famous watchmaker took a visitor through his shop and showed him two different ways of regulating the time of the various instruments on the shelves. In one case a signal was sounded at regular intervals telling the correct time and revealing the error of the time pieces. But this was all the signal could do. It could only reveal how much the clocks were off time. If they were wrong, the signal would reveal the error; but to rectify it, other means were necessary. This is law — it strikes the signal, but it cannot repair the wrong.

In the other case there was a master clock connected electrically to a number of clocks in such a way that the clocks were controlled from the Master Chronometer, "synchronized," to go beat by beat under the control of the constant corrector. This is grace. For what the law could not do, grace is able to do. You cannot keep in step with the Master unless you are in constant communication. Check the lines today and be sure the lines are open.   —M.R.D.

> Step by step I'll walk with Jesus,
>   Just a moment at a time,
> Heights I have not wings to soar to
>   Step by step by faith I climb.—A. B. Simpson

"Cling to God; count on God, and move forward!"

THE CHRIST-LIFE

SUGGESTED SCRIPTURE READING: Ephesians 4:17-24

. . . I live; yet not I, but Christ liveth in me. Galatians 2:20

A young Italian boy knocked at the door of an artist's studio in Rome. When it was opened, he explained, "Please, madam, will you give me the master's brush?" The painter had died, and the boy inflamed with the longing to be an artist wished for the great master's touch. The lady placed the brush in the youth's hand, saying, "This is his brush; try it, my boy." With a flush of earnestness on his face he made a supreme effort, but soon found he could paint no better with it than with his own. The lady then said, "Remember, my child, you cannot paint like the great master unless you have his spirit." So, too, men who have never been born again are doomed to disappointment and failure when they attempt to wield the brush of faith without the indwelling Spirit of Christ.

But you say, I have experienced the new birth; I have Christ's Spirit dwelling within, and yet I seem so powerless. The reason, dear child of God, is to be found in the fact that although you have all of His Spirit, *His Spirit does not have all of you!* The self-life with its pride and ambition must be "crucified with Christ" if the resurrection life of the Saviour is to take full control.

> "Oh, to be saved from myself, dear Lord,
> Oh, to be lost in Thee;
> Oh, that it might be no more I,
> But Christ that lives in me."

The greatness of a Christian's power, is in exact proportion to the measure of his surrender to the Christ-life within. —H.G.B.

> As rays of light from yonder sun,
> The flow'rs of earth set free,
> So life and light and love came forth
> From Christ living in me.—El Nathan

"Christianity is not a cloak put on, but a life put in."

WHY JESUS CAME

SUGGESTED SCRIPTURE READING: Matthew 9:10-13

. . . This man receiveth sinners, and eateth with them.

Luke 15:2

This was the accusation of the self-satisfied, self-sufficient, self-admiring, self-righteous, religious Pharisees, against the Lord Jesus Christ. They felt that if He were the Messiah He should not degrade Himself by consorting with the riffraff of the city and the scum of society. It did not befit His high position. But they misunderstood His mission completely. They did not know that the purpose of His coming was, "to seek and to save that which was lost" (Luke 19:10). He said, "I am not come to call the righteous, but sinners to repentance" (Matt. 9:13).

And how thankful we should be for this, for there is "none righteous." Once we see ourselves as we are in the eyes of God we realize that all our righteousnesses are but filthy rags. We are all as an unclean thing. Have you ever seen yourself as a totally unworthy, filthy sinner in the sight of God? Once we accept God's estimate of ourselves (Rom. 3:9-20) we will abhor ourselves and repent in sackcloth and ashes and flee to Him for mercy.

Is your church seeking the lost? Or is it only a "holier than thou" society which caters to the elite and the cultured and the wealthy and neglects the lost and wandering sheep? In the conduct of many a church the parable of the lost sheep in Luke 15 should read as follows: "A certain man, having lost sheep about him, built a beautiful shelter on the edge of the wilderness. Over it he wrote, 'Any lost sheep straying by, who presents his credentials and gives good references to the official board will be admitted to this shelter after due consideration of his worthiness.'" May God deliver us from the sin of self-righteousness!

—M.R.D.

Ho! all ye heavy-laden, come!
Here's pardon, comfort, rest and home,
Ye wanderers from a Father's face,
Return, accept His proffered grace.—E. Campbell

"The church is not a gallery for the exhibition of eminent Christians but a school for the education of imperfect ones, a nursery for the care of weak ones, and a hospital for the healing of those who need assiduous care!" — BEECHER

A CUP OF COLD WATER

SUGGESTED SCRIPTURE READING: Mark 9:38-41

For whosoever shall give you a cup of water to drink in my name . . . verily I say unto you, he shall not lose his reward.
Mark 9:41

Some years ago near Oxford a new church was to be built. A speaker made an eloquent plea for funds, urging the audience to give all that they could. Many were impressed with the need, among them a small boy. When the offering was taken, he took his prized top out of his pocket along with five marbles and placed them in the collection box. Afterward, one of the deacons was inclined to ridicule the boy's gift but the chairman said: "I will give you 20 pounds for that top and will take the five marbles to Oxford, and I assure you that I will get five of my friends to give 5 pounds each for them." And he was as good as his word. At the laying of the cornerstone of the new building, there was placed within it the little boy's top and the five marbles. They had come to symbolize the truth that a little given with a heart full of love for Jesus can be multiplied a hundredfold by the Master, and will not go unrewarded.

Often in His ministry Jesus emphasized that it was not so much the amount of the gift but rather the sacrifice and the love it entailed which made it of value to God. The "widow's mite" becomes "mighty" when God puts His blessing upon it. In Mark 9:41 Jesus underscored two other principles. First, you must *give the best that you have!* If all you can give is water, then God expects you to "pump a little" so that it will at least be "cold." Secondly, giving must not be done to be seen of men, nor are we to take any credit to self, but rather *do all in His name.* When we give, we must remind people that they should consider it as having come from the hand of the Lord Himself; and, therefore, He alone should receive the glory. Those who take the applause of men here "*have* their reward." How much sweeter to wait the praise of Jesus by and by. —H.G.B.

Give of your best to the Master;
Give Him first place in your heart;
Give Him first place in your service,
Consecrate now ev'ry part! —H. G.

"It is the heart and the purpose, not the gift, that makes the giver."

A BROKEN NET

SUGGESTED SCRIPTURE READING: Luke 5:4-11

> *. . . they enclosed a great multitude of fishes: and their* NET BRAKE. Luke 5:6

There are two accounts of miraculous catches of fish. In the first account in Luke the disciples had fished all night without success (Luke 5:5). When Jesus, therefore, told them to let down the nets, Peter objected, saying it was no use for they had toiled all night without success. Reluctantly, Simon let down the "net" and to his utter surprise the net was so full that it "brake" and he had to call in help from neighboring boats to land all the fish. How many fish escaped through the rent in the net we are not told, but there were enough left to fill both the little boats of the disciples (Luke 5:7).

We are led to ask the question, Why did Jesus permit the net to break with its subsequent loss of fish? He had told them to lower the nets; why then the broken net? It was because of Peter's little faith and disobedience. Jesus had commanded Peter to let down the *nets* (Luke 5:4). He did not say *one* net but *all* the nets. It is in the plural. But Peter felt it was no use (verse 5) and said, "Nevertheless, at thy word I will let down the *net*." It's no use Lord, but I'll let down one net to prove it. There's no use letting them all down. But Jesus had said let down the *"nets."* As a result, fish enough for several nets were caught in one net *and it brake.* Oh, how we limit God by our unbelief! God wants us to expect big things when He works. Let us trust God today for great things for He is a Great God.

—M.R.D.

He knows, He loves, He cares,
Nothing this truth can dim,
He gives the very best to those
Who leave the choice with Him!—Anon.

"In the Christian life . . . the ground and secret of all increase is FAITH-FULNESS!" — F. VAUGHN

AN UNBROKEN NET

SUGGESTED SCRIPTURE READING: John 21:4-11

Simon Peter went up, and drew the net to land full of great fishes, an hundred and fifty and three: and for all there were so many, yet was NOT THE NET BROKEN.

John 21:11

John, who wrote this account, was amazed and surprised that the net full of fishes "held" and did not break. He must have been thinking of the previous experience in Luke 5:6 where they also enclosed a multitude of fishes and the net had broken. And so in surprise he writes, "and for all there were so many *yet was* not the net broken."

The scene is similar to the scene in Luke 5. After the disciples spent a fruitless night of fishing without Jesus, the Lord said to them, "Cast the net on the right side of the ship." Without Jesus in the boat we are always fishing on the *wrong* instead of the *right* side. At Jesus' command they cast the net on the right side and the net was full. But the amazing thing was, the net did not break. The reason is evident. In Luke 5 Jesus had commanded to let down *several* nets. Peter let down only one — and of course it had to break — with the load of fish in one net intended for several nets.

But in this incident in John 21 Jesus had told them to let down *one net* (verse 6) and it had to hold. Oh, that we might learn to obey and trust Him. What loss we too sustain when we refuse to believe His perfect command. What joy when we obey. "To obey is better than sacrifice, and to hearken than the fat of rams" (I Sam. 15:22).   —M.R.D.

When we walk with the Lord
In the light of His Word
What a glory He sheds on our way!
While we do His good will,
He abides with us still,
And with all who will trust and obey.—J. Sammis

"The man who earnestly seeks real success, and the favor of heaven, entrusts his fortunes to Jesus Christ."

GREATER LOVE

SUGGESTED SCRIPTURE READING: I Peter 2:21-25

Greater love hath no man than this, that a man lay down his life for his friends. John 15:13

Some years ago a little girl lay critically injured in a hospital in a small mid-western town. An accident had caused her to lose a great deal of blood. An urgent call went out for transfusions for the dying child, but her blood type was hard to find. Finally, it was discovered that the blood of her seven-year-old brother was the same as hers. The doctor took him to his office, held him on his knee, and said, "Son, your sister is very, very sick. Unless she gets some blood, I am afraid the angels are going to take her to heaven. Are you willing to give your baby sister your blood?" The young boy's face turned pale and his eyes widened in fright and uncertainty. He appeared to be in great mental agony; finally, after a minute or so he half whispered to the doctor, "I'll give my little sister my blood." The doctor smiled reassuringly and said, "That's a fine boy, I knew you weren't afraid." The transfusion took place, but the seven-year-old, watching the tube carrying the life-giving blood to his sister, seemed to be very apprehensive. The doctor said, "Don't be nervous, son, it will all be over before long." At that moment, big tears welled up in the little boy's eyes. "Will I die pretty soon then?" he said. It turned out that *he thought he was giving up his own life* so that his baby sister might live. What power there is in true love! And yet there is greater love than this. It is to lay down one's life for an *enemy!* This is what Jesus did. "For . . . when we were enemies, we were reconciled to God by the death of His Son." This is divine love! Have you experienced it? Remember, lives full of service and praise are the best tokens of gratitude for "so great a salvation." —H.G.B.

Could we with ink the ocean fill,
    And were the skies of parchment made;
Were ev'ry stalk on earth a quill,
    And ev'ry man a scribe by trade;
To write the love of God above
    Would drain the ocean dry;
Nor could the scroll contain the whole,
    Tho' stretched from sky to sky.—F. Lehman

"The music that reaches farthest into Heaven is the beating of a grateful, loving heart."

SHINY SCISSORS

SUGGESTED SCRIPTURE READING: Psalm 34:8-10

> *. . . no good thing will he withhold from them that walk uprightly.*   Psalm 84:11

Have you ever had one of your little children beg you for a pair of sharp scissors? How attractive and inviting the scissors seem to be to young and inexperienced eyes. If they could only have that shiny instrument they think they would be supremely happy. But tiny unsteady hands and precious starry eyes are much too valuable to jeopardize by granting such a dangerous request. Of course, there are tears and protests and feelings that Daddy is mean in his refusal to satisfy such ardent longings; yet, their more mature vision of later years will confirm the wisdom of father's decision.

As children of God, are we not prone with the same lack of discretion to ask for some of the shining bubbles of time that we feel we cannot do without? With insistent prayers and tears we often demand an answer that will gratify our immature desires, and think God unkind when He apparently remains deaf to our pathetic cries! Yet, His wisdom, as the Heavenly Father, is far superior to that of any earthly parent. He sees the future pain that the granting of our blind request would entail, and so He in mercy refuses to heed our persistent pleadings. If Christ loved us so much when we were His enemies, that He was willing to leave heaven's glory to die for us on the Cross, certainly now that we are His children, He will not withhold any "good thing" from us. It is His love alone that bars the way to our unwise desires and their tragic results.

Oh, child of God, believe it, even though you cannot understand it, that the Lord never sends anything to hurt you, but only to bless! He'll make it plain by and by!

Take the handkerchief of faith, dry your tears of self-pity, and stop beseeching God for that "shiny scissors"!   —H.G.B.

> Above the tempest wild I hear Him say,
> "Beyond this darkness lies the perfect day,
> In every path of thine I lead the way!"
> So where He leads me I can safely go;
> And in the blest hereafter I shall know
> Why in His wisdom He hath led me so!—Anon.

"Spin cheerfully, not tearfully, though wearily you plod; spin carefully, spin prayerfully, but leave the THREAD with God!"

THE WOUNDS OF JESUS

SUGGESTED SCRIPTURE READING: Isaiah 53

Who his own self bare our sins in his own body on the tree, that we, being dead to sins, should live unto righteousness: by whose stripes ye were healed. I Peter 2:24

Christ died in our stead. He took our guilt and atoned for it on the Cross. Peter says, "By whose stripes ye *were* healed." It is in the past tense. It is done. In heaven He carries the evidence in His glorified body; the wounds in His hands, His feet, and side (Luke 24:39; John 20:25-27). Those wounds are our certificate of His work for us.

A saint of God lay dying, and as is so often the case, Satan made one last final attack upon her faith and tempted her to doubt. He reminded her of her many sins for which she could not pay. But she roused herself and weakly putting the fingers of one hand upon the palms of the other, she whispered, "There are no nail prints there; but He was wounded for my transgressions." After a brief silence, she lifted her hand to her brow and whispered, "There are no thorns there; but He was wounded for my transgressions." There was silence again for a moment and then she opened her eyes and putting her hand over her heart she said, "There is no spear wound here, but He was wounded for my transgressions," and with those words she fell asleep in Christ.

This, my friend, is the good news of the Gospel: Christ died in our stead. Have you thanked Him for it this morning? Is He that real to you? Yes, "while we were yet sinners Christ died for us."

—M.R.D.

How oft at the touch of the nail-scarred palm,
My storm-troubled soul has at once grown calm.
The tempest that surges I will not fear,
For how can I sink if that Hand is near! —Anon.

"The ground of our glory, comfort, and salvation is in Christ and His perfect redemption of which the cross-wounds are the eternal pledge!"
— H.G.B.

THE REWARD OF FAITH

Suggested Scripture Reading: Psalm 61:1-4

. . . my soul trusteth in thee: yea, in the shadow of thy wings will I make my refuge, until these calamities be overpast. Psalm 57:1

Many years ago a story appeared in the *Covenant Companion* which proved a real blessing to me. It concerned a certain Mr. Richard Cecil, who wished to teach his little daughter the meaning of consecration and faith. Taking her upon his knee in his library one day, he asked her if she loved him well enough to give up a little necklace of glass beads which she greatly prized. She looked up with tears on her face, and sobbed, "Yes, Papa." "Well," said he, "you take them off then and throw them into the grate." With heaving bosom and hesitating steps, she made the great renunciation and then flew back to his arms and sobbed herself to rest, while he patted the little golden head and gently said, "Now Papa knows you love him."

Nothing more was said for several days, but on her birthday her father called her to him, and opening a little plush box handed to her a chain of *real pearls* and asked her to put them on her neck as the gift of his love to her. She looked him full in the face; and then a great light broke upon her countenance, and again throwing herself upon his bosom, she cried, "Oh, Papa; I did not understand, but now I do!"

That is the type of consecration which God loves to recompense. Our sacrifices are real investments that will bring us infinite returns in that day when He shall give us diadems for tears, cities for pounds, and ten thousand per cent compounded interest on all that we laid down for His sake.

Do not fret when God removes the baubles of time from your regretful hands, just trust and assuredly believe that He is planning to replace them with the pearls of His eternal blessing. The rewards of faith are never disappointing. —H.G.B.

Whate'er the crosses mine shall be,
I would not dare to shun,
But only ask to live for Thee,
And that Thy will be done.—J. Maxfield

"Many of God's greatest blessings come to us in rough wrappings, but there is gold inside."

THE EVERLASTING ARMS

SUGGESTED SCRIPTURE READING: Psalm 46:1-11

The eternal God is thy refuge, and underneath are the everlasting arms. Deuteronomy 33:27

Have you ever dreamed that you were falling out of bed or from some great height, to awaken with a sensation of fear and fright? I remember as a boy how often I would be awakened by a sensation of falling. I have heard of a man who regularly had this sensation just as he slipped into sleep and was so rudely awakened by his sense of falling, he dared not go back to sleep, for fear of this dread dream being repeated. He feared he would die and imagined he was falling into a veritable "bottomless" pit.

And then one evening he was strolling in a cemetery and his eyes fell on the phrase engraved on one of the tombstones, "Underneath are the everlasting arms." Yes, there was more than a dead body of a saint underneath that sod. The "Everlasting Arms" were guarding that body in hope of the resurrection. And then the words of the Psalmist came to mind, "Yea, though I walk through the valley of the shadow of death, I will fear no evil" (Ps. 23:4).

He realized that in life and even in death, yes, even in sleep, there are the "Everlasting Arms." That night he fell asleep without fear and alarm and could sing as he was taught in childhood: "Teach me to live that I may dread the grave as little as my bed!"
—M.R.D.

Be sickness mine, or rugged health,
Come penury to me, or wealth;
Though lonesome I must pass along,
Upon my Father's arm I rest,
Whate'er He wills, it will be best!—Missionary Tidings

"Faith is the vision of the heart! It sees God in the dark, as in the day!"

THE FAVOR OF GOD

<small>Suggested Scripture Reading:</small> II Chronicles 26:1-15

And he (Uzziah) did that which was right in the eyes of the Lord, *according to all that his father Amaziah did . . . . And as long as he sought the* Lord, *God made him to prosper.*   II Chronicles 26:4, 5

Uzziah was only 16 years old when he was made king of Judah, but he wisely sought to know the mind of the Lord and to live in the center of God's will. Though he later became proud and drifted away from the Lord, and thus left the place of blessing (verse 16), still the results of his earlier dedication are inscribed in the first fifteen verses of II Chronicles 26 for our encouragement. Those who seek the Lord early, and conscientiously govern their conduct by His Word, will find many of the same blessed fruits of Uzziah's faithfulness springing forth in their lives. Uzziah, as a God-centered man, enjoyed the following benefits:

1. Temporal *prosperity* (v. 5)
2. Perpetual *victory* (vv. 6, 7)
3. Far-reaching *influence* (vv. 6, 15)
4. Increasing *strength* (v. 8)
5. *Far-sightedness* (vv. 9, 10)
6. *Loyal supporters* (vv. 11-13)
7. *Marvelous help* (v. 15)

After all this blessing Uzziah still slipped out of fellowship due to pride. Smitten by the hand of God for his sin (verse 20), he suffered the severe punishment of becoming a leper. He lost his throne and became an outcast.

What a lesson for us! "Wherefore let him that thinketh he standeth take heed lest he fall" (I Cor. 10:12). Often after our greatest victories and our highest mountain-top experiences we fall the most easy prey to Satan and his wiles. Spiritual pride is a terrible monster that will lay us low every time if we do not "watch and pray." May the blessing, but not the curse, of Uzziah be our portion. "Keep yourselves in the love of God."

—H.G.B.

> Oh, to grace how great a debtor,
>   Daily I'm constrained to be!
> Let Thy goodness, like a fetter,
>   Bind my wand'ring heart to Thee!—R. Robinson

"Be careful of pride; the worst and most subtle form is being proud of your humility."

WAIT FOR THE MUSIC

SUGGESTED SCRIPTURE READING: II Corinthians 11:22-30

It is good for me that I have been afflicted. Psalm 119:71

David speaks in the *past* tense. He says "*I have been* afflicted." The affliction is past and now he can look back and say, "It was good." It is not usual to say it at the time we pass through the affliction. How bitterly David complains in many of his Psalms while he is passing through deep waters. But *after* it is over, he sees the tender hand of God in it all.

There is a story of a German Baron who made a great Aeolian harp by stretching wires from tower to tower of his castle. When the harp was ready, he listened for the music. But it was in the calm of summer, and in the still air the wires hung silent. Autumn came with its gentle breezes, and there were faint whispers of song. At length the winter winds swept over the castle, and then the harp answered in majestic music.

The strings of the violin must be made to tremble and quiver before they emit their sweet music.

There are some fruits which are never sweet until after the frost has lain on them. I remember my first introduction to "persimmons." It was early fall and they appeared so luscious and inviting, I sank my teeth into one, only to quickly spit it out as my mouth puckered up with the disappointing bitterness. A friend who knew persimmons laughingly said, "Persimmons are never good until they are frozen." So, too, in God's wisdom there are many elements in our life which never grow sweet until mellowed by the frost of sorrows.

May our prayer be that day by day and as the years pass, we may become sweeter and sweeter by the constant work of our Lord upon our lives.

—M.R.D.

He makes me love the way He leads,
And every fear is put to rout;
E'en with my fondest wish denied,
He gives me grace to do without.—Anon.

"A suffering Christian is one whom God has under treatment."

THE MEANING OF LIFE!

SUGGESTED SCRIPTURE READING: John 10:1-10

For to me to live is Christ.   Philippians 1:21

What does life mean to you? Here are some of the answers that men have given:

"A little work, a little sleep, a little love and its all over!" (Mary Roberts Rinehart)

"This life is a hollow bubble!" (Edmund Cooke)

"We never live; we are always in the expectation of living." (Voltaire)

"Life is the jailer of the soul in this filthy prison, and its only deliverer is death!" (Colton)

"Life is an empty dream!" (Browning)

"Life is a walking shadow!" (Shakespeare)

"Life is a dusty corridor, shut at both ends!" (R. Campbell)

"Life is reasoning on the past, complaining of the present, and trembling for the future!" (Rivarol)

What empty commentaries these are on the subject of the meaning of our existence. How refreshing the inspired words of the Apostle Paul, "For to me to live is CHRIST!" Paul here is saying my strength, my joy, my all is found in the Saviour. He is the object of my heart's devotion. In fact, the source, the fountain-head of my life, is found in the inseparable ties of His precious blood that make me a part of His mystical Body!

Existence is the portion of every man, but LIFE belongs only to those who have been joined to Christ through the operation of the Holy Spirit in the new birth! "This is life eternal, that they may know thee, the only true God, and Jesus Christ, whom thou hast sent" (John 17:3). The "dead" sinner (Eph. 2:1) finds human existence a cemetery of regrets until the resurrection light of heaven becomes his portion! This spiritual resurrection is attained only through a personal union with the Lord Jesus Christ, who emphatically declared: "I AM THE LIFE!" (John 14:6). Is Paul's testimony the thrilling watchword of *your* heart?   —H.G.B.

> "For me to live is Christ," I said.
> And then I knelt and bowed my head
> And prayed that God would take my life
> And use it now to honor Him!   —Anon.

"The reality of being, and the blessing of life are both gifts, the one we receive from our parents, the other from God!" (Rom. 6:23)

I SHALL KNOW

SUGGESTED SCRIPTURE READING: Psalm 84

. . . I know in part . . . then I shall know . . . as . . .
I am known. I Corinthians 13:12

Life without Christ is "chaos." Life with Christ is "order." In Him we have the answer to all life's problems and understand the meaning of all our experiences, whether sad or joyful. He takes the disordered life and makes a perfect pattern. He arranges the jumbled pieces of our jigsaw puzzle into a portrait of heaven.

A class in physics was studying magnets. After a number of experiments the teacher took several sheets of paper and a box of steel filings. At his bidding the pupils sprinkled the filings on the papers. The fine particles looked like grains of sand that might have fallen from the hand of a heedless child. "Now," said the teacher, to one of the boys, "take your paper of filings and place it on the top of that magnet." The boy did so, and there was a sudden stirring among the particles. In a second the filings had arranged themselves in beautiful symmetrical patterns. Every particle on the paper seemed to have found its proper place. Out of confusion the magnet had brought order. How scattered and jumbled life seems at times. How can we reconcile joy and sorrow, love and hate, life and death? How can there be any plan to things? But a day will come when life will appear to us like filings above a magnet. Then shall we see everything in its proper place making a perfect pattern.

God has given us a pattern for our life in the person of His Son, Jesus: "Christ suffered for us, leaving us an example, that we should follow His steps" (I Pet. 2:21). Still, in life, there are many things we do not understand — things that seem contradictory and mysterious, but "up there, sometime, we'll understand." "Now I know in part; but then shall I know even as also I am known" (I Cor. 13:12). —M.R.D.

Called in furnace of affliction?
It must be His sweet will, kind;
Glorify Him in fires—
Be not to His purpose blind.—E. Foss

"The Heavenly Father never sends anything to hurt us, only to bless!"
—G.W.

KICKING JESHURUNS

But Jeshurun waxed fat, and kicked. Deuteronomy 32:15

The name "Jeshurun" is a strange and unfamiliar one. A rare term of endearment, it was a poetical way of speaking of the favored people of Israel. Literally it means "the darling," or the "upright one." As an expression of deepest love it was reserved for those who were God's peculiar treasure and delight. The figure employed here to describe Israel is that of a pampered animal, fattened and cared for like a family pet, which does not return this affection but rather is treacherous and dangerous. Instead of being tame and gentle it responds to its kind treatment by becoming vicious and ugly. In other words, although God guided, blessed, and favored Israel in every way, she returned His love by open rebellion, constant murmuring, and unthankful hostility.

Is this not also true of many of us today? Favored with innumerable material and spiritual blessings, we are still always criticizing, quarreling and complaining. Although God tries by every endearment of His grace to mold us after His will and way, we are unresponsive, and even at times openly rebellious. Oh, what "kicking Jeshuruns" we all are! May God forgive us for our ingratitude.

The story is told of an old lady, who though spiritually a favored and well-fattened "Jeshurun," was still an incurable grumbler. She kicked about everything and everyone. At last the preacher thought he had found something about which she could make no complaint. Her crop of potatoes that year was the finest for miles around. When he met her he said, with a beaming smile, "You must be very well pleased, for everyone is saying how splendid your potatoes are this year." The unthankful one scowled at him, as usual, and said, "True, they're not so poor; but *what am I going to do now for bad ones to feed to the pigs?*"

You can always tell an ungrateful "Jeshurun" by the way it kicks!
—H.G.B.

Let us learn to walk with a smile and a song,
No matter if things do sometimes go wrong;
And then, be our station high or humble,
We'll never belong to the family of Grumble!—Anon.

"Normal Christians are easy to live with. If they are not, they are backslidden and misrepresent their Lord."

POETIC JUSTICE

SUGGESTED SCRIPTURE READING: Judges 1:1-7

. . . they . . . cut off his thumbs and his great toes.

Judges 1:6

This was the punishment which the men of Judah inflicted upon Adoni-Bezek, king of the Canaanites. It was the same treatment which Adoni-Bezek had given to 70 kings whom he had conquered. Seventy kings without thumbs or big toes begged for bread under his table. And now he himself is conquered and given the same treatment. This we call "poetic justice," visiting upon one's own head, the treatment given to others. We have many other examples. Jacob cheated his brother Esau — and later was cheated by his uncle Laban (Gen. 31:7). Haman built a gallows for Mordecai, but was hanged on it himself (Esther 7:10). David stole the wife of Uriah and lived to taste "poetic justice" when his own son Absalom went in to David's wives (II Sam. 16:22).

The purpose of cutting off the thumbs and great toes was to make them unfit to fight or resist. Without great toes they were crippled and hindered in running. Without thumbs they could not use bow and arrow. Adoni-Bezek found out that "what a man soweth that shall he reap," and he confessed, "as I have done, so God hath requited me" (Judges 1:7).

Jesus said, "For with what judgment ye judge, ye shall be judged: and with what measure ye mete, it shall be measured to you again" (Matt. 7:2).

We are sowers also. What are we sowing? What we sow we shall reap.

—M.R.D.

> As here ye sow, so shall ye reap,
> The fruit is sure, the root is deep;
> Each word, each deed may seem to sleep,
> Yet, 'twill spring forth; its harvest keep!—G. Woods

"Our words and deeds return to us to give pleasure or pain; . . . they linger either like barbed arrows in the heart, or like fragrant flowers distilling perfumes!"—J. R. MILLER

"WOODEN" CHRISTIANS

SUGGESTED SCRIPTURE READING: Matthew 10:32-40

*Come and hear, . . . and I will declare what he hath
done for my soul.* Psalm 66:16

Many souls have been brought to Christ by a personal word
of testimony fitly spoken in season. Witnessing is a spiritual
exercise that must not be neglected if we desire the full joy of
the "more abundant" life. Spiritual declarations, however, that
are not backed by a life of consecration and which do not spring
from personal experience tend to have a hollow ring and leave
the listener cold and unmoved. We should not say "Come and
hear" unless we could also add, "Yes, come and *see by my life*
what the Lord has done for my soul." Mere mouthing of empty
religious phrases, mere parrot-like repetition of warmed-over,
stale spiritual experiences which took place years ago and which
have no present reality in our lives, are ineffective. They will
not serve to bring a seeking sinner to the living Saviour and
His dynamic Gospel. Sincerity and warmth are essential to
vital witnessing.

There was once a poor working woman by the name of Sophia,
who loved to speak to others about her Lord. She often said
she was called to "scrub and witness." One day a rather coarse
fellow was making fun of her, saying, "Why, Sophia was even
talking about Christ to a *wooden Indian* in front of a cigar store
the other day." Sophia overheard his remarks and replied, "Perhaps I did. My eyesight is not so good. But talking to a wooden
Indian about Christ is not so bad as being a *wooden Christian*
and never talking to anyone about the Lord Jesus."

Be honest now, how long has it been since you have said to
any individual, "I am so happy in Jesus, I wish you could know
what He's done for me." How long since you have given a
stirring witness to His grace? Are you bubbling over with the
joy of salvation so that in your enthusiasm you could almost
testify to a "wooden Indian," or are you a silent, cold, and
"*wooden*" Christian who has lost his first love?   —H.G.B.

> Come, ye that fear the Lord, and hear
> What He has done for me;
> My cry for help is turned to praise,
> For He has set me free.   —Anon.

"The guess-so Christians are never found among the soul-winners."

OCCUPY TILL HE COMES

SUGGESTED SCRIPTURE READING: Luke 19:11-27

> *. . . occupy till I come.*   Luke 19:13

The word "occupy" in the original Greek is *prag mateuomai* and means literally, "to keep busy." It should read, therefore, "keep busy" till I come. There is nothing so deadening to spiritual life as idleness; it is the "devil's workshop." We should keep so busy for Jesus that we have no time for the devil.

What is your business today? As you move among men and women will you be busy for Him or just a "busybody"? Ponder carefully the words of John 9:4 today and follow the example of our blessed Lord.

There is a quaint legend of St. Thomas, the Apostle, which is worth telling. It is said that some years after his first doubt, he was again troubled with misgiving as to his Lord's resurrection. He sought the Apostles and began to pour his troubles into their ears. But first one and then another looked at him in astonishment, and told Thomas that he was too busy to listen to his tale. Then he was fain to impart his woes to some devout women. But they, as busy as Dorcas, soon made him understand that they were just too busy for such thoughts as these. At last it dawned upon him that perhaps it was because they were so busy that they were free from his torturing doubts. He took the hint; he went to Parthia, occupied himself in teaching the Gospel, and was never troubled with doubts any more.

—M.R.D.

Give the Gospel as a witness,
To the world of sinful men;
Till the Bride shall be completed,
And the Lord shall come again.—A. B. Simpson

"Idleness is the gate of all harms. — An idle man is like a house that hath no walls; the devils may enter on every side." — CHAUCER

NOT ALONE

SUGGESTED SCRIPTURE READING: I Chronicles 16:23-27

My presence shall go with thee. Exodus 33:14

Even as Israel was given this precious promise to encourage and strengthen them on the dreary journey to Canaan, so the true child of God today may experience the fellowship of the Saviour as he walks the spiritual desert of this world. As "temples of the Holy Spirit," we are assured of the divine Presence in an even more intimate way than was possible for God's chosen people of old.

A Christian young lady, crossing on a ferry to New York one night, noticed a man watching her. He finally approached and with insinuating looks said, "Are you alone?" "No, sir," she replied. Some time later, as she was walking down the avenue in the great city, she heard a step behind her and turning slightly she recognized the same individual bearing down upon her. Lifting her heart to God in prayer for protection, she quickened her step. Finally when they came to a deserted section, he caught up with her. "I thought you said you were not alone," he exclaimed sarcastically. "I do not see anyone with you. Who is your company?" Her lips trembled, but there was a ring of conviction in her tone as she answered, *"The Lord Jesus Christ and His guardian angels are with me!"* The man was startled. Lowering his eyes he turned and left her, saying, "Madam, you keep too good company for me. Good night!"

We need not wander into such dangerous situations to experience our Lord's fellowship and protection. In every task, at every opportunity, we may commune "as friend with Friend." Walk and talk with Him today! —H.G.B.

> Not as One to dwell apart
> In the spareroom of my heart,
> But as One to whom my prayer
> May confide the smallest care.
> Thus I pray —
> "Lord, be Thou my Guest today!"—Anon.

"Remember, you can't expect to feel God's presence if you are too busy to commune with Him."

INFINITE — ETERNAL

SUGGESTED SCRIPTURE READING: II Corinthians 12:1-10

. . . unspeakable words, which it is not lawful for a man to utter. II Corinthians 12:4

Paul had been caught up into Paradise and had beheld things so wonderful, so amazing, so indescribably glorious that it was impossible to pass them on. He heard unspeakable words, unlawful to utter. Many have speculated on what it was that Paul saw and heard, but all such attempts are utterly futile. We shall have to wait until we ourselves enter that blessed abode, and then we shall "see" glories we had never dreamed of or imagined. We shall find then how limited our vision here has been, how confined our comprehension of the things God has prepared for them that love Him.

A little boy who had never been in the country before was amazed at what he saw. He had never been outside the narrow streets of the city with its walls of buildings on either side. When he got in the country, he cried, "Oh! Oh! Oh!" His hostess asked the reason for the outburst. The boy replied, "Why, what a big sky you have out here." With unobstructed view he, for the first time, had seen the "sky."

When all the material structures which now obscure and limit our vision are left behind and we enter heaven, we too shall exclaim, "Oh! Oh! Oh! What a great Saviour He is!" We will not be like the old lady who, upon seeing the ocean for the first time, expressed her disappointment by saying she had imagined it to be much bigger. Ah, no, we will not be disappointed!　　　　　　　　　　　　　　　　　　　　—M.R.D.

> When this passing world is done,
> When has set the glorious sun;
> When I stand with Christ above,
> Ransomed by redeeming love:
> Then, Lord, shall I fully know—
> Not till then . . . How much I owe!—M'Cheyne

"One of the glories of heaven will be the thrilling surprises and eternal joys that will ceaselessly unroll before our enraptured gaze. It will take us an eternity to explore all the things of which we will then be joint-heirs." — G.W.

SWEET MEDITATION

Suggested Scripture Reading: Psalm 5:1-3

My meditation of him shall be sweet. Psalm 104:34

Meditation has become almost a lost art. Too many people read the Bible without actually feeding upon it and digesting its meaning. Yet, they wonder why they are spiritually undernourished. Someone has rightly observed, "It is not in the bee's touching on the flowers that gathers the honey, but her *abiding for a time upon them* and drawing out the sweet that is vital. It is not he who reads most, but rather he who prays and meditates upon divine truths that will prove the choicest, wisest, strongest Christian."

Once upon a time there was an apothecary in a certain country neighborhood who was a lazy fellow interested only in making money. He had purchased the establishment from another druggist and had never taken the time to look over his entire stock to see what it contained. When the farmers came in for various remedies, he persuaded them to forget their doctor's instructions and to take their doses from one of the few bottles with which he was familiar. As a result, many died through failing to get the right medicine. One day, however, the druggist's oldest son was taken suddenly very ill, and the doctor who was called in declared with a very sober face that nothing on earth could save the lad except a certain rare prescription. Happily, he said there was some of it in the stock of the late druggist if it could be found. Almost frantic, the foolish apothecary turned his store upside down, fairly throwing the bottles around in his anxiety to hit upon the right one. He had waited too long, however, to become familiar with his stock. While he was searching, his boy died.

Thousands of Christians are just as foolish. The Bible is our pharmacy, crammed by the Great Physician with whatever is needed for a sick soul, but few have ever read it clear through to find out what is in it. When sorrow, doubt, or trial comes, they are consequently not able to put their hand at once upon the right remedy.

God help us to meditate more upon His Word. We shall find such endeavor both profitable and sweet.   —H.G.B.

> In sweet communion, Lord, with Thee
>   I constantly abide;
> My hand Thou holdest in Thy own
>   To keep me near Thy side.—Anon.

"Apply thyself wholly to the Scriptures and the Scriptures wholly to thyself."

BLOOD ON YOUR TOE

SUGGESTED SCRIPTURE READING: Leviticus 14:14-28

. . . put it upon the tip of Aaron's right ear, and upon the thumb of his right hand, and upon the great toe of his right foot. Leviticus 8:23

Blood on the right ear, right thumb, and right great toe, this was part of the consecration of the High Priest. It also was commanded to be done to the lesser priests (Ex. 29:20). It was also part of the ritual for the cleansing of defiled persons (Lev. 14:14, 17, 25, 28). The order was always the same. After the priest had been washed (typical of regeneration, John 13:10) he must now be "consecrated." This was an act of dedication to the service of the Lord. A ram was slain and the blood was applied to the right ear, the right thumb, and the right great toe. The ear is for hearing, the hand is for serving, and the foot is for walking. To be truly consecrated we must first *hear*. We cannot go out to serve until we have first "listened." It is listening to His Word. Then we are to serve, carrying out the orders we have heard. And then comes our walk, our conversation, our conduct before men.

We are New Testament priests. We have been washed by regeneration (Titus 3:5). We are now to be dedicated to Him. First, we must *hear*. Our orders are in His Book, the Bible. Unless you know what God says, you cannot serve Him. First, *read your Bible* (the anointed ear). Then, obey and follow instructions (the anointed thumb). And then, *walk* as becomes the saints of God. Does your walk recommend Christ to others?

—M.R.D.

Not for ease or worldly pleasure,
Nor for fame my prayer shall be;
Gladly will I toil and suffer,
Only let me walk with Thee!—F. Crosby

"The world can always tell the difference between a vessel that is overflowing and one that is simply 'wet on the outside.' 'Be ye FILLED with the SPIRIT!' "

THE LUST OF LAZINESS

SUGGESTED SCRIPTURE READING: Hebrews 6:7-12

*The slothful man saith, There is a lion in the way; a
lion is in the streets.* Proverbs 26:13

*Yet a little sleep, a little slumber, a little folding of
the hands to sleep.* Proverbs 6:10

There is no one who can think up more ridiculous excuses for
not working than the slothful man who dearly loves ease, leisure
and sleep. Some become so lazy that they will even imagine
such unlikely consequences as meeting "a lion . . . in the streets"
if they should bestir themselves.

In *Pilgrim's Progress*, "Sloth" and his companions are seen by
Christian asleep by the wayside; for these unwary ones "pre-
sumed that they should do well at last" despite their lack of industry. Later, when Christiana passes by, she sees the same
men "hanged up in irons a little way off." Yes, those who are
"slothful in business" will soon be rudely awakened from their
slumber by the stark fact of poverty and need which will come
upon them.

The same principle holds true in the spiritual realm. Those
who are lazy about their personal devotions, prayer life, Bible
study, and witnessing will find leanness in their own soul and
many doubts arising to plague them.

It has been said that in these days of gathering gloom there
are four things which we can do with our hands: wring them,
fold them, put them in our pockets or *lay them on some job
which needs doing!* God grant that we may do the last and
be saved from the lust of laziness.

A woman, who occasionally used to employ an old colored
lady, met the washerwoman one day all dressed up and said,
"Good morning, Aunt Celia. Why aren't you washing nowadays?" "It's dis way, Miss Anne, I'se been out o' work so long,
that now, when I could work, I finds I'se done *lost my taste for
it.*" This is evidently the trouble with many nominal members
of the Church today. They have become so accustomed to doing
nothing for Christ that when the opportunity is presented to
them to be of service they have no inclination to engage in
Christian activity. To such Jesus would say, "Awake thou that
sleepest . . . . Occupy till I come!" —H.G.B.

Only this hour is mine, Lord;
May it be used for Thee;
May ev'ry passing moment
Count for eternity. —A. B. Christiansen

"The lazy man aims at nothing and generally hits it."

A HARDENED HEART

SUGGESTED SCRIPTURE READING: Hebrews 12:25-29

To day . . . harden not your hearts.   Hebrews 4:7

The Word of God is like a fire and a "hammer that breaketh the rock in pieces." Each time we are exposed to the hammer and fire of God's Word, we either are drawn closer or driven farther away. We can never be the same again! The same sun which melts the ice, also bakes the clay as hard as a rock. When we preach the Word, Paul says we are a savour of life, or a savour of death (II Cor. 2:16). The more often God's call is rejected, the less the possibility of obeying it later. It is a serious thing to read, or listen to the Gospel, for its nature is such, that it never returns "void." It always has an effect.

How easy it is to drown out the voice of God. Are you too busy to stop and listen to Him *right now? Then you are too busy!* The story is told of a young man in Scotland to whom God spoke early in life, but he put salvation off, until he should first make his fortune. He built a great mill and was a success in the "world." Then God spoke once more to him, "You have made your mark in life, now are you ready to give attention to eternity?" By now he was all too busy and again put it off. Shortly after, he was taken violently ill with a fatal sickness, and his frantic wife called a minister. However, it was too late. His only answer to the minister was, "All I can hear is the clanging of the machinery in my mill. I seem to see Jesus speaking, but I can't hear Him. I see His lips move, but I can't hear what He says for the noise of the machinery." And in that delirium he passed out into a godless eternity. If you close your ear to God *today,* you will find it easier to do so *tomorrow.* "To day . . . hear his voice . . . harden not your hearts" (Heb. 4:7).—M.R.D.

O loiterer, speed thee! the morn wears apace;
Then squander no longer the moments of grace;
But haste while there's time! with the Master agree:
The Lord of the vineyard is waiting for thee!—I. B. Woodbury

"Faith in tomorrow, instead of in Christ, is Satan's nurse for man's perdition." — G. CHEEVER

CHRISTIAN ENVIRONMENT

<small>SUGGESTED SCRIPTURE READING:</small> Psalm 121

> *The angel of the* LORD *encampeth round about them that fear him, and delivereth them.*   Psalm 34:7

The Christian is guarded by the Lord on all sides. What security is ours with:
1. God *before* us (Isa. 48:17); 2. God *behind* us (Isa. 30:21); 3. God to the *right* of us (Ps. 16:8); 4. God to the *left* of us (Job 23:9); 5. God *above* us (Ps. 36:7); 6. God's everlasting arms *underneath* us (Deut. 33:27); 7. And His Holy Spirit *within* us! (I Cor. 3:16).

Therefore, Paul exclaims: "In him we live, and move, and have our being" (Acts 17:28). No matter what the local circumstances may be, this is the Christian's true environment.

An Australian missionary once told a thrilling story concerning the care and faithfulness of God which he experienced while on a lonely and dangerous journey. All was safe and easy on the way out, but upon returning he had entrusted to him a large sum of money. A highway man lay in wait for him at a lonely spot, intending to murder and rob him. The missionary, not knowing this, but still keenly aware of his jeopardy, prayed and talked aloud with God as he rode along, committing himself to His loving care and keeping. The robber, who heard him communing with the Lord, thought that there must be two men; and as he had expected only one, he decided not to make the attack. Later the story came out, and the child of God realized that he had been prompted to pray aloud just as he reached the crisis moment in his journey. He rejoiced afresh in the truth of the Christian's divine protection. Truly, if "God be for us, who can be against us?" "Blessed are all they that put their trust in him" (Ps. 2:12).   —H.G.B.

> Just when I need Him, Jesus is near,
> Just when I falter, just when I fear;
> Ready to help me, ready to cheer,
> Just when I need Him most! —W. Poole

"Because the Christian is protected on all sides by the Lord, he has reason to trust; because of the same divine scrutiny he also has the gravest responsibility to walk circumspectly." — <small>H.G.B.</small>

"CHICKENS COME HOME TO ROOST!"

SUGGESTED SCRIPTURE READING: Esther 7:1-10

So they hanged Haman on the gallows that he had prepared for Mordecai. Esther 7:10

"The mills of God grind slow but they grind exceeding small." It is a law of life that "whatsoever a man soweth that shall he also reap." Haman had made elaborate plans to have Mordecai the Jew hanged on a gallows fifty cubits high, but his scheme was thwarted by the intervention of Queen Esther. And Haman died on the very gallows he had made for Mordecai. His evil intentions had come back upon his own head. His "chickens had come home to roost."

King Solomon said in Proverbs 26:27, "Whoso diggeth a pit shall fall therein: and he that rolleth a stone, it will return upon him."

King David in speaking of the wicked evil doers says in Psalm 7:16, "His mischief shall return upon his own head, and his violent dealing shall come down upon his own pate."

God grant that this day we may serve Him, and treat our fellow men as we ourselves would want to be treated. Before you act, turn the tables around, and ask yourself if you want to be treated the same way. Remember — "chickens come home to roost" — and some day we will be rewarded according to our works (II Cor. 5:10; Rom. 14:12, 13).

"And as ye would that men should do to you, do ye also to them likewise" (Luke 6:31). —M.R.D.

Cover my eyes and make me blind
To the petty faults I should not find.
Open my eyes and let me see
The friend my neighbor tries to be.
Teach me, when duty seems severe
To see my purpose shining clear.
Let me at even rest content
That for the Lord my day was spent!—Anon.

"When you have to swallow your own medicine, the spoon always seems about three times as big!"

WHEN THE "TENT-HOUSE" IS FOLDED!

SUGGESTED SCRIPTURE READING: II Corinthians 5:1-9

For we know that if our earthly house of this taber-
nacle were dissolved, we have a building of God.
II Corinthians 5:1

Paul here is speaking of the future accommodations which
God has prepared for the souls of the righteous. These present
bodies, or tabernacles, he compares to *"tent-houses"* (as the
original should be translated). They are temporary, not built
to last, and consequently subject to change and decay. The
heavenly house awaiting us, however, is pictured as a wondrous
and sturdy *building* that shall abide eternally. It is so glorious
that it cannot be compared to our present imperfect and tottering temple of clay. We are not to be "unclothed," or naked
spirits; we are not going to be invisible vaporlike beings in
heaven, but will rather be dressed in a wondrous cloak of immortality wrapped about us in splendor by the hand of God.
The exact nature of what is here involved is one of the blessed
mysteries that only heaven will disclose.

When the former President, John Quincy Adams, was eighty
years of age, he was met by an old friend who shook his trembling hand, and said: "Good morning, and how is John Quincy
Adams today?" The retired chief executive looked at him for a
moment and then said, "John Quincy Adams *himself* is quite
well, sir, quite well, but . . . the *house* in which he lives at
present is becoming dilapidated. It is tottering upon its foun-
dations. Time and the seasons have almost destroyed it. Its
roof is pretty well worn out. Its walls are much shattered, and
it crumbles with every wind. The old tenement is becoming
almost uninhabitable, and I think that John Quincy Adams will
have to move out of it soon; but he himself is well, sir, quite
well!" It was not long afterward that he had his second and
fatal stroke and John Quincy Adams moved from his "shaky
tabernacle" as he called it, to his "house not made with hands"!
—H.G.B.

On earth I'm a pilgrim and stranger,
No place to abide for aye,
But I have a home in God's heaven,
I'm moving up home some day.—J. Vaughn

**"An aged Christian, with the snow of time upon his head, reminds us
that those points of earth are the whitest which are nearest to heaven!"**

BE A BUSY BEE

SUGGESTED SCRIPTURE READING: Matthew 28:16-20

Let the redeemed of the LORD say so.   Psalm 107:2

Last spring I laid out an incompletely filled comb of honey intending to feed it to a hive of bees removed some distance away. To start the process I captured one bee in a cup, placed it over the honeycomb and waited until the bee had discovered the treasure and was so engaged at gathering up store that it forgot it was a captive. I then removed the cup, but it was so interested in its find, it did not even notice. When it was filled, it flew directly to the hive. After a moment she returned and with her a dozen others. These in turn brought many more until finally a literal swarm of bees covered the comb and soon had carried it all into the hive. How the bee transmitted its knowledge to the others I do not know, but in some way it told the other bees of its discovery. What a lesson for us! Are we telling others about Him whom we have found? Christ has committed to us the proclamation of the good news. Shall we who have found honey in the Rock, Christ Jesus, be less considerate of our fellow men than bees are of their fellow insects?

The four lepers who sat just outside the gate of Samaria, after they had come upon the spoil in the tents of the Syrians, passed on the "good news." They said one to another, "We do not well; this day is a day of good tidings, and we hold our peace; if we tarry till the morning light, some mischief will come upon us: now therefore come, that we may go and tell the king's household" (II Kings 7:9). And the child of God who knows the "good tidings" of the Gospel "does not well" if he or she does not pass it on to others. Andrew came into contact with Jesus, and immediately he went to his brother Simon, and said: "We have found the . . . Christ. And he brought him to Jesus" (John 1:41, 42). Will you tell some hungry soul about *Him* today?

—M.R.D.

Close to your door may be someone in sin,
    Tell him the story true
Of Him who died that poor soul to win—
    Oh, bring the one next to you!—C. Forsythe

"Those are the most valuable sermons where one man is the preacher and one man is the congregation."

WALLS THAT TESTIFY

. . . thy walls are continually before me. Isaiah 49:16

An application from this verse in Isaiah is occasioned by the following true incident from the life of the great Bible teacher, G. Campbell Morgan. It seems that shortly after their marriage, Dr. Morgan's father decided to pay a visit to the newlyweds to see how they were faring, and also to inspect their new home which they had just furnished. They showed him into every room with a great deal of pride and happy satisfaction until he suddenly turned upon his heel and in his gruff, but well-meaning way exclaimed: "Yes, it's very nice, but nobody will know walking through here, whether you belong to God or the devil!" Dr. Morgan was shocked by this outburst, but afterward, when the old man had left, he went through the house again and he thought, "Father is right." Talking it over with his wife, they came to the conclusion that something must be done about it. And from that day forward they made it a point to see that in every room in their home bore some testimony to the fact that they were on the Lord's side. A displayed Bible served for one room, a wall plaque bore silent witness in another, while a picture with a text underneath it enhanced another. And so it was that later the great teacher was able to testify, "There is now no room in our home which does not display some message to tell to all the fact that we serve the King!"

What about the walls in your home? Do they declare the grace of God to all who enter?

"Thou shalt call thy walls Salvation, and thy gates Praise" (Isa. 60:18).   —H.G.B.

Oh, bless that house where faith ye find
And all within have set their mind
To trust their God and serve Him still
And do in all His Holy will!   —Anon.

"Face your home toward the Father's House: in word and deed make it a cathedral of grace where the way to heaven is constantly revealed."
   — G.W.

THE WAY UP – IS DOWN

SUGGESTED SCRIPTURE READING: Luke 14:7-15

He (Christ) humbled himself.
God also hath highly exalted him. Philippians 2:8, 9

The path to *"exaltation"* is the path of *"humbling."* He who is never humbled will never be exalted. Even Christ, in order to become our exalted Saviour, first humbled Himself. An ancient temple in Syria has a door so low that it can only be entered by crawling prone upon one's face through the opening. All entrance is blocked until one is willing to get down in the dust and crawl on hands and feet. It certainly suggests the "strait gate," which leads to eternal life. We must get "down before we can go up." Until we are lost we cannot be found. Until we are sinners we cannot be saved. The Lord "bringeth *down* . . . and bringeth up." This is the testimony of the Word.

Zaccheus "came down" and found salvation (Luke 19:6).

Mary Magdalene "stooped down" and saw the angels (John 20:11, 12).

The leper "kneeled down" and received cleansing (Luke 5:12).

The palsied man was "let down" and got forgiveness (Luke 5:19).

Peter "fell down" before Christ and was humbled (Luke 5:8).

Christ "laid down" His life and thus He got the sheep (John 10:15).

Mary "sat down" at the feet of Christ and learned the Lord's secrets (Luke 10:39).

The lowly place is always the holy place.

Jesus is our great example for He, in order to save us, came *down*. He said in John 6:38, "For I came *down* from heaven." He did this that He might take us *up* to heaven. Let us bow before Him today. —M.R.D.

Looking back the way we've come,
What a sight, O Lord, we see!
All the failure in ourselves,
All the love and strength in Thee!—Anon.

"The doctrine of grace humbles man without degrading him and exalts him without inflating him."

FRUIT IN OLD AGE

SUGGESTED SCRIPTURE READING: Ecclesiastes 12:1-8

Cast me not off in the time of old age; forsake me not when my strength faileth.   Psalm 71:9

The problem of old age has been with the race ever since sin entered into the world. Society tries to cope with it by "old age pensions," retirement plans, social security, homes for the aged, etc. Today, according to the statisticians, a man is old at 65 and ready to be gently put on the shelf. But all these things cannot take the loneliness and disappointment of old age away. Only those who know Jesus Christ can face old age with joy and confidence and fruitfulness. While old age means decline of physical strength, for the believer it means increase of spiritual strength, for though "our outward man perish our inward man is renewed day by day" (II Cor. 4:16).

Physically old age means "declension" but spiritually it means "ascension." Only Christ can make the evening beautiful and fruitful. Someone has said, 'The devil has no happy old people." To grow old and have nothing to look forward to is indeed a grim prospect. The things of the world have faded and they have nothing left. But for the believer the sunset years can be most beautiful. May the prayer of those of us who are on the last lap ever be: "Let the evening be bright." I have made my prayer the prayer of the Psalmist, "O God, thou hast taught me from my youth: and hitherto have I declared thy wondrous works. Now also when I am old and grayheaded, O God, forsake me not; until I have shewed thy strength unto this generation, and thy power to every one that is to come" (Ps. 71:17, 18).

"They shall still bring forth fruit in old age" (Ps. 92:14)!

—M.R.D.

> Lord, keep me sweet when I grow old,
>   And things in life seem hard to bear;
> When I feel sad and all alone,
>   And people do not seem to care.
> Oh keep me sweet and let me look
>   Beyond the frets that life must hold,
> To see the grand eternal joys;
>   Yes, keep me sweet in growing old!—J. Hazard

"There is no retirement for the Christian."

WHY TWELVE BASKETS?

SUGGESTED SCRIPTURE READING: II Kings 4:1-7; John 6:5-14

> . . . *Gather up the fragments that remain, that nothing be lost. Therefore they gathered them together, and filled* TWELVE BASKETS *with the fragments of the five barley loaves, which remained over and above unto them that had eaten.*
> John 6:12, 13

A Sunday school teacher in a modernistic church once had to present the story of Jesus feeding the multitude with five loaves and two small fishes. Being unwilling to accept it at its face value she tried to avoid the miraculous aspects of the narrative by saying, "And, of course, you will understand, children, that it does not mean that Jesus actually fed all those thousands with a few loaves and fishes. That would have been impossible. It just means that He so fed the people with His teachings that they lost all sense of bodily hunger, and went home satisfied." She was put to confusion a moment later when after a thoughtful pause one of the youngsters asked, "But, teacher, why were there *twelve baskets* then? And what were the fragments that filled them?" The child had put her finger upon a sore spot and proved once again that "blind unbelief is sure to err, and scan His work in vain."

What practical lessons may we draw from the "twelve baskets"? Jesus is "the Bread of Life" which is broken for us. His disciples are told to feed the multitudes. The little that they are able to distribute is multiplied by the Holy Spirit so that all are fed and each worker ends up with a full basket of food. This was much more than they originally had. So, too, the grace of God multiplies what we do for Christ and pours out abundant, overflowing spiritual blessings. As we give out to others, not only are they fed but we obtain the "more abundant life," receiving much more than we distribute!

Not only the sufficiency of God's ready supply, but also the folly of wasting its wealth is emphasized in this true story. Do you believe this account? Do you practice its lessons? If so, you will experience its "Twelve Basket" reward! —H.G.B.

When Jesus fed the multitudes their needs to satisfy,
Twelve basketsful they gathered up to prove the rich supply.—Anon.

"To those who believe, no explanation is necessary; to those who do not believe, no explanation will satisfy." — F. WERFEL

MILK YOUR OWN COW

> *As newborn babes, desire the sincere milk of the word, that ye may grow thereby.*   I Peter 2:2

Some years ago we heard a story by a famous preacher which is a striking commentary on our verse.

Pat was wonderfully converted from Catholicism and immediately developed a great love for the Scriptures and read the Bible every spare moment. The priest who had missed him in church, dropped in on Pat and found him reading his Bible, and exclaimed in surprise, "Why, Pat, do you know it is dangerous to read that Book without a 'pater' to explain it to you?"

"Sure," says Pat, "I just read — it's the blessed Peter himself who wrote it — 'As newborn babes, desire the sincere milk of the word,' and sure it's a newborn babe I am, and I'm hungry for the milk of the Word."

"Ah, yes," said the priest, "but the Almighty has appointed the priests and the clergy as the milkmen. We are to take the milk and give it to you as you can take it. Only the priests can get the milk of the Word for you."

Pat thought a moment and said, "You know, I have a cow out in my barn and sometime ago I was sick, and I hired a man to milk the cow, but soon found out he was stealing half the milk and fillin' the bucket up with water, and sure it was awful weak milk I was gettin'. But now I'm milking my own cow and it's cream I'm getting — and not water."

Are you milking your own cow? Have you read the Word today? Or do you depend on someone else? There's nothing like milking the cow yourself. Read II Timothy 2:15. —m.r.d.

> It is Truth sent down from heaven;
>   It is much to be desired;
> It is perfect, pure and cleansing;
>   It is every whit inspired.
> It is manna for the hungry;
>   It is milk to make us grow;
> It is light for every traveler;
>   It is Truth that all should know.—Anon.

"Each verse of Scripture committed to memory becomes an arrow of defense against Satan." — l. g. lewis

THE EVIL DESIRE FOR RICHES

SUGGESTED SCRIPTURE READING: Jeremiah 9:22-23

But they that will be rich fall into temptation and a snare, and into many foolish and hurtful lusts, which drown men in destruction and perdition. For the love of money is the root of all evil: which while some coveted after, they have erred from the faith. I Timothy 6:9, 10

Money in itself is a good and necessary thing, but it is wicked to love and desire it beyond its legitimate use in supplying the basic needs of our earthly pilgrimage. Godly contentment involves perfect satisfaction if only our daily supply of food and shelter is provided (I Tim. 6:6-8). We are not to employ all our energies in seeking luxuries, nor strain every nerve to "keep up with the Jones's"! Those who are so exercised about material things and who spend their entire time in scraping together piled up bank accounts are subject to all the spiritual "booby-traps" that Satan can produce. They invite temptation, fall into snares, entertain foolish and hurtful lusts, and err from the faith. Holiness and love of money are poles apart. To run for one pole, is to leave the other behind!

John Wesley was once preaching his famous sermon on the use of riches. His first point was "Earn all you can." An old miser sitting in the congregation nudged his neighbor and whispered, "I never heard preaching the like of that before. Yon man has good things in him." Then Wesley went on to denounce thriftlessness and waste and said, "Save all you can." The lover of money rubbed his hands together in glee and thought that with all the wealth he had piled up, he was certainly on the right track. But then Wesley made his last point with emphasis, *"Give all you can!"* The old miser was beside himself with despair, "Aw dear, aw dear," he exclaimed aloud, "now he's gone and spoiled it all!"

If this devotional "spoils it all" for you, don't blame me; blame the Word of God and your conscience! —H.G.B.

Once His gifts I wanted, now the Giver own;
Once I sought for blessings, now Himself alone!
—A. B. Simpson

"Riches are a blessing only to him who makes them a blessing to others." — FIELDING

THREE-LEVEL HOUSES

SUGGESTED SCRIPTURE READING: Psalm 11; Hebrews 4:11-13

> ... *and I pray God your whole* SPIRIT *and* SOUL *and* BODY *be preserved blameless unto the coming of our Lord Jesus Christ.* I Thessalonians 5:23

Three-level homes are all the vogue in this age of modern architecture. It is quite fashionable to have the rooms of a house on three different levels. But every Christian already lives in a three-level house, for he consists of a body, a soul and a spirit. On the lower level is the kitchen where man eats and drinks. This is the physical part of man — his body. Many men never get out of the kitchen. There they live and there they die — living only for the material and temporal.

The second level is the soul, where the view is better and wider and more beautiful. Here we gather for worship and fellowship and communion. It is the living room of social exercise. Many Christians spend little time in this room. We need not abandon the kitchen altogether for we must care for the body, but we cannot be properly balanced until we learn the secret of joy in the higher level.

The third level is the highest point in the house — the life of the spirit. It is the secret chamber of prayer and personal intercession. It is the holy of holies into which we enter alone and find the most intimate fellowship with God in quiet meditation, prayer and worship. Few people visit the third level. Dust and cobwebs fill the darkened room, with shades all down. Yet, it is the choicest place of power, victory and peace. Where do you live? Which is the room in which you spend the most time? Your answer will determine your spiritual stature and your fruitfulness in life. Live on the higher level today. Take time to visit the room of prayer.   —M.R.D.

O Thou, by whom we come to God,
The Life, the Truth, the Way,
The path of prayer Thyself hast trod;
Lord, teach us how to pray!   —Anon.

"Meditation is the couch of the soul! The time that a man spends in necessary rest he never reckons to be wasted, because he is thereby refreshed ... for further exertion. Meditation then, is the rest of the spirit." — SPURGEON

UNCLEAN THINGS

SUGGESTED SCRIPTURE READING: Isaiah 64:1-6

But we are all as an UNCLEAN THING.   Isaiah 64:6

A man walked down the street one day and passed a store where the proprietor was washing a large plate-glass window. There was one soiled spot which seemed to defy all efforts to remove it. After rubbing it hard and using much soap and water to no avail, he found what the trouble was and called to someone in the store: "It's on the *inside!*"

So too, there are many earnest souls who are striving to clean their soul from its stains by washing it with the tears of sorrow and scrubbing it with the soap of good resolves, with no result. Folks love to rub the stains on their soul with the chamois of morality, and then wonder why there is still such a consciousness of its power and presence. The trouble is: "It's on the *inside.*" It is the heart which is bad. If the fountain is *bitter,* the stream cannot be *sweet!* The "whitewash" of civic endeavor, moral rectitude, and church membership may make the "sepulchre" more attractive, but it can never gloss over the fact that death and decay still fill the inner chambers of the soul. Many individuals who outwardly appear to be ethically sound and religiously proper are spiritually "full of dead men's bones, and of all uncleanness" (Matt. 23:27b).

Only as one is truly cleansed by the operation of the Holy Spirit from the *inside,* will he be made "every whit whole" (John 7:23b). Only the blood of Jesus Christ, God's Son, can cleanse us "from *all sin*" (I John 1:7b).   —H.G.B.

Have you been to Jesus for the cleansing pow'r?
Are you washed in the blood of the Lamb?
Are you fully trusting in His grace this hour?
Are you washed in the blood of the Lamb?—E. Hoffman

"God does not expect us to live His life without first giving us His nature. 'Ye must be born again.' "

THE WORK OF FAITH

*Remembering without ceasing your work of faith,
and labour of love . . .*   I Thessalonians 1:3

Someone has described the place of faith and works in the Christian life as follows: "I work as though everything depended on me, and I pray as though everything depended on God." Another has stated it as follows: "I am a Calvinist on my knees and an Arminian in the pulpit." It is true that everything depends on God, but it is equally true that there is something we must do. We shall never be able to harmonize the Sovereignty of God and the free will of man. It is true that only those whom God chooses will be saved. Jesus said, "Ye have not chosen me, but I have chosen you" (John 15:16a). But in the same verse He adds, "and ordained you that ye should *go and bring forth fruit*" (John 15:16b). We are to pray in *our helplessness* and work in *His strength.*

The following story is told of a poor colored man in the West Indies. A father of twelve children saw a hurricane coming and tying a rope to his little shack, ordered all his family to "haul away" on the rope to windward, to keep it from blowing away. He, being a pious man, took to praying: "O Lord, we know we is weak, we is powerless, we can't do nothin'. You all must do it, and what we do is no use" — but then he shouted to his family, "Haul away at that rope or I'll use it on your backs, you lazy bones" — and then went on praying.

There is the combination — work and pray, pray and work. They must ever go together — they must never be separated. The "work" of faith is a "labour" of love.   —M.R.D.

Awake, my soul, stretch ev'ry nerve,
And press with vigor on;
A heavenly race demands thy zeal,
And an immortal crown!   —P. Doddridge

**"Faith is the root of all good works; a root that produces nothing is
dead."**

AS TO BELIEVING!

SUGGESTED SCRIPTURE READING: Romans 1:15-17

And they said, Believe on the Lord Jesus Christ, and thou shalt be saved . . . and they spake unto him the word of the Lord.   Acts 16:31, 32

What does saving faith include? It requires first of all believing on Jesus as LORD. By this is meant acknowledging His *deity*, His *supremacy* in your life, and bowing to the *absolute authority of His Word*. He must also be received as JESUS. This means you claim Him as your *Saviour* and as the One, who in taking your place upon the Cross, transferred His perfect righteousness to your account. Finally, you must believe on Him as CHRIST. This involves acknowledging Him as the *only one appointed of God to save your guilty soul*. Casting yourself unreservedly into His open arms of forgiveness, turning away from everything and everyone else, you rest on His *finished work* and just trust Him (Rom. 10:3).

Some years ago after the great ship "Titanic" went down, a young Scotsman arose in a meeting and said, "I am a survivor of the 'Titanic.' When I was drifting alone on a spar on that awful night, the tide brought Mr. John Harper of Glasgow, also on a piece of wreck, near me. 'Man,' he said, 'are you saved?' 'No,' I said, 'I am not.' He replied, 'Believe on the Lord Jesus Christ, and thou shalt be saved.' The waves carried him away from me; but, strange to say, they brought him back a little later, and he said once again, 'Are you saved now?' 'No,' I said, 'I cannot honestly say that I am!' He repeated, 'Believe on the Lord Jesus Christ, and thou shalt be saved.' Shortly afterward, he went down; and there, alone in the night, and with two miles of water under me, I believed. I was John Harper's last convert."

At any moment you, too, may lose your grip upon the slippery spar of life to which you are clinging! Before it is forever too late, publicly acknowledge Jesus as your *Lord, Substitute*, and *only Saviour!* Make your eternal destiny certain, *today!* (Rom. 10:9).   —H.G.B.

Have faith in God! for He who reigns on high
Hath borne thy grief and hears the supplicant's sigh,
Still to His arms, thine only refuge, fly!
Have faith in God!   —Anon.

"There are many heads resting on Christ's bosom, but there's room for yours, too!" — S. RUTHERFORD

ANOTHER BED QUILT

Suggested Scripture Reading: John 16:12-15

. . . he shall give you another Comforter. John 14:16

A little lad, whose poverty-stricken mother was prevented from going with him to church because of illness, asked her little son about the sermon which he had heard. "What did the preacher preach about?" she asked him; and he gave the surprising answer, "The preacher said God was going to send us an extra 'bed quilt.'" Surprised, the poor mother asked if he remembered the text and he replied, "The preacher said 'He shall give you another comforter.'"

We smile at the simplicity of the lad but it suggests many truths concerning the Holy Spirit. There is a close analogy between the work of the Holy Spirit and a bed quilt. He bestows warmth and rest. He can keep us warm in our service and protect us from becoming cold and indifferent. When we retire at night we take off our clothing and need other protection. So too, when we are saved we put off those things of the flesh in which we reveled and found our fleeting pleasure. And then we find a new comfort and new pleasures in the things of the Spirit of God. The Comforter promotes a refreshing sleep, and renews our sense of security and safety. As we are led by the Holy Spirit to do the will of God, we alone can know the peace of God.

"I will both lay me down in peace, and sleep: for thou, Lord, only makest me dwell in safety" (Ps. 4:8).   —M.R.D.

Come, Holy Spirit, heavenly Dove,
    With all Thy quick'ning powers;
Kindle a flame of sacred love
    In these cold hearts of ours.
Come, shed abroad a Saviour's love,
    And that shall kindle ours.   —I. Watts

"As we yield ourselves unreservedly to God, and believe His Word, we may know 'righteousness, and peace, and joy in the Holy Ghost' and exhibit the ninefold fruit of the Spirit which is so sorely needed in the church." — (Gal. 5:22, 23)

"LITTLE PILLOWS"

SUGGESTED SCRIPTURE READING: Psalm 3:1-5

I will both lay me down in peace, and sleep: for thou,
LORD, *only makest me dwell in safety.*   Psalm 4:8

In looking through some of my mother's old keepsakes recently, I chanced upon a tiny book which could easily be concealed in the palm of one hand. It was entitled, "Little Pillows." In it were 365 Bible promises, one for each day of the year, which were to be read just before retiring. The title of the book took on a new meaning. Here were "Little Pillows" of trust on which to rest the soul, so that a peaceful night of heaven-sent repose might follow. Psalm 4:8, quoted above, is just such a "spiritual sleeping pill." Many hours of restless tossing may be traced to a failure to trust all to our Heavenly Father's care. Much of our modern tensions which prevent sleep may be attributed to our refusal to "cast our burdens upon the Lord" and to "come apart and rest awhile" as we are bidden! With the Lord leading, with the Lord protecting, with the Lord giving us His many and exceeding precious promises, it should not be difficult for us to say with the Psalmist, "I will both lay me down in peace, *and sleep!*"

During the last war, an old lady in England had stood the nerve-shattering bombings with amazing serenity. When asked to give the secret of her calmness amid such general terror and danger, she replied: "Well, every night I say my prayers and then I remember 'ow the parson told us God is always watching, so I go to sleep. After all, *there's no need for two of us to lie awake.*"

Roll your care on Jesus; relax: "He careth for you" (I Peter 5:7b). It's as simple as all that; . . . *"for so he giveth his beloved sleep"* (Ps. 127:2).   —H.G.B.

> 'Tis sweet to keep my hand in His,
>   While all is dim,
> To close my weary, aching eyes,
>   And trust in Him.   —Anon.

"Many of us worry and struggle with our nerves at high tension, when all the time we only need to let go and drop into the security of the 'Everlasting Arms' just underneath us."—MOODY MONTHLY

IF IT'S DOUBTFUL — IT'S DIRTY

SUGGESTED SCRIPTURE READING: I Corinthians 10:27-33

Abstain from all appearance of evil. I Thessalonians 5:22

There are some things which in themselves are not evil, but may become so if they give others occasion to stumble. Christian liberty must always consider "others" who may look at certain things in a different light. I may have no conscience about eating certain things, but if another brother is offended by my act, then it behooves me to forego my liberty, lest I cause my brother to stumble. We receive many letters from folks who ask questions about amusements, habits, and the use of certain foods and drinks. Some people see no harm in them, others think they are wrong. What is one to do? If there is any question in your mind — don't do it. Paul says in regard to Christian liberty, "He that doubteth is damned if he eat" (Rom. 14:23).

A good rule to follow in regard to questionable things, not specifically forbidden in the Word of God, is to leave them alone. That is the safe course to follow. The late Dr. H. A. Ironside tells the following story which will illustrate this truth.

Sandy was a thrifty Scot who, in order to save laundry expense, would wear the same shirt several times. On one occasion when dressing for a banquet he took a used shirt from the drawer. Not being sure of its cleanness, he held it up before the window to better examine it. His wife, Jean, noticing him shaking his head with indecision, cried out, "Remember, Sandy, if it's doubtful, it's dirty!" Yes, if it's doubtful, it's dirty!

—M.R.D.

My soul, be on thy guard;
Ten thousand foes arise;
The hosts of sin are pressing hard
To draw thee from the skies.

Oh watch, and fight, and pray;
The battle ne'er give o'er;
Renew it boldly ev'ry day,
And help divine implore.—G. Heath

"An EASYGOING Christian life makes the GOING EASY for the devil."

SHADOW-LAND GUIDANCE!

SUGGESTED SCRIPTURE READING: Isaiah 43:1-2

Yea, though I walk through the valley of the shadow of death, I will fear no evil.　　　Psalm 23:4

In South Africa when a poor savage is about to breathe his last, the witch doctor will place in his hand a dead bone as a sort of passport into the world beyond. What a sad commentary this is on human comfort; what a forlorn hope on which to rest the soul in its last extremity. Praise God for a Saviour who has taken the "sting" out of death and made the "valley" just a "shadow." Through the treacherous ravine, overhung by the cliffs of doom, He has already passed on our behalf. Just the mere shadow of its terror of reality remains. Now we need "fear no evil," for there is light at the end of the road. The "nail-scarred Hand" of the resurrected Christ will tenderly guide our glorified soul to its eternal abode. The loving Bosom of the Heavenly Shepherd, with all its warmth and protection, wards off for us the chill of the valley and stills all our craven fears. With the confidence of faith we may cast off all anxiety. We shall find the dark door of death to be only "the other side of the bright and shining gate of life!"

An old Indian chief was told of the Saviour, but he said, "The Jesus road is good, but I have followed the old Indian road all my life, and I will follow it to the end." A year later, as he lay dying, he groped vainly for comfort and some pathway through the darkness. Finally, he turned in desperation to the missionary who had been called to his bedside and whispered weakly, "Can I turn to the Jesus road now? *My road stops here!* It has no path through the valley."

Friend, are you, like the poor savage, on the devil's "highway of despair"? What is your symbol, the witch doctor's "dead bone," or the guiding, "nail-scarred Hand"?　　　—H.G.B.

> Oh, that we now might grasp our Guide!
> Oh, that the Word were given!
> Come, Lord of hosts, the waves divide,
> And land us all in heaven!　　—Anon.

"The THUNDER of the storm of death may still alarm the Christian, but the LIGHTNING has already spent itself upon his Substitute."
　　　　　　— G. WOODS

"TUNED IN"

SUGGESTED SCRIPTURE READING: I Thessalonians 4:14-18

And they that were with me saw indeed the light, and were afraid; but they heard not the voice of him that spake to me. Acts 22:9

So, too, will it be in the day when Jesus calls the Church unto Himself. Only believers will hear and understand His voice and His call. Now if this seems strange to you, let me remind you that whenever you listen to your radio, you have a perfect illustration of the fact that when Jesus shouts, only certain ones will be able to hear it, and others will be ignorant of anything happening at all.

As I speak over the air, you hear my voice coming through the loud speaker, as clearly as though I were there in your own room. But your neighbor next door does not hear a word I say. He doesn't even know that I am speaking, and why not? Because he is not tuned in on the wave length over which I am talking at the moment. He has a radio, the same ether waves which carry my voice through your set are passing through his room, his set is turned on also, but he doesn't hear a word I am saying, just because he is not tuned in on the proper wave length.

Just so it will be at the rapture. Jesus will shout from the air, but only the ones who are tuned in on Station F-A-I-T-H and B-L-O-O-D will be able to get the message. The rest will hear nothing at all, while we who hear will be instantaneously changed and rise to meet our Lord in the air. As a magnet picks up only the steel and leaves the dross behind, so only the Church, magnetized by the Spirit of God and born again, will respond to His call. As the thief takes only the jewelry, money, and valuable articles and leaves the rest undisturbed, so, too, it will be at the Rapture. —M.R.D.

> Now seated on His Father's throne,
> He soon will come to claim His own;
> Soon shall they join His countless train,
> Nor sin nor death afflict again! —Anon.

"One whose eye is fixed on heaven can trample equally under foot the smiles and the frowns of the world!"

SAYING "OH"!

SUGGESTED SCRIPTURE READING: II Corinthians 1:3, 4

In all their affliction he was afflicted. Isaiah 63:9

In a world of sorrow, trial and disappointment the human heart cries out for sympathy. This is well illustrated in a story I once heard concerning a little girl who in attempting to enter her father's study, caught her tiny finger in the swinging door. Being a very busy man, he was preoccupied with his task and so paid little attention to her crying. He stopped just long enough to call down stairs to his wife and say, "You better come up here and look after your child." The mother rushed to the rescue and taking the sobbing little girl in her arms she planted tender kisses upon her brow while she massaged the aching finger. "Does it hurt so badly, dear?" she inquired. "Yes, mommy," said the child through her tears, "but the worst is that *Daddy didn't even say, 'oh'!*"

How we need and appreciate compassion and understanding when the sorrows of life press us sore. It is so good to feel a warm handclasp, to see a sympathetic tear flow down the cheek of a friend as he or she weeps with us in our bitter trials. Oh, that we as Christians might be more like our lovely Lord whose great heart was always "filled with compassion" when He saw human need. Of Him the prophet declares, "In all their affliction he was afflicted" (Isa. 63:9a). Do you make it a point to call upon the sick and bereaved, and "weep with those who weep" (Rom. 12:15b)? The love of Christ should ever constrain us and make us "kindly affectioned one to another" (Rom. 12: 10a). The world is dying "for a little bit of love"!　　—H.G.B.

> Just a word of yours may lighten
> 　Hearts bowed down 'neath unseen load:
> O give it now! with love's compassion,
> 　Give a lift along the road!
> Go with messages of comfort:
> 　Wipe the tears that long have flowed
> While you heeded not—nor pitied:
> 　Give a lift along the road!　　—Anon.

"If thou art blessed, then let the sunshine of thy gladness rest on the dark edges of each cloud that lies black in thy brother's skies."—ANON.

SMOOTH PREACHERS

SUGGESTED SCRIPTURE READING: II Peter 2:1-3

. . . speak unto us smooth things.   Isaiah 30:10

Isaiah was a preacher of judgment. He declared without compromise the holiness of God, the filthiness of Israel's sin, and as a result he was hated, persecuted and, according to tradition, martyred by being sawn asunder between two boards (Heb. 11:37). The people resented hearing about the judgments of God but wanted the preacher to talk about "love" instead, and so they said to Isaiah, "Speak unto us smooth things." The word for "smooth" means "flattering." They wanted to be flattered and pleased, and when Isaiah refused, he was put to death.

In the last days in which we live, this scene is being repeated according to the words of Paul. "For the time will come when they will not endure sound doctrine; but after their own lusts shall they heap to themselves teachers, having itching ears; And they shall turn away their ears from the truth, and shall be turned unto fables" (II Tim. 4:3, 4). A faithful ministry is not likely to be a popular one.

A certain man who had listened to a sermon, described it as very "moving, soothing and satisfying." It was moving inasmuch as half the congregation left during the service. It was soothing because the rest fell fast asleep. And it was satisfying for they cared for no more of that sort. We have not preached the Word unless it has disturbed the sinner and awakened the saint. May God deliver me from yielding to the temptation of pleasing the crowd who say, "Speak unto us smooth things." I would rather heed Paul's admonition to "preach the Word" (II Tim. 4:2)!   —M.R.D.

How firm a foundation, ye saints of the Lord,
Is laid for your faith in His excellent Word!
What more can He say than to you He hath said,
To you, who for refuge to Jesus have fled? —G. Keith

"The best way to eradicate evil is to publish and practice the Truth!"

FEAR OR LONGING?

SUGGESTED SCRIPTURE READING: Genesis 3:1-10

. . . I was afraid, because I was naked; and I hid myself.   Genesis 3:10
. . . Even so, come, Lord Jesus!   Revelation 22:20

In these two Scriptures we have the first and the last words in the Bible addressed to God. The contrast between the two is so marked that they appear as different as darkness and light, and such indeed is the case. In the first utterance we have fallen man, naked before God because of his sin, seeking to hide in fear from the penetrating and judging eye of his Maker. In the latter address we have the prayer of a redeemed saint of God, eagerly longing to see his Lord and ready by grace to meet Him. The individuals involved are no different in themselves except that one has been touched by the Cross while the other stands fearful in his original depravity. Grace is the only thing that can change our fear of God into love and give us confidence in His presence. Man cannot stand naked before the Lord; he must needs have the garments of Christ's righteousness about him.

When Dr. H. A. Ironside was young, his children loved to have him play like a bear with them. He would fix some chairs in a corner with an opening on one side. This, then, would become his "den" as he got down on all fours and growled and chased them about the room. The last time they played the game the little fellow ran into a corner and covered his face. He was so excited he began to scream and cry in fear as he heard the "bear" approach and felt his hot breath in his neck. Then, suddenly, the youngster turned and ran into his father's arms saying, "I ain't afraid, not a bit afraid. You are not a bear at all. *You are my own papa.*" Dr. Ironside said he thought to himself, "Oh, God, that is just the way I was once. I was running away from You. I was treating You as if You were my enemy, as though the worst thing in the world would be to be brought into communion with You. I thank You for running me down."

Are you afraid of God or are you longing for Christ's appearing? By this know whether you stand in grace or not. —H.G.B.

> Oh, Saviour Lord, do quickly come,
> Our hearts are aching to be home;
> We long to see Thee as Thou art,
> And love Thee with unsinning heart.—Anon.

"One dreads the return of the Holy Christ if there is not a certain knowledge of sins put away."

THE VIRGIN BIRTH

SUGGESTED SCRIPTURE READING: Luke 1:30-37

And Jesus himself began to be about thirty years of age,
being (as was supposed) the son of Joseph. Luke 3:23

We call your attention to three words in parenthesis in this verse in Luke 3. These three words are "as was supposed." Jesus was (as was supposed) the son of Joseph, but Luke under inspiration carefully guards the cardinal doctrine of the virgin birth of Jesus by reminding us that Joseph was *not* the father of Jesus at all and so he inserts the parenthesis (as was supposed). Jesus was born of a human mother but had not a human father. Jesus was conceived by the Holy Ghost according to the clear and incontestable testimony of the Scriptures. Joseph was the husband of Mary, but not the father of Mary's child.

God who could form the first man out of a lump of clay, make the first woman out of a crooked bone, and cause a human being to develop in the womb of a mother as the result of the union of two almost invisible cells, certainly would have no difficulty with a simple matter like a virgin birth. Take a look at your own body, think of the mystery of digestion, of growth, of metabolism, of controlling your body temperature; consider the stupendous fact of mind and memory; study your eye, the most complete moving picture camera in all the world; consider the brain, the greatest library in the world; your heart beating 70 to 75 times per minute, day and night for 50, 60, 70, 80, or even 90 years. I would ask you, is the virgin birth of Jesus any more wonderful, any more miraculous, more incomprehensible than you are yourself? I declare, as a physician who has attended hundreds upon hundreds of childbirths during my practice of medicine, that the mystery of the natural generation of a new life is as mysterious as the virgin birth. Why then not believe God's record on the testimony of His Word?

—M.R.D.

One parent only:—Mary mild
Was used by God to bring this Child.
Holy Seed through Spirit granted
Was in Mary's womb implanted!—H.G.B.

"We build a small world when we reject Christ the 'Chief Corner Stone'!"

THE REUNIONS OF HEAVEN

SUGGESTED SCRIPTURE READING: I Thessalonians 2:17-20

> *. . . many shall come from the east and west, and shall sit down with Abraham, and Isaac, and Jacob, in the kingdom of heaven.*
> Matthew 8:11

The universal desire to be reunited with loved ones after death is a hope that Scripture supports as a certainty. David's attitude at the passing of his little child, recorded in II Samuel 12, shows that this truth was already firmly believed by God's ancient people. David said of his departed loved one, "I shall go to him." Certainly this was poor comfort if there was to be no recognition.

The words in Matthew 8:11 also emphasize the preservation of personality after death. Abraham, Isaac and Jacob are said to be individually distinguishable.

Moses and Elijah on the Mount of Transfiguration were also immediately discerned by the Lord's disciples, even though they had *never seen them before in this life!* Yes, in the Word of God the doctrine of mutual recognition strongly pervades each and every presentation of the future state!

A Christian engineer who was longing to meet his departed loved ones in Heaven once addressed a large group of railroad men as follows: "I can't begin to tell you, men, what Jesus means to me. In Him I have a hope that is very precious. Years ago, every night as I neared the end of my run, I would open the whistle and let out a blast just as we came around a curve, and I would look up to the top of the hill where stood a little cottage. Then my old mother would come to the door and wave to me. As my engine would go shooting into the tunnel, she would go back inside and say, 'Thank God, Father, Benny is safe home tonight.' Now Mother and Dad are both gone, and there are no dear ones to welcome me. Some day when I shall have finished my run and shall draw near to Heaven's gate, I shall see that same little old couple waiting there for me. As I go sweeping through the gate, I shall see my precious Mother turn to my dear old Dad and hear her say, 'Thank God, Father, Benny is safe home at last.'"
—H.G.B.

> Then let us gird once again with hope,
> And give them smile for smile the while we wait;
> For loving, serving, when our Father calls,
> We'll go to find our dear ones wait us at the gate.

"Heaven is called 'My Father's House' — and shall not His children then be known to each other?"

UNDER NEW MANAGEMENT

SUGGESTED SCRIPTURE READING: Titus 2

. . . separated unto the gospel of God. Romans 1:1

The believer has been separated from judgment and has dissolved partnership with the devil. The sinner is in company with the devil, but when saved that relationship is broken, and we go in partnership with God. We are under new management. Can the world tell, and do they know, you have changed partners?

A certain businessman had a very dishonest and disagreeable partner who almost ruined his business by his shady practices and dishonest transactions. The only thing to save the business was to buy out the scamp's interest and get a more reliable partner. Even after that, however, business did not pick up, and he complained bitterly to a friend. The friend said, "I can explain that. No one knows you have changed partners. They still think 'Smith' is with you. You must advertise your change of management. Take down the old sign 'Smith and Jones,' and put up the new partner's name, 'Brown and Jones.' " The old sign came down, and the new one went up. The change was advertised in the papers. It read as follows, "John Smith and George Jones have separated and dissolved partnership. Charles Brown is now a member of the firm in the capacity of manager. Business at the old stand but under new management and with an entirely new policy." Everyone read it, confidence was restored, and business began to boom.

Will men and women know today that you are in partnership with God and under new management? Have you informed the world that you and the devil are "through" forever? Take down the old sign and light up the new one. Tell somebody *today* about Jesus.   —M.R.D.

> Till the whole world knows,
> Till the whole world knows,
> I will shout and sing of Christ my King,
> Till the whole world knows.—A. H. Ackley

"Separation from the world finds its best advertisement in the testifying tongue that is backed by a consistent, consecrated life." — G.W.

STONE TURNED INTO BREAD

SUGGESTED SCRIPTURE READING: I Kings 17:8-16

. . . command that these stones be made bread. Matthew 4:3

One evening some years ago a poor widow and her crippled daughter were eating the last bit of food they had in the house. As their custom was, they read the Scripture and prayed at the table. The verse which caught their attention was the one, "Command that these stones be made bread." The mother pointed out to the daughter that Jesus would not take Himself, or His need, out of His Father's hand by performing a miracle; for had He called in His Deity to alleviate His hunger, He would have fallen into a trap of the evil one. He would have thereby admitted that neither He, nor the first Adam, could possibly withstand Satan as a *man*. If this were true, the human race could not be rightly blamed by God for its fallen condition. Jesus must of necessity, as the last Adam, overcome the devil. This He did, even though He was at the point of starvation, for it was part of His required work as our Redeemer. The little girl listened and not fully understanding said, "But, Mother, *couldn't* God have turned the stone into bread for Jesus?" "Yes, my dear, and He can do the same for us if it is for His glory and our good." After a word of prayer they retired to bed, trusting that the Lord would provide for them, although there was nothing left in the cupboard. The mother had kept them both in food by whatever scant employment she could obtain and by selling the farm tools, one by one. Now there was nothing left but an old grindstone which no one would purchase.

Early the next morning they were awakened by a farmer, who much to their surprise, was eager to buy the decrepit sharpening tool for $5.00. Realizing they now could buy food, the mother, with tears of joy coursing down her cheeks, ran back to her crippled child saying, "He did it! *God turned the stone into bread!*"

Even as the angels were sent to minister to Jesus who kept Himself in His Father's will, so, too, God will ever provide for those who resist evil and put their trust in Him.   —H.G.B.

Father, Thy mercy hath supplied
Our wants from Thine unbounded store;
Oh, may our souls thro' Christ that died,
Be fed, and never hunger more.—H. L. Hastings

"Faith expects from God what is beyond all expectation."

FROM RED TO WHITE

> *. . . though your sins be as scarlet, they shall be as
> white as snow.*   Isaiah 1:18

We usually refer to sin as being black, but in the Bible sin
is said to be crimson and scarlet. I am told that the most difficult color to cover is red. Painters tell me that any other color,
even black, can easily be covered with white paint, but with
red it is different, for it will "bleed through." But God can
change red to white by painting it with the red blood of Jesus.

There is a tradition by Jewish rabbis, that the High Priest
bound a scarlet fillet around the neck of the scapegoat (Lev.
16:7), as the sin bearer; and that when the priest confessed his
own, and the people's sins upon the goat (Lev. 16:21, 22), then
the cloth became white if the atonement was accepted. If it
was not accepted, it remained scarlet. The rabbis further say
that the goat was led twelve furlongs out of Jerusalem where
it was thrown down a precipice and was mangled by the fall.
In case the sacrifice was accepted by God, a scarlet ribbon
which had been hung at the door of the temple would turn
from scarlet to white. They (the rabbis) tell us that this changing of the ribbon from red to white was the thing which Isaiah
refers to when he writes, "Though your sins be as scarlet they
shall be as white as snow; though they be red like crimson they
shall be as wool."

The preceding story is only a tradition, but it is no tradition
that "The Blood of Jesus Christ His Son cleanseth us from all
sin" (I John 1:7b).

> "Have you been to Jesus for the cleansing power?
> Are you washed in the blood of the Lamb?
> Are you fully trusting in His grace this hour?
> Are you washed in the blood of the Lamb?"

—M.R.D.

> Whiter than snow! nothing further I need,
> Christ is the Fountain, this only I plead!
> This is the only assurance I know,
> Wash me, and I shall be whiter than snow!—N. Hall

"Man may whitewash himself, but only God can wash him white."

PART ON, PART OFF

SUGGESTED SCRIPTURE READING: Colossians 3:16, 17

. . . because thou art lukewarm, and neither cold nor hot, I will spue thee out of my mouth. Revelation 3:16

It is strange to note that the Laodicean church which is especially condemned, and literally makes God "retch," is not accused of what we usually consider to be "gross sins." It is not said to be immoral in its conduct, nor idolatrous in its practice, nor even apostate in holding to false doctrine. Its severe condemnation is based on its prideful self-satisfaction and *its lack of zeal and warmth.* What a warning this is to all of us today. We, who pat ourselves on the back for our good moral conduct, our purity of doctrine, and our "going and growing" religious organizations should take special notice. If all of our church-going and religious exercise is but outward show, "warmed-over" piety, and a mere mental "joy ride," we are caught in a snare and a delusion. If there is no deep love for Christ, no warmth of true fellowship with God and each other, no zeal for missions, no burden for the lost, no humble yearning and striving to be like Jesus, no burning desire for true holiness, and no glow of His presence in our breast — BEWARE! This is the nauseating, lukewarm hypocrisy that makes God sick!

A number of years ago in Washington a man was returning from visiting friends one cold night in January when his train stopped suddenly. As it showed no disposition to move, he asked the conductor what was wrong. "A car off the track ahead," he said. As cold as the night was, he got off the train to investigate and found the car in such a position as to block progress entirely. He turned to the conductor and said: "It seems to me that the car is not off the track. If it were, we could go on." "That's right," said the trainman, "the trouble is it is *partly on and partly off.*" So, too, those who hinder the work of Christ, are not so much the avowed unbelievers but rather nominal Christians who are "half on and half off the track." —H.G.B.

I am saved, but do I gladly,
Lord, leave all and follow Thee;
If Thou callest do I answer,
Here am I, send me, send me?—Anon.

"In the service of Christ there is no substitute for thorough-going, ardent, and sincere earnestness!"

RATS AND CATS

SUGGESTED SCRIPTURE READING: Psalm 31:19-24

> . . . *with the temptation (trial) also make a way to escape.* I Corinthians 10:13

The Lord will never test us beyond our ability to bear, but just when all hope seems gone He steps in to deliver us. For each test he gives us strength and for each trial a way to escape. Our troubles are but God's opportunity to make us glad. A little girl who had to sleep in a garret infested with rats of which she was terribly afraid, asked of the Lord, "Please, Jesus, chase away the rats." No sooner had she prayed, than the cat, seeing the door ajar, slipped into the room and scattered the rats from the room. A coincidence you say? Oh, no! There are no "co-incidences" with God when He answers the prayers of His children. God has control of cats and rats as well as kings and rulers, and they obey His command.

If there are rats in your life, God has just the right cats to drive them away. Nothing happens to the Christian without a purpose. "All things" work together for good. *"All things."* God even allows some "rats" to trouble us so that we may appreciate his "cats." The gloomy garret where the little girl slept had holes out of which came the rats, but it also had a door through which came the cat. Our deepest sorrows often lead to the greatest blessings.

1. Jacob found God on a stony pillow (Gen. 28:18).
2. Moses got his commission in a desert (Ex. 3:1-4).
3. David turned the taunt of a giant into victory (I Sam. 17).
4. Joseph went to Egypt's throne by way of the pit (Gen. 37).
5. Paul learned patience through a thorn (II Cor. 12:7).
6. John saw paradise while in exile (Rev. 1:9).
7. Stephen saw Jesus while being stoned (Acts 7).
8. Jesus was made perfect through sufferings (Heb. 2:10).

—M.R.D.

The Father reigneth, cease all doubt;
Hold on, my heart, hold on, hold out!—Anon.

"Nothing will show more accurately what we are than the way in which we meet trials and difficulties."

PREVAILING PRAYER

SUGGESTED SCRIPTURE READING: I Kings 17:1, 17-24

> . . . *The effectual fervent prayer of a righteous man availeth much.* James 5:16

Oh, that Christians might know how to use more effectively the mighty instrument of prevailing prayer! Oh, for a desperate earnestness, a real zeal in our petitions and a spiritual understanding of this vital power. Too often our intercession is but an orderly arrangement of pious phrases beautifully linked together, a meaningless repetition of words we memorize and "run off" at the appropriate time. There is too much of powerless, anemic "saying of prayers" and not enough earnest, genuine supplication. Effective prayer requires a right relationship to God. One must be on "praying ground." Secondly, there must also be a deep earnestness and an understanding of a vital need with a willingness to sacrifice self and all else that is necessary, to obtain the blessing.

When Jonathan Edwards preached his great sermon, "Sinners in the Hands of an Angry God," it is said that he had a little manuscript that he held up so close to his face that no one could see his countenance. He went on and on, but the people in the crowded church were tremendously moved. One man sprang to his feet, rushed down the aisle and cried, "Mr. Edwards, have mercy!" Others grabbed hold of the backs of the pews lest they should slip into perdition. They were under such conviction that they felt as if the day of judgment had already dawned upon them. There was a real spiritual reason behind the power of that sermon. For three days Edwards had not eaten a morsel of food, nor closed his eyes in sleep. Over and over again he had been heard to exclaim, "Oh, God give me New England! Give me New England!" When he finally arose from his knees and made his way to the pulpit, he looked as if he had been gazing straight into the face of God. Before he even opened his lips to speak, great conviction fell upon his audience. Oh, for more effectual, fervent prayer! —H.G.B.

> Send coals of heavenly fire
> From the altar of the skies;
> Fill our hearts with strong desire,
> Till our prayers like incense rise!—A. B. Simpson

"Strength in prayer is better than length in prayer; where prayer focuses, power falls."

THE POWER OF LIGHT

SUGGESTED SCRIPTURE READING: John 9:1-5

. . . men loved darkness . . . because their deeds were
evil. John 3:19

When I was a little lad, we did not as yet have electric lights. Everyone went to bed by the light of a candle or kerosene lamp. The houses were all dark after 9 or 10 o'clock; and if we saw light in a neighbor's house during the late night, we knew someone was sick. The streets were only dimly lighted with lamps on posts, which were lit by lamplighters at dusk as they carried their little ladder from street-lamp to street-lamp. Robberies were an easy matter, for the criminals could perform in the dark and do their work unobserved. As a result people were compelled to guard their possessions with iron bars and locks.

I recall the town jewelry store. In the show window were valuable articles of jewelry: watches, chains, bracelets and stickpins. The window was protected by heavy iron bars to discourage robbers and thieves. Then came the electric lights. Storekeepers installed their lights and left them on all night, flooding the show window with brightness. Soon the iron bars came down, for the light was a greater discouragement and deterrent than bars of iron. Today we do not have the iron bars but the light to discourage theft. Before the LIGHT of the world came, the iron bars of the law were set up to discourage sin. Now we have God to protect us from sin. Jesus said, "Every one that doeth evil hateth the light, neither cometh to the light lest his deeds should be 'discovered.'" There is no better insurance against falling into sin than to "walk in the light" (I John 1:7). "He that doeth the truth cometh to the light" (John 3:21).

—M.R.D.

Thou art the Truth; Thy Word alone
True wisdom can impart;
Thou only canst inform the mind
And purify the heart.　　—Anon.

"Truth reveals crookedness and error, for truth, like light, travels only in straight lines."—COLTON

JABEZ

SUGGESTED SCRIPTURE READING: Genesis 39:20-23

And Jabez was more honourable than his brethren: and his mother called his name Jabez, saying, Because I bare him with sorrow. And Jabez called on the God of Israel, saying, Oh that thou wouldest bless me indeed, and enlarge my coast, and that thine hand might be with me, and that thou wouldest keep me from evil, that it may not grieve me! And God granted him that which he requested!　　　I Chronicles 4:9, 10

This verse is one of the many little jewels which God has cast into the oft-avoided book of Chronicles to reward those who diligently search His Word.

What was the "sorrow" which beset the mother of Jabez that she should give him a name which means "desert" or "dry place"? Was it the physical pain of childbirth? Was it sorrow at having to care for another child when, as she supposed, she already had sufficient children? Or was there a death in the family when this son was born? We do not know! But, as is always the case under grace, the last became *first!* This "desert" one, Jabez, became *the well-watered soul,* the "more honourable" one; a man of prayer that desired spiritual gifts and eschewed evil. A man who could move heaven by his petitions so that "God granted him that which he requested"!

Is it not often the same with us? These things which we count "sorrow" . . . do they not often become the lustrous jewels of His grace? Considering Romans 8:28, let us be slow in calling our pilgrimage experiences "Jabez," for grace will yet cause our "desert" to "blossom as the rose"!　　　—H.G.B.

> When trouble, like a gloomy cloud,
> Has gathered thick and thundered loud,
> He near my soul has always stood—
> His loving-kindness, Oh how good! —Anon.

"Lest the gloom should appall us, God braids the cloud with sunshine!"
　　　— BONAR

DOES IT MAKE SENSE?

SUGGESTED SCRIPTURE READING: Nehemiah 8:1-8

> *They read in the book . . . distinctly, and gave the*
> *sense.* Nehemiah 8:8

Ezra, the scribe, was a good preacher. After Nehemiah had repaired the walls of Jerusalem and rebuilt the temple, a great mass meeting was called of all the people old enough to understand the Word (Neh. 8:2). Ezra stood in the pulpit, while the people stood for an entire half day, from morning until noon, listening to the Word. For five or six hours Ezra read in the Book of the Law. An interesting detail is given in verse 8. Ezra read *distinctly* and gave the *sense*. There is the Bible's formula for "good" preaching. Why preach, if no one can understand us? It must be distinct so a child can understand. It must make sense, or else it is senseless. How many sermons have you listened to and heard only "words" instead of "The Word"? Simplicity and not profundity should be our aim. Some sermons are so far over people's heads, no one can reach the "fodder." God's people are not "giraffes" but sheep, so keep the "feed" where they can reach it.

A person who had finished college boasted to his unlettered friend that he had now become a great orator. When asked what an orator was, he said, "Let me illustrate. When you walk up to a common person like you and ask him how much is two and two, he says, 'Four.' But if you ask an orator like me, I say, 'When in the course of human events it becomes necessary to take the numeral of the second denomination and add it to the figure two, I say unto you all without fear of successful contradiction that the result will invariably be four.' That's an orator!"

—M.R.D.

Make the Gospel clear and plain,
That the world may hear His voice,
"As a little child" explain
So that angels may rejoice! —G.W.

" 'Brevity is the spice of wit' and the pungent flavoring of understanding."

THE "SECOND REST"

Suggested Scripture Reading: Matthew 11:20-30

Come unto me, . . . and I will GIVE *you rest . . . Take
my* YOKE *upon you, and* LEARN *of me; . . . and ye shall*
FIND REST *unto your souls.*   Matthew 11:28, 29

Many fail to distinguish between the two kinds of rest that
Jesus here offers. The first is a *gift;* it is the rest of *salvation.*
The second costs us something in terms of work for Christ and
sacrifice of self. This rest of *sanctification and discipleship*
which we *find* only as we *take the yoke* of Christ upon us and
learn of Him was that to which Wesley referred in his hymn
where he prays:

"Let us *all in Thee inherit,*
Let us find that SECOND REST!"

Many Christians miss God's best because they refuse to crucify their own ego, be a disciple, and take the yoke of verse 29.
Consequently, they never experience the deeper joys of the
"more abundant life."

A Christian, trying to explain these truths to a famous doctor,
found it difficult to make him understand. At last he said, "Suppose you should meet with a patient who entreated you earnestly to take his case under your special care, but who at the
same time refused to tell you all his symptoms or take all your
prescribed remedies. Suppose he should say to you, 'I am quite
willing to follow your directions as long as they commend themselves to my mind as being good, but in other matters I prefer
judging for myself and following my own directions.' What
would you do?"

"Do!" replied the doctor with indignation, "Do! I would soon
leave such a man as that to his own care. I could do nothing
for him unless he would put his whole case into my hands without any reservation, and would obey my directions implicitly."

"And that is consecration," said the Christian worker. "God
must have the whole case put into His hands without any reser-
vations, and His directions must be implicitly followed."

"I see it," said the doctor, "and I will do it. God shall have
His own way with me from henceforth." Christian, have you
attained unto Christ's "Second Rest?"   —H.G.B.

Who answers Christ's insistent call
Must give himself, his life, his all!—J. Oxenham

"If we want an increase of Christ, there must be a decrease of self."

"THREE DAYS' JOURNEY"

SUGGESTED SCRIPTURE READING: Romans 10:9-13

> *We will go three days' journey into the wilderness,*
> *and sacrifice to the Lord our God, as he shall com-*
> *mand us.*   Exodus 8:27

When Moses and Aaron petitioned Pharaoh to let the people of Israel go out of the land of bondage that they might sacrifice to the Lord, that diabolical tyrant presented many objections to their plan. All of his suggestions and counter proposals were subtly calculated to prevent the full deliverance of these op-pressed people. He was violently opposed to their complete separation from Egypt even on a temporary basis. His objections were masterminded no doubt by Satan himself, who desires to keep every soul "in bondage." One of the four unacceptable suggestions that Pharaoh made was that Israel should sacrifice to Jehovah *"in the land"* (Ex. 8:25). Moses, however, was not deceived by this proposal. He recognized immediately that *separation from the world is the first rule of service.* There was no compromise possible on this point. God's people had to be distinct and remove themselves from Egypt; for Egypt was a type of the world. "Come out from among them, and be ye separate" (II Cor. 6:17), was already the Divine principle even in Moses' day. And so he tells Pharaoh that his suggestion is unacceptable and that they must go "three days' journey into the wilderness" as the Lord had commanded them.

All of this is rich in its teaching for us today. Salvation involves deliverance from the world. And pray, what is the distance of the separation needed? The answer is: nothing less than a "three days' journey." What a beautfiul symbol we have here of the deliverance afforded us by the death, burial and resurrection of our Lord!

The world and the Christian have no common ground of fellowship; there must be a "three days' journey" between them!

—H.G.B.

> Vain world, I turn away
> Though thou seem fair and good;
> That friendly outstretched hand of thine
> Is stained with Jesus' blood. —Anon.

"The believer must know where the death and resurrection of the Lord Jesus Christ have forever set him, ere he can be an intelligent worshipper, an acceptable servant, or an effectual witness." — C.H.M.

SEEKING EARLY

SUGGESTED SCRIPTURE READING: Proverbs 8:1-17

. . . those that seek me early shall find me. Proverbs 8:17

Why do we think it so remarkable when an aged man or woman is saved? Is it not because it is so rare and unusual? The very fact that we think it so wonderful proves the danger of waiting until one is older. The majority of people who are saved are saved in their youth, most of them in their teens. Authentic statistics show that if one is not converted before the age of 25 the possibility of his ever being saved diminishes rapidly. The more often the Gospel is rejected, the less possibility there is of receiving it. Therefore, the Bible says, "Those that seek me early shall find me."

There is, however, another reason why we should seek the Lord early in life. When a youth is saved, he has all of life before him to serve the Lord and bear fruit for the Saviour. When an old man is saved, he is saved so as by fire with no days left to serve the Lord. Someone has said, "When you save an old person you save a unit; when you save a child you save a whole multiplication table." Yet we make a great fuss when some aged person with no service to bring to the Lord is converted, but when a little child is saved, we act as though it were either questionable or unimportant. Yet what an opportunity to dedicate one's whole life early to the Lord.

There was once a horse that ran away in the morning and did not return to its master until late in the evening. When the owner upbraided the horse, it replied, "But here I am, I have returned, and you have your horse." "True," said the master, "*but my field is unploughed.*" If a man turns to God in old age, God gets a man, but He has been defrauded of this man's work. My great personal regret is that I did not turn to Christ until after I had given over thirty years to the devil.—M.R.D.

O the years of sinning wasted,
Could I but recall them now,
I would give them to my Saviour,
To His will I'd gladly bow. —C. C. Luther

"Blessed is the man who has the seed of salvation sown in his heart while yet a child, for he shall have a lifetime in which to pluck all the delightful fruits of salvation!" — G.W.

THE HORSE-SHOE CURVE

Suggested Scripture Reading: Psalm 77:1-12

> *. . . thou shalt remember all the way which the Lord thy God led thee.*   Deuteronomy 8:2

I shall never forget my first trip by train to the east coast. As we approached Altoona, Pennsylvania, we came to the famous "horse shoe curve." The tracks follow a gigantic curve around a deep ravine. At the beginning of the curve you can see the track on the other side of the ravine going in the opposite direction. But the real thrill was the second look at the curve, after we had rounded the closed end of the horseshoe. Then we could see the part over which we had traveled. It was an awesome sight. On a narrow shelf, cut out of the mountain, the tracks seemed to hang precariously on the rim of the cut which fell away almost vertically to the yawning chasm below.

I remember how I tried to visualize what could happen should a train leave the tracks. But we had a careful engineer who progressed at such slow speed that there was no danger. And I remembered, I too, had a careful Engineer who knew the curves of life, and was worthy of all confidence. I recalled the words of Moses who said, "Thou shalt remember all the way which the Lord thy God led thee."

What precious assurance comes to us as we begin a new day to remember that He has never failed in the past and His promises for the future are secure. He has promised:

"Lo, I am with you alway" (Matt. 28:20).

"I will never leave thee" (Heb. 13:5).

"As thy days, so shall thy strength be" (Deut. 33:25).

"Be not afraid" (Josh. 1:9).

"Don't worry" (Matt. 6:25).

When the day seems dark and the trials seem too much for you — then remember, He has promised that He will not lay upon you more than you can bear.   —M.R.D.

> Wait on the Lord thou weary one,
> When cares of life oppress;
> In Him find ev'ry need supplied;
> In Him find quietness. —F. Shepard

"We trust as we love. If we love Christ, surely we shall trust Him much." — T. Brooks.

"OLD CAST CLOUTS"

SUGGESTED SCRIPTURE READING: I Corinthians 1:26-31

Put now these old cast clouts and rotten rags under thine armholes under the cords. And Jeremiah did so. Jeremiah 38:12

"Old cast clouts" . . . this is one of the strangest expressions in all of the Holy Scriptures, and yet it contains a message of encouragement concerning the wondrous workings of His grace! These matted bits of patched rags and refuse cloth served a noble purpose: they eased and blessed a prophet of God! Acting as a soft padding under the emaciated arms of Jeremiah, they assisted in bringing him up out of a deep and loathsome dungeon whose very floor was quicksand and mire. Yes, by them he was drawn onto the solid ground. Here he enjoyed the welcome sunlight and was afforded the companionship of a king.

All of us by nature are useless and disgusting "old cast clouts" for "we are all as an *unclean thing,* and all our righteousnesses are as *filthy rags*" (Isa. 64:6). Nothing we do can merit salvation, and even our best works after we are saved are polluted with sin; but, praise His Name, in His grace He deigns to use these "old cast clouts" and will even reward us at His judgment seat in that day when every man shall "have praise of God" (I Cor. 4:5).

Do you feel useless and helpless? Then rejoice, for He chooses the "weak things" to exalt His glory. Perhaps He will yet use you or me to lift some one of His dear children out of the "dungeon-mire" of this world into the sunlight of love and the intimate fellowship of the King! Praise God, there is still service waiting for "old cast clouts" like you and me!   —H.G.B.

> Who does God's work will get God's pay,
> However long may seem the day!
> He does not pay as others pay,
> In gold, or land, or raiment gay;
> But, who does God's work: . . . will get God's pay!—Anon.

"Keep thy spiritual tools ready and sharp, and God will find thee work!"

OPEN YOUR HAND

SUGGESTED SCRIPTURE READING: I Timothy 6:10-19

. . . ready to distribute, willing to communicate.

I Timothy 6:18

It is no sin to be rich in this world's goods if one knows how to use his riches for the glory of God and the good of mankind. It is the "love" of money which is the root of all evil (I Tim. 6:10). Covetousness is severely condemned in the Scripture, and "riches" are often more of a curse than a blessing. Riches alone cannot bring happiness, and some of the unhappiest persons in the world are those who possess most of this world's goods. The ability to make money is as much God's gift as the ability to preach or to sing.

Paul tells Timothy to charge those who are rich in this world not to trust in these uncertain riches, but in the living God (I Tim. 6:17).

The things of a material nature are given to us to "richly enjoy," and Paul suggests that the best way to enjoy "wealth" is to use it for the glory of God. Every man, be he poor or rich, is responsible to God for everything he possesses. Each of us will have to render an account of how we have spent our time, our strength, and our money. Paul says, "Be ready to *distribute*." The word means, "open your hand." Be "open-handed" and ready to share. When we only "hoard," it results in covetousness.

A little boy had his hand caught in a milk bottle. Try as they would, he and his mother could not pull it out until she saw he had his hand closed. Then she said, "Open your hand, Johnny." Johnny said, "If I do, I'll drop the penny I am holding." Is your hand open? Ready to distribute; willing to communicate?—M.R.D.

> We are not storehouses, but channels;
> We are not cisterns, but springs,
> Passing our benefits onward,
> Fitting our blessings with wings;
> Letting the water flow onward
> To spread o'er the desert forlorn;
> Sharing our bread with our brothers,
> Our comfort with those who mourn.—Anon.

"What you do with your money tells what it has done to you."

VICTORY THROUGH YIELDING

SUGGESTED SCRIPTURE READING: II Chronicles 30:7-9

. . . but YIELD *yourselves unto God.*   Romans 6:13

A famous traveler tells the story of how he and his party once tried to climb one of the highest peaks of the Sierra Nevada mountains. "After infinite difficulty, exertion and peril," he says, "we finally succeeded in surmounting the last precipice and reached the summit, only to find on the opposite side the tracks of a wagon and the traces of a social feast!" . . . If only he had taken the other side of the mountain he would have found an easily traveled road all the way up! How like this foolish explorer are many Christians! Faced with a mountain of trouble and besetting sins, they seek to struggle towards victory *in their own strength,* without realizing that God has provided a super highway to the Christian's "Arch of Triumph" atop the "Hill of Difficulty"! It is a strange paradox that victory in the Christian life is not attained by fighting, but rather by *"yielding"!* "Walk in the Spirit, and ye shall not fulfill the lusts of the flesh" (Gal. 5:16). If we will but "deny ourselves," that is, "crucify our old ego" and enthrone the Saviour and His Spirit in our heart, we will find that *God will take over the battle for us.* In our weakness we will find His strength! Jesus did not mean for us to live defeated lives, but rather to revel in the fruits of victory as "more than conquerors" in Him. The secret is in *"yielding* yourself unto God." Are you tired of struggling? Then, just *"Let go* . . . and *let God!"*   —H.G.B.

> I rest upon Thy promise, Lord;
> And trust Thy love and power;
> Oh, make me more than conqueror now,
> And in the final hour!   —Anon.

"The best place to prepare for the duties of life is, like Mary, . . . at Jesus' feet!"

THE ACCEPTABLE OFFERING

Suggested Scripture Reading: Hebrews 9:6-15

*Unto Adam also and to his wife did the Lord God
make coats of skins, and clothed them.* Genesis 3:21

Here is the first mention of sacrifice in the Bible. Adam's fig
leaves had failed and now God comes and slays an animal, takes
the skins, and clothes Adam. His sin is not only covered but
atoned for, in the first mention of sacrifice. Now we find in this
first mention of an atonement, three definite things:

1. Salvation must be God's gift. It was God who provided
the animal.

2. It must be by the shedding of blood.

3. It must be by the death of a substitute.

Now all three of these are found in this passage. God made
the coats of skins Himself, rather than the work of Adam's hands.
In order to get these skins an innocent animal naturally must
die, and its blood must be shed. Now by the law of first mention,
every subsequent sacrifice, to be acceptable to God, must meet
the three requirements of this first occurrence.

1. It must be God's gift.

2. It must be by blood.

3. It must be by the death of a substitute.

Omit one or more and God must reject the offering. We have
an example in the very next chapter, Genesis 4. Cain brought
a sacrifice, beautiful, sincere, costly, no doubt. But God rejected
it because it was the labor of his own hands and not God's gift.
It involved no death by the shedding of blood.　　　—M.R.D.

> Nothing to settle? — all has been paid;
> Nothing of anger? — peace has been made.
> Jesus alone is the sinners' resource,
> Peace He has made by the blood of His Cross.—Anon.

**"I have never seen men that were straight on the Blood, that were not
straight on almost everything else in the Book, . . . or . . . perfectly
willing to be taught!" — PAUL RADER**

"ONIONS, LEEKS, AND GARLIC!"

SUGGESTED SCRIPTURE READING: I John 2:15-17

We remember the fish, which we did eat in Egypt freely; the cucumbers, and the melons, and the leeks, and the onions, and the garlick.   Numbers 11:5

When the multitude of the Israelites "fell a lusting," immediately the sweet manna from heaven became unpalatable to them! The "flesh-pots of Egypt" had a more pungent flavor. They longed for the earthly leeks, onions, and garlic, and the melon patches that were all a part of their old life of slavery and bondage. They were so blinded by their carnal desires that they supposed that these "tokens of the flesh" had been theirs "freely," while in fact they had cost them the sweat, tears and degradation of a life bereft of true freedom and hope! Yes, the onions, leeks, and garlic had a racy dash and thrill that the oily, sweet manna could not equal. But oh, how foolish they were; for despite the outward zest and taste-appeal of these herbs of the earth, *they contained hardly a calorie of true nourishment!* Their value was but for the moment of partaking, no permanent good or blessing was imparted. Rather, they disturb true digestion, impart a disagreeable aftertaste in the mouth, and make foul the breath!

Remembering that all these things happened unto them for our example, we ask: Do you enjoy and long for the flesh-pots of this world? Do you miss the thrill, the glitter of the old vanity fair of sinful Egypt? Yes, there are "pleasures" in sin, but they are only "for a season," impart no true nourishment, and consequently starve the soul! In fact, they disturb the digestion of any "heavenly Manna" that may also be taken by worldly Christians. They leave a bitter aftertaste of remorse! The "breath" of testimony is beclouded and so foul with the stench of "leeks, onions, and garlic" that everyone is offended. The Heavenly Manna, rich with the oil of the Holy Spirit, is the nourishment the starving soul needs! Remember, Christian, you can't play with the things of the world and get away with it! Your "spiritual halitosis" will give you away!   —H.G.B.

Come, for the feast is spread; hark to the call!
Come to the Living Bread, broken for all!—Henry Burton

"Christians that move the world are the ones who do not let the world move them!"

STRANGE PLACES

Then Jonah prayed unto the LORD his God out of the fish's belly.   Jonah 2:1

What a strange place for a prayer meeting. Jonah had gotten himself into real trouble by his disobedience and running away from God. He was cast into the sea, swallowed by a fish and penned up in the stomach of a sea monster. Although Jonah was there through his own fault, God was also there to hear his prayer, and when he confessed, God forgave and delivered him.

God's children get themselves into some strange places and unhappy circumstances because of their folly. Consider the following incidents:

Jonah in the fish's belly (Jonah 2:1);
David in the court of Achish (I Sam. 21:10);
Abram in Egypt (Gen. 12:10);
Lot in Sodom (Gen. 13:12);
Elijah under the Juniper tree (I Kings 19:4), and
Peter in the judgment hall (Luke 22:55-62).

These are but a few examples of the strange places God's children may sometimes be found. They should not be there, but they all too often are. Are you in a strange place today? Are you out of fellowship, defeated and unhappy? Then cry to God, confess your sin and be restored by his abundant mercy (I John 1:9). God is waiting to hear your faintest cry and recognize your first move of repentance.

Walking past my barn one day I heard a plaintive chirping inside and upon investigation found a poor bluejay beating its wings against the glass pane of the window. Had it not "cried and chirped" I would not have heard, but its plaintive note prompted me to open the door wide and it flew out to liberty. Maybe you through your own folly are in a strange place — but He is waiting to hear your cry.   —M.R.D.

> Then I ceased my vain endeavor,
>   And to Jesus yielded all;
> Then He came, the Overcomer,
>   Conq'ring foes both great and small.—J. Complin

"There is nothing so small but that we may honor God by asking His guidance of it, or insult Him by taking it into our own hands."
                                        — J. RUSKIN

A SPECK OF DUST

SUGGESTED SCRIPTURE READING: Job 34:11-16

. . . for dust thou art, and unto dust shalt thou return.
Genesis 3:19

Hear this, proud, self-willed man that would exalt yourself to heaven and become as God: you are but a speck of dust blown up by My breath! You are but a weak creature of time sustained by your Creator! When I withdraw your breath you will revert again, physically, to the earth beneath your feet from which you were formed! . . . Such was the rebuke implied in the words spoken to Adam immediately after the fall. . . . It is well for us to recognize our humble origin and to know that with sin now operative within us, the paths of all earthly glory "lead but to the grave"! Proper spiritual perspective demands that we be aware of our minuteness in the eyes of God, to whom all "the nations are as a drop in a bucket, and are counted as the small dust of the balance" (Isa. 40:15).

Modern science has recently emphasized this truth by confirming the fact that the atoms of which we are composed are almost all empty space! Each atom is similar to the solar system: a few specks of matter scattered through a comparably huge amount of sidereal nothingness. Therefore, they tell us, should all the space in the atoms of the body of a 200 pound man be removed and only the solid substance be retained "he would be no bigger than *a particle of dust*"!

It is expedient that we should recognize with Job that we dwell here in "houses of clay, whose foundation is in the dust" (Job 4:19)! This knowledge should make us reverence our Creator, humble ourselves and seek our salvation apart from our own transitory being, and finally make us aspire to that "house not made with hands, eternal in the heavens" (II Cor. 5:1)! All our boasting and vaunted greatness fall before these words: "He remembereth that we are dust" (Ps. 103:14)!   —H.G.B.

> Without Thy Presence we are poor,
> And trivial trials can not endure!
> The "clay" can only stand the test,
> As Thou dost keep the soul well blest!—Anon.

"The Scripture says: 'He that humbleth himself shall be exalted'; . . . evidently the crowns of heaven are not reserved for swell heads!"

JUST TIED ON

SUGGESTED SCRIPTURE READING: Jude 1:11-20

*He that abideth in me, and I in him, the same bring-
eth forth much fruit.* John 15:5

The evidence of life is fruit, and the nature of the fruit reveals
the nature of the tree. Jesus said, "By their fruits ye shall know
them." But fruit can also be imitated and often is. In our home
is a glass bowl containing a wax pear, peach, apple and a banana.
They look like the real thing, but they are really counterfeits
and totally unfit to eat. So, too, it is in life. Real spiritual fruit
is the result of life, and has within it the seed of life. Morality,
religion, human righteousness, culture and false piety may seem
like the real thing, but are totally unacceptable to God as a payment for salvation. The fruits of our own works are imitations;
only the fruit of the Spirit is real and remains.

A Christian gardener, employed by a wealthy, outwardly religious but unregenerate gentleman, tried in vain to show his
employer that religion without Christ, no matter how sincere,
was not enough. The gardener hit upon a novel idea. In the
garden was a barren tree which never bore fruit. One day the
proprietor saw to his surprise, hanging upon the tree, some beautiful fruit. Imagine his dismay when, as he eagerly tried to pick
the fruit, he found that it was artificial fruit merely tied on to
the tree. The gardener had tied this artificial fruit to the limbs in
an effort to demonstrate to his master the difference between religion and Christ. What kind of fruit do you bear? That which
springs from within, or is it merely "tied on" the outside? It is
an important question. —M.R.D.

> I have a lesson learned
> My life is but a field
> Stretched out beneath God's sky,
> Some harvest rich to yield.—Anon.

"Don't just be good; — be good for something!"

HIMSELF!

SUGGESTED SCRIPTURE READING: I Peter 2:1-7

And if I go and prepare a place for you, I will come again, and receive you unto myself; that where I am, there ye may be also. John 14:3

With the sweet words of consolation recorded in the sublime 14th chapter of John, Jesus seeks to quiet our fears concerning the state of the soul after death. His tone is soothing; His comments simple and direct. He encourages us to put our confidence in Him for the future. His Father's House, to which He is going, is ample and magnificent. It is filled with a multitude of glorious apartments or mansions. There is more than enough room for all. He promises to prepare "abiding places" for our souls which shall be delightsome and perfectly adapted to our needs. It will be a Home such as home on earth, be it ever so sweet, has never been. But, best of all, *it will include eternal fellowship with Himself!* We shall not lose our way to these beautiful mansions, for He has promised to come and personally escort us to the Father's House. There He will be our Friend and Companion forever and we shall "behold His glory" (John 17:24a). When the "veil is lifted" and we at last enter into the joy of our Lord, we shall find the beatific vision of seeing Him "face to face" to be the height of unutterable ecstasy. Luther says we should make this holy and comforting thought our constant "pillow, and a bed of down for our souls."

A young Christian, at the death-bed of an aged saint, said to him, "Shall I read to you the sweetest verse in the Bible?" "Yes," said the other weakly. The lad turned to John 14 and read the second verse concerning the "many mansions." "Yes, that is wonderful, but that is not the sweetest verse. Read on to where it says, 'I will come again *and receive you unto myself.'*" "That is the most precious part," said the dying man. "It is not the mansions so much, it is *Himself* I want!" —H.G.B.

When I look in His face, His wonderful face,
In heaven, that beautiful place! . . .
All the hardships of earth will seem nothing,
When I look in my dear Saviour's face. —L. DeArmond

"Grand, beyond all earthly comprehension, is the thought that the heaven of our Lord is the home of our soul." — G. WOODS

THE BURNED-OVER PLACE

Suggested Scripture Reading: II Corinthians 5:18-21

But he was wounded for our transgressions, he was bruised for our iniquities: the chastisement of our peace was upon him; and with his stripes we are healed. Isaiah 53:5

The following story is told about one of the early settlers of the western prairies. One day a cloud of smoke was detected upon the horizon and to the people's horror, recognized as a prairie fire, fanned by a strong wind, bearing down upon them. As the flames leaped into the air and the smoke billowed upward, one man, to the amazement of the others, quickly set fire to the grass before them. It soon gained in volume and widened its path leaving a charred and barren area behind. As soon as the place was burned over, they quickly moved into the grassless area and standing in the midst of the "burned-over" place saw the fire sweep down upon them till it reached the burned over area and *stopped!* There was nothing left to burn and they were safe while the fire swept around them. They were safe in the "burned-over place."

The fires of God's judgment are descending upon a wicked world, but God has provided a "burned-over place." At Calvary the fire of God's justice was met by Jesus. He bore our sin there and fully paid for our transgressions. He made full satisfaction for our sins, and we who have taken our stand by faith in the finished work of Christ are safe in the "burned-over" place. The "burned-over" place is Calvary. There is nothing left to burn. He bore "our sins in his own body on the tree, that we being dead to sins, should live unto righteousness: by whose stripes ye were healed" (I Pet. 2:24). —M.R.D.

The flames of God's judgment can never touch me,
For Jesus has borne all the wrath on the Tree;
I stand now secure in the "burned-over place,"
A sinner, unworthy, yet saved by His grace!—G. Woods

"Some people who plan to accept Christ at the eleventh hour die at ten-thirty."

"MARAH" AND THE CROSS

Suggested Scripture Reading: II Timothy 4:5-8

> *. . . they could not drink of the waters of Marah, for they were bitter: . . . And he cried unto the Lord; and the Lord shewed him a tree, which when he had cast into the waters, the waters were made sweet.*
>
> Exodus 15:23, 25

Israel had just come out of the bondage of Egypt by way of the miraculous Red Sea experience. They had thus typified God's plan of salvation which triumphs over the world, the flesh and the devil by the simple expedient of taking by faith the heaven-prepared and God-appointed "way" through the waters of judgment! Testifying to this with conviction they sing: "The Lord is my strength and song, and He is become *my salvation*"! (See Exodus 15:2.) Alas, this song of joy was short-lived, not because the redemption was less certain, but because the wilderness path of God's leading was not full of luxury and ease, as they supposed, but rather proved to be a thorny, narrow passage full of tribulation and fiery trial. They found, as do all of us who love the Lord, that "this world is not a friend to grace"! Its experiences are hard, trying and *bitter!* But praise God, "Bane and blessing, pain and pleasure, by the Cross are sanctified." This was revealed in type to Moses in that when the "tree," typical of the Cross, was cast into the Marah of their troubles, all was made sweet! So, too, in the light of Calvary, we see all our trials are sent for blessing; that Christ lifts every burden, sweetens every experience and works all together for our good (Rom. 8:28). Obedience and submission to His will being the basic conditions for the supply of our spiritual needs, we may expect to hear, as did the Israelites, the Divine benediction of His grace: "I am the Lord that healeth thee" (Ex. 15:26). Then what glorious "Elim rest" is ours as we with joy draw water out of the wells of salvation and bask in the refreshing shade of the 70 palm trees of testimony and spiritual victory (Ex. 15:27)!   —H.G.B.

> Hold out! there comes an end to sorrow;
> Hope, from the dust, shall conquering rise;
> The storm proclaims a sunnier morrow;
> The cross points on to Paradise!   —Anon.

"Afflictions are blessings to us when we bless God for the affliction!"

LOOKING AROUND

<small>SUGGESTED SCRIPTURE READING:</small> Ephesians 5:1-17

See then that ye walk circumspectly. Ephesians 5:15

The word "circumspectly" means literally "looking about you." Paul reminds us that we are being watched by others as we travel through this world. What we do makes a far greater impact upon the world than what we say. As we walk through this world, let us look about us and see all the lost men and women who are being influenced by our example. A man said to me one day as I tried to show him the advisability of becoming a Christian, "I would, if I could see more of it in those who call themselves Christians. I have a neighbor who is a member of your church, and gets up in prayer meeting and loudly testifies what Christ has done for him, but I live next door to him and know how he spends his time. I see him abusing his wife, and hear the language he uses, and if that is Christianity — no thanks, I don't care for it." Of course this was no valid excuse, but it is true that many are kept away from Christ through the inconsistent walk of professing Christians. Paul could say, "And herein do I exercise myself, to have always a conscience void of offence toward God, and *toward men*" (Acts 24:16).

A little girl told her preacher one day, "Pastor, I am saved." Elatedly, he replied, "And which one of my sermons brought you to Christ?" The little girl replied, "It wasn't anybody's preaching; it was my Aunt Mary's practicing!" Someone has said, "What you do speaks so loud I can't hear what you say."

—M.R.D.

> I'd rather see a sermon,
>   Than hear one any day;
> I'd rather one would walk with me
>   Than merely show the way,
> The eye's a better pupil,
>   And more willing than the ear;
> Fine counsel is confusing
>   But example's always clear.   —Anon.

"The light that shines farthest shines brightest at home!"

WORKS UNAVAILING!

SUGGESTED SCRIPTURE READING: Romans 10:3-8

Who hath saved us, . . . NOT ACCORDING TO OUR WORKS.
II Timothy 1:9

A dear saint of God, John Vassar, spent much time in spreading the Gospel by house-to-house visitation work. One woman, who heard that he was soon to be in her neighborhood distributing tracts and doing personal work, resolved that she would treat him badly if he asked her to accept Christ. Sometime later John Vassar came to her home and as soon as she recognized him, and ere he could speak, she slammed the door in his face! Realizing that she would not have been so rude if the Holy Spirit were not sending her strong conviction, he decided to sing his testimony upon her door-step. The words were those of the precious hymn:

"But drops of grief can ne'er repay the debt of love I owe."

God spoke to the woman's heart and she found peace of soul at the Cross. Afterward, whenever she gave her testimony, she would say over and over, " 'Twas those 'drops of grief,' that made me realize the value of grace apart from works, and touched my soul with the fire of heaven!"

Works, dear friend, are of no value until *after you are saved.* The Scripture emphasizes this in many places, among them:

1. Ephesians 2:8, 9—"For by *grace* are ye saved through faith; and that not of yourselves: it is the *gift* of God: *not of works,* lest any man should boast."

2. Romans 4:5 — "But to him that *worketh not,* but believeth."

3. Romans 4:6—"God imputeth righteousness *without works.*"

4. Titus 3:5 — *"Not by works of righteousness that we have done,* but according to his mercy he saved us."

Stop *trying.* . . . Start *trusting!*   —H.G.B.

Jesus will save you just as you are,
Jesus will welcome you from afar,
Jesus will heal sin's pitiful scar;
Just as you are, come home. —Wm. Runyan

"The message of the cross is first of all the revelation of the incomprehensible, unconditional love of God."

"FAIR AS THE MOON"

SUGGESTED SCRIPTURE READING: Philippians 2:9-16

Who is she that looketh forth as the morning, fair as the moon, clear as the sun? Song of Solomon 6:10

In Genesis 1:16 we read, "And God made two great lights; the greater light to rule the day, and the lesser light to rule the night." The greater light was the sun; the lesser light was the moon. In the Song of Solomon we see that these two heavenly bodies have a symbolic meaning and a spiritual counterpart. They speak of Christ and His Church. Jesus is called the "Sun of Righteousness" and "the light of the world" (Mal. 4:2; John 8:12; 12:46). He gave light to the earth while He was here in the days of His flesh (John 9:5), and will also be the source of illumination in the ages to come (Rev. 21:23b). However, in the night of this dispensation, while He is away, we are to reflect His glory and "shine as lights in the world" (Phil. 2:15b; Matt. 5:14a).

As you know, the moon itself is a *dead planet.* It only has light and heat as it reflects the sun. So, too, we only have light and joy and spiritual warmth as we reflect the Lord Jesus Christ.

The only time the moon does not shine is when there is an eclipse; that is, when the earth comes between the sun and the moon. In like manner, when there is lack of joy and victory in our life, or when there is spiritual coldness, it is usually due to the fact that *the "world" has come between us and the Lord!*

Is your spiritual life undergoing a chilling "eclipse"; or are you walking "in the light" (I John 1:7a) and shining for Jesus as "fair as the moon"? —H.G.B.

> Nothing between like worldly pleasure;
>   Habits of life, though harmless they seem,
> Must not my heart from Him ever sever,
>   He is my all, let nothing between.
> Nothing between my soul and the Saviour,
>   So that His blessed face may be seen;
> Nothing preventing the least of His favor,
>   Keep the way clear! Let nothing between!—C. A. Tindley

"Keep your light shining for Jesus and God will put it where it will be seen."

"FINISHED!"

SUGGESTED SCRIPTURE READING: Hebrews 9:14, 24-28

When Jesus therefore had received the vinegar, he said, It is finished: and he bowed his head, and gave up the ghost.   John 19:30

"*It is finished.*" With these words the Lord Jesus ended His work and suffering on the cross of Calvary and laid down His life, only to take it up again after three days and nights in the tomb. *It is finished.* In the Latin translation there are two words, *consummatum est,* but in the original Greek, in which John recorded these words, there is only one word used by the Lord Jesus, *tetelestai.* Not three words, but *one, finished.* It was the cry of consummation, the cry of victory, and of completion.

In this one word, "finished," the Saviour declared a fact, a truth so glorious and so wonderful that Satan has been busy ever since trying to hide the meaning of this one last cry from the minds of men and women. As a result, there are millions of earnest, sincere, seeking souls, longing for peace and rest, who have not yet realized that salvation is a *finished* and completed work, and that there is nothing left to do for a sinner in order to be saved. And so these dear souls work and slave and sacrifice, and perform religious duties and place themselves under the law, and struggle and worry and doubt and fret and try to save themselves, or to do things which they feel will merit for them the favor of God and possibly bring down His merit because of their work and goodness and religious activity.

Will you stand with me once more before that Cross, and in that deep darkness when God hid His face, and blackness enveloped the earth hear Him cry with a strength of voice and power that made the earth to quake and the rocks to rend and the graves to open, "*It is finished.*" And can you say with me, Yes, thank God, it is *finished for me?*   —M.R.D.

> Lifted up was He to die,
> "It is finished," was His cry;
> Now in heav'n exalted high,
> Hallelujah! What a Saviour!—P. P. Bliss

"It is not for us, who are passengers, to meddle with the chart and with the compass. Let the All-Skillful Pilot alone with His own Work!"
— HALL

THE NEED FOR ZEAL

SUGGESTED SCRIPTURE READING: Matthew 9:2-8

When Jesus saw THEIR *faith, he said unto the sick of the palsy, Son, thy sins be forgiven thee.*   Mark 2:5

Two words need special consideration here. *Their faith.* I know that men are saved by *their own personal* faith in Jesus Christ and that you cannot be saved by my believing, and yet it is true as well that *men and women are being lost because of our lack of faith.* It is equally true that men do find Jesus through the faith of others. It was through the faith of a Paul who dared to trust God that the Gospel came to Europe, and you and I are saved because of Paul's *faith.* It is true that because David Livingstone had *faith enough* to trust God and blaze a gospel trail into the heart of Africa that thousands were saved.

Men are perishing because we have not faith. There are some whom God wants on the foreign field, but you have *not enough* faith to go, and in consequence men and women will go to hell forever. There are some of you readers who have enough of this world's goods to support a half dozen missionaries, but because you dare not trust God with what belongs to Him, thousands will slip into eternity without Christ. O God, make us dead in earnest. Set us on fire. Help us to break up our homes if need be to bring this old, paralyzed, dying world to Christ. Many of us have a pleasant roof over our heads. With much labor we have made a comfortable place for ourselves while the world is perishing for lack of Christ. Oh, for a zeal that will make us willing to tear up the roof and forget all false propriety and selfish endeavor, to bring the message to those who have never heard it.   —M.R.D.

> Oh, may I learn, in every state,
> To make His will my own;
> And when the joys of sense depart,
> To walk by faith alone!—A. Toplady

"Faith is the bucket by means of which a man may draw water out of the wells of salvation and drink to his heart's content!"

NOW IS CHRIST RISEN!

SUGGESTED SCRIPTURE READING: Revelation 1:12-18

> *But now is Christ risen from the dead, and become the firstfruits of them that slept.* I Corinthians 15:20

If one believes in the actual, physical resurrection of the Lord Jesus Christ he will find no difficulty in believing anything else in God's blessed Book. If he rejects this most cardinal of all Christian doctrines, he would be better off to throw away his entire Bible, for the reading of it will only add to his weight of woe and final damnation. Christ's unique divinity is not only at stake, but man's own redemption and ultimate resurrection is also vitally involved. The hope of immortality is a delusion, if Christ's resurrection is not a reality. Praise God, those of us who have been taught by His Spirit, and who walk and talk with Him daily in spiritual fellowship, know that He lives! If Christ has not risen He has broken His promises, failed in His prophecies, and we are yet in our sins and of all men most miserable.

All other major "religions" in the world adore some great but departed leader or philosopher. Christianity alone declares its faith in a living, resurrected Mediator.

A missionary who sought to impress this truth upon a group of Mohammedans gave them this illustration: "I am traveling, and have reached a place where the road branches off into two ways; I look for a guide, and find two men; one dead and the other alive. Which of the two must I ask for directions, the dead or the living?" "Oh, the living," cried the people. "Then," said the missionary, "why send me to Mohammed who is dead instead of to *Christ, who is alive!*"

The story is told of a little girl who lived near a cemetery. Even though she had to pass through it after the sun was set she never seemed to be apprehensive. Someone finally said to her, "Aren't you afraid to go through the cemetery?" "Ah, no," she replied, "I am not afraid, for *my home is just beyond!*" Christians, are you afraid of the cemetery? You ought not to be, for *now that Christ is risen, your home, too, is just beyond!* —H.G.B.

> Thou art the Life, the empty tomb
> Proclaims Thy conquering arm;
> And those who put their trust in Thee
> Nor death, nor hell shall harm. —Anon.

"Christ has made death but a starlit strip between the companionship of yesterday, and the reunions of tomorrow!"

NO OLD STOCK

SUGGESTED SCRIPTURE READING: Isaiah 40:29-31

. . . I shall be anointed with fresh oil.   Psalm 92:10

Christians are always in great danger of growing "stale" and "insipid." How often we have heard people get up in a testimony meeting and repeat again and again the same old phrases of how they were saved 20, 30, 40 years ago. How often I wished they would bring their testimony up to date and tell of some more recent experience with the Lord. What has the Lord done for you today? We need to be anointed with fresh oil daily. We should keep our spiritual life up to date. How stale our prayers become. We repeat the same old phrases and remember the same old requests over and over again.

Too many Christians are subsisting on the moldy, musty bread of their past experience instead of gathering fresh manna every morning (Ex. 16:4). The manna spoiled after one day (Ex. 16: 19, 20) and became full of worms. Has your testimony become "wormy" because it lacks freshness?

The story is told of an enterprising shop-keeper who opened a shop right next door to another and handled the same goods. Spurred by the new competition the old established store-keeper put a sign over his shop painted in big letters, "ESTABLISHED FIFTY YEARS. PROVEN MERCHANDISE." The next day his competitor displayed a sign, "ESTABLISHED YESTERDAY, NO OLD STOCK."

The only way to keep our life fresh is a daily anointing with fresh oil, as we study His Word, seek His will and witness for Him (Isa. 40:31).   —M.R.D.

> God make us men of steadfast faith,
> Patient, courageous, strong and true;
> With vision clear and mind equipped,
> Thy will to learn, Thy will to do.—F. Gillman

"Determine immediately to get busy for God. Good intentions are like eggs; unless hatched into action they soon run to decay."

DOUBT

SUGGESTED SCRIPTURE READING: Matthew 14:22-33

. . . wherefore didst thou doubt?   Matthew 14:31

These words of Jesus were addressed to Peter. Having trusted Christ's word, he had at first walked securely upon the rolling waves of the sea. A bit later, however, he nearly drowned because he got his eyes on himself and circumstances. Is this not often true of us? Instead of resting on the Word of God and its sure promises, we start viewing the boisterous billows of life, the treacherous winds of adversity, and our own sinfulness and human inadequacy. As soon as we look at anything else but the Lord and His Word and try to go by feeling, we are bound to sink beneath the waves of circumstances. Peter, however, did not need to go down to defeat, and neither do we. All the power of Divine omnipotence is at our disposal. To needy souls Jesus still says, "Come," even as He did to His trembling disciple of old. The Saviour will never disappoint those who put their complete confidence in Him.

A Christian was once in a state of great anxiety concerning her soul. She believed she was beyond hope and "a castaway." To an old minister who tried to comfort her and point her to the assuring Word, she exclaimed with emphasis, "Oh, I'm dead, dead — twice dead and plucked up by the roots!" After a pause he replied, "Well, sitting in my study the other day, I heard a sudden scream, 'John's in the well! John's fallen into the well!' Before I could reach the spot, I heard the sad, mournful cry, 'John's dead! Poor little Johnny's dead!' Bending over the well, I called out, 'John, are you dead?' I was glad to hear from his own mouth the reassuring words, 'Yes, grandfather, I'm dead.'"

We smile at this ridiculous little story, but the doubts of most Christians are just as silly and unreal. The one who fears he is beyond hope shows by his deep concern that spiritual life still surges within him.

Why doubt and be miserable, when you have every right to trust and be happy?   —H.G.B.

Soon shall our doubts and fears all yield to Thy control;
Thy tender mercies shall illume the midnight of the soul.
                                        —A. Toplady

"Unless there is within us yielding to Him who is above us, we shall soon yield to that which is about us!"

ELECTION AND FREE WILL

Having predestinated us unto the adoption of children by Jesus Christ to himself. Ephesians 1:5

This doctrine of sovereign election and predestination has been a real stumbling block to many believers. Because they were unable to reconcile it with the clear teaching of the Bible about man's free will, they reject it, in whole or in part, or ignore the inescapably clear teaching on this important subject. Ignoring the passages which deal with this subject does not do away with them. They are still there, just as surely as the many passages which teach the responsibility of man and the necessity of personal faith. They are both in the Bible, whether we understand them or not. It is God's infallible Word. Before we are saved, we have only one responsibility and that is to believe on the Lord Jesus Christ. If we do this, we are saved. If we don't, we are necessarily lost. Then, after we have been saved, we learn from the Bible the glorious truth that our salvation was already God's work and the work of the Holy Spirit, and not ours at all, for ". . . it is God which worketh in (us) both to will and to do of his good pleasure" (Phil. 2:13).

It is like a train which travels on two rails. The one rail is sovereign grace, the other is human responsibility. They never meet, they never come together, but they are both necessary to keep the train on the track. Remove the rail of man's free will and try to run on only the rail of election and you will land in the ditch of fatalism and hyper-Calvinism. Reverse it and remove the rail of sovereign election and grace, and you wreck yourself in the ditch of a religion of human works and hyper-Arminianism. Keep your wheels on both tracks. —M.R.D.

While passing through the wilderness,
Full of temptations and distress,
What comfort does the thought afford,
Our steps are ordered by the Lord!—Anon.

"Soldiers of the Cross may lose many skirmishes, but they may be assured that the final battle shall see them crowned: 'More than conquerors'!"

"BORROWED AXE HEADS"!

SUGGESTED SCRIPTURE READING: I John 1

But as one was felling a beam, the axe head fell into the water: and he cried, and said, Alas, master! for it was borrowed. And the man of God said, Where fell it? And he shewed him the place. And he cut down a stick, and cast it in thither; and the iron did swim. II Kings 6:5, 6

We have here a telling incident closely related to the Christian life of service and victory. A picture is drawn of certain young men of the "School of the Prophets" eager to enlarge the place of their service, going out as it were to make a building for God. They wisely sought the aid of the prophet and established themselves adjacent to the ever needful living waters. But, being unskilled in their work, they had zeal without knowledge of their task.

One, through improper use of the tools and with much carnal swinging, dislodged the axe head and with it his power to be of service! He was wise enough not to keep on swinging and beating the air with the wooden handle of his own efforts, but asked a man of God for help. How was the loss remedied? The answer of the Prophet gives us direction when we lose our unction in the work of the Lord, for truly our tools, too, are only "borrowed" from the Holy Spirit. Elisha said: "*Where fell it?*" Then taking a stick, perhaps the very one that caused the axe head to loosen, the prophet defies the laws of nature; and lo, a miracle: "the iron did swim"!

If you lose your effectiveness in service, go back to the place where you lost your power: confess your fault, toss in "the stick of contention," get back to your seasons of prayer, your meditation of the Word; and lo, contrary to all expectations, the iron of your power will swim! If you've lost your blessing, Christian, ask yourself: "*Where fell it?*"; go back, and let the Holy Spirit restore your "Borrowed Axe Head" of fellowship!   —H.G.B.

> Now I lay "self" on the altar,
>   That the Christ may live in me;
> Spirit move in mighty power,
>   And from earth-dross set me free!—H.G.B.

"To have full blessing and spiritual J-O-Y; put J-Jesus first, O-others second, and Y-yourself last!"

SINGING LIKE A SPARROW

SUGGESTED SCRIPTURE READING: Psalm 1

*Wherefore come out from among them, and be ye
separate, saith the Lord.*   II Corinthians 6:17

The Lord wants a separated people for His service. No man
can serve two masters. Seeking to convert the world by our
tolerance of their evils will result, not in making the world like
unto us, but rather in us becoming like unto the world. I received a letter some time ago from a Christian wife of an unsaved husband. She tried to interest her husband in going to
church with her and he offered a compromise. He told her he
would go to church with her if she in turn would go to the
tavern and the theater with him. "What shall I do?" she wrote
to me in desperation. Should a wife be subject to her husband
in *all* things? Would her good motive justify her action?

I can best illustrate my answer to her by a little incident I
read some time ago. A certain man had a beautiful singing
canary. His neighbor had a sparrow and wanted to see if he
could teach the sparrow to sing by keeping it with the canary.
The two were placed in their cages side by side. But instead of
the sparrow learning to sing, the canary began to chirp like the
sparrow. It lost its own song, instead of teaching the sparrow
how to sing.

Today, as you go out to your work, you will of necessity contact unbelievers, but you need not enter with them in their
worldly practices. The old Chinese proverb is still true, "You
cannot keep the birds from flying over your head, but you can
keep them from nesting in your hair." As light is contrasted to
darkness, so should we be in this dark world.   —M.R.D.

> Jesus calls us o'er the tumult
>   Of our life's wild, restless sea,
> Day by day His sweet voice soundeth,
>   Saying, "Christian, follow Me."—C. Alexander

**"The real test of a man's conversion is whether he has enough Chris-
tianity to get it over to other people." — S. S. SHOEMAKER**

BLESSING GOD IN ADVERSITY

SUGGESTED SCRIPTURE READING: Job 1:9-22

> . . . *the* LORD *gave, and the* LORD *hath taken away;*
> *blessed be the name of the* LORD. Job 1:21

In London there is a little cabinet-maker's shop. Over the entrance hangs a sign which says, "Living Above." It is a notification to prospective customers that should the door be locked, they can, by ascending a nearby stairway, find the artisan residing in an apartment overhead. As Christians, we also should always be found "living above" our circumstances. It is blessed to be able to retire to a higher altitude and there, in the quietness and the confidence generated by faith, view the hand of God in our lives and say, "All is well . . . All is well! My Father knows!" Was not this the wise and stirring testimony of the much afflicted Job when in singleness of heart he triumphantly declared: "The LORD gave, and the LORD hath taken away; blessed be the name of the LORD"?

Someone has wisely admonished, "Whatever the trouble, take it straight *from God* (that is, look not at the secondary causes), and then as trustfully, take it straight *to God* and thank Him for it."

The deeper our trust in an all-loving Providence, the less we will ask the Lord to explain His sovereign dealings. The cry will not be, "Make plain," but, "Dear Saviour, give grace to bear." The Psalmist rightly remonstrates, "Why art thou cast down, O my soul? . . . hope thou in God" (Ps. 42:5). Indeed, how joyous a sight it is after grief's torrential showers to behold God's rainbow of hope shining brightly in the heart. May we as Christians be able to rejoice in our times of difficulty, feeling no fear, expressing no doubt. May we pray for faith to be a spiritual hero like Job, that the trial of our faith "might be found unto praise and honor and glory at the appearing of Jesus Christ" (I Pet. 1:7).

Do you bless God in adversity? If so, He will bless you!

—H.G.B.

God the Eternal is thy refuge;
Let it still thy wild alarms;
Underneath thy deepest sorrow
Are the everlasting arms.—Anon.

"God's providence we find all good and wise, alike in what it gives and what denies!" — POPE

"FALLOW GROUND"

SUGGESTED SCRIPTURE READING: Matthew 13:3-9

For thus saith the LORD to the men of Judah and Jerusalem, Break up your fallow ground, and sow not among thorns!　　　　Jeremiah 4:3

Fallow ground is ground that is permitted to lie idle and uncultivated, with the result that instead of grain and fruit the land becomes covered with weeds and with thorns and disaster lies ahead. And so the prophet calls out to them, "Thus saith the Lord . . . Break up your fallow ground and sow not among thorns."

The spiritual applications of this expression are many and profitable, but the one that suggests itself first of all is that there can be no blessing without effort, and no harvest without plowing. Before a thing can be made it must be broken. Before the house is built the tree must be broken down. Before the foundation can be laid the rocks must be blasted from their quarry bed where they have lain in peace and quiet for ages. Before the ripe grain can cover the fields the soil must be broken and beaten small and the cutting blade of the plow turn over the sod and the sharp teeth of the harrow pulverize the soil. Before there can be life there must be death; before there can be joy there must be weeping. The joy that floods the mother's heart at the sound of the first cry of her new-born babe was preceded by the tears and anguish of childbirth. Our Lord Jesus stated that principle in just different words when He said, "Except a corn of wheat fall into the ground and die, it abideth alone: but if it die, it bringeth forth much fruit" (John 12:24).

This is the law of life in the natural and it is the law of life in the spiritual. There is no making without breaking. —M.R.D.

Go bury thy sorrow, The world hath its share;
Go bury it deeply, Go hide it with care,
Go think of it calmly, When curtained by night,
Go tell it to Jesus, And all will be right!—M. Bachelor

"Anxiety is the poison of life, and the parent of many sins; but 'perfect love casteth out fear'!"

SPIRITUAL ADVERSARIES

SUGGESTED SCRIPTURE READING: Romans 16:17-20

Lest Satan should get an advantage of us. II Corinthians 2:11

One who believes today in a personal devil and the reality of evil spirits is considered unenlightened, bigoted and a religious fanatic. Satan and his emissaries are not talked about in polite and "educated" circles. Many who stand behind the sacred desk tell us that Satan is not real, but rather "the personification of our unworthy psychological drives." The Bible, however, unmistakably declares that there are evil powers arrayed against man. They are thinking, personal beings who seek his spiritual decline and bankruptcy.

Satan comes oftentimes as an "angel of light" posing as truth, culture, education, or religious reform. Dressed in the garb of supposed spiritual advancement, he seeks to lead men astray. Underneath the pleasing exterior and the thin sugar coating of truth lies the bitter pill of deception and the fatal dose of error.

Satan also comes as a "roaring lion." By sheer brute force he pushes his diabolical schemes across the landscape of time, bludgeoning his victims when he cannot subtly ensnare them.

Finally, when all other methods fail, he gets folks to simply *neglect* their spiritual birthright. If he can induce them to keep so busy, even in worthwhile endeavors, that they have no time for Bible study, prayer, and communion with God, he knows they will soon be spiritual paupers and impotent backsliders.

Some years ago an atheist in Europe bequeathed his farm to the devil. The desire of the deceased to leave the land absolutely untouched by human hands was carried out. In a few decades the farm was a tangled wilderness and an eyesore to the whole community. Plain neglect produced the evil result. So, too, the soul of man becomes unfruitful and a pawn of Satan by failure to appropriate the means of grace. "Neglect not the gift that is in thee" (I Tim. 4:14a). —H.G.B.

> The devil has been voted out,
> Psychologists say he is gone;
> But simple folk would like to know
> Who carries his business on! —Anon.

"If you don't believe in the devil's existence, try resisting him for a while, and you will believe in it." — FINNEY

PRACTICAL CHRISTIANITY

SUGGESTED SCRIPTURE READING: I John 3:14-19

If a brother or sister be naked, and destitute of daily food, And one of you say unto them, Depart in peace, be ye warmed and filled; notwithstanding ye give them not those things which are needful to the body; what doth it profit? Even so faith, if it hath not works, is dead, being alone. James 2:15-17

What an illustration and how practical. What this poor, naked, hungry brother or sister needs is clothing and food. Pious prayers will not help him. Reading Scripture to him will not clothe him. Speaking kind words will not feed him and make him warm. He needs clothes and food and if you are in a position to furnish them, then don't shirk your duty by saying to the poor brother, "We'll pray for you and God will supply your need." You hypocrite, you cover up your penurious, stingy heart and clamp down your fist upon your purse by offering prayers instead of clothing, and pious talk instead of food. Listen! That is what is wrong today. How many times do you say to a brother in trouble, "I'll pray for you," and do it only to get rid of him? The world wants action, not words, and many a cheap, stingy heart is camouflaged under pious cant and hollow prayer. The world is not interested in our prayers. It wants evidence.

How many souls are being kept from Christ through our inconsistency? God help us not to be satisfied with our justification in *His sight* but strive until our faith has been demonstrated before men and we are justified before the world by the life we live and the works we do.   —M.R.D.

> "Giving is living," the angel said,
> "God feed the hungry sweet charity's bread!"
> "And must I keep giving and giving again?"
> My selfish and querulous answer ran . . .
> "Oh no," said the angel, his eyes pierced me through,
> "Just give till the Saviour stops giving to you!" —Anon.

"Carve your name high, above shifting sands on rocks that defy decay. All that you'll hold in your cold, dead hand is that which you've given away!"

RUNNING LIKE ELIJAH

SUGGESTED SCRIPTURE READING: I Kings 18:42-46

And the hand of the Lord was on Elijah; and he girded up his loins, and ran before Ahab to the entrance of Jezreel.   I Kings 18:46

The story in I Kings 18 is a stirring one. Elijah had just engaged in the titanic struggle with the forces of evil on Mt. Carmel. In a wondrous demonstration he had called down fire from heaven thus proving the false character of Baal and vindicating the claims of the God of Israel. At the end of this physically exhausting day he does not eat and drink, as did King Ahab, but rather undertakes another spiritual assignment. He casts himself down upon the earth and having placed his head between his knees (a position of extreme supplication still used in the Orient), he prays most earnestly for rain. Six times his servant goes to look for some gathering clouds that would indicate that the heavens, which had not poured forth their moisture for three long years, would once again refresh the parched earth. Six times he returns with a negative answer. But Elijah prevails in prayer, and the seventh time a cloud the size of "a man's hand" is sighted.

Sure that the Lord has heard him, Elijah tells King Ahab, "Prepare thy chariot, and get thee down, that the rain stop thee not." Hardly had he finished his admonition when the clouds began to pour forth a torrent of water. But now note another astounding event. Elijah girds up his loins and runs with the swiftness and unabated strength of a prize winning athlete the entire *ten-mile* distance to Jezreel. This would seem an almost impossible feat, but when one has the hand of the Lord upon him, he can do great exploits for God.

Do you want to be used of the Lord? Then you must pay the price. You need to be where spiritual power is generated: the place of full fellowship, the place of *self*-denial, the place of prayer. If you will "sell out to God," as did the prophet of old, you too will do incredible things for the glory of the Lord. Are you running like Elijah?   —H.G.B.

> Got any rivers you think are uncrossable?
> Got any mountains you can't tunnel through?
> God specializes in things thought impossible;
> He does the things others cannot do!—O. Eliason

"Faith is dead to doubts, dumb to discouragements, and blind to impossibilities."

THREE KINDS OF WELLS

SUGGESTED SCRIPTURE READING: John 4:6-14

Therefore with joy shall ye draw water out of the wells of salvation. Isaiah 12:3

The Bible has much to say about wells and they are mentioned hundreds of times. Water was a precious and sometimes scarce commodity in oriental lands and many a fierce battle was fought over the possession of wells (Gen. 26:17-21). Various words are used in the Hebrew for wells, the distinction of which is not carried over into our present translations. Among these several words for "well" there are three outstanding ones. There are first of all, man-made wells. Jacob's well was one of these. It was dug by father Jacob himself (John 4:12). It sometimes went dry in the rainless season. It meant hard work to lift the water from its depths. Its water could not permanently satisfy (John 4:13).

The second word translated "well" means a spring or fountain. It did not depend upon rainfall or surface drainage for its supply, but was fed by deep subterranean springs which kept up a constant flow in winter and in summer, in wet seasons and in drought. These wells Jesus compares to the well of salvation and to which Isaiah refers in our text. To drink of these wells means eternal satisfaction. He that drinketh of that water shall "never thirst" (John 4:14).

A third well is mentioned in Scripture and means a "cistern" or a pool which collects water for a time, but soon dries up. Such wells are called "broken cisterns" (Jer. 2:13). Its water is unfit to drink and fails when most needed. Man-made wells and broken cisterns only increase the thirst, but those who have drunk of the fountain of life know true satisfaction. It is found only in Jesus Christ. "For with thee is the fountain of life" (Ps. 36:9).

The last invitation of the Bible is to come and "take of the water of life freely" (Rev. 22:17). —M.R.D.

> We are feeding on the living bread,
> We are drinking at the fountain head;
> And whoso drinketh Jesus said,
> "Shall never, never thirst again."—Anon.

"All Christians are cisterns having living water in them; but few have the spiritual maturity that makes them fountains giving forth to others."
— G. WOODS

THE PRECIOUS WORD

SUGGESTED SCRIPTURE READING: Psalm 119:129-140

. . . I esteem all thy precepts.   Psalm 119:128

When an old minister was asked to give his favorite text, he replied: "When I think of a favorite verse, half-a-dozen dear ones come to my mind. On stormy days I want a cloak; cold days I want the sunny side of the wall; hot days I want a shady path; now I want a shower of manna; now I want a drink of cool living water; now I want a sword. I might as well try to tell which is my favorite eye. The one I might lose is the one I might soon need and want. 'All scripture . . . is profitable'!"

It is true that some parts of God's Word have greater literary beauty than others, and thus lend themselves more to memorization; yet all is equally inspired and valuable. It is a mistake to cling so tenaciously to a few "pet Scriptures" that we fail to grow in mastering new portions that would supply us with fresh insights into the mind of God. Too many of us are content to keep quoting our favorite passages. As a result, we neglect the enriching experience of dwelling on less familiar but equally important sections of the Inspired Record. Are you a good householder bringing forth things "old and *new*," or are you giving the same testimony you did fifteen years ago with the same limited number of quotations from the Bible?

The Holy Spirit did not waste a word when He inspired men to pen the Scriptures. He intended that we should value it in its entirety. Yes, we give mental assent to the thought that every portion of Scripture is profitable, but in practice can we truthfully say, "I esteem *all* thy precepts"?   —H.G.B.

> I love Thy truth, O Lord,
>   The Word which Thou hast giv'n
> Its precepts shall my soul delight
>   On earth as well as heav'n —G. Woods

"A Bible in hand is worth two on the shelf."

WHAT THE LAW COULD NOT DO

SUGGESTED SCRIPTURE READING: Acts 13:33-39

For what the law could NOT DO, in that it was weak through the flesh, God sending his own Son in the likeness of sinful flesh, and for sin, condemned sin in the flesh: That the RIGHTEOUSNESS OF THE LAW might be fulfilled in us, who walk not after the flesh, but after the Spirit. Romans 8:3, 4

What the law could not do! There are some things which the law cannot do. There are some things which the law was never intended to do, and one of them is to create a righteousness in us. On the contrary, it was given to us to reveal our unrighteousness and the sinfulness of our flesh. That is the only reason why Jesus had to die on the Cross, because man could not be justified by the works of the law. There was, of course, nothing wrong with the law; it was the weakness of the flesh, and the law condemns sin in the flesh in order that the righteousness of the law might be fulfilled in us. Notice that it does not say that the law is fulfilled *by* us, but the righteousness of the law is fulfilled *in* us. That is, the righteousness of the Lord Jesus is imputed to and fulfilled in those who, looking away from the law, turn to Calvary for salvation.

Jesus did two things for us. First, He *kept* the law perfectly during His life on earth; and secondly, He *paid* the penalty of the law when He took its curse in death upon Himself. Now the poor sinner turning to Christ receives two things. First, he is free from the curse and the penalty of the law the moment he believes; and secondly, the righteousness of Christ's sinless life by that act is imputed to the sinner. The pardoned sinner becomes a justified saint. Without this clothing of righteousness no man shall ever see God. "For we through the Spirit wait for the hope of righteousness by faith" (Gal. 5:5). —M.R.D.

From shackles of the Law set free,
I bask in perfect liberty;
My chains fell off at Calvary,
And now His love constraineth me!—Anon.

"Salvation is a 'GIFT'; it is grace plus NOTHING!"

AFTERWARD

SUGGESTED SCRIPTURE READING: Psalm 73

Afterward it yieldeth . . . fruit.   Hebrews 12:11

The author of Hebrews is talking about chastening. To chasten means to make "chaste" or pure. God wants His people clean, and to cleanse them from all impurity He often passes them through the fire. At the time this chastening is painful and grievous. We see only the present distress. God sees the future benefit. Only faith can pierce the veil which hides the future — faith in the perfect will of God. Chastening "worketh" for our profit, but it may not be evident till "afterward."

Mrs. C. H. Spurgeon, the wife of the renowned preacher, once lay in a prolonged state of sickness. A log of old oak was burning on the hearth in her cozy little sickroom. The external darkness seemed to enter her soul, and momentarily it obscured her spiritual vision. She fretfully remarked, "Why does my Lord permit this prolonged illness to hinder me from rendering service to His poor servants? Why does He send sharp and bitter pain to visit me?" She was quickly and strangely answered. The old oak log, as the fire licked around it, let loose its imprisoned music from its inmost heart and gave forth a sweet, soft sound, like a tender trill of a robin on the window sill. She was mystified, for it was too late at night and not the season for a robin to be heard. The log again gave forth melodious notes as before. When she saw the reason of the sounds, she exclaimed, "Ah, when the fire of affliction draws music from our hardened hearts, then indeed are we purified, and God glorified." She was thus comforted by this God-sent parable. It was God's grace that enabled Paul to most gladly glory in his infirmities (II Cor. 12:9, 10).

Be patient, suffering one, and trust in God's "afterward."

—M.R.D.

> When I cannot understand my Father's leading,
> And it seems to be but hard and cruel fate,
> Still I hear that gentle whisper ever pleading,
> God is working, God is faithful—only wait!—A.B.Simpson

"The Great Physician never takes down the wrong bottle!"

FLATTERY

Suggested Scripture Reading: Psalm 12:1-4

. . . . meddle not with him that flattereth with his lips.
Proverbs 20:19

The Bible makes at least 21 references to flattery, and none of them are good. It is associated with the lowest type of characters (Ps. 5:9; Dan. 11:36); the worst sins (Prov. 2:17-19; 7:21); and calls down the most severe judgment of God (Ps. 12:3).

Legitimate praise is never out of order, but insincere and lying attention and the baser, selfish objectives that motivate such flattery, is a sin and a stench in God's nostrils. In an effort to "win friends and influence people" such methods of ingratiating one's self into the good graces of another are often used. Even Christians have been known to practice such deception, salving their conscience, of course, by giving the sin the more delicate label of "diplomacy," or "salesmanship." Admittedly, it seems to be the thing to do in this age of false courtesy, cutthroat competition, and insincere self-seeking; but with all its refined sugar-coating, flattery is still the most despicable type of lying.

Not only is flattery an evil from the point of view of the one who employs it, but it also has a tendency to inflate the ego of the hearer so that he "thinks of himself more highly than he ought to think." Human nature being what it is, it is hard enough to "die to self" without others unduly urging us to preen our feathers of superiority.

One day after having preached an exceptionally powerful message, "The Great Methodist" was approached by an admirer who exclaimed to him, "Oh, what a wonderful sermon you preached today, Mr. Wesley." "Ah, sister, you're too late — too late with your flattery, *the devil told me that ere I left the pulpit steps.*"

The Scripture says, "A man that flattereth . . . spreadeth a net" (Prov. 29:5). Judas employed this approach in betraying Christ (Matt. 26:47-49), and flattery will also be a tool of the Antichrist (Dan. 11:21). Christian, you ought to keep better company than that!   —H.G.B.

The lips that speak, the truth to hide,
The tongues of flattery and pride,
The Lord abhors and will requite;
But faithful hearts are His delight.—Anon.

"Flattery is soft-soap, and soft-soap is ninety per cent lye!"

HIGHER AND HIGHER

Suggested Scripture Reading: Philippians 4:1-8

Seek those things which are above. Colossians 3:1

I was on my vacation with two other friends in an isolated cabin on a remote lake in Northern Michigan. There was no sound of automobile or train, no roaring traffic, no clanging telephone. I had been lying on my back on the sand of the shore watching a majestic sight. On an island, just across a little bay, stood the skeleton of a giant tree; and perched on a bare, topmost branch sat a huge bald eagle, his white head and tail gleaming in the sun. He had been preening his feathers, while now and again he cocked his head and looked up into the clear blue sky. Suddenly he spread his huge wings and took off, flapping upward until he reached a current of air. Then his wings became motionless, the flapping ceased and the huge bird merely rested upon the current. With motionless wings he spiraled up and up and up. To the eye he appeared to shrink to the size of a hawk, then he became as small as a robin, finally he was only a mere speck — and then — he was gone altogether: lost in the blue heavens above.

I had been transfixed and had to arouse myself to make sure it was not a dream. Oh, to be like that eagle. Oh, to just open the wings of faith and to rest upon the promises of God. Oh, to look with the eagle's eye, straight up into the "Sun of Righteousness" and live in the heavenlies, far, far above the mundane strife of earth-bound creatures! The Bible says we can! "Seek those things which are above" (Col. 3:1). "Set your affection on things above, not on things of the earth" (Col. 3:2). "Think on these things" (Phil. 4:8). Look "unto Jesus" (Heb. 12:2); and "Consider Him" (Heb. 12:3).

Positionally we are already seated in the heavenlies. Remember, you can live *"above"* the world of defeat and fear today, by a faith which lifts you out of all doubt as it rests upon the promise: "All things work together for good to them that love God" (Rom. 8:28). —M.R.D.

> Jesus, I am resting, resting
> In the joy of what Thou art;
> And Thy love so pure, so changeless,
> Satisfies my heart. —J. S. Pigott

"Stop your carnal flapping, rest on the 'wind' of the Spirit (John 3:8), and soar into the heavenlies of spiritual victory."—G. W.

NEEDED — TRUE ZEAL!

SUGGESTED SCRIPTURE READING: Galatians 4:15-18

Come with me, and see my zeal for the LORD.
II Kings 10:16

These words were spoken by Jehu, who slew the prophets of Baal and exhibited much hearty enthusiasm for God's cause. Yet, in his personal relationship to Jehovah, Jehu was far from what he should have been for he "departed not . . . from the sins of Jeroboam the son of Nebat, who made Israel to sin" (II Kings 10:29). He had zeal without consecration and enthusiasm without full knowledge of God's will. Such zeal may still accomplish some good, but it-is not completely effective and falls far short of God's high requirements.

There are others who swing to the opposite direction. They are consecrated and hold to the full truth, but they err in doing so without luster, sparkle, or enthusiasm. They have the truth, but it is *on ice* rather than *on fire!* Many theologians seem to fall into this unhappy category. Mr. A. J. Gordon has a suggestive word for such. He says, "The sincere milk of the Word may be dispensed from the pulpit, yet be given out so frigidly and unfeelingly as to make it hard to receive. In Siberia, the milkmen sometimes deliver their milk in chunks, not in quarts, it being frozen solid and thus carried to the customers. Alas, is it not in this way that many in the pulpit deliver the milk of the Word? It is the pure article, sound, orthodox, and unadulterated but it is frozen into logical formularies, and hardened and chilled by excessive reasonings. Let us so preach, O men of God, that our sermons shall not have to be thawed before they can be digested."

This same word of admonition is applicable to all of us who seek to witness to others of the grace of God. Love, warmth, and zeal are important. Paul, under inspiration exclaims, "It is good to be zealously affected always in a good thing" (Gal. 4:18a).   —H.G.B.

Set us afire, Lord, stir us, we pray.
While the world perishes, we go our way
Purposeless, passionless, day after day;
Set us afire, Lord, stir us, we pray! —Anon.

"A Christian witness without boldness and enthusiasm is like a smooth file, or a knife without an edge."

HOW MUCH DID HE LEAVE?

As he came forth of his mother's womb, naked shall he return to go as he came, and shall take nothing of his labour, which he may carry away in his hand.

Ecclesiastes 5:15

The patriarch Job said, "Naked came I out of my mother's womb and naked shall I return thither" (Job 1:21). How often we hear the question when informed of someone's decease, "How much did he leave?" If the question refers to material possessions the answer is always an emphatic — "EVERYTHING!" "You can't take it with you" is a common expression of those who advocate "living it up" in rioting and pleasure. Oh, the folly of setting our hearts upon material riches. How insecure and fleeting. How disappointing in the end. After a few years it is all left behind. We leave this world as naked as we came into it. But while we cannot take our wealth with us when we die, we can send some of it ahead to be deposited in the bank of Heaven "where moth and rust do not corrupt." And while we must leave all to others when we go, we, nevertheless, can leave behind some things of abiding worth as "footprints in the sands of time." Yes, some of the poorest saints will leave behind the greatest wealth.

John Wesley left "six silver spoons *and*—the Methodist Church." So the record runs of one who lived and died a poor man, but who belonged to the innumerable company of those who, though poor, made many rich. Great inventions have in many instances come from those who were poor. Such names as Watts and Stephenson and Arkwright are illustrations of this. Bunyan made laces in a prison cell to provide his blind daughter with the necessaries of life. But in that prison cell he wrote his immortal allegory which has caused multitudes of people since his time to possess "unsearchable riches." Our Saviour was so poor that He had "not where to lay his head" (Luke 9:58); yet He has left us "the gift of eternal life" (Rom. 6:23).   —M.R.D.

Go, labor on; spend and be spent,
Thy joy to do the Father's will;
It is the way the Master went;
Should not the servant tread it still?—H. Bonar

"The millionaires of eternity are the givers of time."

THE OVERCOMER'S REWARD

SUGGESTED SCRIPTURE READING: Revelation 3:5-13

He that overcometh shall inherit all things. Revelation 21:7

This passage should be read in the light of Revelation 12:11 and 17:14. Those who overcome the world, the flesh, and the devil, do so always through the blood and power of Christ. Although this is true, yet God in grace provides additional rewards and crowns for those who *after conversion* yield themselves body and soul to Christ, for by so doing they become *clear channels* for His overcoming power. Such, on the basis of their *faithfulness and work,* obtain special honors.

After the Crimean War there was a great celebration in London. Queen Victoria was present to give out medals to the heroes. Some of the soldiers appeared with empty sleeves, some came on crutches, some with bandaged foreheads; but there was the same sweet, royal smile, and the same reward for all. At last, however, there was carried on a litter to the Queen a terribly maimed and battered warrior. His arms and his legs were gone. He had given even more than the rest. At the sight of him the Queen, with tears streaming down her cheeks, went to him, pinned a badge upon the poor fellow's breast, kissed his brow and said with great emotion, "Well done, good and faithful servant!" What a joy it will be if on our Crowning Day we can hear the King of kings say the same to us (Matt. 25:23).

Remember, Christian, men cannot see your heart and consequently may not always appreciate the battle you are fighting; but God, who is the final Judge, will reward you. He has a crown awaiting you. It is the *finish* of the race that counts. Do not despair, nor let oft repeated falls discourage you. Rise up quickly from every defeat and in God's strength go bravely forward. Keep your eye and heart ever on the goal, for "He that overcometh shall inherit all things." At the final roll call you will march down "Hallelujah Avenue" as more than conqueror!

—H.G.B.

Teach me to live Thy purpose to fulfill;
Bright for Thy glory let my taper shine;
Arm me for conflict, Lord, to do Thy will;
Make me a conqu'ror now thro' power divine.—Anon.

"You are a success if you are faithful where God has assigned you service."

BEAUTIFUL HAIR

Suggested Scripture Reading: Proverbs 20:20-29

The beauty of old men is the grey head. Proverbs 20:29

Are you getting "old" or are you merely getting "older"? When once I remarked to the late Dr. Pettingill about his increasing gray hair, he smilingly replied, "Yes, I am getting older but I shall never grow old." Those of us who knew him at the age of 84, when he went home, know the truth of his statement; for he retained the sparkle of youth and an unabated freshness to the end, and died as he had wished — "in his boots."

Gray hairs are not only a sign of "age," but should be the symbol of maturity, mellowness, and experience. Solomon says, "The hoary head is a crown of glory, if it be found in the way of righteousness" (Prov. 16:31).

A close friend of a godly, aging pastor said to him, "You are whitening fast, Pastor." When he stood up to preach, the minister said, "There is a little white flower, which blooms only in early spring. It often comes up through the frost and snow; but we always rejoice to see the little white snow-drop, because it proclaims that winter is past and summer is at hand. A friend today reminded me that I am 'whitening' fast. But it disturbs me not, for it is but proof that my winter will soon be over. I shall soon be done with the cold winds and frosts of earth. My summer — my never ending summer is at hand." A few more frosty nights and then the sunshine of heaven for eternity.

—M.R.D.

We shall reach the Summerland,
  Some sweet day, by and by;
We shall press the golden strand,
  Some sweet day, by and by.
Oh, the loved ones watching there,
  By the tree of life so fair,
Till we come their joy to share,
  Some sweet day, by and by.—F. Crosby

"A graceful and honorable old age is the childhood of immortality."
— PINDAR

MOTHERHOOD

SUGGESTED SCRIPTURE READING: Proverbs 31:10-31

Her children arise up, and call her blessed . . . a
woman that feareth the LORD, she shall be praised.
Proverbs 31:28, 30

Every mother who is worthy of the name must first of all *give herself to the Lord Jesus Christ* so that she will be in a position to train and bless her children in a spiritual way by her words and conduct. Secondly, to fulfill the highest standards of motherhood laid down in the Bible she must sacrificially *give herself to her family* and unselfishly put them *first.* One mother who put this into practice has written the following testimony: "When my children were young I thought the very best thing I could do for them was to give them myself. So I spared no pains to talk to them, read to them, teach them, and to pray with them, and in this way to be a loving companion and friend to my children. I had to neglect my housework often. I had no time to improve myself in many ways that I should have liked to do. I have my reward now! My sons are ministers of the Gospel; my grownup daughters are Christian women. I have plenty of time now to sit down and rest; plenty of time to keep my house in order; plenty of time to indulge myself in many ways, besides going about my Master's business, wherever He has need of me. I have a thousand beautiful memories of their childhood to comfort me. Now that they have gone out into the world for themselves, I have a sweet consciousness of having done all that I could to make them ready for whatever work God calls them to do. I gave them the best that I had — *myself.*"

A young man who was raised by that kind of mother upon hearing a discussion concerning the various versions of the Bible said: "I prefer my mother's version to any other. She has translated it into the language of daily life for me ever since I was old enough to understand it. There has never been any obscurity about her version." Such mothers will ever find their children rising up to call them "blessed." —H.G.B.

> The things in my life that are worthy,
> Were born in my mother's breast;
> And breathed into mine by the fragrance
> Of her life by Jesus blest.   —Anon.

"The mother's heart is the child's schoolroom." — H. W. BEECHER

LEAVE IT ALONE

Suggested Scripture Reading: Proverbs 5:3-13

Come not nigh . . . her house.   Proverbs 5:8

Solomon is here warning his son to shun strange women and to flee from lust and the temptations of sexual impurity. He reminds him that the only safe course is to stay as far away from it as possible. He who plays with fire will be burned. He who plays with temptation will fall into sin. Paul admonishes Timothy to flee "youthful lusts" (II Tim. 2:22). To look at questionable pictures, to read suggestive literature, to indulge in smutty jokes or loose talk about sex, is playing with fire. It can only excite the baser passions and, if indulged, will lead to shameful, open sin. Flee these things. Paul says if we think purely we will live purely (Phil. 4:8). Solomon said, As a man "thinketh in his heart, so is he" (Prov. 23:7). In those borderline cases where it is not clear whether a thing is right or wrong, leave it alone. Don't see how close you can come to the fire without being burned, but stay at a safe distance!

A company of rats once assembled in a cellar to devise some way of getting the bait out of a trap without getting caught. They had seen too many of their number caught. Still they wanted the bait. After many long speeches and elaborate proposals one rat, who thought he was very wise, suggested the following, "It is my opinion that if with one paw we hold down the spring, we can safely snatch the bait with the other paw." All the rats squealed their approval at this sage solution, but they were interrupted by a sad-looking rat, limping on only three legs. He raised the stump of an amputated paw and said, "I tried that method, and you see the result. Now let me suggest a plan to escape the trap. *Don't go near it, let it alone.*" Good advice, I would say. The rat was wiser than many sinners.

—M.R.D.

Shun evil companions, bad language disdain;
God's name hold in reverence, nor take it in vain;
Be thoughtful and earnest, kind-hearted and true;
Look ever to Jesus, He'll carry you through.—H. R. Palmer

"Borderline morality is too close to the devil's territory." — H.G.B.

TO THOSE OUTSIDE

SUGGESTED SCRIPTURE READING: Psalm 92

Ananias . . . having a good report of all the Jews.

Acts 22:12

Ananias, the man who baptized Paul, had a good "reputation." Paul says he had a good "report." He did not hide his light to shine only in his own house, but let it stream out through the windows for all to see. Many Christians "shine" only when they are in the light, but fail in darkness. They witness in prayer meeting and among other believers, but out in the world they are completely silent. No one would ever suspect that they are believers. Outside in the darkness your light is needed most.

At a small country church a famous preacher was once called to conduct a meeting. Long before the service began the place was packed, and every available seat was taken. The rest, who came late, were obliged to remain outside, crowding around the doors and windows. After the preliminaries were over, the speaker arose to address the congregation. He had not proceeded far when a voice from the outside of the church shouted, "Speak louder, we cannot hear you. Remember us who are outside." Yes, indeed, remember those outside who will listen if we only speak loud enough. Do not be content with merely fellowshiping in the church, but remember, too, "those who are outside." Today you will meet many who are "outside." Will your life speak loudly for Christ? Will you witness to them as the occasion arises? Or will they turn away and be left outside forever? Remember those outside and bring them into the place of rest and salvation. —M.R.D.

> You talk about your business,
> Your bonds and stocks and gold;
> And in all the worldly matters
> You are so brave and bold;
> But why are you so silent
> About salvation's plan?
> Why don't you speak for Jesus,
> And speak out like a man? —Anon.

"It is strange how some Christians can withhold from the world, without compunction, the best news that ever came into it."

TRUE ROYALTY

SUGGESTED SCRIPTURE READING: Revelation 5:8-14

And hath made us kings and priests unto God.

Revelation 1:6

The blood of Jesus Christ not only washes away our sins, but it endows us as well with a true royalty. Our divine right is not now recognized by the world, but it will be indisputably admitted in that day when we reign with Christ "on the earth" (Rev. 5:10). As "heirs" with Him, "all things" (I Cor. 3:22) will then be acknowledged as rightfully our royal possession.

A converted shoemaker in Germany, who rejoiced in his salvation and his unique and rightful inheritance in Christ, was constantly heard singing out his joy and gratitude in hymns of thanksgiving to God. One day there passed along the street a Jewish gentleman who had found no rest for his soul in the empty rituals of his father's religion. As he came near the cobbler's door, he was attracted by the joy and confidence of this humble Christian. Stopping, he said, "My friend, you seem exceedingly happy." "Indeed," said the shoemaker, "I have good reason to be, for you must understand, sir, that I am a King's son." The other shook his head disbelievingly and was heard to whisper to himself as he went on his way, "Poor fool." A few days later he had occasion to pass the little shop again. "Good morning your Royal Highness," said the Jewish gentleman with sarcastic scorn. "Good morning," said the cobbler, "please do not hurry away, but give me a moment's opportunity to explain what I meant the other day." The other gentleman halted, and the Christian told in his own sincere and humble way of his Scriptural right to call himself a royal subject. It is said that his testimony later bore fruit and that this Jewish inquirer first became his friend and later by an act of faith, himself became a child of the King.

Hold up your head, weary Christian, soon your true royalty will be disclosed. The crowning day is drawing nigh when we shall reign with our victorious Saviour!   —H.G.B.

A tent or a cottage, why should I care?
They're building a palace for me over there!
Tho' exiled from home, yet still I may sing:
All glory to God, I'm a child of the King.—H. E. Buell

"If the King is indeed near kin to us, the royal likeness will be recognizable."

FELLOWSHIP

Suggested Scripture Reading: I John 3:11-16

We have fellowship one with another. I John 1:7

As you travel through this world, are you ever lonely and hungering for fellowship? Then remember there are others about you in the same condition, who, if they only knew your desire, would rush to your side. Let your light shine and it will attract others to you. John says, "If we walk in the light . . . we have fellowship one with another."

A simple farmer was visiting London for the first time and wandered into the Art Gallery to look around. Presently he stood before a beautiful painting of Jesus hanging on the Cross. He was transfixed; not by the artist's skill alone, but most of all by the picture of the Saviour. As he gazed upon the picture, he became oblivious to all about him. As though he were the only one in the room, he finally cried out with tears in his eyes, "Bless the Lord! Oh, how I love Him, how I love Him."

Others in the gallery heard him; and seeing the tears, as he stood hat in hand before the picture, they were touched and stopped at the picture also. Presently a stranger stepped up and said, "I love Him too." And then another grabbed the farmer's hand and tremblingly said, "And I love Him too." A third one came, and a fourth, and still another until before the picture stood a little knot of men in "fellowship" with one another, perfect strangers but brought together in Christ. And the lonely farmer found fellowship in the heart of a great bewildering city, because he had given expression to His love for Jesus. He had walked in the light and found the fellowship of heaven.

—M.R.D.

Blest be the tie that binds
Our hearts in Christian love;
The fellowship of kindred minds
Is like to that above.

"A true friend is the gift of God, and He only who made hearts can really unite them." — south

THE HEAVEN'S SILENT WITNESS

SUGGESTED SCRIPTURE READING: Psalm 19:1-6

The heavens declare the glory of God; and the firmament sheweth his handywork.   Psalm 19:1

The wonder of God's artistry in the sky; the astounding clock of the heavens that always runs on time; the intricate pattern of whirling spheres, glistening stars, and mysterious planets that hang suspended on unseen bands of energy, amaze the mind of man. To the Psalmist under inspiration, it was a constant stimulus calling forth praise to the great Creator. David, while tending his flocks in the open fields as a boy, had ample time to gaze into the black velvet of the Palestinian night as it sparkled beautifully with the diamonds of God. As he looked, he reveled in their silent witness to the divine glory and wisdom. Let evil men deny the reality of God, still the stars and the planets ceaselessly declare His reality and handiwork.

Does the wonder of the heavens awaken praise in your heart to the mighty God of the universe, who, despite His glory, stoops to love poor mortals such as we? Surely the "music of the spheres" should strike a responsive chord in every thoughtful heart.

It is a well-known fact that during the French Revolution, men determined to abolish Christianity. One fine, clear night an atheist was loudly proclaiming his satanic doctrine to a poor countryman. "Everything," he said, "will be abolished—churches, Bibles, clergymen; yes, even the word, 'God,' itself. *We shall remove everything which speaks of religion!*" The countryman gave a quiet chuckle. "Why do you laugh?" said the other. The peasant pointed to the stars and replied, "I was just wondering how you and your crew would manage to get them down!"

Truly, the glory of the heavens is one silent testimony to God's existence that evil men cannot erase.   —H.G.B.

The sun with royal splendor goes forth to chant Thy praise,
The moonbeams soft and tender their gentler anthems raise;
O'er every tribe and nation the music strange is poured,
The song of all creation to Thee, creation's Lord.—T. R. Birks

"God has not left Himself without a witness. In addition to the Bible He reveals Himself in history, the human conscience, and in the mirror of nature." — G.W.

LAMBS AND TURTLEDOVES

SUGGESTED SCRIPTURE READING: Exodus 31:1-11

If he be not able to bring a lamb . . . bring . . .
turtledoves.   Leviticus 5:7

The Israelite was commanded to bring a "trespass offering" in Leviticus 5. To those who were able, a lamb or a kid from the flock was required. But if a person were poor and unable to bring a lamb, he could bring a pair of turtledoves or two young pigeons. Pigeons were obtainable anywhere just for the taking, and God accepted them just as fully as the more expensive offerings. Many of you complain you can do so little for the Lord, but your "little" is just as great in God's sight as the "much" of others with more opportunities and talents. Some can preach, others can sing, others can only send a letter of comfort or pray. I am thinking of the thousands of you who are bound to your homes and even sickbeds and can only pray. What would we do without you? You have a most important assignment!

A boy was saved from drowning by his brother and carried home unconscious by his group of friends. The father wanted to reward them and said to John, "What did you do?" And John replied, "I jumped in and pulled him out." He received a good reward. "And James and Thomas, what did you do?" "We carried Danny home." "You did well too," said the father, "here is a reward for you." And Mary what did you do?" Mary was only three years old, and she burst into tears and said, "Daddy, I couldn't do anything at all — so I just prayed and prayed." What a surprise for Mary it was when father said, "You deserve the best reward of all, for you did all you could and God answered your prayers through John and James and Thomas." The Lord knows how indispensably important prayer is, and, therefore, puts so many in places where they have time to pray. —M.R.D.

Never a soldier in fierce conflict
Could a higher honor bring,
Than the shut-in who's performing
Secret service for the King!   —Anon.

"If we cannot do the good we would, we ought at least to do the good we can."

CHEER UP!

SUGGESTED SCRIPTURE READING: Proverbs 17:13-22

Then were they all of good cheer. Acts 27:36

A cheerful spirit is a wonderful stimulant! Someone has said, "Most of our ills are imaginary; therefore, they who borrow trouble pay a high rate of interest." Solomon, the wisest man who ever lived, declared under inspiration, "A merry heart doeth good like a medicine." The joy of the Lord in the heart should radiate from the countenance. Jesus does not want us to be gloomy. When He was here in the days of His flesh He said to a man sick with the palsy, "Be of good cheer." When He came walking on the waves in the dark of night, He reassured his frightened and bewildered disciples, and once again exclaimed, "Be of good cheer!" Even at the Last Supper, a time of deepest solemnity, when everyone present was cast into gloom and sorrow by our Lord's predictions, He still admonished them in the same breath to take courage.

Show me a joyful, exuberant Christian and I will show you one who has influence for Christ. With a secure and well-blest soul, with a perfectly guided pathway, and with a blissful future awaiting us, how can we be sad?

I am reminded of the story of the little girl who had been brought up among Christians who thought it was pious and well-pleasing to the Lord to walk around with a dreary "holier than thou" expression. Upon visiting a farm she saw a horse tethered in his stall and was greatly delighted by the friendly animal. She was heard to exclaim, however, "Oh, horsey, you must be a very good Christian, *you have such a long face!*"

Christian, remember: Cheerfulness like charity should begin at home. You may have a bright, flashy personality in public, but what sort of an atmosphere do you radiate in the sheltered seclusion of your family circle? "Now I exhort you (brethren) . . . be of good cheer!" (Acts 27:22a). —H.G.B.

Don't be downhearted, cheer up, . . . cheer up!
For Jesus is on the Throne;
And He will supply every need from on high,
Cheer up! . . . Cheer up! . . . Cheer up! —Anon.

"Remember, you are not only the salt of the earth, but the sugar."

BROKEN SHIPS AT EZION-GEBER

SUGGESTED SCRIPTURE READING: II Chronicles 20:31-37

Jehoshaphat made ships of Tharshish to go to Ophir for gold: but they went not; for the ships were broken at Ezion-geber. I Kings 22:48

Jehoshaphat was one of the best and most spiritual kings of Judah. However, in this story of the broken ships of Ezion-geber (related in greater detail in II Chronicles 20), his sin of compromise and the disaster which followed is graphically displayed. It seems that he had become unduly involved with unbelievers by making an unholy alliance with Ahaziah. With the latter's aid he builds a fleet of ships at Ezion-geber with the intention of sailing them to far-off Ophir, a seaport in southern Arabia on the edge of the Indian Ocean. From that famous region of legend and mystery he meant to take on a cargo of much fine gold to delight his heart and the hearts of his subjects. We are told, however, that the Lord sent a prophet to him who pronounced this severe judgment, "Because thou hast joined thyself with Ahaziah, the Lord hath broken thy works" (II Chron. 20:37). According to the prophetic Word, his fleet of sailing vessels was scarcely past the docks when they met with total disaster upon the rocks that bear the name of "giant's backbone," or Ezion-geber.

Spurgeon, in commenting on this passage, makes the following application: "Would to God that Jehoshaphat's experience might be a warning to the rest of God's people, to avoid being unequally yoked together with unbelievers! A life of misery is usually the lot of those who are united in marriage, or in any other way of their own choosing, with the men of the world. Oh, for such love to Jesus that, like Him, we may be holy, harmless, undefiled and separated from sinners; for if it be not so with us, we may expect to hear it often said, 'The LORD hath broken thy works.'"

Truly, "what part hath he that believeth with an infidel?" (II Cor. 6:15b). Be separate from the world or expect, like Jehoshaphat, to find your "treasure ships" broken before they have fairly left port! —H.G.B.

Where broken vows in fragments lie
The toll of wasted years,
Do Thou make whole again, we cry,
And give a song for tears! —F. Burroughs

"If you wish to avoid great heartaches, don't be yoked to those who refuse the yoke of Christ."

FAMINE IN THE LAND

SUGGESTED SCRIPTURE READING: I Corinthians 6:9-12

*. . . a famine in the land, not a famine of bread . . .
but of hearing the words of the LORD.*   Amos 8:11

I am in the doghouse! All because I didn't know enough to keep my mouth closed. I attended, a little while ago, a lovely dinner party. The food was the very best. At the dinner were some Christian friends whose fellowship I cherished. Afterward the conversation turned to television programs, and each one extolled their own favorite program. One told of this program in the forenoon, another about their favorite one in the afternoon or evening. For a half-hour I sat entirely silent, for I did not want to reveal my ignorance of television "shows." I just sat and thought. For a full half-hour I heard about all the television programs on the air until I concluded that some of my friends did very little besides watching television. And then they discussed a certain quiz program on which a certain man won over $100,000 answering questions about the Bible. The knowledge this man had of the Scriptures was simply amazing. He could answer any question about the Bible. Every one expressed their admiration for this man. And this man was a convert from paganism in Africa only a few years before. Then the opening I was looking for suddenly came, for one dear lady turned to me and said, "Tell me, doctor, how in the world did he learn so much about the Bible?" That was my golden opportunity and I replied, *"He certainly did not get it watching television!"* Well, that must have been the wrong thing to say, for now I'm in the doghouse. But we never learn our lesson, for after my experience, I have related this to you, and now I am in the doghouse with all the rest of you. Oh, well — I am just mean enough to call out from the "doghouse," "It's true anyway." Yes, there is a famine of *hearing the words of the* LORD.

—M.R.D.

For Thy Word and Thy salvation,
Lord, my eyes with longing fail;
Teach Thy statutes to Thy servant,
Let Thy mercy now prevail. —Anon.

"Television gives people what they want; the Bible gives them what they need."

SEEING NO MAN

<small>SUGGESTED SCRIPTURE READING:</small> Matthew 17:1-8

And when they had lifted up their eyes, they saw no man, save Jesus only. Matthew 17:8

Once we have really seen Jesus in all of His glory, as did the disciples on the mount of transfiguration, we will lose sight of self and other men and focus our spiritual eyes entirely upon His blessed Person. We will stop looking at His imperfect followers and their faults and see only in them that which reflects their Saviour (be it in a lesser or a greater degree). Instead of being "faultfinders" we will become "Christ discerners."

Those who have gone on in the Christian life to clearer, spiritual perception always seek to look beyond the messenger to his message. I am reminded in this connection of the incident related in the book, *Saints, Sinners, and Beechers.* In this volume Lyman Beecher Stowe tells of one occasion when Thomas K. Beecher substituted for his famous brother, Henry Ward Beecher, at the Plymouth Church in Brooklyn. Many curiosity seekers had come to hear the renowned Henry Beecher, and when Thomas K. Beecher appeared in the pulpit instead, the "church tramps," sightseers, and spiritually deficient started for the doors. Thomas raised his hand for silence and finally got their attention. Then he made this announcement: "All those who came here this morning *to worship Henry Ward Beecher* may withdraw from the church; all who came *to worship God* may remain."

There are no Christians who are more disappointed in the end than those who follow individuals; for even spiritual giants are human and will fail when put to the exacting test of perfection. Keep from the error of constantly finding fault with the messengers of God, but also from the equally reprehensible extreme of over-exalting those who are outstanding Christian leaders. Human idols have feet of clay. Be careful to "see no man, save Jesus only!" —H.G.B.

Jesus only, let me see,
Jesus only, none save He,
This my theme shall ever be—
Jesus! — Jesus only! —O. J. Smith

"Seeing Jesus only is the sovereign remedy against fault-finding, doubt, and spiritual defeat." — G.W.

DON'T SCARE TIMOTHY

SUGGESTED SCRIPTURE READING: I Corinthians 16:9-24

> *. . . if Timotheus come, see that he may be with you without fear.*   I Corinthians 16:10

Don't scare Timothy when he comes to visit you. So wrote the fatherly Apostle Paul concerning his son in the faith. Timothy was just a lad, starting out in the ministry. In the eyes of Paul, Timothy never seemed to grow old. He was an example of "perpetual youth." Paul knew the proud, carnal church at Corinth and feared that they might be amazed as they beheld this "boyish" ambassador. He could imagine them saying, "Why he is just a boy. What can he do?" But Paul says, "Let no man therefore despise him" (I Cor. 16:11). Ten years later Timothy was still just a "boy" for Paul writes to him in I Timothy 4:12, "Let no man despise thy youth."

Don't scare Timothy! He is young and needs encouragement and not criticism. He needs prayer more than censoring. Is your pastor a young man, still inexperienced and subject to mistakes and blunders? Don't despise him but help him. The best cure for criticizing your young preacher is to pray for him. It is a rule as fixed as the exactitude of mathematics, that your prayers are in inverse proportion to your criticism. Don't scare Timothy!

And this holds for all young Christians. How prone we are to find fault with them and smile at their crude testimonies. How many new converts have been discouraged and "scared" by our lack of sympathy and help, and despising their youth. Speak a kind word today to a beginner. Next time you meet your preacher, tell him you are praying for him, that you appreciate his humble efforts and sincere endeavors. Tell him what you like about him — and the things you don't — *tell them to God alone. Don't* frighten the youthful Timothy!   —M.R.D.

> Life would be a lot more happy
> If we'd praise the good we see,
> Tell each other what is worthy
> In each Christian "Timothy."—G. W.

"Many have fallen by the edge of the sword, but more have fallen by the prick of the tongue."

THE TOUCH OF HIS HAND

SUGGESTED SCRIPTURE READING: Matthew 8:1-4

Behold a man full of leprosy: who seeing Jesus fell on his face, and besought him, saying, Lord if thou wilt, thou canst make me clean. And he put forth his hand, and touched him, saying, I will: be thou clean.

Luke 5:12, 13.

Leprosy is used in Scripture to typify sin, for it is an incurable disease that progressively becomes worse. It is interesting to observe that it is never said to be *healed*, only *cleansed*. In God's sight we are all as "an unclean thing," full of the loathsome disease of sin from which the blood of Jesus alone can cleanse us.

Note that this leper in Luke 5 came to the right Person — he fell on his face before Jesus; He came with the right attitude — praying and recognizing his need; and he came expectantly, that is: with faith. As a result, he was rewarded with the gift of health and cleansing.

If you, too, are "full of leprosy" in a moral and spiritual sense, and come acknowledging your deep need to this same compassionate Physician of Souls, He, in like manner, will give you the cleansing you seek. He has said, "Him that cometh to me, I will in no wise cast out" (John 6:37b).

Some rude children in Madagascar were one day heard calling out, "Leper! Leper!" as they pointed to a poor woman who had lost all of her fingers and toes by that dread disease. A missionary lady who was nearby put her hand on the woman's shoulder and asked her to sit down on the grass by her. The woman fell down sobbing, overcome by her emotions, and cried, "A human hand has touched me! A human hand has touched me! *For seven years no one has touched me!*" The missionary said that at that moment it flashed across her mind why it is recorded in the Gospels that Jesus *touched* the leper. Still today, His hand of blessing bestows that same caress of sympathy and cleansing which is so vital, for He is "ever moved with compassion" (Mark 1:41a) when a disturbed and needy soul calls out for mercy. Yes, His ears are open to *your* cry. Let Him touch you and you will be made "every whit whole."   —H.G.B.

> Just one touch as He passes by,
> He will list to the faintest cry,
> Come and be saved while the Lord is nigh,
> Christ is the Healer divine. —B. Bell

"Every man is spiritually 'unclean' until he is cleansed by the blood."
— H.G.B.

GOD'S CHRONOMETER

SUGGESTED SCRIPTURE READING: Acts 24:10-16

For ever, O LORD, thy word is settled in heaven.
                                        Psalm 119:89

Do you have a chronometer? The word "chronometer" is a scientific name for a "timepiece" — a watch or clock. An absolutely "perfect" timepiece has never yet been made by man. I have a watch which keeps "good" but not "perfect" time. Every few days I must check it by dialing the time service telephone number, or by listening to the radio for the announcement, "At the tone it will be exactly ten o'clock." Usually I am a few seconds off and I must adjust my watch. Who is the authority for the right time? We get the time from the U.S. Weather Bureau, but this agency gets it from the observatory where the time is constantly checked by the stars. The stars never vary. The reason is simple. God made these heavenly "chronometers" and they are perfectly timed. But "chronometers" watches and clocks, are made by man, and no matter how "good," they are never 100% reliable; but they must be checked by God's clock—the stars.

The Bible is God's clock which is the perfect expression of His will. But man, too, has a clock. This is his conscience. It convicts him of right or wrong. Every man must follow his own conscience, but it is not a reliable guide unless checked constantly and adjusted completely to the Word of God. As watches differ in time — so consciences of men differ on many matters. Your conscience must be your guide — but your consicence must be regulated by God's perfect revelation, the Word of God. Before going to catch a train or plane, I always "check the time" so I will not be late. So, too, to begin this day without checking with the Word of God, may result in tragedy. Follow your conscience but be sure it is "on time" by consulting God's "chronometer" — the Bible. Sit down, brother! Don't go until you have made the check.   —M.R.D.

> You've time to build houses, and in them to dwell
> And time to do business — to buy and to sell,
> But none for repentance, or deep, earnest prayer
> To seek your salvation you've no time to spare.
> Then, what of the judgment? Pause, think, I implore!
> For time will be lost on eternity's shore.   —Anon.

"Conscience is like a sundial. When the truth of God shines on it, it points the right way."

THE TOWN CLERK'S ADVICE

SUGGESTED SCRIPTURE READING: Acts 19:23-41

. . . ye ought to be quiet, and to do nothing rashly.
Acts 19:36

These words were not spoken by Peter or the Apostle Paul; but rather by an unknown town clerk of the city of Ephesus. Although not a Christian, he showed himself to be a man of intelligence and diplomacy. His words of wisdom show that God's common grace is still operative even among those who are unsaved. While it is true that man is totally depraved and, therefore, each part of his being is tinged with sin, he is not *absolutely* depraved but still shows marks of his original creation in the image of God. Although not the object of the Holy Spirit's special enlightenment in regard to salvation, yet this town clerk displayed a high degree of discernment by virtue of the light of God which "lighteth every man that cometh into the world" (John 1:9b). There is a lesson here for all of us. Although the worldly man has no *spiritual* discernment, he may have general knowledge and temporal insights granted to him through common grace by which we can profit and expand our *natural* understanding.

Cotton Mather testified that he was greatly indebted to this gentleman in the nineteenth chapter of Acts for his counsel to "do nothing rashly." On any proposal of consequence, Mather would therefore usually say: "Let us first consult a little with the town clerk of Ephesus." Indeed, a great deal of trouble and regret could be avoided if all of us were more in the habit of showing the same caution and common sense as was displayed by this notable Ephesian. It is true that there are some things that should not be put off until tomorrow. There are others, however, which should definitely be delayed in order to give us time for proper consideration and meditation in regard to the advisable course of action.

Before you speak or proceed unwisely today repeat to yourself the motto of the town clerk of Ephesus, *"Do nothing rashly!"*
—H.G.B.

Take time to be holy, be calm in thy soul;
Each thought and each motive beneath His control;
Thus led by His Spirit to fountains of love,
Thou soon shalt be fitted for service above.—W. D. Longstaff

"Hurry is the mother of most mistakes!"

THE BABY RABBIT

SUGGESTED SCRIPTURE READING: Galatians 5:17-24

That which is born of the flesh is flesh. John 3:6

All babies are cute, adorable and sweet. It is hard to imagine that the little gurgling infant in the crib, so pure and innocent, could develop into a vile, law-breaking villain, breaking his mother's heart and bringing disgrace on father's name. Such, however, is the potentiality of that little life, if not touched by the regenerating Spirit of God. That apparently innocent "mother's darling" has a sinful Adamic nature. Unless regenerated, that sweet baby will grow up to be a sinner, destined to eternal doom.

The young of many wild animals may be raised as pets if obtained early in life. My grandson, M. R. the second, found a baby rabbit out of its nest last spring. It was helpless, being only a day or two old. M. R. obtained a small bottle and a "doll nipple," and succeeded in keeping it alive. It became a real, affectionate pet, roaming about the house at will. The children could pick it up anytime. As it developed, it became more restless. It would disappear but always return, until finally it left its coop and was never seen again. For a few weeks, under its care by the children, it seemed tame, but it was not long until its true wild nature conquered and it went astray. The only way it could be made really tame was to give it the nature of a tame rabbit. Until then it would always be "wild." You could only keep it by penning it in a coop; left free, it ran away.

So, too, with a child. It has a sinful Adamic nature. Unless regenerated, it is only a matter of time until this nature asserts itself. We may "fence it in," with the law to restrain it, but left to itself it will go astray. "That which is born of the flesh is flesh." "Ye must be born again." The fence of the law may restrain the sinner; but only the grace of God can give him a new nature. —M.R.D.

> In evil all have gone astray,
> Rebellious is our race,
> In sin from God we turn away,
> Oh, rescue us in grace! —G. W.

"Man talks of the survival of the fittest, but the glory of the Gospel is that it transforms the unfit."

COSTLY SALVATION

SUGGESTED SCRIPTURE READING: I Peter 1:15-25

. . . ye were . . . redeemed . . . with the precious blood of Christ.   I Peter 1:18, 19

A preacher who loved to deal with sinners once paid a visit to some miners to tell them of the grace and truth which came by Jesus Christ. After a simple message concerning God's love for the lost, the time came for the men to resume their work and for the preacher to make his way back along the tortuous tunnels of coal to the elevator where he could ascend to the top of the shaft. The foreman of the crew accompanied him so the servant of God thought to do a bit of personal work by asking him what he thought of God's way of salvation. The man replied, "Oh, it's *too cheap;* I cannot believe in such a religion as that." Without making an immediate reply, the preacher asked him, "Just how do you folks get out of this place?" "Oh, by getting into that cage over there," was the reply. "And does it take long to get to the top?" "No, only a few seconds." "Well," said the preacher, "that certainly is very easy and simple; but say, don't you need to do something to help raise yourself?" "Of course not," replied the miner, "as I have said, you have nothing to do but to get into the elevator." "What about the people who sank the shaft and perfected all this? Was there much labor or expense connected with it?" "Yes, indeed; it was very costly and difficult work. This shaft is 1800 feet deep, but it was necessary, for without this elevator we would never be able to get to the surface." "That's very true," said the preacher, "yet when God's Word tells you that whosoever believeth in the Son of God hath everlasting life, you say to me, 'it's too cheap, too cheap.' But you forget that God's work to bring you and others out of the deep pit of destruction and death was accomplished at a *vast cost:* namely, the price of the precious blood of the Lord Jesus Christ. He died that you might have a way of escape."

Salvation is free, dear friend, but it is not cheap, it cost the best that heaven had! "How shall we escape, if we neglect so great salvation?"   —H.G.B.

> That priceless blood my ransom paid,
> While I in bondage stood;
> On Jesus all my sin was laid,
> He saved me with His blood.—W. McDonald

"True wealth is measured by heaven's gifts to us."

THE ROAD MAP

SUGGESTED SCRIPTURE READING: Psalm 119:89-96

I have chosen the way of truth.   Psalm 119:30.

I have a great respect for "official road maps" when I am traveling from one place to another. They are reliable guides and much time and gas can be saved by following their instructions. How often we have been led astray by ignoring the map and taking a "short cut" to save a few miles. Before taking a trip into unfamiliar places we always get an official itinerary from the Auto Club with the best and most direct routes all clearly marked. As long as we believe the "guide," we get along fine, but when, as we so often do, we begin to plan "short cuts" we run into trouble.

We are touring happily along. Mrs. DeHaan is in charge of the "roap map" and I am at the wheel. Suddenly she says, "There must be a better way to go. This route curves way around, and there's a road which seems to cut off several miles. Let's take that." As often as we have been fooled, we never seem to learn; and so as usual we get into a jam. The short cut is rough, tortuous and narrow. And then that horrible sign, "Bridge out — Detour." And so we turn back, and there is deep silence for several miles.

God's Word is our official road map. It can always be trusted. Study this map if you would travel safely. The devil, however likes to show us some "short cuts." "There is a way that seemeth right to a man, but the end thereof are the ways of death.' Job said, "He knoweth the way that I take." As you travel today over an unknown pathway, be sure to consult the "map" and follow its directions. Before you go to your day's duties will you take time to consult the "WORD," and then pause to pray for light upon your way? Please now — *please* — don't get up before consulting the "Book." To begin the day without the Bible, is to travel in darkness that will only lead to tragedy and defeat.—M.R.D.

> The old Book is my guide, 'tis a friend by my side,
>   It will lighten and brighten my way;
> And each promise I find soothes and gladdens my mind
>   As I read it and heed it today!   —Anon.

"Do not have your concert first and tune your instrument afterwards. Begin the day with the Word of God and prayer, and get first of all in harmony with Him." — J. H. TAYLOR

FEEDING THE CROW

S<small>UGGESTED</small> S<small>CRIPTURE</small> R<small>EADING:</small> Numbers 11:1-6

Tell me . . . where thou feedest. Song of Solomon 1:7

Someone has said, "You are what you eat." How true this is I am not prepared to say, but it certainly applies to the spiritual realm. How much of what you see, hear, and so feed the inner man is spiritual, uplifting, of good report, and profitable in making you more like Jesus? How much of it is worldly, trashy, or even downright obscene and filthy? Tell me, where feedest thou?

The Bible speaks of the carnal man's diet as eating of the "vine of Sodom, and of the fields of Gomorrah." It says he seeks to consume "grapes of gall" whose clusters are bitter (Deut. 32: 32). It is interesting to note that these "grapes" are not the usual nourishing kind, but are of a variety known to the Arabs as "Lot's Sea Orange." This is a highly colored, desirable looking fruit which when plucked explodes like a puff-ball leaving behind only a worthless orange skin and a bit of tough, inedible fiber. In another place the Bible speaks of the diet of Egypt (typical of the world) as being "leeks, and . . . onions, and . . . garlic" (Num. 11:5). Each of these earthly foods has a racy, pungent flavor but scarcely a calorie of nourishment to recommend them. Examples could be multiplied but the truth is the same. The things of the world appeal, but they have no real food value for the soul. Isaiah gives us the conclusion of the whole matter. He tells us that the worldly man "feedeth on ashes" (Isa. 44:20).

The Christian's heart has been likened to a cage in which dwell two birds: *a dove*, and *a crow*. The former represents the new nature, the latter the old man of sin. If you nourish the dove by prayer, Bible study, and witnessing, it will become strong and dominate the nest; if you neglect the things of the Spirit, the carnal bird will soon be in control. *Don't feed the crow!*

—H.G.B.

Jesus has a table spread where the saints of God are fed,
  He invites His chosen people, "Come and dine";
With His manna He doth feed and supplies our ev'ry need;
  O 'tis sweet to sup with Jesus all the time!—C. B. Widmeyer

"The things of God seem unappetizing only when our taste has been impaired by partaking of the forbidden 'leeks and garlic' of the world." — H.G.B.

THE PERFECT SHIP

SUGGESTED SCRIPTURE READING: Genesis 6:8-22

Make thee an ark.   Genesis 6:14

The only unsinkable ship ever built was an ancient one made of gopher wood, 450 feet long, 75 feet wide, and 45 feet high. It was three stories high and sealed with pitch. It was one of three arks mentioned in Scripture, all of them pictures of shelter from death and judgment. The first ark was "Noah's Ark." The second mentioned was the "Ark of Moses," in which the baby Moses was delivered from judgment. The third ark was the "Ark of the Covenant," with its blood-sprinkled mercy-seat. All three of these speak of God's provision for deliverance from death and judgment.

1. The Ark of Noah was designed by God. He was the architect (Gen. 6:14-61).

2. The Ark of Noah was water-tight. It was covered within and without with pitch. The word "pitch" is *Kopher* in the Hebrew and means "atonement." The atonement speaks of blood (Lev. 7:11). We who are in the ark of Christ are made secure by His blood.

3. God was with Noah in the ark for He said, "Come into the ark." It was not "go in," but "Come in with me." So God was "IN CHRIST" our Ark (II Cor. 5:19).

4. There was only one door and that was in the side of the ark. Christ is the only approach to God (Acts 4:12).

5. The Ark had but one window. It was not in the side but in the roof. We cannot see the judgment outside, but only heaven above. We see Jesus (Heb. 2:9).

6. The Ark, therefore, had no outside light of nature, but Noah walked in the light of the ark itself; the Light of the world. The believer walks in the light of Him.

7. The Ark contained food — good food — enough for all its occupants (Gen. 6:21). It was a perfect food which kept all healthy and strong without sickness or death. Yes, all things in Jesus we find!   —M.R.D.

All that I want is in Jesus,
He satisfies, joy He supplies;
Life would be worthless without Him,
All things in Jesus I find.   —H. D. Loes

"Christ is the Ark of Safety, He bears His own through the waters of judgment to 'Mount Ararat,' the 'heavenly places' (Eph. 2:6) of security and divine fellowship." — H.G.B.

THE HOMELAND

SUGGESTED SCRIPTURE READING: I Corinthians 15:51-58

We are confident, I say, and willing rather to be absent from the body, and to be present with the Lord.

II Corinthians 5:8

The expression "present with the Lord," might more literally be translated "*getting home* to be with the Lord." Another has paraphrased it: "We are glad to be exiled from the body and *to come to the homeland,* the presence of our Lord." The refuge that Jesus' bosom will provide, the warmth and joy we shall experience in His presence, is nothing less than *home!* In the safety and repose of those harmonious surroundings we shall be supremely content and forever free from all that might irritate or alarm.

Home on earth is dear to each of us because those things which we cherish most reside there. For the same reason Heaven is precious to the believer. There the longing heart of the world-weary pilgrim sets its affections, for there is the throne of the God he worships; there is the blessed physical presence of the Christ he adores; and there are the kindred spirits of those whom he has "loved long since, and lost awhile."

The story is told of a brave, little old lady who had once lived in an atmosphere of culture and security, but who had to spend her declining years in the poorhouse. However, she always seemed happy and had a testimony for her Lord. When she lay on her deathbed, she called for the Chaplain and said, "I have just one request. When it is all over, I want someone to sing my favorite hymn at the last service." The Chaplain wrote to a friend later, "I shall never forget the day we laid her to rest — all was drab and drear, and disconsolate. Then a transfiguration took place. A deep, rich, contralto voice was singing triumphantly over the pine box: *I'm a Child of the King!* And she was. She had moved out of the poorhouse into her Father's house of 'many mansions.'"

For the Christian death is not a cold, "fearful leap into the dark," it is rather the warm embrace of Jesus and the happy welcome of the eternal Homeland!　　　　　—H.G.B.

> So homesick for Heaven, for Jesus, my Friend;
> One look at His face will earth's heartaches all mend;
> I long for my Saviour, no more here to roam;
> I want to see Jesus, and Heaven, and Home. —Anon.

"To Adam, paradise was home; to his saved descendants true Home is still the same."

A PICKLE IN A BOTTLE

Ye fathers . . . bring them (your children) up in the nurture and admonition of the Lord. Ephesians 6:4

Have you any little "pickles" in your home? I am referring to those little pickles, your small children who will some day be big cucumbers. When I was just a little lad in Zeeland, Michigan, I was tremendously interested and intrigued by a large cucumber. It was no different than any other cucumber, but it was found in the strangest place. It belonged to my uncle and he kept it on a shelf in the "sitting" room. The big cucumber was in a bottle. Now that is not strange either, for grocery store shelves are loaded with cucumbers in bottles. But this particular cucumber was many times too large to go through the neck of the bottle. It was plain to see it could not be removed from the bottle through its narrow neck, but how did it get there in the first place?

I was filled with awe and admiration of my uncle who could perform such a mysterious feat. He was quite a "joker" and told some of the most fantastic tales about how he had "divined" this strange phenomenon. But mother came to my rescue and explained how, when the pickle was still very tiny, it had been passed through the narrow neck and allowed to grow inside the bottle, and now it was impossible to get it out. My mother practiced this same principle in a most effective way. From my earliest memory she surrounded me with prayer and instruction and the Gospel. I grew up in the "bottle" of mother's tears and supplications; and as a result I was brought to Christ and am now safe in the bottle of His salvation. What a lesson for you parents who have little "pickles" in your home. Don't let anything interfere with your first duty toward them. The Jesuit who is credited with the quotation, "Give me a child till he is seven and I care not who gets him after that," knew the value of early training. Don't neglect your "pickles." Soon they will be cucumbers. —M.R.D.

Every life is a preaching life,
With a message it doth proclaim;
And some child who is watching now
Will be trying to live the same. —G. W.

"The parent's life is the child's copy book."

HE KNOWS OUR SORROW

Suggested Scripture Reading: Revelation 21:3-7

And the Lord said, I have surely seen the affliction of my people . . . and have heard their cry . . . for I know their sorrows.   Exodus 3:7

I know thy sorrow, child; I know it well,
Thou need'st not try with broken voice to tell—
Just let me lay thy head here on my breast,
And find here sweetest comfort, perfect rest!
Then trust it all to me today — tomorrow —
Yes, e'en forever, for I know thy sorrow.

On this Memorial Day when many are sad and think of departed loved ones, it is precious to know that there is One who is deeply sympathetic and catches all our tears "in His bottle." As the Heavenly Friend, He understands the aching void in hearts today and seeks to comfort sorrowing ones by drawing them to the security of His bosom.

A little girl was once traveling on a train. No one seemed to know whose child she was, for in her happy glee she romped up and down the aisles apparently at home with everyone. Soon, however, the train plunged into a dark tunnel and the little one with a cry of fear flew like a bird to nest herself in her mother's lap. So, too, in our sunny days of joy we may frolic hither and yon so that there may be little to indicate to whom we belong; but when God allows us to go through some dark tunnel of sorrow and despair, folks will see immediately to whom we flee for refuge, and His name will be glorified. As a mother stills her child, so Jesus lays His loving hand on troubled brows and as it were whispers, "Trust me! I never send anything to hurt you — only to bless. To die is gain, and to be with me is far better! Someday you will understand and know all about it!"

Someone has written, "When crushing bereavement lies like ice on the heart, when the dearest earthly friend cannot enter into the peculiarities of our grief, Jesus can — Jesus does! He who bore my *sins*, also carries my *sorrows* . . . I can think, in all my afflictions, 'He was afflicted'; and in all my tears, 'Jesus wept.'"   —H.G.B.

So resting here my child, thy hand in Mine,
Thy sorrow, to my care, today resign;
Fret not that some new care will come tomorrow—
What does it matter? I know thy sorrow. —Anon.

"Keep your face toward the sunshine of His love, and the shadows will fall behind you!"

A LITTLE CHILD SHALL LEAD THEM

SUGGESTED SCRIPTURE READING: Luke 2:40-52

And a little child shall lead them.   Isaiah 11:6

I have just paid a visit to my grandchild, the latest baby in our family circle. Just a little, tender baby, unable to say a word but what a sermon I heard as I stood by that tiny crib and congratulated myself for being the grandfather to another baby. A baby does something to you. It is the most mysterious thing in the physical world. There is nothing like it. According to our text, babies are born to be leaders. Of course, I realize this refers to the literal millennium and little children leading about wolves and leopards and young lions, but the *prophetic* interpretation does not exhaust its teaching. Have you ever been led by a baby? What a day it is in a woman's life when pressing her very own baby to her breast, she feels the exquisite joy of motherhood. What a day in a man's life when for the first time he tremblingly takes in his arms the dear child of his own body. What happens on a day like that? That baby opens a whole new world of parenthood into a richer, fuller life, a new center and motive for endeavor, something to really live for. Yes, a little child shall lead them.

But there is a deeper lesson still. A little child can lead to the Saviour, for Jesus said we must become like little children if we would be saved. *There is no hypocrisy about a baby!* There is no "sham" and no "put on." It does not hide anything. It lies in complete confidence in mother's arms. So, says our Lord, we are to trust Him. He says, "Except ye be converted and become as little children, ye shall not enter into the kingdom of heaven" (Matt. 18:3). Babies have so much to teach us. Our hearts need their "leading" to keep us tender by their gentle ministries; and so they don't hurry to grow up like other creatures. Yes, a little child shall lead them.   —M.R.D.

How oft a little one has found the road,
The narrow pathway to that blest abode:
A little child! — The Lord oft uses such
The stoutest heart to break, or bend, or touch;
Then by His Spirit bids the conflict cease,
And once, forever, enter into peace!   —Anon.

"What gift has Providence bestowed on man that is so dear to him as his children?"—CICERO

HIDDEN BLESSINGS

SUGGESTED SCRIPTURE READING: Psalm 142

Attend unto my cry; for I am brought very low.

Psalm 142:6

It is said that he who would see the stars sparkling with tenfold luster must dwell in the cold regions of snow. So, too, "he who would know the full beauties of Jesus, the bright and morning Star, must see Him amid the frosts of trouble and adversity." There are certain lessons of grace that can only be learned in the valley of pain and distress. Our affections are directed heavenward best when we have reached such depths of human misery: for there our innate weakness, and the futility of the help of man is emphasized. God alone can truly comfort the soul tortured by sorrow, and heal the sharp, deep wounds of earthly woe. Show me a Christian who has suffered much and allowed his trials to be sanctified to his heart, and I will show you a mellow soul full of compassion for others, and with a deep love for his Saviour.

A king once placed a heavy stone in the roadway. Then he hid and waited to see who would remove it. Many who came by loudly blamed the government for not keeping the highways clear, but none assumed the duty of pushing the offending obstacle out of the way. At last a poor peasant stopped and graciously rolled it into the gutter. To his surprise he found a purse full of gold embedded in the road directly beneath the spot where the rock had stood. A note informed him that it was the king's reward intended for anyone who willingly performed this needed service. The peasant was thus richly repaid for his trouble and inconvenience. So, too, under every trial our King has hidden a blessing. The obstacles on our path are placed there for a purpose. By them God tests our faithfulness, turns our attention heavenward, and gives us opportunity for spiritual reward. There is a hidden blessing under the "rock of trial" that has brought you "very low." Roll the burden on Him and find the divine favor. —H.G.B.

> Whate'er thy grief, whate'er thy care,
> Just bring it unto Me;
> Yes, in thy day of trouble, call,
> I will deliver thee. —S. C. Umlauf

"Where souls are being tried, there God is hewing out pillars for His Temple."

THE REWARD OF SUFFERING!

SUGGESTED SCRIPTURE READING: I Peter 3:14-17

But as his part is that goeth down to the battle, so shall his part be that tarrieth by the stuff: they shall part alike.   I Samuel 30:24

The greatest sermons that I have ever heard preached were not preached from the pulpits, but from sick beds. The greatest, deepest truths of God's Word have often been revealed not by those who stood up and preached as a result of their peculiar preparation and education, but by those humble souls who have gone through the seminary of affliction and have learned experimentally the deep things of the ways of God.

The Bible tells us very distinctly that there is a special reward and a special crown which the Lord has prepared and laid up for those who suffer patiently. This principle is suggested by the incident in I Samuel 30:24. David had gone out to seek the enemy with four hundred strong, healthy men. Two hundred, however, had remained behind because they were weary and faint, probably because of some physical infirmity. These David had left behind to care for the stuff of those who went into the heat of the battle. After the victory had been won the four hundred who had been in the active participation of David's army refused to share with those who remained behind, and said, "We'll give them just a little bit, but we're going to take the spoils"; then it was that David set down the eternal principle in the words of our text!

Yes, those of you who remain by the stuff are not overlooked or forgotten of God; but as I said, there is a special and definite reward laid up for God's patient sufferers.   —M.R.D.

> One little hour of watching with the Master,
>   Eternal years to walk with Him in white;
> One little hour to bravely meet disaster,
>   Eternal years to reign with Him in light;
> One little hour for weary toils and trials,
>   Eternal years for calm and peaceful rest;
> One little hour for patient self-denials,
>   Eternal years for life, where life is blest!

**"Seldom can the heart be lonely, if it seeks a lonelier still,
Self-forgetting, seeking only emptier cups to fill!"**—F. R. HAVERGAL

CHRISTIANS AND CLOCKS

SUGGESTED SCRIPTURE READING: Titus 3:1-8

Be careful to maintain good works.   Titus 3:8

While it is true that a man is saved by grace, apart from the works of the law, it is equally certain that the seed of faith, once it is lodged in the heart, should normally bring forth the fruit of good works. Some have grossly misunderstood the teachings of grace. Forgetting the judgment seat of Christ and the punishment of the "sin unto death" for unfaithful ones, they have become careless in their living. They are much like a native convert who said, "I am under grace; I am *an outlaw!*" Without realizing it, by his improper use of the English language, he probably summarized the secret feelings of many unconsecrated Christians. His being "not under the law but under grace," may have affected him thus; but grace abounding to the sinner should lead to *grace reigning in the saint!* Although the Bible states that one cannot lose his salvation, he can, by his actions, invite the judgment of the Lord in the form of physical sickness and death and also thereby lose all reward in heaven (I Cor. 3:15; 11:30).

Spurgeon, the well-known preacher of grace, was once drawing a word picture of a professing Christian who failed to bring any fruit to perfection. "I once visited a hotel," he said, "where the owner had made it a point to put a clock in every bedroom. In mine there was one with a black marble case; but there was an empty space where the timepiece should have been. It was a mere professor. I fear that there are many in the church who are *without works;* and what a wretched disappointment they are both to God and unto those who fain would make use of them!"

Grace is a "teacher" that does not give us "recess" from responsibility nor license to indulge our appetites, but rather enrolls us in the highly accredited school of Christ's love. Here it instructs us to the end that "denying ungodliness and worldly lusts, we should live soberly, righteously, and godly, in this present world" (Titus 2:11-13).   —H.G.B.

O Thou who died on Calvary
To save my soul and make me free,
I'll consecrate my life to Thee,
My Saviour and my God. —R. E. Hudson

"God measures loyalty to Himself, not by expressions of feeling, but by service."

THE WONDROUS BLOOD!

SUGGESTED SCRIPTURE READING: Leviticus 17:10, 11

For if the blood of bulls and goats and the ashes of an heifer sprinkling the unclean, sanctifieth to the purifying of the flesh: How much more shall the blood of Christ, who through the eternal Spirit offered himself without spot to God, purge your conscience from dead works to serve the living God? Hebrews 9:13, 14

The whole plan of redemption rests upon the power of the blood of the Lord Jesus Christ. The blood is the only tissue which is unlimited in its movement within the body. Almost all other body tissues are fixed, such as muscle, bone, nerve, fat and skin. They remain where they are. There are other fluid products of the body such as saliva and gastric juices, tears and bile, but these are not tissues . . . they are secretions — not parts of the body, but products of that body. The blood alone is the liquid tissue that reaches every single cell in the body and, therefore, unites all the members with the head and the individual members as well.

As essential then as the blood is to our bodies, so essential is the blood of the Lord Jesus Christ to the Body of Christ. It, too, is fluid so that it can reach every single member of that body, no matter how far those members may be removed the one from the other. Just as the blood supplies the food elements for nourishment and life, and then carries off the waste products and poisons due to cell metabolism, so, too, the Lord Jesus Christ is to every believer the only source of life, the only support and substance of life, the One who keeps cleansing us day by day, so that our eternal life is really *eternal,* for the "blood of Jesus Christ His Son cleanses us from all sin." —M.R.D.

Have you been to Jesus for the cleansing flood,
Are you washed in the blood of the Lamb?
Are your garments spotless, are they white as snow,
Are you washed in the blood of the Lamb?—E. A. Hoffman

"Grace is more than 'unmerited favor': it is divine condescension; God's super-abundance filling and overflowing the vacuum of man's abysmal poverty!"

GIVING YET GAINING!

Suggested Scripture Reading: Proverbs 11:23-31

There is that scattereth, and yet increaseth. Proverbs 11:24

There is an apparent contradiction here. How can one scatter his possessions and still find them increased when he is finished? The world heaps up its treasures and clutches its precious things with a grip of selfish greed, but this is not the Lord's way of obtaining a full blessing. In nature He shows this by the fact that while we "waste" the seed in sowing, we later come to reap a greatly multiplied supply in the harvest. The same is true in other realms. As we give out, the Lord gives us in return much more than we ever dispensed. It will not always be in terms of financial gain, but certainly we will amass a wealth of spiritual benefits, true happiness, and treasures of eternal reward that are far greater. Don't be a miser, either of your goods or spiritual blessings, but scatter them to others. The "bread upon the waters" will drift back to you in multiplied abundance.

As soon as you become liberal, however, and seek to put this divine principle into operation, the devil will oppose you. I am reminded in this connection of a well-to-do farmer in New York State, a noted miser, who was gloriously converted. Soon afterward he promised to help a poor man who had suffered the loss of all earthly possessions in a fire. The rich farmer decided that among other things which he would give would be a large ham from his smoke house. On the way to obtain this choice piece of meat, the tempter whispered to him, "Don't be a fool, you are now too liberal; you have given him money; why not give him the *smallest* ham that you have?" The converted miser had a struggle, but finally he took down the largest, most delicious ham he could find. "You're a fool!" the devil seemed to whisper. The farmer thought for a moment and then by the help of God put the evil one to flight with the following spirited reply, "Devil, if you don't keep still, I'll give that poor man *every ham in this smoke house!*" It is said that after this victory he enjoyed the fruits of liberality throughout the rest of his days. The principle is clear: avarice gathers itself poor; charity gives itself rich! —H.G.B.

Not what we gain, but what we give,
Measures the worth of the life we live.—Anon.

"When you rob God, you cheat yourself."

WE ARE ALL DIFFERENT

For the body is not one member, but many.

I Corinthians 12:14

I am sitting in my study meditating on the diversities among believers. There are no two Christians exactly alike. God loves variety. He made no two snowflakes identical, and we are told there are no two blades of grass exactly the same. Yet, unlike as Christians are, if they are true, born-again believers they are still *one in Christ*. Among those who will read this little devotional, there are sharp differences of opinion on doctrines and interpretations. Some of you are Methodist, Baptist, Episcopal, Quaker, Lutheran, Reformed, Brethren, Catholic or something else. But if you are truly born again, we all belong to the one and the same Church — the Body of the Lord Jesus Christ. If we could only realize our common faith, and learn to forget or at least "tone down" our petty differences, we could increase our usefulness a hundredfold. There is no greater evil among the members of the Body of Christ, than quibbling on nonessentials, and riding our particular, petty hobby. Someone has said, "The difference between a 'hobby' and a 'horse' is this — You can get off the horse." I do not mean that we should not have our different convictions but let us differ in love. Even error should be dealt with in love (Gal. 6:1). Most of the bickerings and splits among Christians are so childish they should make us ashamed of ourselves.

The story is told of George Whitefield and a Quaker who had come to some hot words over unimportant things. Finally the Quaker said, "George, we are brothers. We both long to see men come to Christ, but while we are fighting, no souls are being saved. If you will forget to quarrel about my broad brim on my hat, I'll promise to not quarrel about your black clerical gown. Give me your hand." "The members should have the same care one for another" (I Cor. 12:25b). —M.R.D.

> We pray Thee, O Christ, our Saviour and Friend,
> From error and strife Thy children defend;
> Breathe on us, we pray Thee, O Spirit of Love,
> And fit us for union with Thy Church above.—A. Schmidt

"Your own church steeple is not the only one that points to heaven!"

THE BEST PREACHER

SUGGESTED SCRIPTURE READING: Proverbs 28:12-20a

*Moreover it is required in stewards, that a man be
found faithful.* I Corinthians 4:2

A famous preacher recently concluded one of his powerful
sermons with an earnest Gospel appeal. A woman of wealth and
social distinction hastened down the aisle and asked permission
to speak a few words to the audience. "I want you to know,"
she said, "just why I came forward tonight. It was not because
of any word spoken by this good preacher. I stand here because
of the influence of a little woman who sits before me. Her fingers
are rough with toil; the hard work of many years has stooped
her low, she is just a poor, obscure washerwoman, who has
served in my home for many years. I have never known her to
be impatient, speak an unkind word, or do a dishonorable deed.
I know of countless little acts of unselfish love that adorn her life.
Shamefully let me say that I have openly sneered at her faith
and laughed at her fidelity to God. Yet, when my little girl was
taken away recently it was this woman who caused me to look
beyond the grave and shed my first tear of hope. The sweet
magnetism of her life has led me to Christ. I covet the thing
that has made her life so beautiful." The preacher was quite
surprised, but he asked that the little woman be led forward.
She came with her eyes streaming with glad tears, and with
such a shining face as one seldom sees on this side of heaven.
The minister said, "Let me introduce you, friends, to the real
preacher of the evening." The great audience arose spontaneously
in silent, though not tearless, respect.

Many of you who read these words are much like this sweet,
Christian washer-woman. You do not have positions of prominence in the church, nor apparently much opportunity to do
outstanding things for God. Yet, if you shine just where you
are, someday your faithfulness will be revealed. What a thrill
it will be by and by when the Lord Jesus takes you by the hand
and says, "Your whole life was a sermon and your humble deeds
a symphony of praise; well done, good and faithful servant, enter thou into the joy of thy Lord!" —H.G.B.

Shine, shine, just where you are;
Send forth the light into the night;
Shine for Lord where you are. —A. R. Habershone

"It is not success but faithfulness that God rewards."

LISTEN MEN!

SUGGESTED SCRIPTURE READING: I Peter 3:7-12

Likewise, ye husbands, dwell with them (your wives)
according to knowledge, giving honour unto the wife.
I Peter 3:7

Are you a married man? If you are, you should read this carefully. If you are not married, you should read it before you do get married. Being a husband is a difficult task, because very few husbands understand their wives. Peter says, if you want to be happy as a husband, you must use some common sense. That is the meaning of the phrase, "dwell with them according to knowledge." Consider the welfare of your wife before your own. Live to please your wife and not yourself. Consider her desires before your own. And then Peter adds: "giving honour unto the wife." The word "honour" may be translated "dignity." The husband is to make his wife feel dignified, proud of her husband. The word "honour" also may be translated "importance." Do you ever tell your wife how really important she is, or do you make her feel embarrassed and inferior? It's those little things you remember which really count. Do you remember anniversaries? These are important to a woman. Do you ever tell her she is beautiful? It will not make her vain, don't worry. How long since you've told her, "I love you more than ever"? Do you ever comment on her new hat? Does she ever hear a word of appreciation for some special dish? Little things, you say? Oh, no, these are big things — they give dignity to love. They make a woman feel she is needed, important — yea, indispensable. Our great example is Jesus. Paul says in Ephesians 5:25, "Husbands, love your wives, even as Christ also loved the church, and gave himself for it." He *gave Himself!* What are you *giving* to the one *you* love? She wants more than clothes, a home, and gadgets. It is love which gives dignity to a faithful wife and mother. For true lovers — the honeymoon never ends.

—M.R.D.

Honour the wife — in love with her dwell;
'Tis God's command — 'Twill pay you well!

"Woman was taken from man's side—next to his heart—to be loved!"
—J. M. GRAY

ALL THINGS NEW

SUGGESTED SCRIPTURE READING: II Corinthians 6:14-18

Therefore if any man be in Christ, he is a new creature. II Corinthians 5:17

Tremendous changes occur when one is born from above and becomes a new creature in Christ. When the great evangelist, Dwight L. Moody, went to be with the Lord, they found, among other things, a seven-point outline upon the flyleaf of his Bible enumerating the changes which occur when one steps from the darkness of sin into the sunlight of the grace of God. The outline ran as follows:

1. *Justification* — a change of *standing* — before God.
2. *Regeneration* — a change of *nature* — from God.
3. *Repentance* — a change of *mind* — about God.
4. *Conversion* — a change of *life* — for God.
5. *Adoption* — a change of *family* — in God.
6. *Sanctification* — a change of *service* — unto God.
7. *Glorification* — a change of *place* — with God.

Many years ago in the *London Sunday School Times,* Doctor Lawes of New Guinea described how he had seen and heard former cannibals praising God at a prayer meeting. "I heard them pray," he said, "men with tattoos on their chests to indicate that they were murderers and that their spears had tasted blood. I have heard them pouring out their hearts in prayer to God, as sweet as children holding converse with their father, and I knew they had been taught by the Spirit of God." The outward marks of their crimes still remained; but as once these were their pride and glory, now they despised them and did all they could to remove them. Though they could never outwardly take away the scars and tattoos that stood for their murders, inwardly they had become new creatures, known and understood of God. Therefore, the Lord, who looked upon these savages, saw not their marks of shame but rather the redeemed souls of newborn sons and adopted children.

Have you experienced this great change? —H.G.B.

'Twas a great change for me, a great change for me!
Oh, now I am happy! From sin I've been set free!
From out of the darkness I've stepped into light,
And oh, 'twas a great change for me! —J. Oatman

"No life is hopeless unless Christ is ruled out."

THE CHRISTIAN FAMILY

SUGGESTED SCRIPTURE READING: Genesis 1:26-31

And God blessed them, and God said unto them, Be fruitful and multiply, and replenish the earth, and subdue it: and have dominion over the fish of the sea, and over the fowl of the air, and over every living thing that moveth upon the earth. Genesis 1:28

The nearest thing to heaven on this earth is the Christian family and the home where husband and wife, parents and children, live in love and peace together for the Lord and for each other. The nearest thing to hell on earth is an ungodly home, broken by sin and iniquity, where parents quarrel, bicker and separate, and children are abandoned to the devil and all the forces of wickedness.

In this wisdom of God the family is the smallest complete unit of society upon the earth. As goes the family, so goes the nation and civilization and the world. No nation has ever risen higher morally, mentally, or spiritually than the average of the families of which that nation was constituted. All efforts, therefore, at improving moral and spiritual standards in the world, combatting crime, infidelity and violence, must begin with the home and with the family. Attacking these problems anywhere else, anywhere farther down the line, can only be palliative and symptomatic and temporary, only restraining, but never resulting in a cure. Until the homes of America, and that means first of all the parents of America, return to the faith of their fathers and back to the Lord Jesus Christ, this nation must continue to deteriorate morally and spiritually! —M.R.D.

O blessed the house, whate'er befall,
Where Jesus Christ is all in all!
Yea, if He were not dwelling there,
How dark and poor and void it were!
O blessed that house where faith ye find
And all within have set their mind
To trust their God and serve Him still,
And do in all His holy will! —Anon.

"The desire to please God is a continual prayer!"—WESLEY

"LILY WORK"

SUGGESTED SCRIPTURE READING: I Kings 7:13-22

And upon the top of the pillars was lily work. I Kings 7:22

The pillars of Solomon's temple have been considered by many commentators as "emblematic of the Church of God" (see I Tim. 3:15b). Individual Christians are also designated as "pillars" in Galatians 2:9 and Revelation 3:12. It would seem that these cunningly carved works of art, the beautiful ornamental columns that stood at the entrance of Solomon's temple, spoke symbolically of the adorning graces of the Holy Spirit in the lives of the saved. The fruitful beauty of holiness, and the reflected glory of the risen Saviour are typified in the carved chains of pomegranates and the delicate "lily work."

Yet, this most gorgeous and precious ornamentation was reserved for the *top* of the pillar. Again there is a symbolic significance. It is more important that God see the beauty of our consecration and the delicate symmetry of our Christian grace than that men should be able to behold it and praise us for it. Our true beauty is in the "heavenlies" for there God sees us in Christ and reckons us as already seated at His right hand (Eph. 2:6).

Be more concerned with the hidden graces of holiness, and the little acts of devotion that only God may see, than with the outward show of religion that men may extol.

It is said that the handwriting of Napoleon caused him to lose the battle of Waterloo. One of his generals could not read with exactness the message that he sent to him. Was it "Bataille Engagee" (battle is on), or "Bataille Gagnee" (battle is won)? The man who headed Napoleon's rear guard chose the latter significance. Therefore, not believing it necessary to press forward with haste, he arrived too late. All this from the curl of a letter — a pen stroke that was not legible. In other words, the defeat of the Emperor was due to his scrawling handwriting. So, too, it is the tiny, intricate things of the Christian life of which we have to be careful. It is the "little foxes" that often spoil our spiritual vineyard. If you are a "pillar" in the Church watch your "lily work." —H.G.B.

Thus my daily walk shall be in Thy sweet will,
Jesus only, only Thee, my heart shall fill.—J. Hillyer

"The secret of the Lord is imparted to those whose secret life is a thing of beauty and consecration."

DEALING WITH CHILDREN

<small>SUGGESTED SCRIPTURE READING: Luke 18:15-17</small>

But Jesus said, Suffer little children, and forbid them not, to come unto me. Matthew 19:14

Someone has written: "By the time a child is ten he is either a Christian or a pagan. If he is a pagan he has been greatly sinned against. His parents, his neighbors, his teachers and his playmates have done him a great harm." A mother's sheltering arm and a father's watchful eye should ever be exercised to see to it that their child is properly educated in the things of the Lord both at home and in the church.

Being a good parent is one of the most difficult tasks in the world. To temper discipline with love and affection, to encourage spiritual activity without unnaturally forcing it, to lead a child and still develop his individual initiative, these are the things that try a parent's soul. Such exacting duties should make us search the Word for instruction and seek the face of God for guidance. A child is highly impressionable. His early training either develops, or permanently warps, his personality.

When a child spontaneously expresses a desire to be saved, he should never be considered too young. Some of the best Christians I know were converted at a very early age. Some, who have had bitter experiences in sin before they came to Christ, could have been spared years of defeat and heartache if they had been properly dealt with when they first asked for spiritual guidance. One said she came forward at the age of seven when an invitation was given, but the evangelist seemed interested only in the adults and neglected to counsel with her in regard to her soul. It was many years and countless tears later before this lost sheep was rescued.

Are the lambs in your home safe in the Saviour's fold? By word and example are you encouraging them to come to Jesus? Remember, He said, "Forbid them not." —H.G.B.

> I took a piece of living clay
> And gently formed it day by day;
> I came again when years were gone—
> It was a man I looked upon;
> He still that early impress wore,
> And I could change him nevermore.—Anon.

"In all things, parents are their children's most eloquent teachers, whether they wish to be or not."

SOMEBODY CARES

SUGGESTED SCRIPTURE READING: I Peter 5:6-11

Casting all your care upon him; for he careth for you.
I Peter 5:7

God has a tender reason
For everything we face,
Just as each change of season
Makes earth a sweeter place;
For every night — a morning,
For every thorn — a flower,
His rainbow bright adorning
The silver of the shower;
Unfailing comes tomorrow
To work His will and tell—
God cares through joy and sorrow
God lives, and all is well!

These tender words of comfort from the pen of an unknown poet are pasted in my old scrapbook because I feel they summarize well the Christian's viewpoint on suffering. Our precious Saviour is tremendously interested in all our sorrows and trials, and He delights to have us pour out our hearts to Him when the burdens press us sore and the cares distress. All our anxieties are to be brought to His attention in prayer, trusting Him to fully bear the load and make a way of escape. Many of us cast our troubles and cares upon Him, but then, even before we arise from our knees, we take them back upon our own shoulders and seek to choose our own path. This grieves His loving heart. Even as the hymnwriter has admonished, we are to take our burden to the Lord, and *"leave it there!"*

"He knows, He loves, *He cares,*
Nothing this thought can dim;
Only the best He gives to those
Who leave the choice with Him!"

Trust Him with your trials, and He will bless you with His peace! *He careth for you!* —H.G.B.

There is no sorrow that He will not share,
No cross, no burden, for our hearts to bear
Without His help; no care of ours too small
To cast on Jesus; let us tell Him all—
Lay at His feet the story of our woes
And in His sympathy find sweet repose. —Anon.

"If God numbers our hairs, will He not also number our tears?"

TRY SOME DUCKS

SUGGESTED SCRIPTURE READING: II Corinthians 11:21-30

In the world ye shall have tribulation: but be of good cheer; I have overcome the world.   John 16:33

I read recently a story which at first made me smile, and then gave me some very serious thought. A certain man had rented a cottage with a large, light, airy cellar. A beautiful river ran by, and wonderful shade trees surrounded the house. For five years he enjoyed the many blessings of the place and gladly paid the modest rent which the landlord required. He bathed in the brook, fished in the pools, and rested in the shade. He was happy and contented. And then one day the river overflowed its banks, the cellar was flooded and a dozen chickens he kept in the cellar were all drowned. Suddenly he forgot all the past blessings and pleasures the place had afforded him, and all was gloom because of a dozen dead chickens. He bounced off to the landlord. "I have come," he said, "to notify you that I am moving out." Surprised, the landlord asked, "But why, I thought you enjoyed it so much these past five years?" "Yes," replied the tenant, "but it's different now, the river overflowed and all my hens are drowned." The answer of the landlord completely disarmed the grumbler. He said, "Next time, why don't you try ducks?"

Amusing? Yes, but what a lesson. Five years of enjoyment forgotten, because of a few drowned hens. Have you been recently disappointed? Have you been afflicted and suffered losses? Is everything blacked out by this passing misfortune? Have you forgotten all the past blessings? Jesus said, "In the world ye shall have tribulation: but *be of good cheer.*" God knows what He is doing. He has not made a mistake. This may be His way to make you appreciate your many past blessings. If your chickens drown, try some ducks. Cheer up, all things work together for good to the believer.   —M.R.D.

Know this — God's promises are sure,
Trust on through all the days,
And ever patiently endure
With love and prayer and praise.—Anon.

"The silver thread of God's love is woven into each of our trials." —G.W.

SACRILEGIOUS PRAYERS

SUGGESTED SCRIPTURE READING: James 3:1-10

Whose mouth is full of cursing and bitterness.
Romans 3:14

Recently an unsaved man entered the shop of a dear child of God and began to use a great deal of profanity. Almost every sentence he spoke contained an invitation to God to consign something to perdition. With him was his 13-year-old son who took it all in without fluttering an eyelid. Apparently he was accustomed to such language. The Christian proprietor was so disturbed that he suddenly turned upon the customer and said, "Pardon me, sir, but is this the first time you prayed this morning?" "Prayed," said the man with another oath, "what are you talking about?" "Well," said the Christian, "whether you realize it or not, you have been uttering one sacrilegious prayer after another asking God to destroy things. I want you to know, friend, that my God is not in the damning business. When He does have to execute His wrath as a last, extreme measure, it is people and *not things* which are involved. You have a young boy with you who is getting the wrong idea not only of God, but also of my Saviour's loving desire to save rather than to annihilate. I shall pray for you that you may soon come to appreciate His wonderful grace, for once you do, you will not be so interested in calling upon Him to exterminate everything in sight."

You could hear a pin drop in the garage. With blushing apologies the man left the premises. His sacrilegious prayers had been exposed for what they were: terrible blasphemy and a complete misunderstanding of God's love. Our Father in Heaven is "not willing that any should perish, but that all should come to repentance."

Christian, I know you pray, but does your tongue ever slip in anger so that you utter "sacrilegious prayers"? Sometimes "Out of the same mouth proceedeth blessing and cursing. *My brethren, these things ought not so to be*" (James 3:10). —H.G.B.

Be "slow to speak," look well within (Prov. 28:5),
To check there what may lead to sin (James 1:26),
And pray unceasingly for aid (Col. 4:2),
Lest unawares thou be betrayed (Luke 21:34).—Anon.

"Check up on your prayer life; remember, every wish is in reality a prayer!"—H.G.B.

A PREACHER IN A LILAC BUSH

SUGGESTED SCRIPTURE READING: I John 3:1-10

> *. . . in the shadow of thy wings will I make my refuge,*
> *until these calamities be overpast.* Psalm 57:1

My meditation this morning has been about wings. I mean the wings of a bird. I used to think wings were made only to fly, but today I found a much more important reason for wings on a bird. Outside my window is the nest of a robin. I have watched her build it for several days; then watched her cover those little eggs with her wings for about two weeks. Now they are hatched and the fledglings are half-grown. The nest is just outside my study window in a lilac bush. This morning a mighty storm struck suddenly with the force of a near tornado. I saw the branch where the robin sat on her nest, buffeted and tossed and whipped to and fro, till at times it almost touched the ground. And all through that storm and pelting rain that mother bird sat right there, while her brood was safe under her wings. I wondered how in the world she could stay on that nest in that storm. And then it occurred to me she was "glued" to her nest by "love for her brood." Yes, nothing else could have kept those sheltering wings over the "babes in the nest" but love.

Now the storm is over and the sun is shining again but I cannot forget that robin in the lilac bush for it sent me to my Bible to read about the sheltering wings of my Saviour. David said, "Thou hast been a shelter to me . . . I will trust in the covert of thy wings" (Ps. 61:3, 4). In Psalm 63:7 — "In the shadow of thy wings will I *rejoice.*" In Psalm 91:4 he cries, "Under His wings shalt thou *trust*," and now I am resting on the mercy-seat under the wings of the cherubim (Ex. 37:9). What peace! What security! What comfort! Thank You, Lord, for sending that little robin to my lilac bush. The nest will soon be empty but its lesson will remain.

—M.R.D.

> Under His wings, O what precious enjoyment!
> There will I hide till life's trials are o'er;
> Sheltered, protected, no evil can harm me;
> Resting in Jesus I'm safe evermore.—W. Cushing

"When God sends a man to the lions' den He goes there with him."

THE TEARS OF REPENTANCE

SUGGESTED SCRIPTURE READING: Psalm 51:14-17

The sacrifices of God are a broken spirit: a broken and a contrite heart, O God, thou wilt not despise. Psalm 51:17

At the gateway to the famous Parthenon in ancient Athens there stood an altar dedicated to "Tears." No sacrifices were consumed there; no offerings were made. It was simply a place where the penitent and grief-stricken bowed to weep out their sorrows. Although this may have given some psychological relief, it did not touch their basic need. Grief in itself is of little value if it is only the venting of penned-up emotions. It must have spiritual overtones and effect permanent changes in the life and personality if it is to please the Lord. Even worldly and unconverted men usually regret the *results* of their evil deeds because it adversely affects their own opportunities or social standing. On the other hand, those who are truly repentant are disturbed primarily because they have grieved the heart of God and violated His gracious commands. What all of us need today is more such *godly sorrow* over sin. True repentance and saving faith are closely bound together. Repentance without faith is useless. Faith without repentance is impossible. Therefore, *godly sorrow and saving faith are inseparable twins.* True repentance is always accompanied by a sincere attempt to rectify past mistakes, as far as this is humanly possible. The need for such repentance is strongly emphasized in the Scripture. Consult such passages as: II Peter 3:9; II Corinthians 7:9, 10; Romans 2:4; Acts 26:20; Luke 12:3 and Mark 2:17.

Dearer to God than all the pious prayers and superficial penance of the religious Pharisees is the heart cry of one returning prodigal (Luke 15:7). The Father in heaven runs to meet such a penitent while he is yet "a great way off."

A little girl who was asked to define godly sorrow said: "Well, Judas only did penance so he went and hanged himself; but Peter truly repented, and went and wept bitterly." —H.G.B.

Lord, incline me to repent;
Let me now my fall lament,
Deeply my revolt deplore,
Weep, believe, and sin no more!—C. Wesley

"He that lacks time to mourn, lacks time to mend."

A USE FOR EVERYTHING

SUGGESTED SCRIPTURE READING: Romans 8:22-28

God himself that formed the earth . . . created it not in vain.
                                              Isaiah 45:18

The text might better be translated, "He created it not 'useless.'" In the original creation everything God made was for a purpose and for a definite use. It was *"not in vain."* Although sin has marred this creation, it is still true that everything serves a purpose in the plan of God. There was a time when gasoline and kerosene were extracted from petroleum, and the rest was considered waste. Today every part of the crude oil is used to make dyes, medicines, plastics, etc. Things which a few years ago were considered worthless, have proven to be of inestimable value to mankind.

We often think of "deserts" as wasteland, but they have a part in the scheme of things. Predatory animals play their part in maintaining the balance of nature. Nothing is without a purpose and use. What earthly good is the desert of Sahara? What an apparent waste of land with its thousands of miles of arid soil. But wait, we know now that southern Europe across the Mediterranean owes its fruitfulness and productive climate to the winds which are warmed over the Sahara and wafted across the fields of Italy so that even the "burning desert" becomes the mother of paradise.

Are there periods when you are laid aside and are apparently rendered useless? Be assured they have a special value in beautifying character, deepening sympathy, learning patience, giving appreciation of blessings, and in affording opportunities to testify to others of our trust in Romans 8:28. And so, out of our affliction, flows a warmth that only increases the ultimate fruit. He sends nothing upon us *"in vain."*   —M.R.D.

> Our knowledge deeper grows with Him alone;
> In secret oft His deeper love is shown:
> We learn in many an hour of dark distress,
> Some rare, sweet lesson of His tenderness.—Anon.

"The Lord gets his best soldiers out of the highlands of affliction."
                                              —SPURGEON

THE JOY OF A FATHER

SUGGESTED SCRIPTURE READING: Philippians 2:17-24

I have no greater joy than to hear that my children walk in truth.   III John 4

Years ago I frequently made the statement that the greatest joy was to lead some soul to Christ. But as the years passed I was compelled to change my mind. I observed, to my sorrow and great disappointment, that many whom I thought I had led to Christ were never really saved. Under the emotional spell of the moment, or out of fear of sin's consequences, they had made a profession, but never received Christ as their possession. It was seed on stony ground and lasted only for a little season. As a result of too many such experiences, my joy at seeing sinners "profess" Christ was somewhat moderated by the recurring question as to the reality of the experience. It also cured me of "counting converts." Often those whom we counted did not "add up" in the final total, while others we had not counted showed up in the final accounting. Only God is able to count the souls who are really saved.

As the years passed, I began to discover that there is a greater joy than leading a soul to Christ. It is the joy of coming back 5, 10, 25 and 30 years later and finding them "going on" for Christ. And then I found out this was Scriptural also when I read our text, "I have no greater joy than to hear that my children walk in the truth." Again and again we receive letters from afar saying, "Many years ago I found Christ under your ministry and His love grows sweeter every day." This is the supreme joy of a spiritual father's heart.

This is the day on which we are expected to honor "father." No greater expression of appreciation can be given to a Christian father than to hear that his children are walking in the truth. As he receives your "Father's Day" card which you sent him, does it make him sad as he realizes you are not "walking worthy" of Christ? Or does his heart swell with joy to know you are living for Him? Some of you reading this could make father's heart glad by the good news that you have accepted father's God. What better present could you give him? —M.R.D.

O blessed assurance, peace divine,
My father's God today is mine.—Anon.

"A fool despiseth his father's instruction; but he that regardeth reproof is prudent" (Proverbs 15:5).

HE KNOWS OUR NEED

SUGGESTED SCRIPTURE READING: Psalm 84

No good thing will he withhold from them that walk uprightly.   Psalm 84:11

What a remarkable promise with which to begin a new day. Our God promises that this day He will provide us with whatsoever is "good" for us. Whatever God allows to come into our lives is for a reason and will "fit" the purpose for which He sends it.

An interesting anecdote which will illustrate the need of simple faith in trusting God in everything is told of Billy Bray the Cornish miner.

One day Billy Bray was greeted on the street by one of his Quaker friends with the words, "Good morning, brother Bray. I have wanted to see thee for a long time, for I have heard about thee and all the good things thou hast done for my Master. I have asked the Lord whether there was something I could do for thee, and the Spirit told me that a very fine suit of clothes which I have in my home must be given thee. So I want thee to come and get the clothes (provided they will fit thee)." The reply of Billy Bray will illustrate our point. He said, "I certainly thank you so much. I will be after the clothes, and as far as the fit is concerned, don't let that worry you. For if the Spirit of God told you to give them to me, He will see to it that they fit."

But let us add a note of warning: be sure that the testings and trials of the way are the messengers of God, and not the result of our own disobedience and carelessness (read I Pet. 4: 15, 16). "But and if ye suffer for righteousness' sake, happy are ye: and be not afraid of their terror, neither be troubled" (I Pet. 3:14).   —M.R.D.

Upon God's care I lay me down,
As a child upon its mother's breast;
No silken couch, nor softest bed
Could ever give me such deep rest.—Author Unknown

"He who abandons himself TO God will never be abandoned BY God."

FOLLOWING THE LORD

SUGGESTED SCRIPTURE READING: Luke 9:22-25

. . . turn not aside from following the LORD!
I Samuel 12:20

Many Christians seem to rebel against the leading of the Nail-scarred Hand when their pathway dips into the valley of trouble or is beset with the thorns of pain.

When I was at a very tender age the Lord graciously claimed me as His own. I loved to hear about Jesus and sing the hymns of salvation and assurance. At about the age of five I contracted tuberculosis which lodged in my hip-joint. Soon the disease confined me to bed. At night I seldom slept more than ten minutes at a time, for I would be awakened by spasms of excruciating pain that caused me to scream in agony. In the day-time, however, I felt somewhat better and enjoyed singing the hymns which my Christian parents had taught me, including "If Jesus Goes with Me." My condition continued to deteriorate and finally the bones of my pelvis were so eaten away by the disease that they scarcely threw a shadow upon the X-ray. I was ordered to the hospital. Not knowing that singing was forbidden, and being a bit lonely, I warbled in my high, boy-soprano voice my favorite hymn concerning God's leading. A lady from another ward soon entered my room and wept silently as I joyously exulted, " 'Tis heaven to me, where'er I may be, if He is there!" Being only seven, I did not realize the import of her tears. Years afterward I learned that she had come to the hospital a rebellious Christian. She had had much difficulty, and when she finally was ordered in for surgery, she murmured against the Lord and wondered why she had to go to "that place where there would be no Christian fellowship." She was scarcely in her room when she heard a high-pitched voice singing a sweet rebuke, "If Jesus goes with me I'll go *anywhere!*" She thought she would find a very mature, Christian lady; but when she discovered only a seven-year-old boy who had never been away from home singing happily of God's good leading, she was completely broken up. She renewed her dedication and became a real testimony for Christ in her illness.

Oh, Christian, cast not away your confidence; "turn not aside from following the Lord!" —H.G.B.

Friend, you are rich, when by the cross you bear
You earn the right your crown to wear.—Anon.

"No gall, no glory; no cross, no crown!"

ONIONS

Suggested Scripture Reading: Colossians 3:5-9

We remember . . . the onions.   Numbers 11:5

Onions are hypocrites. They are renegades, deserters and traitors. One would never suspect from the appearance and odor of the onion that it belongs to the "Lily" family. Yet botanists tell us onions are members of that fragrant and delightful order of flowers, the "lilies." What has happened to the lily to change it to an onion? Somewhere along the line a branch of the "lily" family went astray and belied all that which is suggested by the name of its family. An onion is a lily with a depraved nature. It is a blot upon the fair family name of "Lilacea," a prodigal son, a disgrace to its lovely brothers and sisters.

No wonder then that onions are mentioned only *once* in the Bible, and then in an evil connection. Onions belong to Egypt, and Egypt is a type of the world. The children of Israel were out of Egypt but had carried their appetite for onions with them, and forgetting all about the God-given manna, they said, "We remember . . . the onions." They did not say, "We remember the Passover Lamb, our deliverance from death, our passage through the sea," but — "We remember the onions." What a picture of the worldly believer. Onions belong to the "old man" of Egypt and not the "new man" of Canaan. How much do you feed on the manna of the Word of God, as compared to the onions of pleasure, worldly habits, entertainment, love of money, success and popularity? Last night you spent over an hour watching TV and all day yesterday you did not spend 10 minutes with your Bible. No wonder you have spiritual indigestion and "halitosis." You can't live on onions. Imagine the children of Israel "mixing" onions with their manna. Your appetite for "manna" is spoiled by onions. There are many kinds of "onions" — but only one manna. The Bible enumerates some of these "onions" in Colossians 3:5-9. How much better to "feed among the lilies" (S. of Sol. 6:3).   —M.R.D.

The dearest idol I have known, whate'er that idol be,
Help me to tear it from Thy throne, and worship only Thee.
                                        —W. Cowper

"Christians who mix worldliness into their spiritual diet ruin their testimony."

AFTER YOUR APPOINTMENT—WHAT?

SUGGESTED SCRIPTURE READING: Isaiah 14:9-11; Luke 23:42-46

It is appointed unto men once to die, but after this the judgment. Hebrews 9:27

There is one appointment which every man must keep — an appointment with God at the end of the road. Death does not end all. There is an immediate judgment which follows that will determine unalterably where the soul will exist for eternity. From the Scripture readings suggested above, it is obvious that both the lost and the saved are conscious in another realm immediately after physical life here is ended.

The story is told of a preacher of the Gospel who was one day speaking to an ungodly crowd about heaven. Afterward a scoffer exclaimed, "I don't believe a word you've said. When we die, we die like dogs, and are buried, and that is the end of us." "Was that what your mother believed?" the evangelist inquired. "No, my old mother loved her Bible and cried over it many nights because I would not accept it." The preacher then asked him, "Is your mother still alive?" "No," said the man; "she has been dead for some time now." "Oh," replied the preacher imitating the sarcastic tone of the unbeliever, "she died just like an old dog then and was buried! Too bad, . . . *that was the end of her!*" "What?" said the man livid with rage, "You say my mother died like an old dog!" "No," was the answer. "*You* say so. I say she died like a saint and is with God in heaven. You see, sir, you do not really believe what you have been saying." The doubter was silenced.

Death does not end all. The termination of physical life and the coming judgment are rightfully a constant source of fear to the unbelieving, but they should not trouble the child of God, for "There is therefore now no condemnation to them which are in Christ Jesus" (Rom. 8:1a).

After *you* keep your unavoidable appointment with God, where will *you* live for eternity? —H.G.B.

Where will you spend eternity?
This question comes to you and me!
Tell me, what shall your answer be?
Where will you spend eternity?—E. A. Hoffman

"When men believe that they die like beasts, they soon come to live the same way."

THE SIN OF JUDGING OTHERS

SUGGESTED SCRIPTURE READING: I Corinthians 8

Let us not therefore judge one another any more.
Romans 14:13

Every man shall give account of himself before God. We will not have to answer for others, but ourselves. Probably one of the greatest sins among believers is the sin of "judging others" when we do not know all the circumstances or temptations of the brother whom we are condemning. Only God is able to judge righteously for He alone knows all the circumstances of our lives. He knows our weaknesses, our temptations and struggles. He considers our disposition, the place we work, the environment we live in, the people we must live with, and all the other circumstances we must face. It is easier for some people to have victory than for others. So let us not judge others when we don't know the peculiar struggle or handicaps which they face.

The story is told of an English professor who was quizzing his class in which one student rose with his book in the left hand instead of his right hand, as they were required. Angrily, the professor thundered at him, "Take your book in your right hand, and be seated!" The student held up his right arm, and it was off at the wrist. The great man hesitated a moment, then went to the student and, with tears streaming from his eyes, he said, "I never knew about it. Will you forgive me?" It ended in the conversion of the young man.

You will never win a man by hasty judgment. What many need is sympathy, encouragement and understanding. Let God be the judge. —M.R.D.

> I used to censure everyone,
> I was a Pharisee;
> Until, quite unexpectedly,
> I got a glimpse of me!—Anon.

"Your neighbors' windows look a great deal better when you first wash your own."

TODAY!

SUGGESTED SCRIPTURE READING: Matthew 6:25-34

As thy days, so shall thy strength be.

Deuteronomy 33:25

This wonderful and comforting assurance given to the saints in the Old Testament was reaffirmed and personalized by the Lord Jesus when He promised us His constant help and abiding presence to strengthen us in each emergency which arises (Matt. 28:20).

A. C. Dixon tells us that when Raphael died at the age of 37, they carried his marvelous painting, "The Transfiguration," only half finished, in the funeral procession as a symbol of the incompleteness of life and the brevity of time. Yes, it is important for us to recognize that "time is a pearl of great price, and the wise merchant man treasures it with great care, turning each present moment to the best advantage."

God, our Heavenly Father, lives in the *eternal present*, and He wants His children to do the same! We are to "forget those things that are behind" (both of triumph and defeat); "Take no thought for the morrow" (that is: don't worry); and *just make this day count for Him!* If we could enumerate the hours which we spend in vain regrets over the past, and tabulate the time and energy we consume in idle worry over the future, we would realize why the Lord warns us not to use up the precious hours of the present in such fruitless endeavor.

"As thy days thy strength shall be
This shall be enough for thee;
He who knows thy frame will spare
Burdens more than thou canst bear!"

To have pleasant memories and much reward in heaven, weave a tapestry of achievement from the golden hours of the present!   —H.G.B.

I have nothing to do with tomorrow,
    The Saviour will make that His care;
Should He fill it with trouble and sorrow,
    He'll help me to suffer and bear. —Anon.

"Do today's duty; that is best; leave unto the Lord the rest."
—LONGFELLOW

SERVING TWO MASTERS

Suggested Scripture Reading: Luke 16:10-13

No man can serve two masters.   Matthew 6:24

The Christian lives for eternity; the unregenerate man lives only for time. But we are in the world, although not of the world. Because we are in the world, we must of necessity mingle with and be in contact with the men of the world. In our business life in the factory, the office, and even in our social life we cannot avoid contact with the world. There may be little to distinguish the believer from the unbeliever as he goes about his duties of his job or profession. But when he leaves his job, and his responsibilities to his worldly employers or associates are done at the end of the day, then the difference between them becomes more apparent, for the believer will go one way and the unconverted another way. The true Christian will then seek the fellowship of other believers, will turn to the study of the Word and prayer and find time to witness and work for the Lord, while the other seeks his pleasure in the world, the tavern, the theater or the idle pleasures of life. When the tensions of life are released, which way do you turn — toward God or the world?

When you see a dog following two men you cannot tell to whom it belongs, but let them come to the parting of the road and we soon find out. He will follow his master. So, too, the believer may engage in the same work and occupation as the worldly person, but when it comes time to make a decision, to choose which way he shall go, then the difference becomes apparent.

How do you spend your time when "off duty"? After work, where do you go; what do you do? Who then is your master? "Ye cannot serve God and mammon!"   —M.R.D.

> Farewell, vain world, my soul can bid adieu;
> The Saviour taught me to abandon you.
> Your charms may gratify a sensual mind,
> But cannot please a soul for God designed.—A. Brainerd

"It's more important for a Christian to be a 'good separator' than a 'good mixer.'"

THE HEAVENLY GUIDE

SUGGESTED SCRIPTURE READING: Romans 8:5-14

For as many as are led by the Spirit of God, they are the sons of God. Romans 8:14

When the Lord Jesus Christ saves a person, He does not thenceforth leave him to shift for himself; rather He gives him the indwelling Holy Spirit as a Comforter and Guide. The sense of direction and leading the Spirit of Truth affords is the birthright of those who are adopted into the family of God (Rom. 8:15). Before we were quickened to spiritual life, we walked "according to the course of this world" lured on by the unholy "spirit that now worketh in the children of disobedience" (Eph. 2:1, 2). But now old affections and desires are superseded by new and holy longing. We now pursue the things of God because we are led on by the Holy Spirit who witnesses to our spirit through the instrumentality of the Word. As we seek His guidance we can feel the tug of heaven upon our soul. The real danger for a Christian is not found in the fact that guidance is not readily available, but rather that sin in the life, and carnal desires, weaken the call of the Spirit and dull the ear of faith. By prayer and Bible study keep yourself sensitive and "in tune" with the call of heaven.

It is said that in the deserts of Arabia there is a certain guide who never loses his way. He carries with him a homing-pigeon with a very fine cord attached to one leg. When in any doubt as to which path to take, the guide throws the bird into the air. The pigeon quickly strains at the cord to fly in the direction of home and in this manner leads his master unerringly. They call that guide the "dove-man." So too, the Holy Spirit, the heavenly Dove, is willing and able to lead us if we will only allow Him to do so and in humble self-denial and submission follow his unerring guidance.   —H.G.B.

Holy Spirit, faithful Guide,
Ever near the Christian's side;
Gently lead us by the hand,
Pilgrims in a desert land.—M. M. Wells

"The secret of an unsatisfied life lies in an unsurrendered will."

PERSONAL EXPERIENCE

SUGGESTED SCRIPTURE READING: Acts 9:1-6

For I know whom I have believed. II Timothy 1:12

Paul says, 'I know *whom* I have believed." He does not say, I know *in* whom I have believed, but I know *Him.* There is a great difference between knowing *about* Christ and *knowing* Him. Paul had heard about Jesus, but one day he met Jesus and it revolutionized his life. Dr. E. Schuyler English tells of an experience which wonderfully illustrates this truth.

While traveling on a train, his conversation with a gentleman seated next to him turned to Florida. Much to his surprise he found his companion expressing his distaste for the "sunshine" state.

When the man had finished speaking, Dr. English said: "Well, however you may feel about Florida, you must admit that its climate is remarkable and the tropical foliage beautiful. When you are in the North in the winter, as you are this year, don't you miss the sunshine, the balmy weather, and the wonderful climate?"

Hesitating just a moment, the gentleman replied: "Well, to tell you the truth, I've never been to Florida. But I have some friends who have gone there for years." The man had not been speaking from experience.

The wonderful, matchless blessings of the Christian life do not follow a merely intellectual knowledge of Christianity, but they accompany a heart-experience with the Lord Jesus Christ. Only such can say with feeling: "I count all things but loss for the excellency of the knowledge of Christ Jesus my Lord" (Phil. 3:8).   —M.R.D.

Loved with everlasting love,
Led by grace that love to know;
Spirit, breathing from above,
Thou hast taught me it is so.—W. Robinson

"In the spiritual things, unless head knowledge becomes heart knowledge, it were better one had no knowledge at all."

THE PRUNING KNIFE

SUGGESTED SCRIPTURE READING: I Thessalonians 1:1-7

Every branch that beareth fruit, he purgeth it, that it may bring forth more fruit. John 15:2

Sorrow and trouble are God's pruning knife with which He strips away that which is sapping our spiritual energy and retarding our fruitfulness. The dead wood of outward profession and carnality must be trimmed away. Our relationship to the life-giving Vine must thus be brought into full focus. Perhaps we were leaning too heavily on someone or something in our life other than the Everlasting Arms. Perhaps we were idolizing a person other than our blessed heavenly Friend. Or perchance our being "careful and troubled about many things" had made us neglect those eternal pursuits which were more needful. Whatever the cause, if we are now suffering under the sharp knife of trial it may well be due to the fact that the Heavenly Gardener has seen the need for painful, yet profitable pruning. He may cut away what we consider to be the most beautiful and luxuriant aspects of our existence, because He realizes that these are the very things that are preventing us from coming into a period of true, spiritual productivity. God is faithful and all-wise. He weighs our eternal good against our present earthly joys; and invariably His love chooses for us what we might consider temporal loss, but which He knows to be heavenly gain! We, short-sightedly, revel in the brilliant blossoms of earthly ease and contentment, and the full-leafed shade of much profession; but God is interested in "more fruit."

A skilled physician, who was about to perform a delicate operation on a patient's ear, said reassuringly, "I may *hurt* you, but I will not *injure* you." The Great Physician speaks to us that same message when He uses the knife to cut away that which is retarding our productivity. Pray that His pruning may cause you to flourish luxuriantly! —H.G.B.

"Afraid of troubles?"—Needed for true growth,
To stir from sleep, and to arouse from sloth;
The need for troubles is a humbling thought,
But when God chooses, would we alter aught?—Anon.

"Sanctified afflictions are spiritual promotions."

WHERE CHRISTIAN TESTIMONY SHOULD BEGIN

SUGGESTED SCRIPTURE READING: II Corinthians 9:10-15

They made me the keeper of the vineyards, but mine own vineyard have I not kept. Song of Solomon 1:6

Too often we have seen Christians in their zeal running all over the land holding meetings, while their children were left at home to shift for themselves. I have known wives, who should be better mothers, leaving their children in order to accompany their husbands on their evangelistic tours, trying to save other people's children, while their own were going lost. Well might these folks heed the words of Solomon in Canticles 1:6.

I have a Negro preacher friend, a dear brother, who once gave the answer to this question in a striking way. A group of students at a Bible and Missionary Institute came to him, and said: "Brother So-and-So, you will be greatly pleased to know that we are planning to go as missionaries to Africa in a few months when we complete our training here, and bring the Gospel to your people there." They imagined, of course, that he would be elated, and they were sadly taken aback when he asked them: "How many of my Negro people have you tried to win for Christ here at home? You have gone to school three years and lived a stone's throw from one of the densest Negro populations in the city. What an opportunity to reach my people right here at home! How many of these have you won for Christ?" It was a good question, and I cannot blame him for his blunt rejoinder, for I know what a burden this brother has for his colored brethren. Oh, I know there is more glamor, more romance, in the work far away, but the commission is still: "Beginning at Jerusalem"!   —M.R.D.

Give me a faithful heart, likeness to Thee,
That each departing day hencefore may see
Some work of love begun, Some deed of kindness done,
Some wand'rer sought and won, Something for Thee.
                                        —S. D. Phelps

"Do what you can, where you are, with what you have!"—D. L. MOODY

SINGING OR WORRYING

SUGGESTED SCRIPTURE READING: Psalm 81

I will sing of the mercies of the LORD for ever
Psalm 89:1

When you worry you are not trusting. When you worry you are not singing. The happy Christian is the trusting one. It is now an established fact that a large percentage of the ills for which people seek a doctor are not organic but psychic. A famous stomach specialist says that 80 per cent of stomach disorders are not organic but functional. The trouble is in the head instead of the stomach. The symptoms of indigestion are due to wrong mental and spiritual attitudes. These "ulcer patients" are victims of wrong thinking. A large percentage of our ills are caused by worry and fear and doubt. Faith is often more important than diet in treating stomach ulcers.

A wealthy but very unhappy man had in his employ a poor colored servant, who was always either humming or singing from morning till night. The wealthy employer was greatly annoyed by her happy disposition, for he spent the days taking pills, while he grumbled about business and worried about investments. At last he said, "Mandy, either stop that exasperating singing or else give me the secret of your happiness." "Secret! Secret! It's no secret, Master, I just don't have anything to worry about, so I just sing. I have no money to lose, so I needn't worry about that. The little bit of furniture in my shack belongs to the Lord, and if it burns up or is stolen, the Lord done burned up His own stuff. He never burned up 'nuthin' of mine. I don't worry about my health, for if I gets sick and dies, I'se going right to be with Jesus, so I never worry about that. I haven't got anything to worry about, but I'se got to do somethin' — so I just sings."

Why not relieve your "dyspepsia" with liberal doses of the promises of God, washed down with a song of praise and thanksgiving? Remember, "a man's life consisteth not in the abundance of things which he possesseth" (Luke 12:15b).   — M.R.D.

> Sing and smile and pray, that's the only way;
> If you sing and smile and pray,
> You'll drive the clouds away! — V. Brock

"Happy is the man who can set his worries to the music of heaven, and thus sing them into oblivion."

"FIVE SMOOTH STONES"

SUGGESTED SCRIPTURE READING: I Samuel 17:40-54

> *And he ... chose him five smooth stones out of the brook*
> *... and his sling was in his hand: and he drew near to*
> *the Philistine.* I Samuel 17:40

In I Samuel 17 we have the thrilling story of David, the spiritual and modest shepherd-boy, slaying the arrogant, ten-foot giant of Gath named Goliath. The drama of the moving events so occupies our attention that often the spiritual lessons contained in the more minute details escape our gaze. Yet it is remarkable how much blessing and instruction has been condensed by the Holy Spirit into every passage of Scripture so that no matter where you set your mental spade, you can unearth some rare jewels of learning in the way of righteousness. Let us consider for a moment the import of the expression, "five smooth stones."

Why *"five"*? ... Was not David a man of faith? Did he doubt that God would direct him and give him perfect timing and aim as he hurled the stone out of his trusty sling at the enemy of the Lord? Certainly he needed only one. But wait, did you know that Goliath had four brothers? (II Samuel 21:15-22) Knowing that they might rally to Goliath's defense, even if the rest of the Philistines did not, David was ready for them. He had great faith; one stone for Goliath, and one for each of his brothers was all that he needed.

Why did he choose *"smooth* stones"? One can shoot much more accurately with the proper ammunition! He had faith, but he also used sanctified common sense. He didn't get fanatical and say, "Well, the Lord is going to do it anyway, so I'll just take anything that comes to hand." No, he recognized human responsibility as well as divine providence.

Keep your spiritual balance like David. He came thoroughly prepared with a sufficient number and the proper kind of stones, but he still relied upon God for the actual victory after he himself had done all that he could. Show your faith *BY YOUR WORKS!* (James 2:17) — H.G.B.

> Faith and works together shine,
> In Thy most holy will divine! — Anon.

"Works do not justify a man, but a justified man works."

"TELLING" AND "SHOWING"

I Corinthians 4:8-16

Be ye followers of me, even as I also am of Christ.
I Corinthians 11:1

What a daring and remarkable statement by the Apostle Paul, "Be ye followers of me"! Paul assures the Corinthians that if they will follow his example it will never lead them astray. In I Thessalonians 1:6 he declares, "And ye became followers of us and of the Lord." How I covet for myself the ability to say in all sincerity, "Follow me and it will lead you to Christ"! It implies living a life fully conformed to the will of God.

Some time ago a friend related the following experience. He was traveling through Detroit on his way to Canada and being unacquainted in the city he inquired at a filling station for the route to the tunnel leading to Windsor. The station attendant replied, "You want to know the best way to Windsor? Why that is as simple and easy as can be! Go to the third traffic light and turn left two blocks. Then take the angling road to the right for one block, turn left again until you come to a filling station; turn right there and you will be at the tunnel." My friend set out to follow the directions and after wandering around for 30 minutes had lost his way entirely. As he stopped at a traffic signal, a car drove along side. My friend opened the window and said, "Please sir, can you tell me the way to the tunnel?" The man replied, "Certainly, I'm going there myself. Just *FOLLOW ME!*" ... And sure enough, he followed the car and in a few minutes arrived at the tunnel. ... *Follow Me!* There is a great difference between "telling" a person the way, and "showing" him. You may be able to tell a man how to live the Christian life, but it is another thing to *SHOW* him the way! May we be able with Paul to say, "Be ye followers of me"! (I Cor. 4:16)   — M.R.D.

The life most blessed is not the one
That speaks, but never leads;
For Christ wants us to SHOW the way
And HELP the soul in need! — H.G.B.

"God never fore-announces His examinations; ... what you ARE flashes out when you do not know anyone is likely to be watching you critically!" —G. CAMPBELL MORGAN

IF GOD BE FOR US!

SUGGESTED SCRIPTURE READING: Psalm 33:8-22

Except the LORD *build the house, they labour in vain that build it.*   Psalm 127:1

It was the summer of 1776. Delegates had come from 13 colonies to make a momentous decision. Conditions were troubled in the New World and something had to be done. Apparently however, there was no good choice. Faces were gloomy in the old Statehouse in Philadelphia. One suggestion after another was offered and discarded. Finally, in the midst of their dissension and debate as to whether a new nation should be created or not. the men turned to Benjamin Franklin, the oldest and most renowned of the delegates, and requested his opinion. Franklin hesitated, then rose to his feet and delivered a brief message centered around Psalm 127 that became the spiritual foundation stone of America and resulted in the Declaration of Independence. Although few today have ever heard of these words, they were jewels of truth and wisdom. Said he, "I have lived a long time; and the longer I live, the more convincing proofs I see of this truth, that God governs the affairs of men. And if a sparrow cannot fall to the ground without His will, is it possible for an empire to rise without His notice? We have been assured in the sacred writing that except the Lord build the house, they labour in vain that build it. I firmly believe this, and I also believe that without His concurring aid, we shall succeed in this political building no better than the builders of Babel." He then suggested that they have a season of prayer. His advice was followed. Chaos soon resolved into unity and the United States of America was born July 4, 1776.

Our forefathers laid the foundation of this nation not only on Plymouth Rock, but also on the much surer rock of prayer and the Word of God! This is our heritage; but, alas, in many ways we have drifted far from our spiritual moorings. America must acknowledge anew her *dependence* upon God if she wishes to continue to proclaim her *independence* from slavery! For "where the Spirit of the Lord is, there is liberty" (II Cor. 3:17). — H.G.B.

> Thy love divine hath led us in the past,
> In this free land by Thee our lot is cast;
> Be Thou our Ruler, Guardian, Guide, and Stay;
> Thy Word our law, Thy paths our chosen way.
> — D. C. Roberts

"Faith in our God is indispensable to successful statesmanship."
— ABRAHAM LINCOLN

THE FUTILITY OF "ROWING HARD"!

SUGGESTED SCRIPTURE READING: Romans 10:9-13

Nevertheless the men rowed hard to bring it to land; but they could not: for the sea wrought, and was tempestuous against them. Jonah 1:13

The men in the ship which carried the disobedient prophet Jonah were in mortal danger. Because of Jonah on board the Lord had sent judgment upon the sailors and the ship was nigh to be broken. There was only one way to still the storm. Jonah must die and so he had told them to cast him overboard; but instead of throwing Jonah overboard, they only rowed the harder. "Nevertheless the men rowed hard to bring it to land but they could not." Their own efforts were futile — they could be saved only by the one who bore the guilt. This is a picture of salvation. Because of Jonah's sin, the sailors were under sentence of death. By one man's sin came death. Father Adam had brought judgment upon all. "By one man's offence, death reigned by one" (Rom. 5:17).

There is only one remedy — the sinner must die. The Lord Jesus (though without sin) took the sinner's place and like Jonah offered to die that the others might be saved. Jesus gave His life, but proud man refuses to accept this remedy and like the sailors in Jonah 1 they still imagine they can save themselves by their own efforts and labor. "Nevertheless the men rowed hard." This is the tragedy today. Men reject God's remedy and seek to save themselves by their works, religion, tact, morality and self-righteousness. Peace came only when they cast Jonah "forth into the sea and the sea ceased her raging." Only by the death and resurrection of Christ can peace be restored.

"But to him that worketh not, but believeth on him that justifieth the ungodly, his faith is counted for righteousness" (Rom. 4:5). — M.R.D.

The tempest's awful voice was heard —
O Christ, it broke on Thee!
Thou wast sore stricken of Thy God;
There's not one stroke for me!
All for my sake, my peace to make;
Now sleeps that sword for me! — A. R. Cousin

"Grace is most simply defined as: God's Riches At Christ's Expense!"

THE SAFETY OF THE LILIES

SUGGESTED SCRIPTURE READING: Song of Solomon 2:1-4

I am . . . the lily of the valleys.   Song of Solomon 2:1

The lilies referred to here are not to be confused with the snowy white ones to which we in America are accustomed. The lily of Palestine is a flower of brilliant hue which emits an exquisite fragrance. These "sweet flowers" are likened in the fifth chapter of the Song of Solomon to the scarlet mouth of the bridegroom whose "lips like *lilies*" are ever "dropping sweet smelling myrrh" (S. of Sol. 5:13). Jesus, in His discourse recorded in Matthew 6, compares their hue to that of the gorgeous apparel worn by Solomon who was known to be clothed in scarlet and deep purple. Those who have seen these blood-red blossoms say that they are more than two inches in diameter, in many places forming a beautiful and fragrant carpet that at certain seasons of the year almost completely covers the ground. Their very color seems to speak of redemptive blessings.

When these flowers are in bloom, hunting is brought to a standstill, for the delightful odor of the lilies is so strong that the scent of the game is lost and the dogs cannot trace the prey. The small game can wander and browse, therefore, without fear among the lilies. Dr. R. F. Horton, who has seen the same thing happen in southern France in connection with a similar flower that grows there, feels that the protection afforded by these extraordinary plants points up a spiritual lesson: "That is why we call Jesus 'the Lily of the Valley.' Because where Jesus is, we are safe; we can walk among those lilies and no 'hounds' can reach us or track us. How wonderful it is that Jesus Christ protects us, not by the methods of war, but by the Lily of Peace!"

The sweetness of Christ will cover the undesirable scent of your old nature if you will but dwell in His shadow. Satan will be helpless against you if you stay very close to Him who is "the Lily of the Valley!"   — H.G.B.

I have found a Friend in Jesus, He's everything to me,
He's the fairest of ten thousand to my soul;
The Lily of the Valley, in Him alone I see
All I need to cleanse and make me fully whole. — Anon.

"God is not only a present help in trouble, but a great help in keeping us out of trouble."

BROKEN THINGS

<small>Suggested Scripture Reading:</small> Lamentations 3:22-33

I am like a broken vessel.   Psalm 31:12

There are few entirely unbroken lives in this world that are useful to God. There are few men and women who can fulfill their own hopes and plans without interruption and disappointment all along the way. But man's disappointments are ever God's appointments, and the things which we believe are tragedies are only blessings in disguise, the very opportunities through which God wishes to exhibit His love and grace. There are some lives in which human plans are so completely thwarted that their story is most pathetic as we read it and look at it from the mere human standpoint. Yet we have but to follow through these lives to the end to see that the life that has been afflicted was better and more effective than if it had had its own plans and purposes carried out.

Are you, my friend, being broken today? Has the dearest in life been torn away? Have your dreams all faded? Have your hopes all failed? Then remember, that if you could see the purpose of these things in your life from the standpoint of God and the standpoint of eternity, if you could interpret these things in the aggregate of life's blessings, you would be able to dry those tears and praise the Lord for it all. We have His promise that "He will not withhold any good thing from them that walk uprightly," and if the best thing in our lives is not our way but His way, the way of testing and trial and sorrows, it will still be the best for us. Remember, "whom the Lord loveth He chasteneth" (Heb. 12:6).

— M.R.D.

Not now, but in the coming years,
It may be in the better land,
We'll read the meaning of our tears,
And then, sometime, we'll understand.
Then trust in God through all thy days,
Fear not, for He doth hold thy hand.
Though dark the way, still sing and praise,
Sometime, up there, we'll understand.
— M. N. Cornelius

"God grinds the axes He means to use!"

MIDNIGHT MELODIES

SUGGESTED SCRIPTURE READING: Psalm 42

. . . God my maker, who giveth songs in the night.
Job 35:10

Throughout most of his life the famous composer Beethoven lived in fear of deafness. He felt the sense of hearing was of the essence when it came to creating musical portraits of lasting value. You can imagine what feelings swept over him when he discovered that the thing he feared most was becoming a reality. When the first symptoms of infirmity in his hearing became apparent, he was so upset that his anxiety bordered on despair. Doctors and quacks alike were consulted, and every possible hearing aid was tried in the vain hope of assisting his weakening sense. The deafness, however, increased until at last he communicated with others only by means of writing. Finally he found the strength he needed to go on despite his handicap. To the amazement of all concerned, it was only after he was dead to all sense of outward sound that Beethoven wrote his grandest music. Shut out from the distractions of the world, new melodies and harmonies flooded in upon him as fast as his pen could write. His deafness had become a blessing.

So, too, children of God often find new joys in their night of sorrow and unexpected grace in their time of need. When God shuts us away from the things of this world, then it is that we may expect to hear more perfectly the matchless harmonies of heaven. When we tread the deserts of despair, then we seek our joy on a higher plane and find that the river of God is still "full of water." Though all is shrouded in the blackness of night, yet by His grace we shall find that we can still joy in the God of our salvation. We may wonder how we will face the future darkness; but we need not despair for He is a very present help in trouble. We do not have to compose our own symphony since it is our *Maker* who "giveth songs in the night." Wait upon Him for the music. You will find that there is never a song so sweet as His "midnight melodies."
— H.G.B.

When the clouds of affliction have gathered,
And hidden each star from my sight,
I know if I turn to my Father,
Sweetest songs He will give in the night.
— N. A. Montgomery

"Turn care into prayer and God will turn midnight into music."

THE SOLAR SPECTRUM

SUGGESTED SCRIPTURE READING: II Corinthians 4:3-6

. . . the light . . . hath shined in our hearts, to give the light of the knowledge of the glory of God in the face of Jesus Christ.   II Corinthians 4:6

Science has discovered that sunlight is a perfect blend of seven different visible colors. When a beam of sunlight is passed through a transparent prism, it is broken into seven colors called the solar spectrum. At one end of the spectrum is the violet, and at the opposite side is the red, and between these are arranged the other five colors. What a wonderful picture of the Word of God, and the living Word Incarnate. Seven colors, all blended together in the Word — both the written and the Incarnate.

1. Light is *REVEALING* in its ministry. Paul says that the light gives us the "knowledge" of the glory of God. In the new birth, God opens our eyes to see. "Except a man be born again, he cannot see" (John 3:3).

2. Light is *SWEET*. In Ecclesiastes 11:7 we read — "Truly the light is sweet (sweetening)." The sugar in the fruit is made by sunlight.

3. Light is *HEALING*. "Then shall thy light break forth as the morning, and thine health shall spring forth speedily" (Isa. 58:8).

4. Light *TRANSFIGURES*. As Jesus was transfigured on the mount, so dwelling in the light should transfigure us.

5. Light is *PURIFYING*. It is like a "refiner's fire and like fullers' soap" (Mal. 3:2).

6. Light brings *JOY*. How welcome the first ray of light after a long night of tossing upon a bed of suffering (John 5:35).

7. Light is *PROTECTING*. It is called "the armour" of light. It prevents us from stumbling and falling.   —M.D.R.

> How beautiful to walk in the steps of the Saviour,
> Stepping in the light, stepping in the light;
> How beautiful to walk in the steps of the Saviour,
> Led in paths of light.   — E. Hewitt

"We must be washed in the blood to walk in the light." — C. N. BARTLETT

GOD IS LOVE

SUGGESTED SCRIPTURE READING: I John 4:5-10

. . . for God is love.   I John 4:8

A simple peasant believer once had a weather vane on top of his barn on which were inscribed the words, "God is love." One day an infidel came to visit him and on seeing this weather vane changing position in the wind he turned to the peasant and with a ridiculing smile upon his face said, "You mean to say that your God is as changeable as the wind?" The peasant shook his head. "No," he said, "What I mean to say is that *no matter which way the wind blows*, GOD IS LOVE!" The infidel was put to shame.

This profound, three word statement implies much more than that God *displays love*. It means that love is the heart and essence of the Divine Being. The depths of His love we shall never be able to plumb even in eternity, but the Apostle John points out that our deepest, present understanding of it is realized as we view the Cross. As we see the Prince of Glory dying there for us unworthy worms of the dust, we catch a glimpse of the reflected beauty of the throbbing, loving heart of God. John goes on to point out that if God is love, His children should resemble Him. Consequently, if we find no warm glow in our bosom for our brother, if we do not thrill to the lovely Name of Jesus, we may well question the reality of our conversion experience. Someone has said, "Christ did not die that God might love man; He died *because* God loved man. The atonement is not the cause, but the effect of the love of God." God shows us His love in many ways. In the Cross He shows us His *heart*, in Providence He shows us His *hand*, and by and by in Glory He will show us His *face!* Well did Beecher say, "My God is a God who loves out of His nature, and not on conditions. It is not needful that I should be beautiful in order that He should love me. It is not needful that I should be patient in order that He should love me. He loves me because of Himself. We are saved by grace. Our salvation does not depend upon what we are, but upon what God is."   — H.G.B.

> God is love, His mercy brightens
> All the path in which we rove;
> Bliss He wakes, and woe He lightens;
> God is wisdom, God is love!   — J. Bowring

"To have no personal knowledge of love is to have no personal knowledge of God."

NO PLACE FOR THE DEVIL

SUGGESTED SCRIPTURE READING: Ephesians 6:11-18

Neither give place to the devil.   Ephesians 4:27

A teacher in a Bible school gave his students two subjects for their examination paper. They were to write a half hour on each of the two subjects, the Holy Spirit, and the devil. One student wrote steadily for an hour on the first subject, the Holy Spirit, and then wrote a note at the bottom of his manuscript, "I had no time for the devil." He had been so busy with the Holy Spirit that he had no place for the devil.

This is the only way in which we can resist and overcome Satan. The Holy Spirit has left us the Word of God. If we fill ourselves with God's Word and prayer and witness for Christ, then we shall not "give place to the devil." The word "place" is significant. The devil cannot occupy the same "place" as the Holy Spirit. When we are saved we receive the Holy Spirit, but it is possible for a true believer to give place to Satan. The only remedy against it is to be "filled with the Holy Spirit" (Eph. 5:18). To be "filled" means to be so full that there is place for nothing else. It means a full and complete surrender to the will of God. And you can only know the will of God as you know the WORD OF GOD. Before you launch out into the world today — have you stopped to read the Scripture suggested at the head of this article? Have you prayed? Are you filled? Then go forth to conquer with the shield of faith and quench all the fiery darts of the wicked.   —M.R.D.

> I am sinful, full of weakness,
> At Thy sacred feet I bow;
> Blest, divine, eternal Spirit,
> Fill with pow'r, and FILL ME NOW!
> — E. Stokes

"Satan trembles when he sees the weakest Christian on his knees."

MISHANDLING THE BIBLE

These . . . searched the scriptures daily.   Acts 17:11

It is regrettable that more Christians do not consult the Scriptures in the intelligent and thoughtful way exhibited by the "noble Bereans" of Paul's day. Too many either superficially scan the contents of the Word so that its full import is completely missed by them, or else they treat it like a book of magic. That is, they open it at random and expect to be guided by the first passage that they see. Such impious treatment of the Bible is a form of superstition which should be discouraged. We are told to *"study"* if we wish to be "approved" (II Tim. 2:15).

A missionary who used to get his directions by just opening the Bible at random was cured of this misconception by a startling experience. Desiring to know how he would be received at the end of life by the Lord of the harvest, he opened the Scripture and was shocked beyond measure when he found the text his finger indicated read: "Hell from beneath is moved . . . to meet thee at thy coming" (Isa. 14:9a).

"At one time I read so many chapters of the Bible a day," said Dwight L. Moody, "that if I did not get through my usual quantity, I thought I was getting cold and backsliding. But, mind you, if a man had asked me two hours after as to what I had read, I could not tell him; I had forgotten it nearly all.

"When I was a boy, I hoed corn on a farm; and I used to hoe it so badly in order to get over so much ground, that at night I had to put down a stick in the ground so as to know the next morning where I had left off. That was somewhat in the same fashion as running through so many chapters every day. A man will say, 'Wife, did I read that chapter?' 'Well,' says she, 'I don't remember.' Neither of them can recollect. Perhaps he reads the same chapter over and over again; and they call that 'studying the Bible'."

Are you a Bible-taster or a Bible student?   — H.G.B.

> Sweet Word of God, my soul to bless,
> Upon thy tenets fair I muse;
> Oh Word of Power of pure design
> Help me thy sword-thrusts well to use.
> — G. Woods

"I have yet to find the first man who ever read the Bible from cover to cover who remained an infidel." — D. L. MOODY

DON'T LOOK BACK NOW

SUGGESTED SCRIPTURE READING: Colossians 3:1-4

No man, having put his hand to the plough, and looking back, is fit for the kingdom of God.　　　　Luke 9:62

This is Jesus' own formula for plowing a straight furrow. All believers are plowmen, but all believers do not plow a straight furrow. In this passage in Luke, Jesus is talking about discipleship. All disciples are believers, but all believers are not disciples. To become a believer one does nothing and brings nothing. He only receives the free gift of God's grace. But to be a disciple means sacrifice (Matt. 8:19-22). It may mean suffering (Matt. 10:24, 25), separation (Luke 9:61), and bearing a cross (Luke 14:27). Discipleship costs something — salvation is God's free gift. But God wants all believers to become disciples and in our text gives the requirements.

He uses the figure of plowing to make a straight furrow. I remember well my uncle, many years ago, teaching me how to plow straight. I watched him start the field. He would first plow a "back furrow" in the middle of the field. If this back furrow were straight, all the other furrows would be the same. And then came the time for me to try. I had seen him make a furrow as straight as an arrow, and he told me the secret. He said, "Don't look at the furrow you are plowing. Keep your head up. Never look back to see how you are doing — look straight ahead." Then, when he had put the plow point in at one end of the field, he gave me the reins and said, "I'll stand at the other end and you keep your eye on me and plow straight toward me. Don't look down, don't look back — just keep your eyes on me."

This is the secret of the victorious Christian life. "Looking unto Jesus the author and finisher (both ends of the furrow) of our faith." Today — *keep your eyes on Jesus. Follow Him* and He will make you a fisher of men.　　　　— M.R.D.

We know not where the path may lead,
　As yet by us untrod;
We "look not back" but sweetly trust
　The providence of God! — G. Woods

"If God has called you, don't spend time in looking over your shoulder to see who is following you."

THE UNFINISHED CORNICE

SUGGESTED SCRIPTURE READING: Hebrews 11:8-16

. . . and confessed that they were strangers and pilgrims on the earth. For they that say such things declare plainly that they seek a . . . better country, that is, an heavenly.
Hebrews 11:13, 14, 16

People who pass Lord Rothschild's mansion in Piccadilly are surprised to notice that the end of one of the cornices of his beautiful home is unfinished. Many think it strange that a rich man such as he could not afford to put the final touches on this otherwise superb residence. The explanation, however, is very simple. Lord Rothschild was an orthodox Jew; and every pious Jew's house, tradition says, must have some part unfinished to bear testimony to the fact that its occupants, like Abraham, are but pilgrims and strangers on earth. The incomplete cornice on the mansion says to all who understand its meaning: "This is not Lord Rothschild's *final home;* he is traveling to *eternity."*

We, too, are in the world, but not of the world. We should always remember not to build our nests too strong here. Can others recognize by our conduct, our words, and our deeds, that we are living with "eternity's values in view"? When depression strikes, when privations and trials increase, or when death comes and sits upon our doorstep, these are the acid tests which determine how much we have set our heart upon the things of this life. You and others will know then very soon whether you have "an unfinished cornice" in your life. If you have, you will triumph by faith over all these things and emerge from every circumstance as more than a conqueror in Christ. The mature Christian recognizes that this life is not an end in itself, but rather a pilgrimage toward the Heavenly Land where our true citizenship resides and where our eternal treasures lie. If you have "an unfinished cornice" you will know the deeper fellowship with Christ that is so precious, for those who set their affections above are the objects of God's special blessing. By them God is honored, and He is therefore "not ashamed to be called their God."   — H.G.B.

I'm but a stranger here, Heav'n is my home;
Earth is a desert drear, Heav'n is my home.
Danger and sorrow stand round me on ev'ry hand;
Heav'n is my fatherland, Heav'n is my home.
                    — T. R. Taylor

"He who makes God first will find God with him at the last!"

A CHICKEN IN THE STORM

. . . as a hen gathereth her chickens under her wings.
Matthew 23:37

Whoever invented the word, "chicken-hearted," didn't know his chickens. "Chicken-hearted," according to Webster, means to be timid, afraid, fearful or cowardly. In modern teenage jargon, anyone without courage is called "chicken." I spring to the defense of the grossly maligned fowl, for a chicken is just the opposite. I have never seen a greater demonstration of courage, fearlessness and loyalty than I saw displayed by a chicken in time of grave danger. Chickens are not "chicken-hearted," and whoever made the statement owes the noble hen an apology. Take the case of my hen. I had placed 14 eggs under her and she faithfully hatched all 14. That took courage and stamina and patience for 21 long days. I made a coop for her with slats across the open end, so the chicks could pass in and out while the mother hen remained confined inside. The coop is outside my study window. One afternoon a storm arose, and before it broke I could hear the frantic "cluck cluck" of the mother hen as she called her brood to shelter. It was a terrible storm. Trees were blown down, and the air was filled with debris. Suddenly a gust of wind lifted the coop into the air and sent it tumbling across the lawn. I was expecting hen and chicks to be blown away all over the place. But there she sat on the open lawn, without shelter, exposed to a gale violent enough to blow a man down. As though cemented to the ground she squatted motionless till the storm was past. Don't ask me how she did it. *Love* made her immovable — love for her little chicks. Now we can understand better why Jesus compared His own love to that of a hen who "doth gather her brood under her wings" (Luke 13:34b). Remember today, child of God, that under *His* wings you are safe and secure. — M.R.D.

Under His wings, what a refuge in sorrow!
How the heart yearningly turns to His rest!
Often when earth has no balm for my healing,
There I find comfort, and there I am blest.
— W. Cushing

"Be sure if God sends you on stony paths, He will provide you with strong shoes."

GOD'S CARE

SUGGESTED SCRIPTURE READING: Psalm 116:1-9

I love the Lord, because he hath heard my voice and my supplications.   Psalm 116:1

The unknown author of the 116th Psalm here praises the Lord for His gracious watch-care and ready help. God has taken him from the brink of despair, delivered his soul from death, dried his tears, and established his goings. Such compassion and tender ministrations call forth an answering response of thankful gratitude. With impassioned zeal he exclaims, "I love the Lord, because He Hath heard my voice and my supplications."

How often we, too, have seen the Lord undertake in a marvelous way when human help seemed vain. We rejoiced when His loving hand made level the unscaleable heights of some mountain of difficulty, and blessed His Name when He smoothed the rough pillow of care till it became the downy cushion of contentment.

Rosalind Goforth tells this touching incident which further illustrates God's loving help in time of need:

"One day when my grandfather was a small boy, he went to visit his cousins in the south of England, their home being situated close to a dense forest. The children, lured by the beautiful wild flowers, became hopelessly lost in the woods. After trying in vain to find a way out, the eldest, a young girl, called the frightened, crying little ones around her and said: 'When mother died, she told us always to tell Jesus if we were in any trouble. Let us kneel and ask Him to take us home.' They knelt, and as she prayed, one of the little ones opened his eyes to find a bird so close to his hand that he reached out for it. The bird hopped away, but kept so close to the child as to lead him on. Soon all were joining in the chase after the bird, which flew or hopped in front almost within reach. Suddenly it rose into the air and flew away. The children looked up to find themselves on the end of the woods in sight of home." Yes, "God leads His dear children along." Do you love and praise Him for it? The Psalmist did; so should you!

— H.G.B.

He has not failed thee in all the past.
And will He go and leave thee to sink at last?
Nay, He said He will hide thee beneath His wing;
And sweetly there in safety thou mayest sing. — Anon.

"The school of suffering graduates rare scholars!"

MEMBERS OF HIS BODY

SUGGESTED SCRIPTURE READING: Ephesians 5:25-32

For we are members of his body.   Ephesians 5:30

The body of Jesus Christ is spoken of in both a literal and symbolic way. Jesus had a literal body in which He was born, lived, died, ascended and in which He is coming again (John 2:21, Heb. 10:5). But this literal body of *Jesus* is a figure of the spiritual body of *Christ*. Christ is the Head of this body and believers are the members. When God looked upon the body of His Son on the Cross, He saw more than a physical body. He saw a spiritual body consisting of Christ and all the redeemed. This body is called the "Church" (Eph. 1:23, Col. 1:18). When God saw Christ dying on Calvary, He also saw the members of His body dying with Him there. As members of the body of Christ, everything which happened to our Saviour as Head is reckoned as having happened to us as well.

As members of Christ's body we were:

1. *Crucified* with Christ (Gal. 2:20)
2. *Buried* with Christ (Rom. 6:4)
3. *Raised* with Christ (Col. 3:1)
4. *Ascended* with Christ (Rom. 6:4)
5. *Seated* with Christ (Eph. 2:0)

Christ is in heaven today as our Head, and positionally as members of His body we, too, are already there.

A certain minister once severely rebuked an old saint for saying, "I am eternally secure in Christ." She quoted the verse, "No man shall pluck me out of his hand." The minister replied, "But you might slip out between the fingers and so yet be lost." But the dear saint replied, "I cannot slip out between the fingers; for, you see, I am one of the fingers." We are members of His body, of His flesh, and of His bones.   — M.R.D.

> I'm leaning on His arm alone,
> I cannot know defeat;
> The glory shall be all His own
> When vict'ry is complete. — J. Gray

"Noah's faith led him into the ark, and the ark, not his faith, saved him. So, too, Christ is the ark in which we find eternal security."

THE "FLOWER-CLOCK" OF LIFE

SUGGESTED SCRIPTURE READING: Job 9:1-10; 25, 26

My days are swifter than a weaver's shuttle.　　Job 7:6

History records that Linnaeus, the noted botanist, once constructed a clock of flowers. Each of the blooms opened in turn at a set time of day. God, too, has a similar order and beauty in the garden of life. Carefully, steadily, He unfolds the petals of time before us that from them we may extract the nectar of His sweet will and the honey of His never-failing blessing. Realizing that "the path of the just is as a shining light that shineth more and more unto the perfect day" (Prov. 4:18), we are never to approach His dealings with pessimism. The Word reveals that His will for us is ever kind. We should be always praising no matter how lamentable our lot at the moment seems to be; for the clouds are "big with mercy," and the rainbow of promise gleams in every storm of adversity. The close-sealed buds that circle the clock of time will open in beauty at their appointed hour as the "kindly light" of heaven steals across the horizon of our life. Then we shall find that each "cup of the hours" will contain the needed nectar of grace for its own appointed trial. The perfume of benediction that will issue forth from the unfolding petals will shed the beauty of God's love upon us.

The more mature we become as Christians, the more we realize that we must measure our years "not by the water-clock of falling tears, but by the flower-clock of thankfulness and praise!" The lightning movements of the weaver's shuttle will then not alarm us, but graciously teach us to number our days so that we may "apply our hearts to wisdom."

"Redeem the time" this day by filling it with service and humble adoration. — H.G.B.

Not till the loom is silent
And the shuttles cease to fly
Shall God unroll the canvass
And explain the reason why.
The dark threads are as needful
In the Weaver's skillful hand
As the threads of gold and silver
In the pattern He has planned. — Anon.

"Every day, like the weaver's shuttle, leaves a thread behind; and each shall wear, as he weaves."

WHY WASTE IT?

Suggested Scripture Reading: Mark 14:3-9

... Why was this waste of the ointment made? Mark 14:4

A woman took a very costly vase of precious ointment and poured it upon the head of Jesus. Some of those present took offense at the apparent waste, but Jesus points out that what we do for Him is never wasted. It is thought that this woman had been saved from a life of awful sin, and this ointment was designed to perfume *herself* in order to allure and to entrap her unfortunate victims. But now she was saved and takes that which she had prepared for herself and used it on Jesus instead. Here is a lesson. How lavishly we spend our time and money for the things of self before conversion, and how stingy we are with our time and money *now* for the cause of Christ.

A man complained to Sam Jones because the church had assessed him $20.00 a year. Jones asked him, "How long have you been saved?" He replied, "Four years." "You were a drunkard and God saved you; and how much did you spend on drink before you were saved?" The man replied, "About $250.00 a year." "You are a rascal," replied Jones, "from the crown of your head to the sole of your foot. Stop and figure your own ratio, brother! Think of the price you had to pay for your life of sin — now isn't salvation worth as much?"

"Well," said the saloon keeper to an old customer, "I see you've been to the revival meeting and given the evangelist your last nickel. Now you'll have to walk home." "Yes," said the new convert happily, "and many a time I've given *you* my last nickel and *couldn't* walk home!" Billy Bray was digging potatoes and the devil came along and upbraided him on the small potatoes. Said the devil, "You say the Lord loves you but look at the small potatoes He gives you." "Listen, devil," said Billy, "when I was serving you I didn't have any potatoes at all!" How much do we appreciate our salvation? "All to Him we owe."   — M.R.D.

We give Thee but Thine own,
Whate'er the gift may be;
All that we have is Thine alone,
A trust, O Lord, from Thee. — Anon.

"When the heart is converted the purse will be inverted!"

THE FAITH OF JENNY BITSY

SUGGESTED SCRIPTURE READING: Psalm 61:1-4

What time I am afraid, I will trust in thee. Psalm 56:3

Jenny Bitsy was a pretty little Indian girl. Some years ago she was taken into the missionary hospital in New Mexico in order that she might receive treatment for rheumatic fever. She was a sweet child of eleven years, but was very weak physically. She had been given a hymnbook and a Bible and these she always cherished and often carried with her. Jenny was a model patient; always kind, obedient and cheerful. In fact, the matron often stated that Jenny seemed almost too sweet and angelic for this evil old world. Her health continued poor and it was noticed that her tonsils were tremendously enlarged and would have to be removed. Surgery, in her case, would be dangerous, but, as it was absolutely necessary, preparations were made. Jenny said she was not at all afraid, for she loved the Lord Jesus and trusted Him very much. A very strange thing happened when she was on the operating table; although she was under ether, she unexpectedly regained consciousness and said just six words, *"Dear Jesus, take care of me!"* Said the missionary pastor, "We shall never forget those words, they were the last ones this little girl ever spoke on earth, for after the operation was completed and they were about to wheel her to her room, she stopped breathing. Jesus took Jenny Home! Everyone at the mission station was heartbroken and yet, when the other Indian children sang at her funeral, 'Safe in the Arms of Jesus,' all seemed to realize that Jenny's prayer had been answered in a manner which God knew was best. Jesus was taking care of her in a most glorious way, showing her all the wonders of His precious Home above."

Oh, for the faith of a Jenny Bitsy so that in all of life's circumstances we may be smiling and unafraid, confidently trusting our all into His hand of love with the simple prayer, "Dear Jesus, take care of me!" Such faith will find a rainbow in every dark cloud, and the sparkle of God's love in every teardrop! — H.G.B.

Nothing is hid from His all-seeing eye,
Never a teardrop, nor even a sigh;
"Careful and troubled" you never need be,
Trust Him completely and doubtings will flee.
— W. Nienhuis

"A firm faith in the promises of God is the best theology."

COUNT YOUR BLESSINGS

SUGGESTED SCRIPTURE READING: Luke 12:16-26

> *. . . a man's life consisteth not in the abundance of the things which he possesseth.* Luke 12:15

The secret of happiness does not depend upon material possessions, but upon our spiritual appreciation of what we have in Christ. Two persons may look at the same object and yet see two different things. Looking at a bouquet of flowers one will see the beauty of the bouquet while the other will see only the one faded bloom. Some people can only see the one "poor" apple in a whole bushel of good ones. How easy to see the one fault in a Christian and be blind to all his finer qualities. Someone has said, "You see only what you look for."

Two ladies were visiting a lumberyard with large rafts of timbers floating in the stained, foul-smelling river. Said the one, "How fragrant those pine boards smell." "Pine boards!" exclaimed the other, "all I can smell is this foul river." "No, thank you," replied the other, "I *prefer to smell* the pine boards instead." How easy to overlook our blessings, when we become occupied with the unpleasant things of life. The sign of Christian growth is the ability to overlook, or even be unconscious of the little eccentricities of others and see only their finer Christian qualities. Today don't be a "spiritual policeman," always on the lookout for trouble. Don't be "down in the mouth," thinking only of your troubles. But begin to count your many blessings and you will find the blessings far outweighing your troubles. Someone has recommended counting sheep if you cannot sleep. I have better advice than that. Try counting God's favors and even the devil will put you to sleep, for he does not want you to "count your blessings." A little girl begged her mother to read to her the story of Daniel at bedtime. "I am afraid," said the mother, "that you will dream about the lions if I do." "Oh, no," answered the little one, "I will only dream about Daniel and leave out the lions." May God help us to remember the pleasant things, and forget the others. —M.R.D.

> It will help your disposition,
> It will brighten up your face;
> If you stop to count your blessings
> And appreciate God's grace. — I. Honcy

"Where love is thin — faults are thick!"

WHY?

SUGGESTED SCRIPTURE READING: Romans 5:3-5

He knoweth the way that I take. Job 23:10

One of the words most frequently used by little ones in the home is the word, "Why?" Those of us who are God's spiritual children seem to be infatuated with the same expression. "Why does the Lord allow me to suffer so?" ... "Why did the Lord take my loved one from me?" ... "Why doesn't the Lord answer my prayers?" ... Why? ... *Why?* ... WHY? God does not always choose to give us the answer here, but we may rest assured that there is a sufficient and weighty reason for everything which He sends. All is shaped by His hand of love and is dispensed according to His unerring wisdom. Trials, sickness, disappointment, *everything* is working together for our eternal good. We are receiving exactly what we would request if we could see as God sees! Therefore, whatever comes of apparent good or ill, *give thanks for it!* (Eph. 5:20) Our insistent and often faithless "WHY" finds its sufficient answer in the gracious and comforting words, HE KNOWETH!"

—H.G.B.

I promised a doll to my dear baby girl;
I pictured a treasure most fair,
With exquisite features, and teeth of pure pearl,
Moving eyes, walking limbs and real hair!
We entered a shop, and the dear little maid
Clasped a cheap, tawdry doll to her breast;
To make the exchange I was really afraid,
Though I wanted to give her the best.
I took it away, and the tears filled her eyes,
Till I gave her the one I had planned;
Then the dear little face glowed in joyous surprise
That a dolly existed so grand...
Oh, Saviour, I too am a child in Thy sight,
I choose the first things that I see;
I struggle to keep them, I do not know quite
Why the Father should take them from me.
But when I look back, through the wisdom of years,
When my faith is age-old and sublime,
I know I shall see, through a rainbow of tears,
That my Father planned best, all the time! — Anon.

"Trial is the school of trust!"

WHICH IS FAR BETTER!

SUGGESTED SCRIPTURE READING: Philippians 1:8-23

. . . to be with Christ . . . is far better. Philippians 1:23

The Apostle Paul had caught a glimpse of the glory on the other side, and at times was literally homesick for heaven. He knew that his deepest afflictions were permitted by God, and even his imprisonment in Philippi was for the "furtherance of the gospel" (Phil. 1:12). He could sing with his feet in the stocks, and in the middle of the night. It is easy to sing and praise the Lord when all is bright and prosperous; but to be able to sing when all is dark and there seems no way out except "UP," is evidence of a truly victorious faith.

You do not find it hard to praise the Lord as you sit in your comfortable home, but suppose you were kneeling on a lonely spot on a hill in far-away China with an executioner's sword raised above your head; what would be your thoughts? This situation faced the Rev. and Mrs. R. W. Porteous in the spring of 1931. They were taken prisoners by Communist bandits in China. Led to a lonely spot on top of a hill, the officer said, "This is the place." The executioner took the knife from its holder, raised it above the necks of the courageous couple, and certain death seemed imminent. However, instead of cringing and begging for mercy, they began to sing. The executioner's knife did not fall. The officer stared open-mouthed as the missionary couple sang:

> Face to face with Christ, my Saviour,
> Face to face — what will it be?
> When with rapture I behold Him,
> Jesus Christ who died for me.

These two saintly souls were ready for certain death, but to their surprise, no order was given. The executioner returned the sword to its sheath and Mr. and Mrs. Porteous were released. Subsequently, they were returned to their homeland in England, and there they told the story of the perfect peace which the Lord Jesus gives to His children in the face of certain death.   — M.R.D.

> Face to face I shall behold Him,
> Far beyond the starry sky;
> Face to face in all His glory,
> I shall see Him by and by! — Mrs. F. Breck

"Grace comforts the soul, puts to flight the devil, and makes a Christian equal to any situation." — G.W.

NEVER FORSAKEN

SUGGESTED SCRIPTURE READING: Hebrews 13:5-8

*. . . for he hath said, I will never leave thee, nor forsake
thee.*
Hebrews 13:5

Charles H. Spurgeon, the prince of preachers, often spoke of
God's faithfulness and watch-care over His own. One time when
he went into the country to preach, he had rich opportunity to
test his own faith in this regard. As he was riding along he was
shocked to find that he had lost his ticket. The only other occupant
of the compartment noticed him fumbling in his pockets and said,
"I hope you have not lost anything, sir." Mr. Spurgeon told him
that his ticket was missing and that by a remarkable coincidence
he also found that he had neither watch, nor money, nor anything
valuable with him. "But," said Spurgeon, "I am not at all troubled,
for you see I am on my Master's business and have had so many
evidences of Divine Providence in small mattters, as well as in
great ones, that I am bound to experience His aid in this difficulty
as well." Shortly thereafter a ticket collector came into the coach.
He tipped his hat to the preacher's companion, who in turn said
something to him in low tones. The man immediately left the compartment. "It is very strange," said Mr. Spurgeon, "that the collector did not ask for my ticket." "No, Mr. Spurgeon," said his
companion, "it's only another illustration of what you have been
telling me about the Providence of God watching over you, even
in the little things. You see, I am the general manager of this line.
No doubt it was divinely arranged that I should happen to be your
companion just when I could be of service to you." Once again
God had rewarded Spurgeon's faith.

Someone has said concerning our text that it is hardly possible
to give the word order as it is found in the Greek. There are actually five negatives in the one sentence. Literally translated it
would probably read: *"Not will I fail thee! Nevermore! No! Never
and by no means will I forsake thee!"* God will never desert us
in any circumstance. No! Five times no! Trust in His faithfulness
and take new courage!
— H.G.B.

I know that He is close to me, My Guard — my Guide;
He leadeth me, and so I walk quite satisfied. — Anon.

**"When you are at your wit's end — God is still in no perplexity, and
HE CARETH FOR YOU!"**

SEARCH THE SCRIPTURES

SUGGESTED SCRIPTURE READING: Luke 24:44-48

Search the scriptures: — they are they which testify of me. John 5:39

This was the advice Jesus gave to His critics who refused to recognize Him as the Messiah and accept Him as the Son of God. There is only one Book in the world which contains the revelation of the Lord Jesus, and therefore, no one can know Christ apart from the Word of God. To be saved, one must believe what the Bible says about Jesus (I John 5:10-11). The "new birth" is the result of receiving God's Word concerning the Son of God. It is the "seed" which alone can produce eternal life by the power of the Holy Spirit (I Pet. 1:23).

And for the believer the "Word of God" becomes the necessary food for proper spiritual growth and development. We are admonished to "grow in grace, and in the *knowledge* of our Lord and Saviour Jesus Christ" (II Peter 3:18). This knowledge is found only in His Word, therefore, we must "feed" upon it. It is not enough to just read a passage as a custom or habit, but Jesus said "*Search*" the Scriptures. Paul says in II Timothy 2:15, "Study to show thyself approved." The virility of your spiritual life is in direct proportion to the time you spend prayerfully in this Book. Take a few minutes extra today and see the difference. Let nothing keep you from it.

An Irishman was once reading the Bible, when the priest entered and remonstrated with him for so doing. But Pat replied, "It says, 'search the Scriptures,' your reverence, and when you came in I was just reading, 'Ye shall read it to your *children*,' and the priests have no children. How do you account for that?"

Others cannot "search" the Scriptures for you. The fruit you pick yourself is always the sweetest. — M.R.D.

I could not get along without my Bible,
Its words are life and spirit to my soul,
Revealing all there is for me in Jesus,
Renewing, cleansing, burning, making whole.
— L. Nankivell

"Re-Bible and revival are closely related."

AARON'S WONDERFUL ROD!

SUGGESTED SCRIPTURE READING: John 3:14-17

> *For they cast down every man his rod, and they became serpents: but Aaron's rod swallowed up their rods.*
>
> Exodus 7:12

Have you ever pondered the meaning of the phrase, "but "Aaron's rod swallowed up their rods"? To understand its typical significance you must realize that the serpent, due to his activity and use by the devil in causing man to fall, is always associated with evil and frequently is emblematic of Satan himself! (Rev. 12:9). Aaron's rod was symbolic of life and grace. But more than this, it typified the Lord Jesus Christ! A careful reading of Numbers 17 will verify this, for Aaron's rod, though dry and dead, some years later came to life, budded, blossomed, even yielded almonds, and was then laid up in the ark of the covenant as a testimony of God's revivifying grace (Heb. 9:4). Aaron's rod thus speaks eloquently of the Divine Son of God who after the night of death on Calvary burst into the bloom of new life in the tomb of Joseph of Arimathaea and came forth to bear all "the fragrant fruit of resurrection"! But you say, if "serpents" stand for sin why did this wondrous rod of Aaron take the same form? The answer is found in John 3:14 and II Corinthians 5:21! "For he hath *made him to be sin for us,* who knew no sin; that we might be made the righteousness of God in him." Do you see now the typical significance of Aaron's rod devouring the rods of sin? It is all a picture of marvelous grace. Christ took our sin and expiated it. Thus we all become a part of this Branch of Righteousness that blossomed to eternal life! Even more than this, Satan, the personification of sin, with his power of death, is to be defeated. All shall one day be "swallowed up in victory"! (I Cor. 15:54). Such beauty of type and figure underscore the truth of inspiration!

— H.G.B.

> Oh, glorious height of vantage ground!
> Oh, blest victorious hour!
> In Him to trust and fully know
> His resurrection power! — P. P. Bliss

"The Bible is the window in this prison of hope through which we look into eternity!"

GOD'S INSOMNIA

He that keepeth thee will not slumber.   Psalm 121:3

God never sleeps and for this we may be truly grateful. The devil is on the watch and if our God should withhold His providence from us for a single moment we would perish immediately. The story is told of a sentinel of the army whose duty was to keep constant watch. He dozed for just a moment but in that moment the enemy attacked and overwhelmed the garrison. But our God watches over His own every moment of the day and night. And because He is awake — we can peacefully sleep. We have the precious promise, "Behold, he that keepeth Israel shall neither slumber nor sleep (Psa. 121:4).

Two different words are used in the Hebrew. The word for slumber is *noom* and means to be drowsy. The word for sleep is *yashen* and means to be off guard or slack. Our Lord is never "off guard." He cannot be taken by surprise.

A little orphan girl upon retiring inquired of her mother one moonlit night, "Mommy, is the moon God's lantern?" The lamp had just been put out and the only light in the room came through the window from the moon. "Yes, darling," replied the mother, "that is God's light up in the sky." After a pause the little girl asked tremblingly, "Will God turn off the light and go to sleep, too?" "No, my child," said the mother, "Gods lights are always burning." The little girl replied as she turned over to go to sleep, "Then, Mamma, while God's awake I am not afraid." Oh, for the faith of a little child. Remember today your heavenly Father watches over you.   — M.R.D.

I'll walk in faith this day, O Lord,
No foes or storms I'll fear;
But trusting in Thy precious Word,
I know I'm safe while Thou art near. — Anon.

"The beginning of anxiety is the end of faith, and the beginning of true faith and trust is the end of anxiety. — G. MUELLER

THE "ALTHOUGH" AND "YET" OF FAITH!

SUGGESTED SCRIPTURE READING: Psalm 13

> *Although the fig tree shall not blossom, neither shall fruit be in the vines; the labor of the olive shall fail, and the fields shall yield no meat; the flocks shall be cut off from the fold, and there shall be no herd in the stalls: Yet I will rejoice in the LORD, I will joy in the God of my salvation.*
>
> Habakkuk 3:17, 18

The eye of the Christian should be focused on the Lord, not things! He should live above the shadows of fear and bask in the sunlight of faith! With the prophet Habakkuk he, too, may have a long column of adverse circumstances listed under the caption "Although"; but with true spiritual discernment he should "X" them all out with the "Yet" of faith!

I shall never forget the story of the Christian lady who was very downcast because of her earthly troubles. As she walked along the street she met a Spirit-led man of God who asked her of the state of her soul. With a sour look and a bitter shrug of her shoulders she replied, "Oh, not too bad, *under the circumstances!*" With his characteristic frankness and discernment he aptly replied, "Well, get *above the circumstances,* sister, that's where Jesus is!"

The prophet was of the same mind. He refused to let circumstances quell his faith or crush his certain hope. He calculates the prospects of the future not with the doleful "Althoughs" of earthly reverses, but with the "Yet" of faith and the tape measure of God's favor! When the fig tree does not bloom and the fields yield no meat, then the very sun of adversity that turns our garden into a desert will also melt the snows of God's higher supply so that once again "the river of God is full of water"! Faith's answer to human disappointment must always be: "Yet I will rejoice in the LORD, I will joy in the God of my salvation!" — H.G.B.

> Although my trees are fruitless,
> No grapes are on the vine,
> Yet Christ is all my fulness,
> And all His sweetness mine. — Anon.

"One day we shall bless God not more for what He has granted than for what He has denied!" — H. E. MANNING

THE MIRROR OF GOD'S WORD

SUGGESTED SCRIPTURE READING: II Kings 12:1-10

For if any be a hearer of the word, and not a doer, he is like unto a man beholding his natural face in a glass: For he beholdeth himself, and goeth his way, and straightway forgetteth what manner of man he was.

James 1:23, 24

The Bible is a mirror in which we can see ourselves as we are by nature. In Psalm 14 God presents us with a "bust" of the sinner, but in Romans 3 we have a full-length portrait. Yet men will either refuse to look in this mirror or else promptly ignore what they see and forget what God says about them. We can see the faults of others, little realizing that they are our own faults.

The story is told of an elderly man, very nearsighted, who took great pride in posing as a critic of art. One day he visited the art museum with some friends and immediately began to give his criticisms of the various paintings. Stopping before a full-length portrait, he began to take it apart. He had left his glasses at home and could not see the picture clearly. With an air of superiority he began: "The frame," said he, "is altogether out of keeping with the picture. The subject (a man) is too homely and shabbily dressed. In fact he is ugly, and it was a great mistake for the artist to select such a shoddy subject for his portrait." The old fellow was going on in this way, when his wife managed to get to him and pulling him aside, whispered in his ear, "My dear, you are looking in a mirror." He had been criticizing himself. What a lesson for us all. Our own faults, which we do not recognize, seem so big when we see them in others; but we are blind to them when they are our own. David was quick to condemn himself (unknowingly) when he condemned the man who stole one little lamb. It is not what we think of ourselves, but what God says about us that counts.

— M.R.D.

It takes much grace to judge yourself,
For vanity is strong;
But God will bless the soul who cries,
"O Lord, forgive; I'M WRONG!"

— G. Woods

"Other men's sins are before our eyes; our own are behind our back."

THE "COME" AND "GO" OF SERVICE!

SUGGESTED SCRIPTURE READING: Matthew 17:24-27

Come now therefore, and I will send thee unto Pharaoh, that thou mayest bring forth my people the children of Israel out of Egypt.
Exodus 3:10

Once in the arm of the flesh Moses had attempted to be the leader of his oppressed people and failed utterly. Rejected by the very race he sought to aid in his unsanctified zeal, he spent forty years on the backside of the desert! (Ex. 2:11-15). Moses had made the mistake so commonly encountered among God's people; he had failed to realize that *the Lord never says "go" before He first says "Come"!* Not until we have answered His loving call to seek fellowship with Him and to receive His unction does He send us! When we are thus qualified, however, our natural inability and the immensity of the task has no bearing on the glorious outcome of our mission. For when He sends, He empowers! Although Moses had several things in his favor, such as his mother's early training, his schooling in all the learning of the Egyptians, and his practical and devotional experiences on the backside of the desert, yet there was no one who at the time looked less likely to succeed in leading Israel out of bondage! Having slain one of Pharaoh's overseers, his return to the court might mean his death! Secondly, he had met with only resentment and ridicule in his first attempt at being a leader, and he had no guarantee that he would not be similarly rejected now! Thirdly, as a natural pretender to the throne of Egypt (as "the son of Pharaoh's daughter") he would be eyed with suspicion and probably marked for extermination by the new potentate who had taken over in his absence (Ex. 2:23). Finally, he was not possessed of some of the necessary qualifications of a leader. He was very meek, rather than dynamic, and "slow of speech" rather than a persuasive orator! Yet, Moses' success was assured in the words: *"I will send thee!"* In Christian service nothing outweighs the call of the Lord!
— H.G.B.

He marks the steps, he goes before,
From this time forth, for evermore,
Then from thy heart let praise outpour —
He leads us on! — Anon.

"The measure of your usefulness is determined by the measure of your consecration!"

THE "WALK" OF "FAITH"!

SUGGESTED SCRIPTURE READING: II Corinthians 4:16-18

For we walk by faith, not by sight. II Corinthians 5:7

The Christian not only "lives" by faith, but he is to "walk" by faith as well. Walking implies going forward, moving and making progress. It implies that we are going some place. We hear much about our standing in Christ and our inheritance and security, but "standing" is not enough. Because of our "standing" in Christ we are to go forward in our Christian experience. Walking is good exercise. Just standing makes us weak and flabby and lazy. It makes us prey to many temptations which we do not experience when we walk and press on. If we "walk in the Spirit, we shall not fulfill the lusts of the flesh."

But we are not only to walk, but to walk by faith. We must depend in faith upon a reliable guide who can see in the dark and who knows the path which lies ahead. We do not know the path one step ahead and so we follow our guide. How little we know of what lies before us this very day! But we can trust our Guide. The Holy Spirit is our Guide and the Bible is our road map. Jesus said in John 16:13, "Howbeit when he, the Spirit of truth, is come, he will guide you into all truth." Is your walk directed by the Holy Spirit? Only as you seek His will as revealed in the Bible can you walk in the dark. Now indeed we "walk by faith and not by sight." How fortunate that we cannot see everything about us! If we could see the roughness of the road we might despair. If we could see the mountains just ahead we might become discouraged. And so we walk by faith in Him Who can give strength for the way and lead us around the obstacles or carry us over if need be.

— M.R.D.

All the way before, He's trod,
And He now the flock precedes,
Safe into the fold of God,
Jesus leads, Jesus leads. — J. R. Clements.

"If the Great Pilot is at the wheel, why should the captain pace the deck?"

STOP, THIEF!

Suggested Scripture Reading: John 10:1-9

. . . He that entereth not by the door into the sheepfold, but climbeth up some other way, the same is a thief and a robber. John 10:1

Some years ago there appeared in a religious periodical the story of a man who was quite content to trust in his own merits for salvation. He dreamed one night that he was occupied with the task of constructing a ladder which would reach from earth to heaven. Whenever he did a good deed the ladder was extended upward, and occasionally when an extra good act was performed progress was correspondingly accelerated. He dreamed that in the course of years the ladder finally passed out of sight of the earth up almost to the gates of heaven itself. Alas, however, when the builder was about to step off the topmost rung onto the floor of heaven, a voice cried, "He that climbeth up some other way, the same is a *thief and a robber!*" Down came the ladder with a terrific crash! The startled dreamer awoke. He was set to thinking and finally realized that if he was to obtain salvation it would have to be apart from his own "righteousness."

Even our best works are imperfect, but were they jewels of grace, still human merit would be insufficient to atone for *past* mistakes. The ladder of self-righteousness is no way to enter the fold of the Good Shepherd. God has provided a *Door*, and it is only as we enter through Him and His atoning merits that we can expect to find eternal shelter. Jesus said, "This is the work of God, that ye *believe* on him whom he hath sent" (John 6:29). Christ's righteousness is imputed "without (human) works" (Romans 4:4-6). God will not be *robbed of His glory* by allowing you to "climb up some other way." To those who would seek to be saved by human effort and "work-righteousness," the grace of God shouts out a warning. Its language is simple and unmistakable: "Stop, Thief!" — H.G.B.

Not the labors of my hands
Can fulfill Thy law's demands;
Could my zeal no respite know,
Could my tears forever flow,
All for sin could not atone;
Thou must save, and Thou alone. — A. Toplady

"Why try to buy or 'steal' salvation when you can have it as a gift?"
(Romans 6:23)

THE ASCENDED LORD'S FIRST MESSAGE!

SUGGESTED SCRIPTURE READING: John 14:1-4

> *Two men stood by them in white apparel; Which also
> said, Ye men of Galilee, why stand ye gazing up into
> heaven? this same Jesus, which is taken up from you into
> heaven, shall so come in like manner as ye have seen him
> go into heaven.* — Acts 1:10, 11

This was our Lord's first message from heaven after His ascension. *I am coming back again! I will return,* and when I do, then the Kingdom promises will all be fulfilled without a single exception. Now a number of things are important in this verse:

1. It will be the very same Jesus, the very same One who was born of a virgin, taught among men, died on the Cross, and arose from the grave. Yes, *this same Jesus* in a human body with the prints of the nails in His hands and feet — *this same Jesus* is coming back again.

2. He will come in the same manner as He went away. He went away visibly; He will return visibly. He left them from the Mount of Olives; He will return to the Mount of Olives (Zech. 14:4). He went away leaving the promise of the Kingdom as His last message before He ascended; His first message after He ascended was the assurance of His return to set up this Kingdom.

3. When He ascended He lifted up His hands to bless His disciples (Luke 24:50, 51). When He returns it will be to bring in the full and complete blessing upon Israel and the nations, and the entire earth.

Yes, indeed, Jesus Christ is coming again. He is coming literally, visibly, bodily, in like manner as He has gone away. He *may return today!* — M.R.D.

> Lord, we wait for Thine appearing;
> "Even so," Thy people say;
> Bright the prospect is, and cheering,
> Of beholding Thee that day. — T. Kelly

"If you want to know if you REALLY believe in the imminent return of Christ, see if it has affected your life; for 'every man who hath this hope in him PURIFIETH HIMSELF' "!

NEEDED: A ROD!

SUGGESTED SCRIPTURE READING: Exodus 4:1-5; 17-20

. . . and Moses took the rod of God in his hand.
Exodus 4:20

When Moses was commanded by God to lead the people of Israel out of bondage, he was told to take with him the rod which he held in his hand. He probably was surprised that he was commissioned to take this old, weatherbeaten staff into Pharaoh's throne room, but he soon found that "little is much when God is in it." This simple shepherd's rod was to become the wonderful wand which would be used to divide the Red Sea, bring forth water out of the rock, and be turned at will into a serpent. It was to serve as a scepter of power and authority as he led Israel through the wilderness.

This rod had another function too — it would remind Moses of his forty years on the "back side of the desert." Originally he had sought to lead the children of Israel out of bondage in his own strength and had failed miserably. Discouraged, he sulked in seclusion. Yet Moses needed this communion with the Lord to prepare him for his task. For a full four decades he tended sheep in relative obscurity. Here he was empowered and mellowed for his life's important mission. This rod, therefore, was a *humbling reminder* of his early mistakes. But, he also held it in his hand when he had his wondrous "burning bush" experience. It would hence also serve as an encouragement to him, assuring him that his was a *Divine mission whose success was guaranteed* by the power of God.

We, too, need to carry our *rod* with us! If we would only admit our past mistakes and profit by the lessons the Lord has taught us, we would not allow ambition or pride to hinder our present service. On the other hand, our true calling and the source of our power should keep us from becoming discouraged. Take a firm grasp on your rod, Christian, for humility and spiritual vision will result in *power*. Remember, it was through the instrumentality of His rod that Moses wrought miracles for the Lord! — H.G.B.

Oh Master, let me walk with Thee,
In lowly paths of service free;
Tell me Thy secret; help me bear
The strain of toil, the fret of care. — W. Gladden

"For effective service for God, both surrender and vision are necessary."
— G.W.

THE PRAYER OF A CHILD

SUGGESTED SCRIPTURE READING: I Samuel 3:1-18

And the child Samuel ministered unto the LORD.

I Samuel 3:1

Jesus said concerning children, "Take heed that ye despise not one of these little ones." God loves to use little children in the carrying out of His program, and many are the examples in Scripture where children like Samuel "ministered unto the Lord." Isaac Watts, the hymn writer, was converted at the age of nine years, Jonathan Edwards at the age of seven, Henry Ward Beecher at five, Richard Baxter at six; and what lessons these little ones teach us. In a certain hospital a little girl of four was to undergo a serious operation. After placing her on the table the attendant began to prepare her for the anesthetic. Bewildered, the little one said, "What are you going to do to me?" The kind doctor replied, "Before we can make you well, we must put you to sleep." And the little girl replied, "Then wait just a moment. If I am going to sleep, I must say my prayers first." She closed her little eyes and repeated the child's prayer: "Now I lay me down to sleep," and then said, "I am ready now." Afterward the surgeon testified that he himself prayed for the first time in thirty years, and was converted. Yes, "a little child shall lead them."

A little boy, whose father was publisher of the "Daily Press," was studying his Sunday school lesson and came across the verse, "He sought to see Jesus . . . and could not for the press" (Luke 19:3). "Oh, Dad," he cried, "is that why you cannot accept Jesus; because of your press?" The simple words struck home and brought conviction. How we ought to win the children for Christ for they are often His best witnesses. D. L. Moody returning from a meeting reported "two and a half" conversions. "Two adults and a child?" asked his friend; and Moody replied, "No! Two children and an adult. The children gave their whole lives — the adult had only half his life to give." Take good care of the lambs and there will be no trouble with the sheep.   — M.R.D.

"A little child shall lead them" —
How often it is true,
Men marvel at their simple faith
And trust their Saviour too! — G.W.

"Faith shines brightest in the heart of a child." — H.G.B.

THE ACID TEST

SUGGESTED SCRIPTURE READING: James 5:7-11

Behold, we count them happy which endure. James 5:11

The acid test of a true disciple of the Lord is to be able to endure with Christian grace any and all affliction and "evil treatment" that may be his portion. We must learn in this world of sin to expect tribulation and with God's strength to endure it not only patiently, but triumphantly. The great men of Scripture, including Job and the Prophets, despite the fact that they were in the center of God's will, had difficulties as they traveled the pathway of duty. Often they had to go forward alone, suffering dire and unjust persecution. How can we, therefore, expect to escape trouble if we would do His bidding? Yet God encourages us by promising glory and reward for those who stand firm and hold the fort in the battle against the world, the flesh, and the devil!

It is said that when one crosses the higher Alps, oftentimes it has to be along narrow ledges only broad enough for a mule to get a foothold. These ribbons of rock on the edge of the towering mountains skirt dreadful precipices that descend thousands of feet to the valley below. The safest way for a traveler is not to attempt to guide the course of his mule, nor even grasp the bridle, for the slightest touch may easily throw both the mule and the rider over the cliff to death and destruction below. So, too, as Guthrie says, "There are times and circumstances in the believer's life when, if he would keep himself from sinful doubts, if he would keep himself from falling into despair, he must, as it were, shut his eyes, lay the bridle on the neck of Providence, commit his way to God, and however things may look, make this his comfort, 'He will never leave me, nor forsake me.' In such circumstances the only thing is to trust in God; 'walk by faith, and not by sight.'"

To those who thus endure, there is a reward. Of him the Psalmist says, "Blessed (happy) is the man whom thou chasteneth, O Lord" (Ps. 94:12a).   —H.G.B.

> Great Shepherd! Firmly grasp my hand
> And lead me while I go,
> For thou hast said thy purpose grand,
> Which yet I do not understand,
> Hereafter I shall know!

"Child, thou art come into the world to suffer; endure, and hold thy peace!" — LONGFELLOW

IS ISHMAEL IN THE TENT?

SUGGESTED SCRIPTURE READING: Psalm 4:1-6

Wherefore she said unto Abraham, Cast out this bond-woman and her son: for the son of this bondwoman shall not be heir with my son, even with Isaac. Genesis 21:10

As long as Ishmael was alone in Abram's tent, everything went along seemingly fine, but when Isaac came there was trouble. And that is true of the Christian believer. When we are born again, we begin to realize what a struggle there is within us. The evidence of really being saved is the fact of the struggle with the flesh, of which we become conscious more than ever after we have been saved. For thirteen years before the Isaac type of spiritual man was born, there seems to have been no trouble in Abram's tent; but no sooner is Isaac born than the strife begins. I find also that the people who are really saved are most conscious of their own utter, complete unworthiness. The true test of holiness is this; that the closer we live to God the more we see our own unworthiness. So if you are having a struggle, believer, if you are conscious of your own weakness, yes, even if you fail, and have to cry out, "Oh God, I am making so little progress, I am having such a battle, such a struggle with my old nature and such difficulty overcoming it," it is a sign of life, and not of death. If there is no struggle at all in your Christian life, it is a sign that there is no life within. And that is true not only of the individual, but also of groups and churches. May God deliver us from the complacency of death and from a life which has not enough activity even to be conscious of the struggle.

God grant us to search our lives and honestly judge every known and doubtful sin, confess it, and repent, and know the victory of yielding our all to Him. — M.R.D.

Our bodies to Thee, Lord, we give,
A living sacrifice to be;
O come, and in these temples live;
Abide in us, and we in Thee! — H. J. Zelley

"It is in the Christian life as in the art of horticulture: it is not enough for the gardener to love flowers; he must also hate weeds!"

DESTROYING OUR ENEMIES

SUGGESTED SCRIPTURE READING: Luke 6:27-36

> *But I say unto you, Love your enemies, bless them that*
> *curse you, do good to them that hate you, and pray for*
> *them which despitefully use you, and persecute you.*
>
> Matthew 5:44

People are always eager to get rid of their enemies. The devil's formula is to get men to physically annihilate those they dislike. Christ, too, gives us advice on how to eliminate our enemies, but He would have us destroy not them but their animosity. By the power of His grace and love they are to be turned into friends.

The story is told of Hudson Taylor, dressed in Chinese costume, who was one time waiting for a boatman to take him across a river. As he stood on the dock, a richly dressed Chinese came and also awaited transportation. When the boat came near, this man, not seeing that Mr. Taylor was a foreigner, struck him on the head and knocked him over into the mud. Taylor said his first impulse was to smite the man, but God immediately stopped him. When the boat drew alongside, the man looked more closely at Mr. Taylor whom he had abused and suddenly recognized that he was a foreigner. He could hardly believe his eyes and said, "What, you a foreigner and you would not strike me back when I struck you like that?" The missionary replied, "Friend, this boat is mine. Come in and I will take you where you want to go." On the way, Mr. Taylor poured into the Chinaman's ear the wondrous message of salvation. When the missionary left, tears of repentance and joy were running down the face of his former attacker. Such is the power of the Gospel to transform enemies of God and man into eternal friends.

Act upon Jesus' advice this moment by thinking of someone who has "despitefully used you" and "pray for them" right now.—H.G.B.

How our lives would speak for Jesus,
If we ever kept in view,
Every word and thought and action,
"What would Jesus do?" — A. B. Simpson

"A little of the oil of Christlike love will save a lot of friction."

GOD'S MAGNET

SUGGESTED SCRIPTURE READING: John 11:20-28

... the dead in Christ shall rise first. I Thessalonians 4:16

The most certain thing in all the world is the return of Jesus Christ. He said to His disciples, "I will come again and take you unto myself" (John 14:3). Death is not the "surest" thing in the world for "we shall not all sleep" (I Cor. 15:51). When Jesus comes (and each day brings us one day nearer), He will shout from the air and two things will immediately happen. First, all the dead who have died in faith shall be resurrected (I Thess. 4:16). Then, all living believers shall be instantaneously changed (I Thess. 4:17), and be joined with the resurrected ones and together be caught up to meet the Lord. But all the rest of the wicked dead shall remain in their graves, and the wicked living ones be left behind to perish in the Tribulation.

The coming of Christ will be like a magnet. If I place on my desk a mixture of dust, paper scraps, pieces of glass and wood, and steel shavings, it may be impossible to see all the bits of steel hidden among the scraps. But now I take a magnet and hold it above the pile of material and immediately something happens. The magnet lifts out every bit of steel to itself and separates it from the refuse, leaving everything else behind. It is the nature of steel to be attracted to the magnet. There may be bits of metal which look like steel but when the magnet is applied they fail to respond. The magnet makes no mistakes. It reveals the true nature of the metal and distinguishes the true from the false.

It may be impossible now to tell the difference between the true and the false, but when Jesus shouts from the air, all deception will be revealed. Only the dead *in Christ* shall respond to the "pull" of His blessed voice. Have you received the new nature, the nature of *Him* whose voice will soon be heard? Make your calling and election sure, by receiving Jesus Christ as your personal Saviour. Yield now to the "pull" of His Spirit. *The magnet makes no mistakes!* — M.R.D.

Will you meet me in the air, when the reaping day shall come?
Will you greet me over there in the joyful harvest home?
Christ will draw us to His side, that with Him we may abide,
Will you meet me in the air? — A.B.S.

"Only those tuned to station B-L-O-O-D will hear the shout: Come up hither!" — M.R.D.

GOD IS NOT DEAD!

SUGGESTED SCRIPTURE READING: Psalm 46

*God is our refuge and strength, a very present help in
trouble. Therefore will not we fear.*   Psalm 46:1, 2

"At one time," said Martin Luther, "I was sorely vexed and tried
by my own sinfulness, by the wickedness of the world, and by the
dangers which beset the church. One morning I saw my wife
dressed in mourning. Surprised, I asked her who had died. She
replied: 'Don't you know? . . . God in heaven is dead.' . . . I said
to her: 'How can you talk such nonsense, Katie? How can God
die? He is immortal, and will live through all eternity.' . . . 'Is that
really true?' she asked. 'Of course,' I said, still not perceiving what
she was aiming at, 'How can you doubt it? As sure as there is a
God in heaven, so sure is it that He can never die.' 'And yet,' she
said, 'Though you do not doubt that, you are still so hopeless and
discouraged?' . . . Then I observed what a wise woman my wife
was, and mastered my sadness."

It is ludicrous to presume that God is dead, and yet from a
practical point of view, have not all of us at times acted as if He
were? His ear is ever open to the cry of His child, and He is fully
able to meet our every need. Nothing goes by Him unnoticed,
nothing is out of His control. He who guides the immense universe in its hurried flight through space, also marks the sparrow's
fall and decrees even the exact instant when a minute hair shall
fall from our head. Nothing is left to chance, all is conceived in
His providence. If God then be for us, "who can be against us?"
"Like as a father pitieth his children, so the Lord pitieth them
that fear him" (Ps. 103:13). He loves; He cares; He controls.
God is not dead; stop acting as if He were!   —H.G.B.

Oh God, our help in ages past,
Our hope for years to come,
Be Thou our guide while life shall last
And our eternal home. — I. Watts

"To look around is to be distressed. To look within is to be depressed.
To look up is to be blessed." — R. BECKER

SCARECROWS IN THE GARDEN

SUGGESTED SCRIPTURE READING: Numbers 13:26-33

And there we saw the giants . . . and we were as grass-hoppers.
Numbers 13:33

In my garden I have four rows of everbearing strawberries; a fact which has evidently been proclaimed from the housetops to all the robins, starlings, and brown thrashers in the neighborhood, and they have been having a picnic. So I spent quite some time building a scarecrow from a couple of broom sticks, over which I draped an old coat, a pair of trousers, and conspicuously frosted the whole with a white hat, set at a jaunty angle. But I was in for a surprise, for this morning a wise robin was perched right on top of the hat singing at the top of his voice, "Free strawberries here." I found out there are two kinds of birds; wise ones and stupid ones. The stupid ones sat in the trees about the garden but dared not come near. They were fooled by a scarecrow. But the wise ones welcomed the message. They know a scarecrow is simply an advertisement in disguise. It is an invitation to a banquet.

The Bible tells of some scarecrows and some birds, both wise and stupid. Moses sent twelve spies to bring in a report of the promised land, a land of milk and honey, of fabulous fruits and blessing. But ten of them never tasted the fruits for they saw the scarecrows (the giants and the walled cities). But there were two wise "birds": Caleb and Joshua, who believed God had given them the land, and they were not fooled, but said, "Let us go up at once and possess it."

The Lord has prepared a rich feast for His children, but the "scarecrows" of doubt and fear, of sacrifice and toil prevent many from ever enjoying all the Lord has for them. The ten "stupid," faithless, fearful birds lost out — the ten spies never reached Canaan. Only the two who had faith — Caleb and Joshua — entered to occupy their possession. Go in and possess the land by faith. The giants will all fall before the ones who dare to trust! — M.R.D.

Others saw the giants, Caleb saw the Lord;
They were sore disheartened, he believed God's Word!
— A. E. Richards

"Satan always provides us with an enlarging glass for our troubles, and a blindfold for obscuring God's power!" — G.W.

"HOLY GROUND"

SUGGESTED SCRIPTURE READING: Exodus 3:1-5

. . . the place whereon thou standest is holy ground.

Exodus 3:5

Men often distinguish between what they call "sacred" and "secular," but for the Christian all of life is "sacred" to a greater or lesser degree. All that we do and say is to be colored and motivated by our Christian position and testimony. At home, in the busy market place, in the business office — in fact, everywhere, the light of Christ which is within us should fall upon our task and illumine it with a holy glow of blessing. If it does, we shall find our holy ground leading to "higher ground."

Over a hundred years ago there lived in Oxford a little boy whose business it was to clean the boots of the students at a famous university. He was poor but brilliant. His task was menial, but he considered it holy ground. He did what he was supposed to do with all his might, that His Saviour might be glorified through his efforts. This lad, whose name was George, grew rapidly in favor with the students. His prompt and hardy way of doing things and his industrious habits and faithful deeds won their spiritual admiration. They saw in him a man of promise. "A boy who can blacken boots that well can also be depended upon for other things, and to study well," said one. And so they began to teach him a little every day even though he could not afford the expense of actually attending the school. Eager to learn, George accepted their help and surprised all of his teachers by his rapid progress. We cannot stop to tell you of the patience and perseverance of young George, but he went on from step to step realizing that all of life was "holy ground." He soon became a great and learned man preaching the Gospel with burning zeal until thousands were swept into the kingdom of God. Thus a bootblack became the renowned pulpit orator, George Whitefield.

Go forward with God today with the same vision, realizing that the "place whereon thou standest is holy ground." — H.G.B.

It may be on a kitchen floor, or in a busy mart or store,
If faithful by thy Lord thou art found,
The place thou standest on is "holy ground." — M. Colley

**"There is nothing so small as cannot be done well
and to the glory of God."**

NEITHER FISH NOR FOWL

SUGGESTED SCRIPTURE READING: Revelation 3:14-22

. . . choose you this day whom ye will serve. Joshua 24:15

The story is told of a battle between the animals and the birds. Among them was a bat which has the body of an animal, yet flies like a bird. When the animals were victorious and rushed upon the birds, the bat would fold its wings and cry out, "I am an animal." But when the birds seemed to be winning and threatened the animals, he spread and stretched out his wings and cried, "I am a bird." It's only a story, but it gives a real picture of many people who parade as Christians on Sunday and live for the devil on Monday. They are neither fish nor fowl. They take on the local color of the group with which they happen to be associated. They are people without convictions of their own, and you can never depend upon them, for you never know where they stand. They are neither birds nor mice.

God expects every true believer to have convictions and to stand for them no matter what the cost. Today it is popular to be "tolerant" and "compromising" with the world. Separation is almost unknown. This is the Laodicean age of the lukewarm Church, which God says He will spue out of His mouth (Rev. 3:16). Woe to the man or woman who "rides the fence" and compromises with everyone to avoid persecution. If we are to be true to the Word, and "come out" from the world, it will cost a price which few are willing to pay. But Daniel paid the price. Peter paid the price. John paid the price. And so did Jesus!

Don't be a bat! The bat sought to be friends with both the birds and the animals. Dr. Pettingill said to me many years ago, "The preacher who is true to the Book and refuses to compromise will find himself very lonesome at times." It is becoming popular today to be "cooperative" and "charitable" and "tolerant" even at the expense of truth. Be true to Him today, no matter what the price may be. Faithfulness — not success — is God's requirement.

— M.R.D.

Ye that are men now serve Him, against unnumbered foes:
Let courage rise with danger, and strength to strength oppose.
— G. Duffield

"In the battle of right against wrong, one cannot afford to be neutral."

RADIANT CHRISTIANS

They looked unto him, and were lightened: and their faces were not ashamed.   Psalm 34:5

Psalm 34 breathes with the spirit of exuberant confidence and faith in God. The Lord, says David, delivers us from all fears; and not only that, but those who look up to Him with a heaven-born confidence reflect the light of His countenance so that they become (as one translation has it) "radiant-faced"! You remember how Moses' face shone after he had been long communing with his Lord on the mount? So, too, shall we exhibit spiritual contact if our hearts are in tune with heaven! The inner joy is bound to "bubble over" and be displayed in our eyes and face. The artist and the psychologist alike tell us that what a man is *inside* is soon eloquently depicted *upon his countenance;* for "a merry heart doeth good like a medicine"! (Prov. 17:22). "God is light" and when you get "The Sun of Righteousness" shining in your heart some of the inner illumination is bound to beam forth and alter your outward appearance!

A dear Christian lady, over eighty years of age, wrote to me some years ago and related a personal experience along this line which had influenced her life profoundly. "I recall in class-meeting when I was a child," she said, "that I used to watch a precious old saint as with closed eyes he sang with head thrown back and with tears trickling down over a perfectly radiant face, 'Come Thou Fount of Every Blessing'! Sometimes he sang in tune, and sometimes way off, but nobody cared, because he sang with his whole soul. I do not remember a single word that he ever *said,* but I was profoundly impressed by his *face.* I wanted to be a Christian like that! Since then I have often prayed, 'O Father, help me to be a radiant Christian!' "

Take a look in the mirror, dear friend; does your face "say" a good word for Jesus Christ?   H.G.B.

> You don't have to tell how you live each day,
> You don't have to say if you work or pray,
> A tried, true barometer serves in its place;
> However you live, it will show in your face! — Anon.

"We've a lot of folks today with their dispensations all right and their DISPOSITIONS ALL WRONG!" — VANCE HAVNER

POOR FISHING

Suggested Scripture Reading: Matthew 4:12-20

And that night they caught nothing.   John 21:3

What an embarrassing situation! A group of seasoned fishermen fishing all night and not a minnow to show for their efforts. Fishing without Jesus is always unproductive. The scene in our text is *after* the resurrection. Three and a half years before, Jesus had called them from their nets and said, "Follow Me and I will make you to become fishers of men." They had left their old nets and boats and become fishers of men. But now their master had died and while He had arisen they saw but little of Him. Their hopes of a kingdom were shattered and Simon Peter's suggestion they go back to their old life again; but their empty nets were to teach them the lesson that there is no going back, once we have taken up His cross and followed Him.

That night they caught nothing. Then Jesus came. As if to drive home the lesson He asks, "Children have ye any meat?" and they could speak only the discouraged word - "No." Now comes the miracle. They had confessed their failure and He says, "Cast the net on the right side of the ship." Notice that it was the *right* side. They had been fishing on the *wrong* side. Without Jesus in the boat you are always fishing on the wrong side. And when they obeyed - the net was full! Have you, too, neglected the Lord and gone back from your early fellowship with Him? Then all your efforts count for nothing. Confess your failure *now* - and begin fishing on the right side of the boat.   —M.R.D.

He was not willing that any should perish;
Am I His follower, and can I live
Longer at ease with a soul going downward,
Lost for the lack of the help I might give,
Perishing, perishing! Thou wast not willing;
Master, forgive, and inspire us anew;
Banish our worldliness, help us to ever
Live with eternity's values in view!
                    — L. R. Meyer

"True Christianity is holiness put into action! It is faith gone to work!"

THE PERSPECTIVE OF AFFLICTION

SUGGESTED SCRIPTURE READING: Exodus 33:18-23

And it shall come to pass, while my glory passeth by, that I will put thee in a clift of the rock, and will cover thee with my hand while I pass by.   Exodus 33:22

Someone has beautifully described the darkness and momentary lack of earthly vision that frequently attends our trials as follows: "Affiction is but the hand of God, which He places before our face to enable us, like Moses, to see the train of His glory as He passes by. The saint has had many a pleasant view of God's loving kindness from the top of the hills of mercy; but *tribulation is very frequently the Lord's Pisgah by which He gives them a view of the land in all of its length and beauty.*" Yet, if we are properly exercised by our trials and learn to say, "Thy will be done," momentary darkness and difficulty is replaced by a new and heavenly perspective that broadens our spiritual horizons and lifts the curtain on new aspects of God's love and tender grace.

Moses was placed in the cleft of the rock before his wondrous experience; and only as we too are hidden in the Rock, the Lord Jesus Christ, can we see the glory and goodness of God in all of our trials. Well does the poet sing:

Bane and blessing, pain and pleasure,
By the Cross are sanctified.

A poor shoemaker in a dreary little shop in a large city found by accident that there was one small place in his dark establishment from which he could get a view (through a window) of green fields, blue skies, and distant hills. He immediately changed his working bench so that at any free moment he could lift his eyes and catch a glimpse of beauty. So, from the dark confines of sorrow and the gloom-filled areas of life, there is always a point from which we may gaze on glory and see the face of Christ. When once we have directed our life toward the window of full surrender, we will have attained the serenity and joy that comes from affiction's perspective!   — H.G.B.

Whatsoe'er my lot may be,
In this I calmly rest,
If I could see as Thou dost see,
I'd choose it, as the best! — Anon.

"Dark clouds make a traveler mend his pace and mind his home."

FIRE AND THE FINISHED WORK!

Suggested Scripture Reading: Galatians 5:1-6

> *There came a fire out from before the LORD, and consumed upon the altar the burnt offering and the fat: which when all the people saw, they shouted, and fell on their faces.* Leviticus 9:24

The fire upon this altar was kindled from heaven. It fell from God and kindled the sacrifice on the occasion of the dedication of the tabernacle when it was completed. No human hands brought the kindling fire, no man-made fire burned upon this altar, for when the tabernacle had been completed, all the furniture set in its place, and put within the Holy of Holies, Moses and Aaron came out. There was no one left in the tabernacle, and then it happened! The fire fell from heaven, not kindled by human hands.

Salvation is entirely and exclusively of the Lord (Jonah 2:9). No human effort, no human help, no human contribution was made to kindle the fire upon this altar. It had to be all by the grace of God, wholly apart from all human help and merit, religion and works. To do otherwise meant certain death. The two sons of Aaron, Nadab and Abihu, in Leviticus 10, brought strange fire and were smitten with immediate death by the fire which fell upon them from heaven. How the fire upon this altar was kindled, we do not know. Whether a bolt of lightning, or fire from the fiery pillar, or some other means was used, it came from heaven directly. This was God's method of showing His approval upon an acceptable sacrifice.

The lesson, of course, is evident. We are not to add anything at all to the finished work of the Lord Jesus Christ. There is nothing we can do until we have come to Calvary and received God's own finished salvation by faith in the shed blood of the Lord Jesus.

—M.R.D.

> Thy cross all my refuge. Thy blood all my plea —
> None other I need, blessed Jesus, but Thee!
> In Thee have I trusted, and cheerfully lay
> My hand in Thy hand for the rest of the way!
> —Anon

"Man's way says: 'Do,' But God says: 'It's Done!'; All now is 'Finished.' Believe on the Son!" — H.G.B.

THE IMPORTANCE OF "TRIFLES"

SUGGESTED SCRIPTURE READING: Ephesians 4:22-32

. . . Behold, how great a matter a little fire kindleth!

James 3:5

Men are concerned about big things, but often fail to recognize the importance of "trifles." In Jesus' day, for instance, men looked at the imposing gifts of the rich, but our Lord who could discern hearts took special notice of a poor widow who threw into the treasury her paltry "two mites." God, you see, delights to use little things to exalt His glory. Think of Gideon and his handful of men overcoming a tremendous army; Elijah, a lonely servant of the Lord, successfully putting to flight the prophets of Baal; and little David with a stone and sling, slaying the towering giant of the Philistines!

Little things of an evil nature are also worthy of our corrective attention for they can result in great damage if left unchecked. A few ill-chosen words can wreck a life and ruin a career. A tiny spark can flame into a four alarm fire. So, too, one sin can start a frightening chain of events that will end in disaster.

I am reminded of the true story of a stolen bucket that started a war and ended a career. It began when a soldier in a playful mood snatched an attractive bucket from a public well. The receptacle was passed from hand to hand until at length it came into the possession of young Prince Henry of Sardinia. A great fuss was stirred up about it, and finally a battle was fought to secure it. Prince Henry himself was made a prisoner, and it is said that his imperial father offered a golden chain seven miles long for his ransom which was refused in anger by the enemy. For twenty long years the Prince lay in prison, until he pined away and died. The war continued until most of the governments of Europe were involved and thousands of lives and much property was lost. All this because as a practical joke a soldier committed a "little sin" and stole a public bucket! Guard against the pitfall of little things! In life there are no trifles. "Behold, how great a matter a little fire kindleth!"

—H.G.B.

Great oaks from little acorns grow —
And character from deeds you sow! — Anon.

"The smallest tendency toward evil, left uncorrected, may wreck a character or spoil a life."

WE ARE MILLIONAIRES

SUGGESTED SCRIPTURE READING: Colossians 1:9-14

For all things are yours . . . And ye are Christ's.
                                        I Corinthians 3:21, 23

The heart-warming story is told of a father who with his family had moved to a new house, where the accommodations and luxuries were so much more ample and rich than the old house from which they came that it seemed almost impossible. His little boy, still a lisping babe, ran around in every room, scanning every new thing in ecstasy, and called out in childish wonder at every new sight, "Is this ours, Father, and is this ours?" The child did not say "yours," and the father, as he listened, was not offended with the freedom. You could read in his glistening eye that the infant's confidence in appropriating as his own all that his father had was an important element in his satisfaction.

Such, I suppose, will be the surprise, joy, and appropriating confidence with which the child of our Father's family will count all his own, when he is removed from the comparatively mean condition of things present and enters the infinite of things to come. When the glories of heaven burst upon his view, he does not stand at a distance, like a stranger, saying, "O God, these are Thine." He bounds forward to touch and taste every provision which these blessed mansions contain, exclaiming, as he looks in the Father's face, "Father, this and this is ours!" The dear child is glad of all of the Father's riches, and the Father is even more glad for His dear child.

Why, oh, why do we live as paupers in doubt and fear and worry, when we are "heirs of all things" and spiritual millionaires?
                                        —M.R.D.

> My Father is rich in houses and lands,
> He holdeth the wealth of the world in His hands,
> Of rubies and diamonds, of silver and gold,
> His coffers are full, — He has riches untold.
> I'm a child of the King, a child of the King!
> With Jesus, my Saviour, I'm a child of the King!
>   — H. Buell

"That man is poor indeed who lives without Jesus, and he alone is rich with whom Jesus abides."

INVITATION TO PRAYER

SUGGESTED SCRIPTURE READING: Matthew 18:18-20

. . . watch unto prayer.   I Peter 4:7

Someone has said that when a Christian suddenly awakens in the night for no apparent reason, he can be quite sure that he has received a special invitation from the Lord to engage in prayer, either for himself or others. Whether this is always true I would not dare to say, but certainly I have heard of some remarkable experiences in this regard. Perhaps the most outstanding incident occurred one Sunday evening in April, 1912. On that night the supposedly "unsinkable" *Titanic* went to the bottom of the Atlantic, carrying hundreds of passengers to their death.

Among those on board was Colonel Gracie. After he helped launch the few lifeboats that were available for the women and children, he resigned himself to death. When the *Titanic* slipped beneath the waves, he was sucked down in the great whirlpool of water and thought he had breathed his last. Calling on God for help he tried desperately to swim for the surface. Meanwhile, his wife in far away America awoke from a deep sleep. Her mind was suddenly filled with great concern. There was no way of her knowing, and yet she felt that her husband was in grave danger. Believing that she had been awakened for a purpose, she prayed most earnestly for several hours beseeching the Lord for her husband's safe return. Finally, about five o'clock in the morning, peace came into her heart and she fell into a restful slumber.

Meanwhile, out in the Atlantic, Colonel Gracie had bobbed to the surface near a capsized boat. Comparing notes later, he and his wife found that while she was agonizing in prayer, he had been clinging desperately to this overturned craft. At about five o'clock in the morning, when she had finally found peace of soul, another lifeboat had come alongside and rescued him. Remember this story and the next time you awaken in the middle of the night without apparent reason, consider it an invitation from heaven to repair to your prayer closet.   —H.G.B.

> We cannot tell how often as we pray
> For some bewildered one, hurt and distressed,
> The answer comes; but many times these hearts
> Find sudden peace and rest. — Grace Noll Crowell

"Prayer moves the Hand that moves the world!" — J. WALLACE

NOW AND HEREAFTER

SUGGESTED SCRIPTURE READING: Psalm 23

He that dwelleth in the secret place of the most high shall abide under the shadow of the Almighty. Psalm 91:1

A dear friend of mine, an old lady now with the Lord, once related her experience with an insurance salesman. When he explained his policy to her, she replied, "but Mister, I have all that and more in an insurance policy I already possess and it doesn't cost all that money you are asking for yours." When the salesman, moved to curiosity, requested to see this policy, she produced her Bible, turned to Psalm 91 and said, "There it is — every imaginable insurance in the world. In verse 1, I have social security — 'abiding under the shadow of the Almighty.' — In verse 2, I have insurance against damage in war — 'He is my refuge and my fortress.' In verse 3, I have health insurance from the noisome pestilence, neither 'shall any plague come nigh thy dwelling.' In verse 12, I have collision insurance — 'lest thou dash thy foot against a stone.' In verse 13, I have accident insurance. In verse 15, is fire insurance — 'I will deliver him', and then in the last verse, life insurance — 'With long life will I satisfy him and show him my salvation.'"

The life insurance agent made no further attempt to sell his policy.

"Godliness is profitable unto all things, having promise of the life that now is, and of that which is to come" (I Tim. 4:8b).

—M.R.D.

Saviour, let me walk beside Thee,
Let me feel my hand in Thine;
Let me know the joy of walking
In Thy strength and not in mine!
— J. Sidebotham

"The circumference of blessing cannot be small when God is the center!"

WHOSE LOVE?

Suggested Scripture Reading: John 16:22-26

Herein is love, not that we loved God, but that he loved us.   I John 4:10

A man who was a professed Christian was one day taken seriously ill. As is so often the case when we are in weakened physical condition, Satan began to attack him so that he was beset by many doubts and fears. He was especially troubled about the little love he felt in his heart for God, and he spoke of his lack of spiritual warmth to one who called to see him. His friend was a wise counselor and far along on the Christian pathway and so he answered him as follows: "When I go home from here, I expect to take my baby on my knee, look into her sweet eyes, listen to her charming prattle, and, tired as I am, her presence will rest me; for I love that child with unutterable tenderness. She, however, loves me little. If my heart were breaking, it would not disturb her innocent sleep. If my body were racked with pain, it would not interrupt her play. Even if I were dead, she would probably forget me in a few days. Besides this, she has never brought me a penny, but is a constant expense to me. I am not rich, but there is not enough money in the world to buy my baby. How is it? Does she love me, or do I love her? Do I withhold my love until I know she loves me? Am I waiting for her to do something worthy of my love before extending it?"

This pointed illustration concerning the love of God for His children caused the tears to roll down the sick man's face. "Oh, I see," he exclaimed, "it is not my love to God, but God's love for me that I should be thinking of. And I do love Him now as I never loved Him before!"

Oh, doubting Christian, stop looking within; you will only make yourself more miserable. Look away to Jesus, think of His warm, tender, undying love for you, and your assurance will return. "Herein is love, not that we loved God, but that *he loved us*" (I John 4:10a).   —H.G.B.

There is Someone who cares all along through the years,
Always Someone who cares;
Who's abundantly able to banish our fears,
Always Someone who cares. — H. S. Tool

"None live so pleasantly as those who rest on God's great love rather than on their own fickle feelings." — G.W.

TATTLERS AND BUSYBODIES

SUGGESTED SCRIPTURE READING: II Thessalonians 3:6-15

Tattlers also and busybodies, speaking things which they ought not. I Timothy 5:13

The Apostle in denouncing tattlers and busybodies immediately adds the definition of a "busybody." He says they speak "things which they ought not." Repeating things which should not be spoken is Paul's definition of a tattler and busybody. Do you ever gossip about others? It is one of the most common sins. Many people indulge in it. Gossip is repeating something which may damage someone else. The fact that the thing may even be true is no excuse for repeating it. Solomon says, "A talebearer revealeth secrets: but he that is of a faithful spirit concealeth the matter" (Prov. 11:13). Again he says in Proverbs 17:9, "He that covereth a transgression seeketh love; but he that repeateth a matter separateth very friends."

As we move among men this day, let us take heed to our tongue and speak only that which can edify and do good. Let us not repeat anything we hear which is injurious to another. Yea, better, let us not even listen to it. We may not know the circumstances and the facts, and none of us are in a position to judge others when we ourselves have so much in our own lives which would not sound so good if it were blazed abroad. The word "tattler" in the original means a "bubbler" in the sense of gushing out everything. Gossip is a greater sin than stealing, for stolen goods may be returned, but gossip robs men of their good name and reputation, which can never be recalled. What trouble could be avoided among friends in the home and in the church if all gossip and evil speaking could be stopped. It causes the separation of more friends than anything else in the world. May our prayer be: "Set a watch, O LORD, before my mouth; keep the door of my lips" (Ps. 141:3). —M.R.D.

"They say!" O pause and look within —
See how thine heart inclines to sin;
And left in dark temptations hour,
Thou, too, should'st sink beneath its power.
Pity the frail, weep o'er their fall,
But speak of good — or not at all. — Anon.

"Be careful what you say for you speak for all eternity!"

RAINBOWS

SUGGESTED SCRIPTURE READING: Genesis 9:1-17

I do set my bow in the cloud. Genesis 9:13a

Do you like to look at rainbows? Have you ever thought of the fact that while you are observing it, God, too, is making it the object of His *special attention?* Next time that "child of the storm" — that spectrum of beauty — bends over the landscape, take time to view it in the light of His certain promise to Noah, "the bow shall be in the cloud; and *I will look upon it* that I may remember the everlasting covenant" (Gen. 9:16).

After the flood, the rainbow became the gracious pledge to man and every living creature that God would never again use *water* to destroy the earth. The Apostle Peter points out, however, that there is a worse calamity coming. He warns the wicked that . . . "The heavens and the earth, which are now, by the same word are kept in store, reserved unto FIRE against the day of judgment and perdition of ungodly men" (II Peter 3:5a, 7).

Typically, the rainbow, seen upon the billows of justice, spoke of grace. It looked ahead to the Cross where God's wrath against sin would once for all be visited upon the believer's Substitute, Jesus Christ. When the *Light* of the World and the storm *clouds* of judgment met at Calvary, a beautiful bow of promise and forgiveness came into view. Its soft beauty and gracious promise of eternal life ever delights the spiritual eye. It is a token that we shall someday live with God in fellowship with all the saints around the rainbow circled throne (Rev. 4:1-3).

Just a practical application: The clouds of life, too, will always produce the rainbow of His promise if we allow the light of God to fall upon them. His comfort in sorrow is assured for He has said, "When I bring a cloud . . . *the bow shall be in (it)* . . . and I WILL REMEMBER!" —H.G.B.

> Though today the clouds are drifting
> Far across the stormy sea,
> There's a rainbow shining somewhere
> That will someday shine for me. — A. Campbell

"In the tears of His saints God sees a rainbow."

SIXTY-SIX CHAPTERS

SUGGESTED SCRIPTURE READING: II Timothy 4:1-8

All scripture is given by inspiration of God.

II Timothy 3:16

We commonly speak of the 66 Books of the Bible from Genesis to Revelation, but in reality there is only one book of the Bible, consisting of 66 chapters. They are all written by the same author, the Holy Spirit, and have one message, redemption. There is no other book like it. 40 different writers were used, from Moses to John. Written over a period of some 1600 years by all sorts of men, including shepherds, kings, fishermen, and philosophers, they never contradict one another, but all are in perfect agreement and harmony.

Can you imagine 40 different physicians and surgeons writing entirely independently of each other, from seven different countries speaking many different languages, and bringing forth over a period of 1600 years a reliable textbook on medicine? Then think of taking these writings composed by these 40 men independent of each other and using them as a textbook for the treatment of any particular disease! Imagine putting all these writings into one volume. What a mess it would make! All the superstitions of 1500 years ago, all the blunders of ancient medical practice, from the days of darkness when men used spirit incantations, witchcraft, and all sorts of foolish expedients and traditions for the treatment of disease, down to this time with our ultra-modern, scientific methods of treating the illnesses and the weaknesses of men. How would you like to treat a patient from that kind of a book, or rather, how would you like to be treated by a doctor who used that kind of book? You see immediately how absurd the entire thing becomes. But not so with the Bible. It is unique. Moses, writing 1600 years before the last book of the Bible was penned, was just as modern and scientific as Paul, John, or any other author or present day investigator.

DON'T NEGLECT THIS MIRACLE BOOK!   —M.R.D.

Holy Bible, book divine,
Precious treasure, thou art mine. — J. Burton

"Man by himself could not have written the Bible if he would, and would not if he could." — J. WESLEY

BALM FOR THE PERSECUTED

SUGGESTED SCRIPTURE READING: John 15:18-25

The servant is not greater than his lord.   John 15:20

When one is persecuted it is easy to indulge in self-pity. Sulking and complaining, however, is not the path of spiritual victory. Jesus set us a better example of patient endurance and sweet submission. This should ever be our pattern, for "the servant is not greater than his lord."

I recently read a true incident that well illustrates this truth. It seems that some years ago, a pastor of a small church in a little village became exceedingly discouraged due to persecution. Because of his trials he soon became an inveterate grumbler. He found fault with his brethren and complained that they did not treat him fairly. Sometime went by and then one day a fellow minister came to assist him in special meetings. At the close of one of the services, the persecuted pastor took his visitor into his confidence while they were awaiting dinner. "You have no idea of my troubles here," he said. "My congregation treats me very badly." "Oh," said the other, "Did they spit in your face?" . . . "No, they haven't come to that." . . . "Did they ever smite you?" . . . "No" . . . "Did they ever crown you with thorns?" . . . The complaining pastor bowed his head and said nothing. The other replied, "Your Master and mine was thus treated and yet He opened not His mouth." The effect of this conversation was wonderful. After a few more words of exhortation they both bowed in prayer and earnestly sought to possess the mind that was in Christ Jesus.

During the ten day's meetings that followed, the discontented pastor had a radical change in his attitude. Things improved for him and he became a power for God, winning many to the Saviour. He was never heard to complain again, and his parishioners knew him from that day on as a dedicated man who had "sold out to Christ"!

Our Lord was willing to suffer, are you?   H.G.B.

> And so, whate'er thy cross may be,
> From God accept it willingly;
> But reckon Christ, — His life — His power
> To keep, in thy most trying hour. — Anon.

"Persecution separates the wheat from the chaff."

THE WONDERFUL CHANGE

SUGGESTED SCRIPTURE READING: II Timothy 2:11-19

Ye turned to God from idols.　　I Thessalonians 1:9b

Salvation by faith in Jesus Christ is one of the most momentous transactions imaginable. We are made alive after being dead in trespasses and sins. The greatest evidence of the power of the Gospel is the change it produces in the believer. The thief is made honest, the harlot virtuous, the blasphemer a worshiper, and the liar dependable. The world has no answer to a changed and godly life.

The story is told of an old Fijian chief and an English earl, an infidel, who visited the islands.

The Englishman said to the chief: "You are a great chief, and it is really a pity that you have been so foolish as to listen to the missionaries who only want to get rich among you. No one nowadays would believe any more in that old Book which is called the Bible; neither do men listen to that old story about Jesus Christ. People know better now, and I am only sorry for you that you are so foolish."

When he said that, the old chief's eyes flashed, and he answered: "Do you see that great stone over there? On that stone we smashed the heads of our victims to death. Do you see that native oven over yonder? In that oven we roasted the human bodies for our great feasts. Now, you! If it had not been for these good missionaries, that old Book, and the great love of Jesus Christ, which has changed us from savages into God's children, you! you would never leave this spot! You have to thank God for the Gospel, as otherwise you would be killed and roasted in yonder oven, and we would feast on your body in no time!"　　—M.R.D.

What a wonderful change in my life has been wrought
Since Jesus came into my heart!
I have light in my soul for which long I have sought,
Since Jesus came into my heart. — R. McDaniel

"There is no solid basis for salvation, or true civilization either for that matter, but in the Word of God."

"BOOK OF REMEMBRANCE"

SUGGESTED SCRIPTURE READING: Revelation 20:12-15

Then they that feared the LORD spake often one to another: and the LORD hearkened, and heard it, and a book of remembrance was written before him. Malachi 3:16

The other day a dear Christian friend visited me at my office and unburdened his heart concerning a spiritual matter. We spoke then of God's leading, of the sweetness of our Saviour, and how the "steps of a good man are ordered by the Lord"! We rejoiced in the God of our salvation and bowed together in a heart-felt moment of prayer. As he rose to go, he shook my hand and said, "Isn't it wonderful to know that when two or three of us who love the Lord get together and meditate, and pray, and talk of His preciousness, that He is not only in our midst, but writes it all down in His 'Book of Remembrance'?" . . .

I had not thought of it quite like that before, but was blessed when a bit later I read the thrilling confirmation in Malachi 3:16! Perhaps this was not the primary interpretation, I thought; but certainly it was a warranted application of the text. It refreshed my soul anew when the Holy Spirit brought to my attention the corroborating words of the Psalmist: "I am poor and needy; yet *the Lord thinketh upon me!*" (Ps. 40:17)

In Malachi the word "remembrance" in the original denotes "a memorial." It reminded me of the "Hanging Gardens" of Nebuchadnezzar and the Pyramids of the Pharaohs. What insignificant monuments of time these are compared to the eternal scroll of God's "Book of Memories"! . . . How many words of memorial have been written there on your account? If you are writing only upon "the sands of time" that are reserved unto fire, the words of Job will apply: "Your remembrances are like unto *ashes*"! (Job 13:12) But if your deeds are penned in glowing letters of light upon God's Book, then the Psalmist was speaking of you when he exclaimed, "The righteous shall be *in everlasting remembrance*"! (Ps. 112:6)　　　　　　　　　　— H.G.B.

Nothing is lost that is done for the Lord,
Let it be ever so small,
The smile of the Saviour approveth the deed,
As though it were the greatest of all!
— Author Unknown

The world may little notice us, but the word in Isaiah stands fast: "Yet will I not forget thee!" (Isa. 49:15)

TRUE AND FALSE REPENTANCE

SUGGESTED SCRIPTURE READING: James 1:22-27

I have sinned.   Exodus 9:27

Seven different men in the Bible are recorded as uttering the three words, "I have sinned." Five of these did not manifest true repentance, and their words were uttered in unbelief. These five men were Pharaoh (Ex. 9:27), Achan (Josh. 7:20), Balaam (Num. 22:34), King Saul (I Sam. 15:24), and Judas Iscariot (Matt. 27:4). The other two who confessed, "I have sinned" were believers; namely, Job (Job 7:20) and the returning prodigal (Luke 15:18).

1. Pharaoh said "I have sinned," because he was gripped with fear caused by the terrible plagues which had come upon Egypt. It was a repentance of fear, not sorrow for his sin.

2. Achan said "I have sinned" because he was caught in the act and hoped to mitigate his punishment by a "forced" confession.

3. Balaam uttered his confession as an excuse of ignorance. He said he did not know God was speaking through the ass about an angel in the way.

4. King Saul's confession came because he was rejected by God as king. It was a confession of remorse.

5. Judas' confession of sin was a cry of hopeless despair, which resulted in suicide.

6. Job's confession, "I have sinned," was a cry of agony, from a believer, seeking light.

7. Another true confession was uttered by the returning prodigal. It was sorrow over sin. There are two kinds of repentance. When Jane's little brother after being mean to her said, "I am sorry," she replied, "What kind of sorry, the kind of sorry that you won't do it again?"

There is a sorrow over the punishment of sin, and a sorrow for sin, itself.   —M.R.D.

> I've wasted many precious years,
> Now I'm coming home;
> I now repent with bitter tears,
> Lord, I'm coming home. — W. Kirkpatrick

"True repentance means not only a heart broken FOR sin, but FROM sin."

"KILL THE SPIDER"!

If any man would come after me (Jesus), let him deny HIMSELF. Matthew 16:24

Except a corn of wheat fall into the ground and DIE, it abideth alone: but if it die, it bringeth forth much fruit! John 12:24

Many misinterpret the words of Jesus in Matthew! They suppose that He is here advocating abstinence from certain worldly joys and pleasures: a sort of year-'round "Lent!" What Jesus is really saying, however, as is obvious especially from the original, is that a man who would follow Him must deny that "which is *of himself.*" In other words, *crucify* the "ego!" For unless we "die to self" and let Christ live in us, we cannot bring forth "much fruit!" Lopping off a few sins or pleasures here or there is not the answer. That is merely pruning a tree which should be *uprooted!*

Someone has rightly observed:

> The last enemy destroyed in the believer is *SELF!* It dies hard. It will make any concession if allowed to live. Self will permit the believer to do anything, give anything, sacrifice anything, suffer anything, be anything, go anywhere, take any liberties, bear any crosses, afflict soul or body to any degree. . . . *ANYTHING* . . . if it can only live. It will permit any rival if it can only have first place.

How we cherish the "I" in our life and conversation! But hear Jesus' Word: "He that loveth his life shall lose it; and he that hateth his life in this world shall keep it unto life eternal" (John 12:25)! The story is told of an old deacon who used to pray at prayer meeting and invariably concluded with the words: "And, oh Lord, clean all the *cobwebs* out of my life!" Finally it got too much for one fellow who lived next door to this self-seeking, carnal Christian, so one Wednesday night when the old man made that prayer again this fellow jumped to his feet and shouted, "Lord, don't do it! Don't do it! Make him KILL THE SPIDER!" Beloved, we too need to do the same! —H.G.B.

Wholly Thine, my Lord, to go when Thou dost call;
Thine to yield my very self, till Thou art all in all.
— Annie Hawks

"The Christian life is full of paradoxes: 'Poor, . . . and yet rich; dead to self, yet alive unto God; the world's dirt, but God's jewels!'" — T. MANTON

THREE DELIVERANCES

Who delivered us from so great a death, and doth deliver: in whom we trust that he will yet deliver us.

II Corinthians 1:10

Three "deliverances" are mentioned in this verse: a "past" deliverance, "present" deliverance, and a "future" deliverance. Our salvation is a complete salvation, but it is not experienced all at once. Part of our redemption is past, part of it is going on now, and part still lies in the future. Spiritually we have been justified once for all (Romans 5:1); but the sanctification of our soul is a daily process (Peter 3:18). The redemption of our bodies is future at the return of Christ (Rom. 8:23; Phil. 3:20, 21).

There is far more to salvation than merely escaping hell or going to heaven when we die. Our salvation includes more than "saving our souls." It includes also the redemption of our bodies (I Cor. 15:51-54).

Jesus "hath" delivered us, He "doth" deliver us, and He "will yet" deliver us. Our salvation includes justification of our "spirit," sanctification of our "soul," and glorification of our "body." When man fell the fall was complete. His spirit died immediately, his soul degenerated progressively, and his body died ultimately. Redemption follows the same order. We are justified in the spirit *IMMEDIATELY*. We are sanctified in our souls progressively, and will be glorified in our bodies ultimately. Christ is a complete Saviour. As prophet, He justified; as priest, He sanctifies; as king, when He comes again, He will glorify us. These bodies of pain, suffering and death will also be transformed into painless, deathless, sinless bodies to dwell in perfect bliss forever and ever.

Praise ye the Lord! —M.R.D.

There is a song of triumph
They sing upon that shore,
Saying, Jesus has redeemed us
To suffer nevermore:
Then, casting our eyes backward
On the race which we have run,
We'll shout there loud, Hosanna,
DELIVERANCE HAS COME!
— J. Matthias

"Heaven is the day of which grace is the dawn!" — GUTHRIE

THE MUCH TRAVELED "BROADWAY"

SUGGESTED SCRIPTURE READING: Psalm 1

Wide is the gate, and broad is the way, that leadeth to destruction, and many there be which go in thereat.
Matthew 7:13b

A certain earl, who once held the office of King's Jester, always enjoyed a practical joke. One day when he was out driving along the English countryside, he decided to have some fun with a little urchin he saw playing in the fields. Bringing his horses to a stop and winking slyly at his riding companions, he called to the boy, "I say, lad, . . . which is the way to hell?" Possibly the boy misunderstood his question, but at all events he replied without a moment's hesitation, "Go straight on sir; *you'll soon be there!*" The smile faded from the man's face, and it is reported that through this simple conversation the Holy Spirit brought conviction and salvation to his soul.

All of us by nature are on the "broadway" of death that slants toward perdition. In Psalm 51:5 we read, "Behold, I was shapen in iniquity, and *in sin did my mother conceive me.*" Galatians 3:22 declares, "the Scripture hath concluded *all* under *sin*"; and I Kings 8:46 reminds us that "there is *no man* that *sinneth not.*"

The "broadway" of sin is an easy road, filled with a pleasure-mad, hilarious crowd; yet at the end it drops off into the abyss of eternal doom (Rom. 6:23; Matt. 13:41, 42). The wicked, without exception, "shall be turned into hell" (Ps. 9:17). Only as we seek the "narrow way" of the Cross and turn to the Lord Jesus Christ, can we expect to enter eternal life (Matt. 7:14).

"Don't trouble yourself about me, sir; I'll slip into heaven with the crowd someday," said a careless sinner to a Christian worker. "But, my friend," said the soul winner, *"the crowd is going the wrong way.* If you slip in with them, you will slip into hell!" The young man was shocked. He had not thought of that . . . Have you?
—H.G.B.

The "narrow road" points heavenward;
It is the upward path.
The way of sin is easy now;
But, oh, its end is wrath. — G. W.

"Hell is easy to locate. It lies at the end of a Christless life."

THE BLESSING OF BURDENS

SUGGESTED SCRIPTURE READING: II Corinthians 12:6-9

. . . . Most gladly therefore will I rather glory in my infirmities, that the power of Christ may rest upon me.
II Corinthians 12:9

Paul, the great Apostle, has set us a blessed example in regard to suffering. In the face of crushing conditions he exclaimed, "I take pleasure in infirmities, in reproaches, in necessities, in persecutions, in distresses for Christ's sake: for when I am weak, then am I strong" (II Cor. 12:10). As Christians we have no right to allow ourselves to stagger into spiritual defeat beneath the load laid upon us, crushing though at times it may seem to be. Our trials are to cause us to rejoice and glory, for we should realize that God is making us *weak* that He may bestow upon us *the power of Christ!* He would teach us not to glory in our own insignificant, self-centered, sham vitality, but rather in His Almighty, never-failing strength!

There was once an old "grandfather's clock" that had stood for three generations in the same corner, faithfully ticking off the minutes, hours and days. In it was a heavy weight that was pulled to the top each night in order to keep the clock running. "Too bad," thought the new owner, "that such an old clock should have to bear so great a load." So he took the heavy weight off the hook and removed it from the clock. At once the old clock stopped ticking. "Why did you do that?" asked the clock. "I wanted to lighten your burden," said the man. "Please," said the clock, "put it back. *That is what keeps me going!*" Too many are looking for an easy way out of life. They think that if they had no burdens they could live pleasantly and triumphantly. They do not realize that God often keeps us *up spiritually* by keeping us *down physically!* The weight of trial gives our feet spiritual traction. Not only does our burden bless us here, but remember, it also "worketh for us a far more exceeding and eternal weight of glory" (II Cor. 4:17). —H.G.B.

One day at a time, and the day is His day:
He hath numbered its hours, though they haste or delay,
His grace is sufficient; we walk not alone;
As the day, so the strength that He giveth His own!
— Annie Johnson Flint

"Your present burden is but the weight of the Potter's hand forming you for His eternal purpose." — G.W.

FAITH AND WORKS

SUGGESTED SCRIPTURE READING: James 2:21-26

Ye see then how that by works a man is justified, and not by faith only.   James 2:24

We have no right to expect God to do things for us which we are able to do for ourselves. We must use the means and do our part, and then God assumes the responsibility of blessing. If we do not sow the seed — faith in God for a harvest is sheer mockery. If we do not use the remedies God has placed within our reach, it is useless to trust Him for healing. If we do not witness for Him, we cannot expect souls to be saved; for praying alone will not do it.

I read a story somewhere about a father who took his little boy on a fishing trip to his cottage beside the river. Upon arrival they baited a number of hooks on a trotline, strung it out into the stream, and then retired to the cabin. After an hour they lifted the line, and sure enough, there were several fish. Gleefully the little fellow shouted. "I knew it, Daddy. I knew all the time that we would catch fish." The hooks were re-baited and visited again after an hour, and again they removed several fish from the line. Once more the little lad shouted, "I knew it all the time, Daddy, even before you pulled in the line." To the question how he knew, the little lad replied, "I prayed to Jesus for fish on the line and I knew they would be there." Again the line was reset and just at sundown they pulled it in and — *not a fish!* Sadly the lad looked at his father and said, "I knew there would be no fish this time because I didn't pray about it." "And why didn't you pray this time?" asked the father; and the lad replied, "Because you forgot to bait the hooks."

Are your hooks baited with prayer, testimony, a godly life, faithful distribution of tracts and gospel literature and a life of separation and holiness? You can't catch fish on a bare hook. Before you go to work today, take time to bait your hooks.   —M.R.D.

You are writing a gospel, A chapter each day,
By deeds that you do, By words that you say.
Men read what you write, Whether faithless or true,
Say! What is the gospel according to *YOU*? — Anon

"God can't use anybody until they are willing, if necessary, to be 'fools for Christ's sake.'"

SCARLET LINES AND RED RIBBONS

SUGGESTED SCRIPTURE READING: Joshua 2:1, 9-21

> . . . and she (Rahab) bound the scarlet line in the window.
>
> Joshua 2:21

Rahab was a harlot living in the doomed city of Jericho; but by faith she "perished not with them that believed not, when she had received the spies with peace" (Heb. 11:31). She associated herself with the line of Christ and the blood of redemption by hanging an identifying scarlet cord in her window. She thus escaped the judgment that overtook those not under the blood (Joshua 6:22-25).

The story is told of one who in passing through a village in Basutoland noticed to his surprise some chickens with little red ribbons fastened to their backs between their wings. Asking the owners of the flock what the ribbons were there for, he received the following reply: "They protect the chickens from the many vicious hawks that otherwise would attack them. The hawks are afraid of the red ribbons. During my fifteen years in this African village, I have never known of a chicken with a red ribbon being taken by a hawk, while hundreds of others, not so shielded, have fallen prey to the danger from the sky. Neither blue, nor green, nor any other color will provide the needed immunity from attack." What a lesson for all of us. We too need the protection of the "scarlet ribbon of Christ's blood," for He alone can shield us from the just wrath and doom which awaits unredeemed sinners, and keep us from the onslaughts of Satan who otherwise would take us "captive at his will."

Rahab and her household were safe while dwelling under the shelter of the scarlet cord. Are you securely tied to the love of God by the red ribbon of the atoning blood? —H.G.B.

> For Jesus shed His precious blood
> Rich blessings to bestow;
> Plunge now into the crimson flood
> That washes white as snow. — J. H. Stockton

"Our scarlet sins viewed through the blood of crimson Calvary are white as snow (Isa. 1:18)."

TOO BUSY

SUGGESTED SCRIPTURE READING: Ecclesiastes 3:1-14

And as thy servant was busy here and there, he was gone.

I Kings 20:40

God's prophet told a sad story about himself to king Ahab. It was the sad confession of a soldier to whom had been committed the safe-keeping of a prisoner of war. To allow such a prisoner to escape was a crime of the gravest nature. His one duty was to guard that prisoner day and night. He was excused from every other duty but this one, to see that the prisoner did not escape to carry valuable information to the enemy. But this servant neglected his important duty and busied himself with unimportant and non-essential details. His sad but honest confession was "while thy servant was busy here and there — he was gone." This man was busy, but not with the most important things. What a lesson for us today. We, too, have a responsibility to be witnesses for Christ and to win others to Him. But how often we are too busy "here and there" and forget the most important task.

A visitor in America once drove to Niagara Falls about which he had heard so much. He had come hundreds of miles to see the great sight. When about seven miles from the falls he thought he could hear the roar of water, and seeing a man in a field, inquired. "Are those the falls I hear?" The man replied, "It could be, I don't know, but it could be. What of it if it is?" With surprise the visitor asked, "Do you live here?" "Born and raised here," was the answer. "And yet you don't know if that is the thunder of the falls?" "No, stranger," he said, "I have never seen them; I am too busy with my farm."

Are you missing God's best today, because you are *too busy?*

—M.R.D.

> Slow me down, Lawd, I's agoin' too fast,
> I can't see my brother when he's walkin' past
> I miss a lot o' good things day by day,
> I don't know a blessin' when it comes my way.
> Slow me down, Lawd, *I'S AGOIN' TOO FAST!*
> — Old Spiritual

"Let it be a subject of daily prayer, as well as an object of daily endeavor, to do our right work at the right time." — N. MAC LEOD

PROFITABLE LABOR!

S<small>UGGESTED</small> S<small>CRIPTURE</small> R<small>EADING</small>: I Timothy 6:1-12

*For as much as ye know that your labor is not in vain in
the Lord.*   I Corinthians 15:58

On Labor Day you'll hear much about "enobling toil" and the
glory of industry. Yet, social inequality, physical disabilities, and
many other considerations often result in disillusionment, frustration and heartbreak; but, praise God, there is One who regards
all our efforts and properly evaluates our labors. If all our work
is sanctified by being done for His glory, then it shall have its
abundant reward by and by. Especially is this true of our spiritual
endeavors.

Some years ago a young girl lay dying. She already had tasted
the bitterness of life's sorrows, having lost her mother when only
eight years of age. A visitor asked her: "Are you afraid to die,
dear?" "Oh, no!" she whispered weakly. "But what shall I say to
Jesus when I meet Him, for I do not remember doing anything
worthwhile for Him? You see, mother died when I was eight. I
tried to do as she had done, and took care of the four little ones;
I kept the house tidy, and then I was too tired to do more!" Taking the rough little hand of the dying girl in her own, the Christian
lady, eyes filled with tears, said tenderly, "I would not say a thing,
dear, but just show Him your toil-worn hands, and He will understand and say, 'Well done'!" Thus encouraged, the faithful "little
mother" soon went to be with the Righteous Judge who gives
praise to every faithful servant.

We, too, may rejoice knowing that our "labor is not in vain in
the Lord."   —H.C.B.

Grant me, Oh Lord, the strength today
For every task which comes my way.
Grant me to live this one day through
Up to the best that I can do!
Through Jesus Christ our Lord, Amen! — Anon.

**"Work is not a curse, but rather God's boon; the more pious a Christian
is, the more industrious will be his labors!"**

BAD MEMORIES

Suggested Scripture Reading: Romans 16:1-16

Alexander the coppersmith did me much evil.
II Timothy 4:14

The only memory Paul had of Alexander was that he had done him much evil. How sad to be remembered only for the evil which one has committed. How much better to be remembered for the good we have done. A boyhood friend and I were talking and reminiscing on our childhood experiences. Said my friend, "Do you remember John . . . ?" "Yes," I replied, "I remember just one thing about him and that is all. I recall how he once threw a rotten tomato in my face." That was the only thing I remembered about this fellow. That one thing stood out in my memory. I remember another person for just one act. It was a dear old lady. I never learned her name, but she took me as a little lad, bandaged a cut finger for me, and gave me a cookie.

Just a little thing. I never saw her again, but that little act stands out in my memory. For what will you be remembered? For the good you have done or the evil? Will people remember you as a true Christian by your words and conduct today, or will only unpleasant thoughts be suggested when your name is mentioned?

All Paul seemed to remember about Alexander was the evil he had done. How different with the list of names in Romans 16: Priscilla, Aquila, Epaenetus, Mary, Andronicus, Junia, Amplias, Urbane, Apelles, Herodion, Tryphena, Tryphosa, Persis, Rufus, etc., etc. All these were remembered by Paul for "their work of faith and labor of love." As you go to work today, will men see Christ in you? Will they think of *Him* when they remember you?

—M.R.D.

When sunset comes and life is o'er,
And we set sail for heaven's shore,
What works will follow us below;
What mem'ries bless through afterglow?
— G. Woods

"When the seed of faithfulness to God is sown, it brings forth the blossoms of blessed memories here and the fruit of eternal reward over there." — G.W.

RETRIBUTION

SUGGESTED SCRIPTURE READING: Matthew 7:1-5

> *. . . with what measure ye mete, it shall be measured*
> *to you again.* Matthew 7:2

Making hasty, unjust judgments concerning others is sin. The Pharisees of Jesus' day seemed to be especially adept at back-biting and attempting to elevate themselves by tearing down and slandering the character of others. Those who have true piety, however, exhibit love and charity toward their neighbors. The easiest way to lose humility and end up upon the prideful pedestal of self-satisfaction is to attempt to judge others. Also we will find that there is a law of retribution operative in life. If we are censorious, we can expect others in turn to be critical of us. We will reap what we sow *with interest!* The spoon will seem twice as large when we have to take a dose of our own medicine.

A baker living in a small town made it a habit to buy his butter from a certain neighborhood farmer. One day he became sus-picious that the butter was not of the same weight as it had been at first. He concluded that the rolls were gradually diminishing in size. This angered the baker so that he had the farmer arrested. "I presume you have weights," said the judge. "No sir," replied the farmer. "How then do you manage to weigh the butter that you sell?" "That's easy," said the farmer, "when the baker com-menced buying his butter from me, I thought I had better get my bread from him, and it's his own one pound loaf that I have been using as the weight for the butter I sell. If the weight of the but-ter is wrong he has only himself to blame." Sin is like that. If it becomes the rule of our lives, it turns upon us to betray us when we least expect it. The deceiver then becomes the deceived. De-pend upon it; the law of retribution will catch up with you!

—H.C.B.

> Don't be too hard on the man who sins,
> For the yardstick you lay on another
> Will someday be used to measure you;
> Oh "judge not," be gracious, my brother! — G.W.

"The best Christians are those who are always more interested in re-forming themselves, than in censuring others."

BAREFOOTED BUT HAPPY

SUGGESTED SCRIPTURE READING: Psalm 111

. . . I have learned, in whatsoever state I am, therewith to be content. Philippians 4:11

I read a story somewhere of a Christian who was reduced to such poverty that he had only one pair of shoes, with the soles worn through and his toes sticking out. Depressed and discouraged he walked down the street mumbling to himself: "I might as well be barefooted as to wear these miserable, uncomfortable shoes." He felt himself becoming more and more bitter, when suddenly he came upon a man sitting on the sidewalk begging. The poor fellow had no feet—not even legs. Then the discouraged Christian realized that there is something worse than "old shoes." It is having no feet to put shoes on! Are you given to complaining? Then look about you and see how much worse it could be.

In Hebrews 13:5 the author says, "Be content with such things as ye have." Why? Listen to the answer: "for he hath said, I will never leave thee nor forsake thee." No matter how dark the day, the believer has with him One who knows all about it and will not permit us to be tested "above that we are able" (I Cor. 10:13). True contentment is a "state of faith" and a frame of mind. The most miserable people are often those who have the most of this world's goods, while some of the happiest are those humble believers who have *nothing but Christ*. A poor, penniless old lady was asked, "Why are you so happy all the time? I see you have only two teeth left in your mouth." Her answer is a lesson in appreciation, "Yes," said the aged Christian, "I have only two teeth left, but I thank God each day, these *two are opposite each other*, so I can still chew with them." —M.R.D.

O for the peace of perfect trust,
My loving God in Thee;
Unwavering faith that never doubts
Thou choosest best for me.
So may I learn to be content,
Whate'er my lot may be! — Anon.

"Anxiety springs from the desire that things should happen to us as we wish, rather than as God wills."

FRUIT AFTER DEATH

SUGGESTED SCRIPTURE READING: II Corinthians 9:6-10

. . . he being dead yet speaketh. Hebrews 11:4

When a Christian dies many people say, "Well, he has gone to his *reward.*" We understand what they mean, but technically they are incorrect, for long after a Christian is dead his reward continues to add up. You see, every act we do for the Lord here sends out ripples of influence which touch lives until the end of time. That is what the Scripture means when it says, "the fruit of the righteous is a *tree of life*": what we do continues to *branch out* so that when we stand someday before the Lord, we will be amazed at what has developed from the seed we have sown. The man who led Dwight L. Moody to the Lord will have part interest in all of the souls and the good work which Moody did, and then in turn a smaller fraction of what Moody's converts accomplished, etc., etc. Only God, therefore, could possibly mete out a just reward to each of His own children, and then only at the time of the harvest after the full fruit of their deeds has become manifest.

"Mother," said a sweet Christian girl one evening, "I want you to give me a little apple tree in our orchard." "Why, my child? They are all yours for they belong to our family." "Yes, but I mean something different. I should like to have a little tree for my very own and the apples which it bears I would like to give as a present to the Lord." The child was allowed to choose a tree. Placing her hand on the trunk, she said, "Little tree, now you belong to the Lord Jesus." Sometime later the mother sent a gift to some missionaries and after relating the above incident, continued: "Our little one was suddenly taken home to be with the Lord. She has now been a year in heaven, and this year the tree bore fruit for the first time. I am enclosing what we received from the sale of the apples." Yes, Christians may "rest from their labors; (but) their *works do follow them.*" —H.G.B.

When on that day we all shall meet
Our Saviour at the judgment seat,
The seeds now scattered far and wide
Will — with His blessing — sheaves provide. — C.H.F.

"The present moment is divinely sent. Make good use of it that it may bear fruit to the end of time."

SELF- INSPECTION

Suggested Scripture Reading: Psalm 32.1-11

I acknowledged my sin unto thee.   Psalm 32:5

How easy it is for us to see the faults of others, and how unpleasant and difficult to acknowledge our own. The three hardest words in our language are, "I was wrong." It is a mark of real grace in the heart when one is not ashamed to admit his own sin. It is so easy to find fault with others when we ourselves may be unconscious of even greater faults in our own lives. Sensitiveness to other's faults is very often only a smokescreen to draw attention away from our own failures. The easiest thing in the world is to find fault with others, when we should be doing something constructive. A dog who had been trained to pull a lawn mower stopped pulling the mower to bark at another dog passing by. The boy who was guiding the mower said to a boy watching him, "Don't mind the dog, he is just barking for an excuse to rest. It is easier to bark then to pull this machine."

It is easier to be critical than to be correct, easier to bark than to work, easier to burn down a house than to build one, easier to hinder than to help. Destruction of reputation is easier than construction of character.

It is said that when the judges met to consider their humble address to the Queen of England on the occasion of her Jubilee in 1887, not a little opposition was raised to the insertion of the words, "conscious as we are of our shortcomings"; and that thereupon Lord Justice Bowen suggested, in his gentlest tone, that the phrase should run, "conscious as we are of one another's shortcomings."

We are not admonished to confess our neighbors' faults, but to confess *our* faults one to another. "If we confess *our* sins, he is faithful and just to forgive." As long as a mule is *kicking*, he makes no progress.   —M.R.D.

I used to censure everyone,
I was a Pharisee;
Until quite unexpectedly,
I got a glimpse of me. — Anon.

"Knockers are the folks who try to cover their own faults by talking about the faults of others."

TOO LARGE A PURSE?

Charge them that are rich . . . that they be rich in good works, ready to distribute, willing to communicate.
I Timothy 6:17, 18

The story is told of a prosperous Scotsman who was often asked by his pastor to give liberally to the work of evangelizing the poor in the city of Glasgow but who always received the reply: "Na, I need it for myself." One night this miser dreamed that he was at the very gates of heaven, which were only a few inches ajar. He tried to get in, but could not. Soon he was in agony because of his inability to squeeze through the narrow opening. Suddenly the face of his minister appeared before him admonishing him as follows: "Sandy, why stand ye glowering there? Why don't ya gae in?" "I can't; I'm too large and my pocketbook sticks out whichever way I turn." "Sandy, think how mean ye have been to the Lord's poor, and you will be small enough to go through the eye of a needle," said the reprimanding pastor. Suddenly Sandy awoke and determined by the grace of God to reduce his pocketbook. Fortunately he had found, before it was too late, that a bulging purse can be a great hindrance to an abundant entrance into heaven.

You may not have much money but what are you doing with that which the Lord *has* entrusted to you? Remember *a man can drown in a pond as well as in an ocean!* You can set your affection on a hundred dollars as well as on a thousand.

Dispense earthly treasures with a heart full of love for Jesus and you will receive heavenly reward, for "the liberal soul shall be made fat." Don't let your purse become a curse!   —H.C.B.

I ask not ownership of vast estates
Nor piles of gold —
But make me generous with the little store
My hands now hold. — Anon.

"People with large purses find great difficulty in making progress on the narrow way." — G.W.

MUTTON AND TURNIPS

SUGGESTED SCRIPTURE READING: Philippians 4:10-20

But my God shall supply all your need.

Philippians 4:19

The prince of preachers, C. H. Spurgeon, tells of an incident in the orphanage which he sponsored. They were in need of food for the orphans. One day a huckster at the market stopped Mr. Spurgeon and said, "Here are six dozen bunches of turnips for the orphans, and I hope someone else will supply the mutton." When he arrived at the orphanage with the turnips, here was a farmer waiting with a sheep that he had fattened, killed and dressed for the orphanage. A coincidence you say? Yes, but who ordered it? There was no human conspiracy or agreement between the huckster and the farmer, for neither knew about the other or his intentions. There may be an affinity between turnips and mutton, but no chemical law attracted them to the door of an orphanage at the same time.

Surely God had ordered that meal, for the Father of the fatherless by the promptings of His Spirit can command the simplest agencies to provide for His own. Had the huckster withheld the turnips and the farmer brought the mutton; or had the farmer sold the sheep and the huckster given the turnips, the meal would have been incomplete. But "My God shall supply *all* your need," yes *all!*

To refuse to give mutton because we cannot give turnips, or to withhold turnips because we cannot furnish a sheep is to forget that God can bring our *need* together. God is a God of detail. Giving what we have is to trust God to supply the rest. Give what you have — He asks no more. Thus God sets the table for all.

—M.R.D.

He clothes the lilies, feeds the birds;
Would He to you, then, pay less heed?
Look up to Him with prayerful heart,
He will supply your every need. — Anon.

"Nothing with God is accidental. The steps of Providence are often only comprehended as we look back upon them."

ON BEING KIND

SUGGESTED SCRIPTURE READING: I Corinthians 13:1-4a

And be ye kind one to another, tenderhearted.

Ephesians 4:32

We used to have a neighbor who would remark about every little kindness we would show her as follows: "Oh, thank you — thank you; that is so nice. Christians would all have so much more influence if they would only remember that *the world is dying for a little bit of love!*" Although we have long moved from that neighborhood, I have never forgotten her thoughtful words of wisdom. Kindness is indeed often the only key that will open a hardened heart to the Gospel. The Rev. Ira Gillett, missionary to Portuguese East Africa, tells of a group of natives who made a long journey, walking past a nearby government hospital to come to his mission station for treatment. When asked why they had traveled the extra miles to reach the mission hospital when the same medicines were available at the government institutions, they replied, "The medicines may be the same, but *the hands are different.*" The loving kindness shown by the Christians had opened their hearts, and they listened to those who practiced what they preached.

The love of Christ should constrain us to go the extra mile and do the added deed of special consideration which will show that our heart has been made tender by the grace of God. Such conduct will make others realize that we are followers of Him who came "not to be ministered unto, but to minister, and to give His life a ransom for many."

A mother asked her son what loving-kindness meant. "Well," he said, "when I ask you for a piece of bread and butter, and you give it to me, that's good; but *when you put jam on it, that's loving-kindness!*"

Christian, when you give others the "bread of life" do you seek to make it more palatable by adding the "jam of loving-kindness"? Oh that we would follow Paul's admonition and approve "ourselves as the ministers of God . . . by *kindness,* by the Holy Ghost, and by love unfeigned" (II Cor. 6:4, 6).   —H.C.B.

> God, make me kind!
> So many hearts are needing
> The balm to stop the bleeding
> That my kind words can bring.
> *GOD, MAKE ME KIND!* — D.M.

"If you are not very kind, you are not very holy!"

TOO CLOSE TO THE EDGE

SUGGESTED SCRIPTURE READING: II Timothy 2:1-10

. . . go forward. Exodus 14:15

The day of our conversion is but the first step in a journey which can never end until we reach the final goal of perfection. We are to go constantly forward (see Luke 9:6). This was God's command to Israel as they faced the Red Sea. They were out of Egypt but their goal was the land of Canaan — the place of victory. And so the Lord says, "Go forward." We are not to look back at our old life, but to press on and on, growing in "grace and in the knowledge of our Lord and Saviour Jesus Christ." When Israel looked back to Egypt and said, "We remember the onions, leeks and garlic," they were delayed in the progress and turned back to wander in the wilderness. When Lot's wife "looked back" she was turned into a pillar of salt.

Are you going forward? As you review the years of your Christian experience, how much progress can you see? The farther we go toward Canaan, the farther we will leave Egypt behind. Too many Christians try to see how closely they can live to Egypt, without going back into it. They try to see how close they can drive to the edge of a cliff without actually falling into the gorge. Today, as you mingle with people, don't live close to the world but stay as far away from the line of separation as possible.

A little boy fell out of his bed while he was asleep. His mother asked him, "Tommy, why did you fall out of bed?" The answer was childishly simple but emphatically true. He said, "I guess, mamma, it was because I stayed too close to the gettin' in place." Some Christians are always falling out of bed because they stay too close to the "gettin' in place." Will men know today you are a separated Christian or will you walk so close to the line which distinguishes the saved from the unsaved, that none can see the difference? Keep thyself pure (I Tim. 5:22). —M.R.D.

> I'm pressing on the upward way,
> New heights I'm gaining ev'ry day;
> Still praying as I onward bound,
> "Lord, plant my feet on higher ground."
> — J. Oatman, Jr.

"A pint of Christian living is worth a gallon of mere idle profession."

DON'T FEAR THE SHADOWS

SUGGESTED SCRIPTURE READING: Luke 1:68-79

Yea, though I walk through the valley of the shadow of death, I will fear no evil.   Psalm 23:4

Too many Christians live in doubt and fear. We should realize, however, that "our life is hid with Christ in God" (Col. 3:3), and instead of worrying, our heart should be calm and our spirit trusting, for our Saviour is ever faithfully protecting us. He averts all evil, or otherwise turns it to our profit (Rom. 8:28).

A certain governess once frightened a child in her care with the shadows of the garden, seeking thereby to keep her from wandering away. As time went on, however, the little one became more and more obsessed with fear concerning all that lay beyond the hedges of her own estate. In reality, beyond the shadowy borders were flowers and fruits rich beyond compare and freely accessible to her. One day her elder brother took the nurse's place and sought to entice the child to run through the hedge into the neighboring garden. She cried out in the grip of mortal fear. Try as he would, he could not persuade her to advance through the shadows. She could not believe that the nurse's stories were only idle and there was actually nothing to dread. The brother then asked her if she would believe that there was no danger if he went through the hedge and came back? When he did, the child immediately took his hand and walked boldly through the momentary darkness to the bright sunshine of the glorious garden beyond. So, too, our Elder Brother, the Lord Jesus Christ, braved for us the terrors of death and came back from the shadows to tell us that the grave and earthly difficulty should no longer hold us in the grip of fear. Beyond lies the more abundant life and "pleasures forevermore." The Psalmist, anticipating these glories, exclaims, "Yea, though I walk through the valley of the shadow of death, I will fear no evil: for thou art with me." —H.G.B.

When the clouds are hanging low,
Look beyond, look beyond;
Soon the skies will overflow
With the sunlight's cheery glow,
Look beyond, look beyond. — E. E. Hewitt

"When fear knocks at your door send faith to answer it and you will find that there is no one there."

UNHAPPY IN HEAVEN

SUGGESTED SCRIPTURE READING: Revelation 22:1-7

And there shall in no wise enter into it any thing that defileth. Revelation 21:27a

The unhappiest place in the universe for an unsaved sinner would be heaven. The unregenerates, who have despised Jesus here below, would feel very much out of place with the redeemed. There would be more fellowship in hell with his old companions.

"I have just been thinking," said a Christian traveler to a profane and half-drunken coach driver with whom he had been journeying, "what would you do in heaven? There will be no coaches, horses, or harness to swear at; no saloons to drink in; no stable companions to quarrel with. What would you do in heaven?"

The question was startling, well-timed, and unexpected. It proved to be a nail in a sure place, and by the blessing of God it brought him to repentance.

There are few people, however sinful their lives, who do not cherish a vague hope that in some way they will go to heaven when they die. It does not occur to them that they might not be happy there.

What a disappointment awaits the lost when they wake up and find it is to late. What wouldn't the lost be willing to give for one last chance. The legend is told of a preacher who was addressing a listless, sleepy audience. A dark looking stranger came to him after the service — so goes the legend — and said, "Come down to hell and make us just *ONE* such offer." Today is day of salvation!

—M.R.D.

I dreamed I had gone to that city,
That city where never comes night,
And I saw the bright angels in glory,
I saw the fair mansions of light;
Then I dreamed, I searched heaven for you.
Searched vainly thru heaven for you;
Friend, won't you prepare to meet me up there?
Lest we should search heaven for you.
— M. E. Wiess

"If it were possible for one to enter heaven void of holiness, the hell of sin within would keep that one from happiness."

"DUMMY" CHRISTIANS

SUGGESTED SCRIPTURE READING: Psalm 107:1, 2

Be ready always to give an answer to every man that asketh you a reason of the hope that is in you.

I Peter 3:15

Several years ago at a Gospel meeting in the Orient a Chinese gentleman arose at the end of the service and began to cry for mercy with sighs and tears. When at length he found utterance, he prayed, "Oh, God, forgive me; I have been a *dummy Christian.* When I was converted, the devil came to me and said, 'There are preachers to do the preaching; you need not bother about it.' I listened to the devil's lie, and all these years I have been living in ease while souls have been lost." He had suddenly came to realize that the words of the Lord Jesus, "Ye are my witnesses," apply to all of His followers.

There are some sincere individuals who mistakenly believe that if they just live a Christian life, that is all that is required of them to be well pleasing to the Lord. Although of course such dedication is necessary, it loses its force unless the tongue gives the testimony point. If the redeemed do not "say so," the world usually gives the credit for the clean moral life to the individual himself. He is considered a "swell fellow," a "good sport," or a "real straight shooter." "Dummy" Christians are like beautiful road signs with words of direction painted off.

"Well, I never knew before that you were a Christian," said one man to another in a Michigan logging camp, "although we've been on the job together here for two years. In fact when the traveling evangelist was here last winter and talked to me about my soul, I told him if so clean a chap as you could get along without religion I believed that I could take a chance on it myself." The silent Christian realized that he had been disloyal to Christ.

Are you ready "always to give an answer to every man that asketh you a reason of the hope that is in you"? —H.C.B.

Only a word for Jesus!
Oh, speak it in His dear name;
To perishing souls around you
The message of love proclaim.
— F. J. Crosby

"Let your lips as well as your life speak for Christ."

OPERATION SUCCESSFUL — PATIENT DIED

SUGGESTED SCRIPTURE READING: Colossians 2:1-8

Beware lest any man spoil you through philosophy and vain deceit, after the tradition of men, after the rudiments of the world, and not after Christ. Colossians 2:8

In II Corinthians 11:3 Paul the Apostle fears that the Corinthian Christians might be "corrupted from the simplicity that is in Christ." I wonder what Paul would say if he were here today and saw our modern churches. What a beehive of complicated activity. Organizations, committees, boards, teams, programs, and entertainment without end. We have gymnasiums, poolrooms, recreation rooms, swimming pools, etc., etc. But the worship services have been reduced to one hour, with no services at night and no prayer meeting. Some call this *IMPROVEMENT* over the simple program of our forefathers; but is this progress?

A German woman when taken seriously ill was sent to the hospital. In the evening her husband inquired how she was getting along and was told that she was "improving." Next day he called again and was told she was still improving. This went on for some time. Finally, one night he was told that his wife was dead. Seeing the doctor, he went up to him and said: "Vell doctor, what did she die of — improvements?" There is a moral here for some of our churches. We know of a church that died of improvements. The first improvement was to get a "new theology" minister. The next was to get a highly trained but godless quartet; then to change the prayer meeting into a weekly literary debating society; and finally, to give up the pulpit prayers — the minister saying that God knew far better what the people needed than he could tell Him. But the church is dead — dead as a doornail, and that is as dead as anything can be. Now, if someone wants to put up a tombstone over its grave, we suggest these words and a truthful and appropriate epitaph: "Died of Improvements." —M.R.D.

A glorious band, the chosen few on whom the Spirit came;
They met the tyrant's brandished steel, the lion's gory mane;
They bowed their necks the death to feel;
WHO FOLLOWS IN THEIR TRAIN? — R. Heber

"The church had never such influence over the world as in those early days when she had nothing to do with the world."

EARS THAT HEAR!

He that hath ears to hear, let him hear!　　　Luke 14:35b

Spiritually man is *"dead* in trespasses and sins" and unless he is given new life by the Holy Spirit he "cannot *see* the kingdom of God" (John 3:3) or *hear* the voice of the Saviour! That is why unregenerated men can listen to the Gospel, read the Bible through from cover to cover, and still remain blind and deaf to the things of the Lord.

Jesus often used parables and stories to illustrate spiritual realities, and when He sought to underscore the fact that there were deeper meanings involved than those which lay upon the surface, He consistently used this phrase: "He that hath ears to hear, let him hear!" Have you by faith heard the voice of the Son of God, or have you turned away your "ears from the truth"? (II Tim. 4:4)

This story is told of John Wesley's meetings: A certain ungodly tavern keeper who was very fond of music determined to attend one of the Methodist gatherings in order to hear the singing. He resolved, however, to stop his ears as soon as this was over and not to listen to the sermon. Therefore, after the hymns were concluded he sat with his head down and his fingers in his ears. But when God will speak to a soul He can make His voice heard, even if He uses what may seem to us strange and contemptible means. As the man sat there a fly lit upon his nose. For a moment he moved his hand to drive it away, and in so doing, nine words of the speaker were brought to his attention: "He that hath ears to hear, let him hear." From that moment the man had no rest in his soul. He came to the next meeting, listened eagerly to the Gospel, and became converted!

Have *you* heard the Saviour's voice? — "Hear and your soul shall live!"　　　　　　　　　　　　　　　　　　　　　　　　—H.G.B.

I hear Thy welcome voice,
That calls me, Lord, to Thee
For cleansing in Thy precious blood
That flowed on Calvary.
　　　　　　　— L. Hartsough

"Of all the acts of men, repentance is the most sublime. The greatest of all faults is to be conscious of none." — T. CARLYLE

HE MUST INCREASE

SUGGESTED SCRIPTURE READING: Galatians 2:17-21

He must increase, but I must decrease.   John 3:30

Two little saplings grew up side by side. Through the action of the wind they crossed each other; by and by the bark of each became wounded and the sap began to mingle, until in some still day they became united together. This process went on more and more, and by and by they were firmly compacted. Then the stronger began to absorb the life of the weaker. It grew larger and larger, while the other grew smaller and smaller; then it began to wither and decline, till it finally dropped away and disappeared. Now there are two trunks at the bottom and only one at the top. Death has taken away the one; life has triumphed in the other.

There was a time when you and Jesus Christ met. The wounds of your penitent heart began to knit up with the wounds of His broken heart, and you were united to Christ. Where are you now? Are the two lives running parallel, or has the word been accomplished in you, "He must increase, but I must decrease"? Has the old life been growing less and less and less? More and more have you been mortifying it, until at last it seems almost to have disappeared? Blessed are ye, if such is the case. Then you can say, "I live; yet not I, but Christ liveth in me; and the life which I now live in the flesh, I live (not of myself, but) by the faith of the Son of God, who loved me and gave Himself for me" (Gal. 2:20). Henceforth "for me to live is Christ" (Phil. 1:21) — not two, but one. Just how far has this vital union been expressed in your experience? We are "one" with Christ. Can the world see *Him* when they look at you, or do they only see *you?* Oh, to become nothing!

—M.R.D.

Ready and willing Thee to obey,
Silent, if need be, have Thine own way;
In full submission all do I give,
Nothing withhold, Lord, in me now live.
— C. F. Warren

"The man who bows lowest in the presence of God stands the straightest in the presence of sin."

September 21

"WHOSOEVER" — MEANETH ME

Suggested Scripture Reading: Luke 15:1-10

. . . This man receiveth sinners, and eateth with them.
Luke 15:2

In Luke 15 the Lord Jesus tells three interesting and pointed stories concerning a lost sheep, a lost coin, and a lost son. These taken together illustrate the marvelous plan of redemption and form one parable of rebuke in answer to the contemptuous remarks of the Pharisees and scribes concerning our Lord's association with publicans and sinners. In the first part of the parable Jesus graphically sets forth the reason for man's unhappiness — he has wandered away from God. The second word picture, concerning the lost coin, shows man's resultant useless and helpless condition. In the last story, that of the prodigal son, we are shown the part that man has to play in the plan of redemption; he must acknowledge his condition, repent, and return to his loving Heavenly Father by the power of grace. Although God hates sin, He loves the sinner and is eager to welcome man back into the fellowship of heaven if he will only repent and believe.

A group of children one cold night decided to slip inside of a church to get warm. Soon a service began, and the preacher took for his text: "This man (Jesus Christ) receiveth sinners and eateth with them." Afterward a little girl about eight years old went up to him and said, "Please, sir, I didn't know my name was in the Bible." "And what is your name, little girl?" "Edith, sir." "No," he said, "Edith doesn't appear in the Bible." "Oh, yes, sir," she replied, "you said very plainly: Jesus Christ, receiveth sinners and EDITH with them." Her hearing may have been at fault but her theology was good. The Lord Jesus saves every John, Mary, Peter, Edith, etc., who will acknowledge their lost condition and flee to Him for salvation. If you have any *desire* to become a child of God, then remember, "Whosoever *will*" includes you!
—H.G.B.

I am happy today and the sun shines bright,
The clouds have been rolled away;
For the Saviour said, "Whosoever will"
May come to Him today. — J. E. McConnell

"Sin's worst, brought to God, is no match for His grace."

I LOVE STRAWBERRIES

SUGGESTED SCRIPTURE READING: Psalm 126

. . . Be fruitful, and multiply.　　　　　　　Genesis 1:28

I love strawberries. They are my favorite fruit. And I love strawberry plants even though I cannot eat the plants. I love them because they preached such a powerful sermon to me once. I have never been able to forget it. I was on my hands and knees in the strawberry patch, pulling out weeds, when suddenly I noticed something I had seen hundreds of times but never had caught the lesson. It was the "runners" on the berry plants. From the parent plant a number of slender shoots like arms reached out in all directions. They were thin, green stalks creeping along the ground, being pushed out by that mysterious power in the mother plant. After reaching out about six inches, the end developed roots which penetrated the ground, while the leaves of a new baby plant shot upward. All the while, before the little infant plant was able to sustain itself, it received its nourishment from the parent through the "runner." When the little plant was fixed in the ground, the "runner" resumed its journey and reached out another six inches still nourished by the mother plant. Here the process was repeated and a second plant was born. Soon the runner began to move again and a third plant resulted. And while this one "runner" was multiplying, there were several others doing the same in other directions. I forgot all about the weeds and saw only that mother plant sending out its runners in obedience to God's command, "Be fruitful and multiply." I found myself crying out, "Oh God, make me like that strawberry plant, reaching in all directions to multiply and bring forth fruit." The Christian must reproduce or the fruit-bearing soon ends. In a few years the old "plant" dies off, but its life is perpetuated through others who are our spiritual offspring. This was the sermon I listened to on my knees in my strawberry patch.

　　　　　　　　　　　　　　　　　　　　　—M.R.D.

> Go, labor on: spend and be spent,
> Thy joy to do the Father's will;
> It is the way the Master went;
> Should not the servant tread it still? — H. Bonar

"We are not merely to be 'enlightened' ourselves; but to be as lights enlightening others!" — A. R. FAUSSET

HOLY QUIETNESS

SUGGESTED SCRIPTURE READING: I Timothy 2:1-3

Be still, and know that I am God. Psalm 46:10

All of us by nature are murmurers and complainers. We question almost every act of God and man. In our arrogance and self-will, we secretly think that we could do much better if things were in *our control.* Yet, how much better off we would be, how much more sanctified and blessed, if we would only heed the words of our text, and those of the Apostle Paul to the Thessalonians, and "study to be quiet" (I Thess. 4:11).

J. R. Miller says in regard to the need for spiritual tranquillity: "Once I went to visit a friend who lay with a broken arm. 'Does it hurt you very badly?' I asked. *"Not when I keep it still!"* was the answer. This is the secret of much of the victoriousness we see in rejoicing Christians. They conquer the pain and the bitterness by keeping still. They do not ask questions, or demand to know why they have trials. They believe in God and are so sure of His love and wisdom, that they are pained by no doubt, no fear, no uncertainty. Peace is their pillow, because they have learned to just *be still.* Their quietness robs trial of its sharpness, sorrow of its bitterness, death of its sting, and grave of its victory."

Down beneath the surface of the restless sea that is agitated by storms and driven by the winds, we are told there is a deep layer of water that is never stirred. So, too, the peace of God is that *eternal calm,* which like the cushion of the sea, should lie far too deep down to be reached by external trouble.

Let us pray that we may ever have the grace to be *still* and rest our all in the compassionate and tender hands of our Father—God.

—H.G.B.

Cease your thinking, troubled Christian,
What avails your anxious cares;
God is ever thinking for you,
Jesus ev'ry burden bears.
Casting all your care upon Him,
Sink into His blessed will;
While He folds you to His bosom,
Sweetly whisp'ring, "Peace be still."
— A. B. Simpson

"The secret of peace is the constant reference of all things to the care of God."

LEFT-OVERS FOR GOD

And the residue thereof he maketh a god.   Isaiah 44:17

The residue for God! This is divine irony and sarcasm. The passage describes in detail the story of a man who cuts down a tree and uses part of it for firewood to warm himself (Isa. 44:15), and part of it is to cook his food (Isa. 44:16). He takes care of his bodily needs first. He looks after his physical comforts, using the tree to roast his meat, to warm himself and says, "Aha, I am warm, I have seen the fire." And then he gathers up the remainder of the tree. His conscience smites him, for he remembers that he had grown the tree for the purpose of making of it a god. But he has used most of it for self and there is little left of the tree but some knotty chunks and chips and shavings. He gathers them up and fashions them into a god. "And the residue thereof he maketh a god." Of course, this is divine satire and a caricature of the folly of Israel in their idol worship. God brings out in satirical irony the folly of idolatry.

But it has a lesson for us. How prone we are to be more interested in our own personal comforts and material needs than in our responsibility to God. Many parents are more concerned with the material prosperity of their children than their spiritual welfare. How often we give only the "left-overs" to God. We first take care of our comforts and bodily needs and give what is left to God instead of first giving God His part. We find little time for Bible study, prayer and testimony. Will you today — this day — put God first in your devotion, in your giving, in your responsibilities, in witnessing — or will it be only the fag ends, the shavings, and left-overs for God?   —M.R.D.

My life on the altar for Jesus
In glad dedication I lay,
To be used when and where as He pleases,
Or just set aside, as He may.
— Mrs. Morris

"They that deny themselves for Christ, shall find their joy in Christ!"
— J. MASON

PRACTICAL PRAYER

SUGGESTED SCRIPTURE READING: James 2:14-20

. . . Thy prayers and thine alms are come up for a memorial before God. Acts 10:4

What a happy combination: *prayer* and *alms* — faith and works. Works without prayer is unspiritual; prayer without works is usually hypocritical. Prayer *and* works, coupled with the will of God, is a mighty dynamo of power that gets results and comes up before God as a lasting and worthwhile "memorial."

An incident is related of a company of people that had gathered to pray for a family who were in great financial straits. While one of the deacons was offering a fervent prayer for blessing upon the family, there was a loud knock at the door. The door was opened and there stood the sturdy son of one of the local farmers. "What do you want, boy?" asked one of the elders. "Pa couldn't come, so I brought *his prayers* in the wagon," replied the boy. "What do you mean?" asked the astonished churchman. "I brought Pa's prayers. Just come and help me, please, and we'll bring them in." When they reached the wagon the fact was disclosed that "Pa's prayers" consisted of potatoes, flour, beef, oatmeal, turnips, apples, jellies, and clothing. It is said that the prayer meeting adjourned on short notice.

Prayer and alms, faith and works, should go together. It is only when there is nothing else left that we can do, that prayer has a right to stand alone. —H.G.B.

He needs them all — the open hand,
The willing feet, the praying heart —
To work together and to weave
A threefold cord that shall not part.
— Annie Johnson Flint

"Prayer that has the most power with God is that which is most consistent with our spiritual action and practice." — G. W.

THIRTY ASS COLTS

SUGGESTED SCRIPTURE READING: Matthew 6:16-24

And he (Jair) had thirty sons that rode on thirty ass colts, and they had thirty cities. Judges 10:4

Jair the Gileadite was the eighth judge of Israel, during the unsettled days before God gave the nation a king in the person of Saul. Only three verses are devoted to the record of "Jair" who judged Israel for twenty-two long years. Only three verses sum up everything he did in twenty-two years. What an empty life! The record tells us (1) that he judged Israel, (2) that he had thirty sons, (3) that these thirty sons rode on thirty ass colts and had thirty cities. And finally, (4) he died and was buried. The most important thing the historian could think of recording concerning this man was that his thirty sons rode on thirty ass colts. It must have been an impressive sight. Thirty able bodied men riding three abreast on ass colts, clothed I suppose in gaudy riding habit with all the latest foppery and vagaries of fashion, with tight breeches and blue ribboned whips and polished puttees. It was a sight one must not miss when visiting Camon.

But ludicrous and mirth provoking as all this may seem, it contains a serious thought. Not a single word is mentioned about one worthwhile thing being done by Jair in twenty-two years. The outstanding thing was a family of boys whose only ambition was to ride an ass. One wonders who were the greatest asses in the story, the sons of Jair or the mounts they rode. And the story closes with, "And Jair died and was buried." Nothing remained of all his works but thirty asses. It is the story of an empty life.

How rich and fruitful is your life, my friend? If God should call you today, how much of abiding worth would you be able to take along? —M.R.D.

Not what I have, but what I give,
Not what I know, but how I live;
Not what I wish some day to be;
But how I stand at Calvary! — Anon.

"A man of words and not of deeds, is like a garden full of weeds!"

THE "SITTING" HEART

SUGGESTED SCRIPTURE READING: Philippians 4:1-9

Peace I leave with you, my peace I give unto you.

John 14:27

There are literally hundreds of languages and dialects into which the Scripture has not yet been translated. Those who are seeking to reach these savage and little known tribes with the Gospel tell us that one of the greatest difficulties they encounter is the fact that the most significant words in the Bible have no counterpart in these languages. How do you set about telling of redeeming grace and glories of the Christian life, when there are no words like "love," "peace," "joy," or "happiness" in the dialect into which you desire to do your translating? Many of these benighted people live in such darkness and sin that these concepts of faith and blessing are completely outside of their experience.

Recently a missionary ran into this situation in trying to translate the word "peace" into very primitive, tribal jargon. There was no word that expressed it. Finally after weeks of difficulty a native, who new both his mother tongue and the more common "trade language," came running into the compound with the answer. "I have it, missionary," he said, "I know how we can make my people understand what Jesus does inside those who trust Him." "You mean you have found a word for 'peace'?" said the translator eagerly. "No! There is no *one* word, Master, but you can make them understand by telling them — *Jesus will make your heart sit down!*"

Oh, dear saint of God, are you always in a turmoil of worry and anxiety? Are you constantly fretting; or is your spirit at rest in the confidence that you are living in the blessed center of His perfect will where all evil is averted or turned to your profit? Is your heart "in your throat"; or has God made your heart "*sit down*"?

—H.G.B.

If your heart is often troubled
And you wonder what to do,
Just look up and simply trust Him,
For He'll surely take you through! — Anon.

"Peace rules the day when Christ rules the heart."

A MOUTHFUL OF GRAVEL

SUGGESTED SCRIPTURE READING: John 6:30-51

The bread of deceit is sweet to a man, but afterwards his mouth shall be filled with gravel.　　　　Proverbs 20:17

A mouthful of gravel! What spine-chilling feelings are suggested by this homely figure. It pictures a man anticipating a piece of sweet bread which he had obtained by dishonest methods — only to find upon biting into it that it is filled with stones. Have you ever had this happen? You had a bag of peanuts and you sank into a comfortable chair anticipating the relaxing exercise of doing a bit of munching! You take a handful and begin chewing with eagerness. Suddenly your teeth crash upon something other than a peanut. Like lightning a stab of pain shoots across your face — and spitting it out you find among the peanuts a pebble — and a piece of broken tooth! If you have ever experienced this, as I have, you can understand our Scripture.

The lesson is pertinent. Solomon is speaking of the bread of deceit. What is more deceitful than sin? To expect that sin will not be punished is a deception and a delusion. He who lives only for pleasure and temporal enjoyment will find himself at last with only a mouthful of gravel. Shady practices and questionable methods in business may seem to "pay off" at the time, but afterwards his "mouth shall be filled with gravel." To imagine that the things of this life can satisfy is "eating the bread of deceit." Jesus said, "Labour not for the meat that perisheth but for the meat which endureth unto everlasting life" (John 6:27). May this be our motto *TODAY*.　　　　— M.R.D.

> Let worldly minds the world pursue,
> It has no charms for me;
> Once I admired its trifles too,
> But grace has set me free! — Anon.

"As long as we feed on the husks of the world, and are in love with it, we are neither willing nor able to taste the comforts of God's love."

TRUE GREATNESS

SUGGESTED SCRIPTURE READING: Luke 22:24-30

But whosoever will be great among you, shall be your minister. Mark 10:43b

We live in an age of power where "greatness" is a byword. This desire to dominate, this struggle for superiority has even touched the Church of Jesus Christ. Men vie with one another for places of prominence and influence. The ones who can generate the largest meetings or build the greatest organizations are considered models of spiritual excellency. Although there are men of God who are doing extraordinary things for the Lord today, we are prone to forget that many obscure but faithful servants of Christ are working the stony, unproductive places. These, although unnoticed and often unrewarded, are no doubt more outstanding in the eyes of God than the former. True greatness is attained by those who humbly serve the Lord without attempting to push or elevate themselves in the eyes of men.

A farmer once went with his son into a wheat field to see if it was ready for the harvest. "See, father," exclaimed the boy, "how straight those stems hold up their heads? They must be the best ones. Those that hang their heads down I am sure cannot be of much account." The farmer plucked a stalk of each kind, and said, "See here, foolish child! This stalk that stood so straight is light-headed and almost good for nothing, while this that hung its head so modestly is full of the most beautiful grain."

F. B. Meyer is quoted as saying, "I used to think that God's gifts were on shelves one above the other; and that the taller we grew in Christian character the easier we could reach them. I now find that God's gifts are on shelves one beneath the other; and that *it is not a question of growing taller, but of stooping lower;* and that we have to go down, always down, to get His best gifts."

To this agree the words of the Lord Jesus, "but whosoever will be great among you, shall be your minister" (Mark 10:43b). Yea, "if any man desire to be first, the same shall be last of all" (Mark 9:35).
—H.G.B.

Lord, take my life, and make it wholly Thine,
Fill my poor heart with Thy great love divine;
Take all my will, my passion, self and pride;
I now surrender: Lord, in me abide. — J. E. Orr

"The branches that bear the most fruit, hang the lowest."

THE BEE-STING CURE

SUGGESTED SCRIPTURE READING: Romans 5:12-21

The sting of death is sin.   I Corinthians 15:56a

What an expression! Death had a sting. It was sin. But Jesus took the sting out of death by paying the price of eternal death. Death for the Christian is robbed of its sting when we understand the truth of grace.

I have at my home a beehive. Some years ago while I was walking in the field with my two boys, one of these insects made a bee-line for the elder of the two and, before he was aware of it, had stung him just above the eye. He quickly brushed it away and threw himself in the grass, kicking and screaming. No sooner had the bee been brushed away when it went straight for the younger son and began buzzing around his head while he, too, hid his head in the grass, screaming and yelling for help. But I picked him up and told him to stop crying. Said I, "That bee is harmless. It cannot hurt you. It has lost its sting." As you may know, a bee stings only *ONCE*. When it does, it leaves its stinger in the victim and from then on is perfectly harmless. So I took him over to his elder brother, showed him the little black stinger in his brother's brow, and then said, "The bee can still buzz and scare you, but it is powerless to hurt you. Your brother took the sting away by being stung."

Then I explained this verse in I Corinthians 15 to them. The sting of death is sin. But our Elder Brother, the Lord Jesus, hung on the Cross and took the sting out of death, *NAMELY SIN*. He took our sin; since death has only one sting and the law can ask satisfaction only *once*, death from now on is powerless to hurt those who have accepted the *WORK* of the Elder Brother, Jesus. The only thing that makes me fear death is to face God with *SIN*, but that was taken care of when death left its sting in Jesus. Now it may buzz around and scare us badly, but it cannot hurt us any more. All it can do is open the door to Glory.   —M.R.D.

Hail, Thou agonizing Saviour,
Bearer of our sin and shame!
By Thy merits we find favor:
Life is given through Thy name. — J. Bakewell

"The defeated tyrant, 'Death,' has become for the Christian a servant charged by God with the responsibility of opening the gates of Paradise." — G. W.

BREAKFAST - DINNER - SUPPER

<small>SUGGESTED SCRIPTURE READING: Luke 11:1-10</small>

Evening, and morning, and at noon, will I pray, and cry aloud; and he shall hear my voice. Psalm 55:17

David had made one definite resolve, that come what may, he would not neglect to pray. Prayer is the Christian's bulwark and defense against temptation. To neglect constant prayer is to open the door wide to the adversary of our souls. As we need three meals a day — breakfast, dinner, and supper so too the believer needs his three regular periods of prayer to sustain his soul. It is of course not limited to three times only, but David suggests that three times a day for *AUDIBLE* prayer is a minimum. It was not a silent prayer, but he said he would cry "aloud." There is a blessing when we stop to pray with our familes as regularly as we eat our meals. Daniel was cast into a den of lions because he defied the king's command and *THREE TIMES* a day kneeled down to pray, where all could see him — *breakfast, dinner,* and *supper.*

The order given by David is significant. It is not as we might suppose; morning, noon, and evening, but "evening, and morning, and at noon." The evening is put first. That is when we have the most time and temptations are the greatest. It was in the *EVENING* that David saw Bathsheba taking her bath in the courtyard. Had David been on his knees for his *EVENING DEVOTIONS*, the sad story of David's great sin would never have been written. I wonder, could this be the reason David mentions first the "evening prayer"? Will you take time *right now* — to pray? —M.R.D.

> Ere you left your room this morning,
> Did you think to pray?
> In the name of Christ, our Saviour,
> Did you sue for loving favor,
> As a shield today?
> Oh, how praying rests the weary!
> Prayer will change the night to day;
> So when life seems dark and dreary,
> Don't forget to pray. M. A. Kidder

"Soldiers of the Lord do their best fighting on their knees!"

STANDING STILL

SUGGESTED SCRIPTURE READING: Exodus 14:1-14

Stand still, and see the salvation of the LORD.

Exodus 14:13

Stand still! That is a difficult thing for anyone to do. We like to be active and busy, but sometimes God says "Stand aside for awhile." After years of an active ministry I was laid aside some years ago for several weeks as I hovered between life and death upon my sick-bed. There I learned the lesson that I was not indispensable. While I "stood still," the work went on. Before this we rushed and hurried and fretted in our busy life, and then the Lord had to teach a lesson learned only by "standing still." Have you learned the lesson? You had to learn as you were laid aside that your business and your family and loved ones just had to get along without you. You found to your surprise that God did undertake, and they did get along without you, and you found that God was there and knew all about it before and made provision for it.

I must confess that I had to learn that hard and difficult lesson. It is hard on our pride. It makes us humble. It takes something out of us, and yet it teaches us this great lesson — the Lord can get along without us and we must learn to depend upon Him. In Exodus 14:13, when the Israelites stood before the sea, the Egyptians behind them and on each side deserts and mountains, the Lord said, "Stand still, and see the salvation of the LORD." Oh, the precious lesson He teaches us when we learn that God can undertake for us and do things far beyond our comprehension!

Are you one of God's shut-ins? Did you have to learn some of these lessons? Ah, then your life has been enriched, and I know that even now you can praise God for His wonderful dealings in your life.

Stand *STILL* — God wants to talk to you! —M.R.D.

> Be still, my heart; for faithful is thy Lord,
> And pure and true and tried His Holy Word;
> Through stormy flood that rageth as the sea,
> His promises thy stepping-stones shall be!
> — Anon.

"Sanctified afflictions are spiritual promotions!"

THE TROUBLES GOD ALLOWS

Suggested Scripture Reading: Job 1:12-22

. . . for this thing is from me.   I Kings 12:24

There is a legend concerning an old violin maker who was much envied by his fellow artisans because of the superior quality of the instruments he produced. Finally, he disclosed the secret of his success. While the others went into the protected valleys to cut wood to make their violins, he climbed the rugged crags of a nearby mountain in order to secure trees which had become severely twisted and gnarled by the storms. From these weather-beaten monarchs of the forest he then fabricated his violins — famous for their tone and beauty. He knew that the fierce trial of the mountain gales caused such trees to strengthen and toughen their fibers. It was this — their storm-tortured heart and grain — that produced the deep, colorful tones when the instrument was played.

So, too, the Lord often allows sore difficulties to come into our lives that we may more fully bring forth the music of His grace when our soul-trying experiences have done their sanctifying work. Sometimes God allows Satan "inside the hedge" of our divine protection. When this occurs, deep distress and unexplainable afflictions come without reason or apparent design. At such times there may be a terrific battle against fear and doubt. Our prayers for deliverance seem to beat themselves weak against skies of iron. In such times, when we are tempted to despair, let us fall back upon God's eternal love and promises, and *trust* Him even though we cannot *trace* Him. Christians are to recognize at all times that their troubles are divinely sent. He controls the severity of the storm and whispers reassuringly, "This thing is from Me!"

Job is a shining example of seemingly unreasonable trial and distress. Oh, for a faith like his to see God's hand ruling over all, and to testify triumphantly. "The Lord gave, and the Lord hath taken away; blessed be the name of the Lord" (Job 1:21). Then, even as in the case of Lazarus, our "sickness" and difficulty will prove to be "for the glory of God."   H.G.B.

When health gives way, the body breaks,
When seized by darkest mood,
E'en yet God maketh no mistakes
My God is wise and good. — H. J. Hager

"This thing is from Me — these five words furnish a silver lining to the darkest cloud." — H. HOFFS

THE FIRST MARTYR

SUGGESTED SCRIPTURE READING: I John 3:7-12

Cain rose up against Abel his brother, and slew him.

Genesis 4:8

Abel, the righteous man (I John 3:12), was the first man to taste the curse upon sin, namely physical death by violence at the hand of his brother. Death did not first strike Adam, the first sinner, nor Cain, the first murderer; but it struck the innocent and the righteous one (Heb. 11:4). One would hardly expect such a surprise, for we would suppose that death would strike first the guilty and not the innocent and the righteous. In all this we have in the very dawn of history a picture of redemption by the One whom Abel foreshadowed.

The first soul who met death by death and overcame it, the first man who left earth and went to heaven, was Abel. Yes, the one whom God loved most died first, while the guilty faced eternal death. Cain remained alive, while his righteous brother Abel died. But the curse remained upon Cain; and today Abel is with Christ, while Cain is in the place of the damned. Yet Cain had the same opportunity; he had the same parents, the same early training, and the same message of salvation (Gen. 3:21). But by one act of rejection he was lost. Instead of faith in a bloody sacrifice, he brought the work of his own hands. That was the step which led to his later act of murder.

On the top of a hill in a midwestern state stands a courthouse so situated that raindrops falling on one side of the roof travel by way of the Great Lakes into the Atlantic, while drops on the opposite side find their way through the Ohio and Mississippi to the Gulf. Just a breath of wind one way or another may determine whether a single raindrop will end up either in the Gulf or in the Atlantic. Even so, one single decision is enough to determine man's destiny, either heaven or hell. Have you made the right decision?

—M.R.D.

Far dearer than all that the world can impart
Was the message that came to my heart;
How that Jesus alone for my sin did atone,
Now Calvary covers it all. — Mrs. W. G. Taylor

"A man may be almost saved, yet entirely lost."

THE INNER VOICE

SUGGESTED SCRIPTURE READING: Acts 24:10-16

. . . their conscience also bearing witness, and their thoughts the mean while accusing or else excusing.

Romans 2:15

All of us have heard the old maxim: "Let your conscience be your guide." Now it is true that God speaks to man through that still, small, inner voice, but we must not forget that because of his fall into sin, man's nature is now so twisted and distorted that conscience by itself is no longer an infallible guide. We need a conscience enlightened and sensitized by the Word of God if we are to safely follow its leading. Another reason why conscience alone cannot be relied upon is this: If its admonitions are often disregarded and its warnings left unheeded it becomes "seared as with a hot iron." The inner voice then becomes inaudible.

An Indian was once asked by a missionary to define conscience. The copper-skinned native pointed a finger at his breast and said, "It is a little three-cornered thing in here. When I do wrong, it turns around and hurts very much. If I keep on doing wrong, it will turn until *it wears the edges all off, and then it will not hurt me anymore.*"

A negro had applied for a job as a teamster. "Are you familiar with mules?" asked the employer. "No, sah!" replied the applicant. "I knows mules too well to git familiar wid 'em." So, too, there is great danger in hurting our conscience by becoming familiar with sinful practices. How important it is to keep our hearts tender and in touch with the Word of God. Do not allow yourself to grow dull to sin because of its prevalence. Do not mute the 'inner voice."

How happy is the man who has a conscience "void of offence toward God, and toward men" (Acts 24:16). "For if our heart condemn us, God is greater than our heart, and knoweth all things" (I John 3:20). If your conscience is bothering you, confess your sin, make the necessary restitution, and you will find the peace of mind you so much desire; for "if our heart condemn us not, then have we confidence toward God" (I John 3:21). —H.G.B.

Thy blessed cross has sealed my peace,
Thy sorrows make my own to cease;
Thy pow'r has cleansed me from all sin,
Thy presence keeps my conscience clean. — C. A. Miles

"Conscience is our compass, but the Word of God is our chart."

A CHEERFUL GIVER

SUGGESTED SCRIPTURE READING: II Corinthians 8:1-15

> . . . *God loveth a cheerful giver.*   II Corinthians 9:7

The word translated "cheerful" in the original is *hilaros*. It might also be translated "hilarious." So our text should read: "God loveth a hilarious giver." The only giving which deserves any credit is that which is done willingly, joyfully and without pressure. There is no legality in acceptable Christian giving. Tithing was a minimum under the law, but under grace we do not figure percentages, but are to give liberally, according to each one's ability. If Christians knew the true "grace of giving" (II Cor. 8:7), we would not have to devise schemes and tricks to get folks to contribute. We would not have to stress the need of the work. The world has a saying, used in the past war, "Give until it hurts." But that is not Christian giving. As long as it hurts you have not yet given enough. Rather we should "Give till it feels good." If giving does not make you "hilarious" you had better give some more.

The story is told of a very wealthy man who, upon the occasion of his daughter's marriage, sent a check for $5000.00 to the bridegroom as a wedding present. He sent it by the hand of the bride's sister and when she returned, the man eagerly asked, "What did your new brother-in-law say when you gave him the check?" The girl replied, "He didn't say anything, but when he looked at it he began to cry." "And how long did he cry?" was the question, and she replied, "Oh, I imagine for about a minute." "Only a minute?" roared the disappointed giver, "Why, I cried for an hour after I had signed the check!"

When we consider how Christ gave Himself for us, it should compel us to lay ourselves and our all at His feet. The secret of the liberality of the Corinthians was this, that they "first gave their own selves to the Lord." (II Cor. 8:5).   —M.R.D.

> Saviour, Thy dying love Thou gavest me,
> Nor should I aught withhold, dear Lord, from Thee:
> In love my soul would bow, my heart fulfill its vow,
> My all I bring Thee now, something for Thee.
> — S. D. Phelps

"If truth takes possession of a man's heart, it will direct his hand to his pocketbook."

NEEDED: MORE EMPTY VESSELS

SUGGESTED SCRIPTURE READING: II Kings 4:1-7

And . . . she said unto her son, Bring me yet a vessel. And he said unto her, There is not a vessel more. And the oil stayed. II Kings 4:6

What an interesting and thrilling story this is. A widow, who had been married to one of the prophets associated with Elisha, had come to the point of destitution. The creditors were about to take her two sons as slaves to make up for what she owed. When she cries to Elisha for aid, he asks her what she has in the house of value and she lists her assets as "one pot of oil." He tells her to borrow as many empty containers as she can, go into her house, shut the door, and begin to pour out the oil into the vessels. Her sons quickly gather for her some pans and bottles and she does as the prophet has commanded. When she has filled them all to the brim, the original pot of oil has not yet run dry. She asks her son for an additional container, but there are no more to be had; then, and only then, does the oil stop running. *Had there been more vessels, there would have been more oil!* God had worked a miracle to deliver this poor widow, for she subsequently sold the oil and paid her debts. The lesson is plain: There is no limit to God's grace. He freely fills "empty vessels." "God giveth not the Spirit by measure" (John 3:34). *It is we who limit God; the oil never stops as long as we have room to receive it!* Yes, you are His child, but have you received *"abundance* of grace"? (Romans 5:17) Someone has said we are like wicks. Our light for Christ in this world is proportionate to the oil to which we have access. There is a little parable about one who asked of a lamp, "Will you not soon burn to an end with your poor wick?" "No, I do not fear that, for the light does not burn *me,* though it burns *on* me. I only bear to it the oil which saturates my texture. I am but the ladder upon which it climbs. It is not I, but the oil that is in me, that furnishes the light!"

Vessels, empty of self, can hold the most oil and provide the most light! —H.G.B.

Like the cruse of oil unfailing is His grace forevermore,
And His love unchanging still;
And according to His promise with the Holy Ghost and power,
He will every vessel fill. — Mrs. C. H. Morris

"The Holy Spirit flows to those who are empty of self."

NOT FOR SALE

SUGGESTED SCRIPTURE READING: Romans 4:1-5

Buy . . . without money. Isaiah 55:1

The prophet Isaiah invites all who are athirst to come and "buy wine and milk without money and without price." It is free to whosoever will come and receive it. In Romans 4:5, Paul says, "But to him that worketh not, but believeth." If there is one thing which is clear in the Bible, it is the fact that salvation is the "free gift of God's grace." It cannot be earned, merited, or bought. An old man said that it took him forty years to learn three simple things. The first was that he couldn't do anything to be saved; second, that God didn't expect him to; and third, that Christ had done it all and all he needed to do was accept it.

I read somewhere a touching story which will illustrate this great truth. On a cold winter's day a poor woman stood before the window of the king's conservatory looking eagerly at a cluster of luscious grapes. She had a sick child and this poor mother wished that she could cheer her with this fruit. She went home, worked day and night making a blanket, sold it for a small sum, and offered the king's gardener the few coins for a bunch of grapes, but was driven away. She went home, snatched her blanket from her bed, pawned it for a few coins, and again offered it to the gardener and again was driven away. But the princess walking through the garden heard it, and said, "You have made a mistake, madam. My father is not a merchant, but a king. His business is *not* to sell, but to *give*. And so saying, she plucked the largest cluster of grapes and with a smile gave it to the poor woman.

"Our God is not a merchant but a King!" His salvation is not for sale—but free! —M.R.D.

> Nor silver nor gold hath obtained my redemption,
> Nor riches of earth could have saved my poor soul;
> The blood of the cross is my only foundation,
> The death of my Saviour now maketh me whole.
> I am redeemed, but not with **silver;**
> I am bought, but not with gold;
> Bought with a price, the blood of Jesus,
> Precious price of love untold. — J. M. Gray

"Salvation is free to you because Somebody Else paid for it."

MORE BLESSED TO GIVE

Suggested Scripture Reading: Acts 20:28-35

. . . It is more blessed to give than to receive. Acts 20:35

These words of the Lord Jesus are not found in the Gospels as such, but are mentioned by Paul as having been spoken by our Lord while He dwelt here on earth. This principle, however, was enunciated by our Lord in Luke 14 when He said, "When thou makest a dinner or a supper, call not thy friends, nor thy brethren, neither thy kinsmen, nor thy rich neighbors; lest they also bid thee again, and a recompense be made thee. But when thou makest a feast, call the poor, the maimed, the lame, the blind: And thou shalt be blessed; for they cannot recompense thee: for thou shalt be recompensed at the resurrection of the just" (Luke 14:12-14). How seldom we practice this precept of our Lord. At our festive occasions and banquets we usually invite our close friends and loved ones, rather than the poor and needy, to partake of our bountiful fare. Do not all of us have to admit that even our prayers are to a great extent selfish? We seem much more interested in receiving than in giving. Our Lord knew the deceitfulness of covetousness and riches. He recognized that instead of satisfying our deepest needs, they only increase our desire for even more "things" which leave the soul barren and unblessed. Let us determine today to begin to think more of others; to be more willing and more anxious to distribute, than we are to grasp greedily for personal gain.

For a number of weeks a Sunday school class had been studying the subject of "stewardship." At the end of their course they were asked to write out what they thought it meant. One boy wrote this: "Stewardship means that life is a great ship, loaded with a rich cargo of many things to be delivered to many people, in many places. God is the owner, but I am the captain of the ship." — Is this your point of view, or are you just a "gimme" Christian? A faithful steward is happiest when he is "delivering the goods" to others in the name of his Saviour.   —H.G.B.

> Oh, the heart grows rich in giving;
> All its wealth is living grain;
> Seeds which mildew in the garner,
> Scattered, fill with gold the plain. — Mrs. Charles

"You cannot love without giving, and you cannot give without blessing!"

ONLY ONE STEP TO HELL

SUGGESTED SCRIPTURE READING: Matthew 10:25-33

> *. . . fear him which is able to destroy both soul and body in hell.* Matthew 10:28

Jesus had just commissioned His disciples for the great task of preaching the Gospel to the people. He had warned them that their message would not be popular but would result in persecution and tribulation. He had said, "Behold, I send you forth as sheep in the midst of wolves; be ye therefore wise as serpents, and harmless as doves." The Gospel has never been popular with the masses. When God's servants fearlessly preached the whole counsel of God it invariably resulted in persecution, reviling, and tribulation. It was so with Isaiah, and Jeremiah, and Daniel, with John the Baptist, and Peter, and Paul. If our preaching meets with no opposition then is the "offence of the cross ceased." If ever I cease to receive criticism and persecution for preaching the Gospel, I will know I have omitted something.

Today men will listen to a message of love and compassion, but the preaching of "hell" is rejected. Yet if there is no "hell" then the Bible is a lie, Jesus and the apostles were mistaken, and all Christians are stupid fools. Billy Sunday once said, "You may not believe in hell now, but you will one minute after you get there."

A miner going down the shaft in the elevator was much annoyed by the profanity of one of the men. As they descended the shaft deeper and deeper into the earth it became hotter and hotter till it was stifling. With an oath, the profane passenger said, "It's so hot here we must be close to hell. How far is hell from here?" The Christian miner had the answer. Said he, "The distance for you to hell is the length of one link in the chain on which hangs this car. If one link gives way you will be in hell in a moment." For the unsaved there is only one breath between himself and eternal doom; but thank God, Heaven is just as close to the believer.

—M.R.D.

Only a step to Jesus! Come, He waits for thee;
Come and thy sin confessing,
Thou shalt receive a blessing;
Do not reject the mercy He freely offers thee.
— F. J. Crosby

"For the unsaved, hell is only a heartbeat away!" — M.R.D.

DESIRED HAVEN

SUGGESTED SCRIPTURE READING: Psalm 107:21-31

*He maketh the storm a calm . . . Then are they glad
. . . so he bringeth them unto their desired haven.*
Psalm 107:29, 30

The waves and billows of this life often beat loudly against the hold of our ship as we pass through the sea of time; but every hard trial and duty which lies in our path, though it cost us pain, has a blessing in it if we are "exercised" by it. We need not despair, for the floods shall not overflow us. We shall someday anchor safely in the Glorious Haven of the redeemed.

The story is told of a beautiful young girl who lay dying. Although a Christian, she was filled with doubts. When her pastor arrived she cried in anxiety, "Oh, Dr. Donald, I am horribly afraid to die! I feel as if I am being thrust out of my happy life into the darkness. I cannot see anything! I cannot believe anything! What shall I do?" The preacher's grave, strong face grew tender as he looked at her. He knew she was a child of God and that Satan was attacking her in her final moments. "Jenny," he said, "a year ago there came into your sister's household a sweet, lovely baby; do you remember all that was done for her? Everyone in the family tried to think of some new service for that tiny bit of helpless humanity. Dainty linens and laces were made ready before she came; her food was scientifically prepared; and the love that was shed forth in watching her day and night to assure her comfort was wonderful to behold. That is the kind of care we humans give to a new life when it comes into *this world;* well, *do you suppose that God is less loving than we?* In that Home He is calling you to enter, He too has made ready every device for your happiness, and every protection by which His love may make you feel at home!" A light broke over the face of the dying girl. "I see what you mean," she said, "He went to *'prepare a place' for Me!*" Her last moments were spent in peace, and there was a smile upon her lips as she entered the "desired haven."   —H.G.D.

Earth's trials and its headaches, rough pathways that we tread,
Should never cause a worry, with "Heaven just ahead"!
Where shadows now are lingering, the sun will shine instead,
So cheer up brother, cheer up, for "Heaven lies ahead"!
— Mrs. M. E. Rae

"Oh, what sweet truths He often whispers to His saints from behind the clouds."

SELF-DEFENSE

SUGGESTED SCRIPTURE READING: Ecclesiastes 4:1-6

A soft answer turneth away wrath.   Proverbs 15:1

The natural tendency of the human heart is to requite evil with evil and to stand up for our so-called "rights." What terrible tragedies are enacted as the result of some trifling remark which should simply have been ignored. But such is the propensity of human nature that we meet insult with insult. In my experience I have dealt with many a problem of a broken home or friendship which began with an insignificant remark of a cutting nature. Instead of ignoring it or meeting it with a kind reply, it was answered in "kind" rather than in kindness. One harsh word led to another until it resulted in a complete breakup of fellowship. All of it could have been avoided if we had only followed the example of Jesus, "who when he was reviled, reviled not again." We can best defend ourselves against unkind acts by meeting them with kindness.

"Do you think it would be wrong for me to learn the noble art of self-defense?" a religiously-inclined young man inquired of his pastor. "Certainly not," answered the minister; "I learned it in youth myself, and I have found it of great value during my life." "Indeed, sir! Did you learn the old English system, or Sullivan's system?" "Neither, I learned Solomon's system." "Solomon's system?" "Yes; you will find it laid down in the first verse of the fifteenth chapter of Proverbs: 'A soft answer turneth away wrath.' It is the best system of self-defense I know."   —M.R.D.

> A careless word may kindle strife;
> A cruel word may wreck a life;
> A bitter word may hate instill;
> A brutal word may smite and kill;
> A gracious word may smooth the way;
> A joyous word may light the way;
> A timely word may lessen stress;
> A loving word may heal and bless. — Recorder.

"The most glorious victory over an enemy is to turn him into a friend."

HONORING THE MASTER'S NAME

SUGGESTED SCRIPTURE READING: Exodus 20:1-7

> . . . *if then I be a father, where is mine honour? and if I be a master, where is my fear? saith the* LORD *of hosts.*
>
> Malachi 1:6

A Christian gentleman was once in the company of one who embellished his conversation with constant references to Satan. It was "what the devil" this, and "what the deuce" that, etc. Finally, he took the name of God in vain. "Stop, sir!" said the Christian, "I said nothing to you when you only used the names of *your master*, but I insist you shall *take no freedom with the Name of mine.*"

God is so holy, so glorious, so far above us, so greatly to be praised that to frivolously or irreverently use His name is a sin of tremendous magnitude.

A poor shepherd addicted to the habit of swearing was once reminded by a minister of the Gospel concerning the Scriptural precept, "Swear not at all"; to which he replied that he meant no harm; "'tis only a way I've got." "True, my friend, but the same Book tells you and me, 'There is a way which seemeth right unto a man, but the ends thereof are the ways of death.'"

We live in an age where "reverence" is little understood and even less displayed. In fact, Christians have in many cases forgotten the supreme holiness and greatness of God. They would not openly swear or blaspheme, but they think nothing of looking around the church while the preacher is praying, or of whispering and causing disturbances when the message is being delivered. Humorous stories about God, heaven, and Biblical characters are carelessly and lightheartedly repeated. If we expect the worldly man to stop using God's name in vain, we had better show a bit more reverence ourselves. God says, "If then I be a Father, *where is mine honour?* and if I be a master, where is my fear?" Is Christ your Master? (Matt. 23:8) If so, render to Him the honor due His Name! —H.G.B.

> That Name I just heard is delightfully sweet,
> Jesus is Lord! And Him you must meet;
> He hears you blaspheme; but, oh, if you knew
> How much He loves sinners, how much He loves you,
> You'd fall at His feet, and adoringly sing,
> "Jesus My Saviour! My Lord! And My King!"—J.H.W.

"Live and speak so that no man can despise either you or your Master."

THE POWER OF THE WORD

SUGGESTED SCRIPTURE READING: John 12:44-48

Is not my word . . . like a hammer that breaketh the rock in pieces?   Jeremiah 23:29

On Highway No. 2 in the upper peninsula of Michigan is a boulder close by the road called the "split rock." It is a huge stone split in two massive sections with a tree growing in the crevice. Years ago a little seedling took root in a crack of that great rock, and as it grew its roots dug deeper and deeper into the split, and silently but surely pushed it apart. The seedling had "life" and was able to break the rock in pieces. Such is the power of the Word of God. It is a living seed, an incorruptible seed, with life and power. The power of this seed of the Word is compared by Jeremiah to a hammer that "breaketh the rock in pieces." Nothing can stand against this Word for "heaven and earth shall pass away" but the Word of the Lord will endure forever.

Some years ago an infidel in Germany, who scoffed at the Bible, lay dying. To the pleas of friends to renounce his atheism, he replied, "This is the end of me. You may bury me, for I shall never rise." Then he gave orders that his grave should be covered by a huge granite slab, cemented securely in place with the following inscription cut in the granite: "This burial place is my house for eternity — It shall never be opened." The man died and his wishes were carried out. Years passed, and wind, sun, rain, and erosion did their work, and then one day a little seed was carried by the wind and fell into a tiny crevice in the joint between cement and granite. As the tiny rootlet pushed downward, it grew larger and stronger, lifted the slab, and pushing it completely aside, opened the grave. A large tree now stands over the place, proclaiming the message of the power of the Word. The hammer of God's Word will crush all the rocks of infidelity and silence every skeptic's sneer.   —M.R.D.

Thy Word like a hammer the flinty rock breaks,
And sinners from death into new life awakes.
Though hell's dark dominion against it convene,
Yet ever triumphant the Bible has been! — G.W.

"One evidence of the value of the Bible is the character of those who oppose it!"

THE COMFORTING ADVOCATE

SUGGESTED SCRIPTURE READING: John 16:7-14

And I will pray the Father, and he shall give you another
Comforter, that he may abide with you for ever;
I will not leave you comfortless. John 14:16, 18

An interesting story is told of a missionary in Africa who sought for a proper term or phrase by which he could translate the Scriptural word for the Holy Spirit or "Comforter" into the native language. One day, after three long years of frustration, he heard in the court of an African village the name *"Nsenga-Mukwashi"* frequently mentioned. He asked the old chief, after court closed, what this man had to do with the proceedings. The chief smiled and explained that "Nsenga-Mukwashi" was a title given to the one whose duty it was to interest himself in all the native people and stand by them when they were in any trouble. On that particular day this official had brought to the court an old woman who had been ill treated. He eloquently pleaded her just cause. "He is known to my people as the *comforting advocate,*" said the chief. The missionary was overjoyed with these words for he recognized that he now had a term worthy of expressing the work of the Holy Spirit, our Helper and Comforter.

Have you often wondered at the way your poor stammering prayers have been answered so gloriously; how your life is still so richly blessed, though your faith is so weak? The answer is to be found in the One who "maketh intercession for us with groanings which cannot be uttered." Yes, He prays and pleads for the saints "according to the will of God" (Rom. 8:26, 27). Have you ever wondered, after your times of trial and sorrow, how you were able to bear up under it so well, and how it was that you experienced such unexpected grace? It was due to the heavenly "Nsenga-Mukwashi." He ever stands by us in trouble and pours in the balm of Gilead. How blessed is the ministry of our "Comforting Advocate." —H.G.B.

Holy Spirit, faithful Guide,
Ever near the Christian's side;
Gently lead us by the hand,
Pilgrims in a desert land. — M. M. Wells

"Men at best are but 'miserable comforters'; only God the Holy Spirit can effectively minister to bleeding hearts!" — G.W.

THE SIN OF WHISPERING

SUGGESTED SCRIPTURE READING: James 3:6-12

A whisperer separateth chief friends.   Proverb 16:28

We are quick and ready to condemn the thief and the drunkard, but how slow we are to judge the more polite sins of gossip, coveteousness, jealousy and envy. Just because we are not guilty of the grosser sins, we condone and tolerate the so-called lesser sins in our own lives. But the Bible has just as much to say about lying, gossiping and whispering as many of the coarser sins. Whispering and gossiping are more serious than stealing or wounding a man. The stolen goods may be restored and a wounded body will heal; but idle gossip can never be recalled.

A minister, seeking to rebuke a notorious "whisperer" in his congregation, asked her to go to the market, buy a freshly killed chicken, and pluck its feathers on the way home. Nearing her home with the chicken half plucked she was met by the minister who said, "Now go back and gather up all the feathers you have strewn by the way." In surprise she exclaimed, "But that is impossible! The wind has blown them in all directions!" "Just so," said the minister, "are the words of slander; they go hither and yon and can never be recalled."

Watch your tongue today and you will watch your whole life. For, "If any man offend not in word, the same is a perfect man, and able also to bridle the whole body." May our aim be this day, "I will take heed to my ways, that I sin not with my tongue: I will keep my mouth with a bridle" (Ps. 39:1).   —M.R.D.

"They say!" ... Ah, well, suppose they do!
But can they prove the story true?
Why count yourself among the "they"
Who whisper what they dare not say?
Suspicion may arise from naught
But malice, envy, want of thought.
Pity the frail, weep o'er their fall,
But speak of good — or not at all. — Anon.

"A ready accuser is usually a self-excuser."

DEEP WATERS AND GOD'S LOVE

SUGGESTED SCRIPTURE READING: Ephesians 2:1-7

Many waters cannot quench love.   Song of Solomon 8:7

Water in large quantities in Scripture always speaks of trouble and judgment. To appreciate this one has to think only of the flood of Noah's day or of the words of the Apostle John, that in the new heaven where all judgment is past, there will then be *"no more sea"* (Rev. 21:1b).

The deep billows of judgment one day swirled ever so angrily at the foot of the Cross, but they could not quench our Saviour's self-sacrificing and redeeming love. He won the victory over sin's torrent of terror. Now in the light of His life and atonement we walk securely. Nothing can ever separate us from His love in regard to our salvation (Rom. 8:31-39).

There is another application that can be made of this Scripture as to our pilgrim walk. It is to be noted that no matter how high the waters of distress may rise, His love like the sunrise will ever be present to shed its warming beams of blessing upon the troubled sea.

The touching story is told of a father and his little daughter who had just buried the mother of the home. They were brokenhearted when they returned from the funeral, for things at the old homestead seemed so different. The child was placed in her bed for the night as usual. The father, too, retired, but could not sleep. Presently the little daughter called to him, "Papa, it's so dark." He reassured her in soothing tones saying there was nothing to fear and urged her to just try to go to sleep. For a while the child was quiet, and then she said trustingly, *"Papa, you love through the dark, too, don't you?"* "Yes, dear," he said with a quivering voice; and with that he looked up into the face of Jesus and prayed silently, "Thank you, Lord, for using my little one to remind me that Thou dost love me, Thy child, even though the way is dark."

Friend, are you going through the "deep waters"? Then let these words cheer you: "I have loved thee with an everlasting love" (Jer. 31:3a).   —H.G.B.

None can be so o'erwhelmed with grief,
But he in Christ may find relief;
All misery, however great,
His comforts can alleviate! — Unknown.

"Darkness cannot put out the lamp: it can only make it shine the brighter."

PREPARING FOR THE WEDDING

SUGGESTED SCRIPTURE READING: Ruth 3:1-16

Wash thyself . . . anoint thee . . . put thy raiment upon thee. Ruth 3:3

These were the instructions Naomi, the clever matchmaker, gave to Ruth, her daughter-in-law, when she was to go and meet her lover. Ruth, the widow, had labored all day in the field of Boaz and now the harvest was over and the night drew on. This was the night Ruth was to spend with her future husband. On the morrow she was to become Mrs. Boaz! Naomi tells Ruth, "and you must be your very prettiest. You must be clean and sweet and pure and spotlessly attired. Wash yourself — anoint yourself — dress up, for this is the day of days."

All this is a prophetic picture of the Church in these latter days. The harvest is about over, the last gleanings are almost gathered in, and the night of threshing of the nations is at hand; but during that dark Tribulation the Church will be with her Lord. The day is almost gone. We must prepare to meet the Bridegroom for He may come at any moment — even today! How fitting the advice of Naomi to us, the waiting bride. To be ready for Him, we must *wash* ourselves. The water is the Word of God (Eph. 5:26). We are to cleanse ourselves from every spot and stain. Then we are to be anointed. This speaks of the Holy Spirit in sanctifying power. As we obey the Word (washing), we shall be filled (anointed) with the Spirit. And then put on your best garments. These are the deeds of service and works of love and devotion we give to Him (Rev. 19:8). Are you ready to meet Him today — washed by the Word, anointed by the Spirit, and dressed in "good works" and righteous deeds? Then you can join in the closing prayer of the Bible, "Even so come Lord Jesus" (Rev. 22:20b).

—M.R.D.

Finish, then, Thy new creation;
Pure and spotless let it be:
Let us see Thy great salvation
Perfectly restored in Thee;
Changed from glory into glory
Till in heaven we take our place,
Till we cast our crowns before Thee,
Lost in wonder, love and grace! — Charles Wesley

"Belief in Christ's imminent return is the secret fountain of holiness."

THE SOUL WINNER'S HEART

SUGGESTED SCRIPTURE READING: I Corinthians 9:16-22

. . . yet have I made myself servant unto all . . . that I might by all means save some.   I Corinthians 9:19, 22

The Scripture says, "he that winneth souls is wise" (Prov. 11:30). While the Holy Spirit must do His *primary work* in the heart of the unbeliever (Acts 13:48), it is also true that "faith cometh by hearing . . . the word of God"; and this Word is only brought to the attention of the sinner by the faithful testimony of God's witnesses (Rom. 10:14). Our prayerful earnestness and Scriptural methods are important factors. We read that the apostles *"so spake,* that a great multitude . . . believed" (Acts 14:1). The "so spake" is our part. Will you, like Paul, go to almost any length to reach others for Christ that you might "by *all means* save some"?

Paul Rader had many times dealt with a banker in New York concerning his soul, without avail. One day God seemed to speak to Mr. Rader urging him to go immediately and seek out this individual again. Obediently he caught a train and went with all speed to the place where the banker was staying. As he came near he saw him standing in the doorway. "Oh Rader," he said, "I am so glad to see you. I wrote a telegram begging you to come, but I tore it up and did not send it." "That may be so," said the evangelist, "but your message came by way of heaven." Under deep conviction of sin, the man was impressed by Rader's earnestness and his special effort to reach him with the Gospel; consequently, that very hour he accepted the Lord. In his new-found joy he exclaimed, "Rader, did you ever see the sky so blue or the grass so green?" "Ah," said the soul winner, "we sometimes sing: 'Heaven above is softer blue, earth around is sweeter green; something lives in every hue Christless eyes have never seen.'" Suddenly the banker leaned against Mr. Rader and then with a gasp fell into his arms — dead! He had been saved on the very brink of eternity. What if Paul Rader had delayed to come, or had pressed home the claims of the Lord with less urgency? Do you have the same soul winner's heart?   —H.G.B.

Jesus I long, I long to be winning
Men who are lost, and constantly sinning;
Oh, may this day be one of beginning
The story of pardon to tell. — H. B. Tovey

"Guess-so Christians are never found among the soul winners."

A SQUASH OR AN OAK?

SUGGESTED SCRIPTURE READING: Philippians 3:7-15

*But grow in grace, and in the knowledge of our Lord and
Saviour Jesus Christ.*   II Peter 3:18

The moment we believe on the Lord Jesus Christ we are potentially made perfect *in Him.* This is our justification in the Spirit, but this is not the end. We still need to be daily sanctified in our souls and ultimately our bodies, too, must be redeemed. And so the Christian life is both complete and incomplete. It is "potentially" complete and finished; it is "experientially" still incomplete. We are perfect in our standing; we are imperfect in our state. Our new nature is perfect; our old nature is unimproved.

Hence the admonition of Peter, "*Grow* in grace." This is a lifelong process. It is an idle unscriptural delusion that our old nature can be instantaneously eradicated and that we can attain absolute perfection here below. In God's infinite wisdom He knows that the constant battle and victory over temptation makes us strong. A great educator was asked by a farmer to admit his son to his school, but asked him the question, "Can't you give my son his education in one term instead of taking four years?" The educator replied, "Yes, but it depends on what you want to make of him. You can grow a squash in three months. It takes a hundred years to grow an oak." God wants us to be oak trees and as such we must be "patient in tribulation," never satisfied with *our* progress and attainments.   —M.R.D.

From strength to strength go on;
Wrestle and fight and pray;
Tread all the powers of darkness down,
And win the well-fought day! — C. Wesley

**"We're saved for a purpose! It isn't enough to be good; be good for
something!"**

TWO KINDS OF BELIEVING

SUGGESTED SCRIPTURE READING: I John 5:1; 10-13

> *If we receive the witness of men, the witness of God is greater.* I John 5:9

Martin Luther once said: "There are *two kinds of believing* — first, a believing about God which means that I believe that what is said of God is true. This faith is rather a form of knowledge than of faith. There is, secondly, a believing God which means that I put my trust in Him . . . and believe without any doubt that He will be, and do to me according to the things said of Him. *Such faith which throws itself upon God*, whether in life or in death, alone makes a man a Christian." In other words, although believing things *about God* is important, it is only personally *believing God* that saves a man.

A student at Cambridge was once brought under the preaching of the Gospel and came forward to accept the Lord. Before leaving he said to the preacher, "If I have any difficulty may I call and see you?" "Certainly," replied the man of God. The next morning he did call to say, "I am afraid I decided too hastily last night. I have been looking for some *token* that I have been saved, but I cannot find any." "Well, didn't I tell you that you could see me this morning if you had any difficulty?" "Yes," he said. "Well, why didn't you ask *me* for my watch as a token that I would keep *my word*? If you could believe me by faith; if you could put your confidence in a fallible mortal, why should you now look for a *token* from *God* — can't you also take Him at His Word?" The young convert saw the point, and by resting on the Scriptural, "thus saith the Lord," he found the assurance he needed. Remember, believing about God is knowledge, but believing God is faith!

—H.G.B.

I simply take Him at His Word
I praise Him that my plea is heard,
And claim my answer from the Lord,
I take — He undertakes! — A. B. Simpson

"Faith is saying amen to God and resting confidently in his promises."

TEN STRINGS

SUGGESTED SCRIPTURE READING: Ephesians 5:6-20

Upon . . . an instrument of ten strings.   Psalm 144:9

An old man at a prayer meeting prayed like this: "Oh, Lord, we will praise Thee, we will praise Thee with an instrument of ten strings." People in the service wondered what the ten strings were, but presently they discovered them. The old saint prayed on, "We shall praise Thee with this instrument of ten strings. We will praise Thee with our *eyes* by looking only unto Thee. We will praise Thee with our *ears* by listening *only* to Thy voice. We will praise Thee with our *hands* by working in Thy service. We will praise Thee with our *feet* by running in the way of Thy commandments. We will praise Thee with our *tongue* by bearing testimony to Thy loving-kindness. We will praise Thee with our *heart* by loving only Thee. An instrument of ten strings, Lord, keep the instrument in tune. Lord, play upon it; Lord, play upon it. Lord, ring out the melodies of music; keep it in harmony. Make it to speak out Thy glory — 'an instrument of ten strings.'" Two eyes, two ears, two hands, two feet, one tongue, and one heart. Let us take Miss F. R. Havergal's hymn, "Take my life and let it be consecrated, Lord to Thee, etc." and go through it verse by verse, and lay every member of our body on the altar in full consecration to our Master. "Neither yield ye your members as instruments of unrighteousness unto sin; but yield ye yourselves unto God, as those that are alive from the dead, and your members as instruments of righteousness unto God" (Rom. 6:13).

Our bodies belong unto the Lord. (Rom. 12:1, 2) Someone has said, "The Lord has no hands but ours, no eyes to search out the lost but ours, no feet to carry the message but ours, and no hands to be reached out to a lost world but our hands." We are ambassadors for Christ!   —M.R.D.

Two eyes to look to God, two ears to hear His Word,
Two feet to serve the Lord, two hands to wield His Sword,
One heart to love His ways, One tongue to sing His praise,
Take them, Saviour, let them be
Always busy, serving Thee! — Anon.

"Praise is one of the eternal delights that will outlive time. The devil fears a thankful, praising Christian!"

SAFE IN THE ROCK!

SUGGESTED SCRIPTURE READING: Psalm 18:1-6

The LORD *is my rock . . . in whom I will trust.* Psalm 18:2

Spurgeon used to tell this true story. A Welsh lady, when she lay dying, was visited by her minister. He said to her, "Sister, are you sinking?" She answered him not a word, but she looked at him as if she could not believe her ears. He repeated the question, "Sister, are you sinking?" With a supreme effort she raised herself a little in the bed, and then she said triumphantly, "Sinking! Sinking! Ah, no! Did you ever know a sinner to sink through a rock? If I had been standing on the sand, I might sink; but, thank God, Pastor, I am on the Rock of Ages and there is no sinking there."

The word for stone in our text if literally translated should read *"cleft rock."* What a picture of the Lord Jesus Christ, the Rock of our salvation, whose side was pierced that His own might find there a place of concealment and safety! In Him we may confidently put our trust. His blood shelters us for time and eternity.

Even as Jacob found a stony pillow an adequate cushion in preparation for his angelic vision and his view of the "gate of heaven" (Gen. 28:11, 17), so we, too, can find a place of blessed assurance when the "sleep of death" approaches if we are resting our all upon the Rock of Ages.

Are you hiding in Jesus? No need then to fear the storms of life or the waves of death. You're safe in the Rock.   —H.G.B.

> Hide me, O my blessed Saviour,
> Till the storms of life are past;
> Hide me till I reach the harbor
> Where Thy ransomed rest at last.
> Hide me, hide me, Saviour, hide me,
> Hide me sweetly in the cleft;
> In Thy bleeding side, O hide me,
> Hide me, hide me in the cleft.
> — Mrs. H. Jones

"The steps of faith fall on the seeming void, yet find the Rock beneath."
— WHITTIER

LISTEN TO THE SPARROWS

SUGGESTED SCRIPTURE READING: Luke 12:1-7

Are not five sparrows sold for two farthings, and not one of them is forgotten before God?　　　Luke 12:6

A farthing is the equivalent of about one penny. Two farthings were the price of five sparrows. Sparrows are the most common, widely distributed, most numerous of the birds. They were of little value and were sold cheap. In the days of Christ they were evidently sold for food and were a boon to the poor because they could be bought for so little. An extra sparrow was of little consequence for they sold two for one cent, or five for two cents. If you bought only two of them they were a penny, but if you bought two cents worth they threw in an extra sparrow for good measure.

In Matthew 10:29 we read, "Are not *TWO* sparrows sold for a farthing?" But in Luke 12:6, they are five for two farthings. The extra one was thrown in for free. It is like selling an item today — five cents each and six for a quarter. But Jesus says that God values every one of these sparrows and not a one falls on the ground without His will. Luke says, "Not one of them (not even the extra fifth one) is forgotten before God" (Luke 12:6). Then he says, "Fear not therefore: ye are of more value than many sparrows" (Luke 12:7).

Will God, who provides for the sparrows, forget His own redeemed children? Oh no, we can fully trust Him today. Remember the sparrows when things today become difficult — remember *He cares.* See how He cares for you:

He calls His sheep by name. (John 10:3)
Our very hairs are numbered. (Matt. 10:30)
He counts our every step. (Job 31:4)
He records our fears. (Mal. 3:16)
He bottles our tears. (Ps. 56:8)
He holds our hand. (Isa. 41:13)
And He supplies every need. (Phil. 4:19)
TRUST HIM TODAY!

　　　　　　　　　　　　　　　　　　　　　　—M.R.D.

Through every moment of the day,
Whate'er may meet thee on life's way,
This thought shall be thy strength and stay,
"HE CARES"! — Anon.

"Faith beholds God in the smallest hair that falls and is content in knowing that what is controlled by his Father's Hand must be sent for our good."

SENDING TREASURES AHEAD

. . . lay up for yourselves treasures in heaven.
Matthew 6:20

A lady was once visiting at the home of a pastor who had two sons well instructed in the things of the Lord. When she arrived these youngsters were amusing themselves with some beautiful and instructive toys. The lady remarked, "Well, boys, are these your treasures?" "Oh, no ma'am," said the preacher's oldest son, "these are not our *treasures;* these are only our *playthings. Our treasures are in heaven!*" So, too, the things which we have on this earth may be interesting, desirable, and helpful in a limited degree, but they are transient and will not last. We are not to set our heart upon them for the "fashion of this world passeth away." How important then to lay up treasures where they cannot be lost, spoiled, consumed, or stolen.

A young couple were spending their honeymoon traveling abroad. They intended to build a home when they returned; so whenever they could secure a beautiful picture, statue or vase, they purchased it and sent it back to America to await their coming. These rare and curious treasures which they secured would afterward be linked with happy memories and would serve to bring future enjoyment. I love to think that those of us who are Christians are doing the same in connection with our heavenly home: Sending treasures on ahead while we spend our pilgrimage days here on earth. The kindly deed done for Jesus' sake that makes a rare picture in someone's life, the little sacrifice that blossoms into joy, the helpful friendship, etc., — all these we shall find again. Whatever of beauty, tenderness, faith, or love we can put into other lives through the power of grace, will be among our cherished treasures in heaven.

In this life have you dedicated yourself to Christ, putting God first, others second, and yourself last? This is the only way to "lay up treasures in heaven." —H.G.B.

Cast thy bread upon the waters,
Others' wants to satisfy
Angel eyes will watch above it,
You will find it by and by. — Anon.

"Worldly treasures are dangerous; they bring moths, consumption, and thieves into the heart. — LANGE

MOTES AND TIMBERS

SUGGESTED SCRIPTURE READING: Luke 6:41-46

> *. . . why beholdest thou the mote that is in thy brother's eye, but considerest not the beam that is in thine own eye?*
> Matthew 7:3

This is divine sarcasm and irony. What a ludicrous situation. Here is man with a great big timber sticking out of his eye and offering to remove a little speck of dust from his brother's eye. How foolish! He couldn't even get near his brother because of the beam. What a picture of too many professing, pious, sanctimonious Christians, who are always finding fault with everyone else, while they themselves condone things in their own lives which are a hundred times worse. They find fault with the preacher's sermon, his grammar, and his gestures; criticize Mr. Prosperous for being a spendthrift, etc., etc. But all the while they are carrying around a beam in their own eye. These folk are proud, "holier than thou," cantankerous, faultfinding, carping, and judges of everyone else except themselves. Jesus calls them hypocrites. Beware when you think everyone is wrong except *YOU*. You are in a bad way! I often tell a rather "smelly" story to illustrate this. Grandpaw was sleeping in his chair. His grandchildren found some very ancient — very putrid Limburger cheese, and gently stroked some of it on grandpaw's mustache. When grandpaw awoke he sniffed and grumbled, "This room stinks." He went into the kitchen and said, "And the kitchen stinks." He went outdoors and met Mr. Smith his neighbor and rudely remarked, "And you stink too!" Finally he shouted, "the whole world stinks!" The trouble, however, was right under grandpaw's own nose. All he needed to do was "clean his own nose" and everything else would become sweet again.

Are you sour, bitter, critical and faultfinding? Then try to "examine yourself" (I Cor. 11:28), and clean your own nose first. Remove the "beam" and you won't be looking for "motes." —M.R.D.

Let me be a little kinder, to the faults of others blinder;
Let me praise a little more.
Let me walk in "full surrender", and like Jesus be more tender;
Blessing all who pass my door. — I. Honcy

"Faults are like headlights on a car; those of others always seem more glaring than our own."

THE VINE AND THE BUDS

SUGGESTED SCRIPTURE READING: John 15:1-5

I am the vine, ye are the branches. John 15:5

A Sunday school teacher who was trying to make his class understand the dependence of the branches on the Heavenly Vine, said, "Remember, children, Jesus is the Vine and we are the branches. We draw all of our life and happiness from Him." When the lesson was finished a young boy named Buddy spoke up. "Teacher," he said, "if Jesus is the Vine and grown-up people are the branches, then we children must be the *buds*." The Sunday school teacher was struck by the thought, for he realized that if a blight strikes the buds there can be no branches and no fruit. He saw with fresh insight the importance of bringing up children "in the nurture and admonition of the Lord" (Eph. 6:4).

Think it through: are the "buds" being blessed or blighted by your life and testimony? Do you have a family altar? Have you personally dealt with your children concerning spiritual things? Have you suggested that they have a brief "morning watch" or quiet time for personal Scripture reading and prayer? Have you set them a worthy example by your life, testimony, church affiliation, and social connections? *Don't neglect the buds!* —H.G.B.

The soul of a child is the loveliest flower
That grows in the garden of God,
Its climb is from weakness to knowledge and power,
To the sky from the clay and the clod.
To beauty and sweetness it grows under care,
Neglected, 'tis ragged and wild.
'Tis a plant that is tender, but wondrously rare,
The sweet, wistful soul of a child.
Be tender, O gardener, and give it its share
Of moisture, of warmth, and of light,
And let it not lack for the painstaking care,
To protect it from frost and from blight.
A glad day will come when its bloom shall unfold,
It will seem that an angel has smiled,
Reflecting a beauty and sweetness untold
In the sensitive soul of a child. — Anon.

"A torn jacket is soon mended, but the bruised heart of a child may never heal."

THE GOD-PLANNED LIFE!

SUGGESTED SCRIPTURE READING: Job 42:1-6

But he knoweth the way that I take: when he hath tried me, I shall come forth as gold. Job 23:10

This was the hopeful cry of the suffering Job, when darkness had enveloped him on every side. All hope seemed to be cut off, he was beset on every side. Walled in completely without a visible door of escape, Job exclaims his faith in God. He says in Job 23:8 and 9:

> Behold, I go forward, but he is not here; and backward, but I cannot perceive him. On the left hand, where he doth work, but I cannot behold him: he hideth himself on the right hand, that I cannot see him (Job 23:8, 9).

All was darkness round about. It seemed that God had forsaken him and he saw no human way of escape. And then with the eye of faith he pierces the gloom and rejoices in that fact that God still knows the way. Job could not see one step ahead, but he knew that God was there. Today we stand before a brand new day. We know not what lies ahead. It is all unknown to us what will befall us of pleasure or pain, success or failure, sickness or health, life or death. What will this day bring forth — only God knows and so we turn confidently with Job to Him and say, "HE knoweth the way." And though we be tried it will be for our good because "When he hath tried me, I shall come forth as gold." Maybe this will be the day of days when Jesus will come and we shall emerge as gold to shine forever in the Saviour's crown, and when He comes, our faith will give way to sight and doubts and fears be forever gone. Precious saint of God, let this be your strength today as you face an unfriendly world: *"He knows the way."*

—M.R.D.

> What need to worry then, or fret?
> The God who gave His Son,
> Holds all my moments in His Hand
> And gives them, one by one! — B. C. Ryberg

"God writes with a pen that never blots, speaks with a tongue that never slips, and acts with a hand that never fails!"

THE SONG THAT WON A BATTLE!

SUGGESTED SCRIPTURE READING: II Chronicles 20:20-30

And . . . he appointed singers unto the LORD . . . to say, Praise the LORD; for his mercy endureth forever. And when they began to sing and to praise, the LORD set ambushments against the children of Ammon, Moab, and mount Seir, which were come against Judah; and they were smitten!   II Chronicles 20:21, 22

This is indeed a thrilling account! A great multitude had set themselves in battle array against the relatively small kingdom of Judah. Fearful, not knowing what to do, Jehoshaphat, their leader, prayed and sought the help of the Lord. The answer he received was almost unbelievable. The Lord would save them by a *SONG!* They were to stand still, praise the Lord in the beauty of holiness by a psalm of adoration, and to have no fear. In faith they did as they were told, and God honored His Word. He caused confusion to reign in their enemies' ranks until soon every man's sword turned against his neighbor's. There was such a slaughter that not a one of the opposing host was left alive. The wonder of it all was that *the victory came when the song began.*

What a lesson for us! When we come to "wits end corner" and there is nothing more we can do, then we are to stand still and by faith await the salvation of the Lord. We are to praise Him for the certain victory we know is coming, even though at the time we cannot understand how He will accomplish it. In our hours of crisis the song of the Lord must always be heard in our life. Oh Christian, with your heart against a thorn, let your sweet notes of praise arise. The victory will come when the song of perfect trust and testimony begins. Sing the clouds away!

—H.G.B.

Not by cries, or groans or fears,
Are our conflicts to be won;
But by faith that claims and sings,
Ere the battle is begun.
Onward, then, with nobler strains
Songs of victory let us sing,
Marching through Emmanuel's ground,
Waiting for our coming King,
Victory comes while we sing. — A. B. Simpson

"Do you believe in the sun when it is hidden behind the cloud? Then doubt not the goodness of God when He seems to hide His face."

IT FELL ON A LAMB

Suggested Scripture Reading: I Peter 2:21-25

The Lord hath laid on him the iniquity of us all.

Isaiah 53:6

The Bible teaches the glorious doctrine of substitutionary atonement. It is an exchange of place, whereby Jesus took the sinner's place on Calvary, and we take His place as sons of God. It is a divine act which cannot be explained fully but is abundantly taught in the Scriptures. The good Samaritan in Luke dismounted from his beast and came down to where the wounded man lay. There he lifted up the poor victim and placed him on his own beast while he walked beside him. This is substitution. Jesus took our sin upon Himself and then imparted His own righteousness to us. God sent His own Son in the likeness of sinful flesh, that the righteousness of the law might be fulfilled in us. "For he hath made him to be sin for us, who knew no sin; that we might be made the righteousness of God in him" (II Cor. 5:21).

A gentleman traveling in Norway tells how he went to see the church in a certain town. Looking up at its tower he was surprised to see the carved figure of a lamb at the top. He inquired why it was placed in that position, and he was told that when the church was being built a workman fell from the high scaffold. His fellow workmen saw him fall and rushed down, horror stricken, expecting to find him killed. But to their surprise and joy he was almost unhurt. A flock of sheep was passing at the time of his fall, and he fell upon the crowded flock — right upon the top of a lamb. The lamb was crushed to death, but the man was saved. So they carved a lamb on the tower, at the exact height from which he fell, to commemorate the miraculous escape.

"Behold, the Lamb of God that taketh away the sin of the world" (John 1:29b). —M.R.D.

If you from sin are longing to be free,
Look to the Lamb of God;
He, to redeem you, died on Calvary,
Look to the Lamb of God. — H. Jackson

"Substitution is the touchstone of grace; without it, Calvary is a tragedy and salvation an impossibility." — H.G.B.

THE SEED OF THE WORD

SUGGESTED SCRIPTURE READING: I Peter 1:18-25

> . . . . *my word . . . shall not return unto me void, but it*
> *shall accomplish that which I please, and it shall prosper*
> *in the thing whereto I sent it.*   Isaiah 55:11

Dr. Malan of Geneva, on a trip to Paris, one day fell into a conversation with a man who began to reason with him about Christianity. The doctor answered every argument with a quotation from Scripture — not venturing a single personal remark or application. Every quotation his companion evaded or turned aside, only to be met by another passage. The skeptic became enraged. "Don't you see, I don't believe your Bible! What's the use of quoting it to me?" he shouted. But Dr. Malan's reply was another thrust of the sword of the Spirit, "If ye believe not that I am he, ye shall die in your sins." Years passed. Then one morning Dr. Malan received a letter. Opening it he read, "You took the Sword of the Spirit and stabbed me through and through one day, and every time I tried to parry the blade and get you to use your hands, and not the Heavenly steel, you simply gave me another stab. You made me feel I was not fighting you, but God." It was signed by the former skeptic in whom the "seed of the Word" had finally been mixed with faith.

Even as the natural seed changes soil into plants, so the living seed of the Word changes the character of the individual who comes in contact with it. For example, in the night of the Dark Ages when the Word of God was planted by the Holy Spirit in the hearts of chosen men, it brought forth the fruit of the Reformation. There was a rediscovery of the truth, that salvation is not by ritual or works, but by the free grace of God. The words, "The just shall live by faith," lodging in the soul of Martin Luther, broke the bonds of his ecclesiasticism, and bloomed forth into 95 theses of freedom. These awoke the world to the truth concerning justification and many other cardinal doctrines of the faith.

The same Word is still the "power of God unto salvation!"

—H.G.B.

> Oh, may I find my armor there!
> Thy Word my trusty sword,
> I'll learn to fight with every foe
> The battle of the Lord. — E. Hodder

"The Bible is the only Book that always finds me." — COLERIDGE

REST IN THE STORM

SUGGESTED SCRIPTURE READING: James 3:13-18

Thou wilt keep him in perfect peace, whose mind is stayed on thee: because he trusteth in thee. Isaiah 26:3

Two artists each painted a picture to illustrate his conception of rest. The first chose for his scene a still, lone lake among the far-off mountains. The second drew on his canvas a thundering waterfall, with a fragile birch tree bending over the foam. At the fork of a branch, almost wet with the cataract's spray, a robin sat on its nest. The first was only *Stagnation;* the last was *Rest.* For in rest there are always two elements — tranquillity and energy; silence and turbulence; creation and destruction; fearlessness and fearfulness.

This is the victory of faith. It is easy to "rest" when all is quiet and peaceful; but to rest in the midst of storm, this is perfect peace! Today as you go forth to meet the trials and testings of life, you can know the "peace of God" which passeth all understanding. And how is it obtained? By turning everything over to Him.

"Be anxious in nothing; but in everything by prayer and supplication with thanksgiving let your requests be made known unto God" (Phil. 4:6). Before you go forth to work, pause to tell Him all about it and trust Him for everything.   —M.R.D.

O for the peace of a perfect trust,
My loving God, in Thee;
Unwavering faith, that never doubts,
Thou choosest best for me! — Anon.

"Trust God where you cannot trace Him. Do not try to penetrate the cloud He brings over you: rather look to the bow that is on it. The mystery is God's; the promise is yours." — MACDUFF

INSTEAD OF THE BRIER

SUGGESTED SCRIPTURE READING: Zechariah 1:7-11

> *. . . instead of the brier shall come up the myrtle tree.*
> Isaiah 55:13

Hear the parable of the brier and the rose: Once there was a brier growing in a ditch. A gardener came along and with his spade he dug around the ugly weed and lifted it out of the ground, placing it in his wheelbarrow. The brier said to itself, "What is he doing that for? Doesn't he know that I am just an old worthless brier?" But the gardener took it home and planted it with his flowers, while the brier again said, "What a mistake he has made, planting an old brier like myself among such beautiful roses as these!" A little later the gardener came once more. He took his knife, made a slit in the brier and budded it with a flower and when summer came, lovely roses were blooming on the old brier bush. Then the gardener said, "Your beauty is *not due to that which came out, but to that which I put into you.*" What a picture of the processes of grace! Alongside of the useless brier of our old nature, God grafts in His new, perfect life. By the power of His Holy Spirit we then bring forth all the beautiful flowers of testimony and the fruit of grace so adequately typified by the myrtle tree. It is said that this luxurious plant, which grows in the Orient, produces a profusion of snow-white flowers bordered with purple, and emits a perfume more exquisite than that of the rose. It also has many tasty seeds which we know as the flavorful allspice. Thorns, thistles and briers are reminders of the curse brought on by sin; but the myrtle tree speaks of the wonders that God performs in and through us by His grace.

Has your life been joined and engrafted by the Rose of Sharon? If it has, the perfume of His love will radiate from you. Which is most prominent in your life — the unlovely brier of the old nature, or the fruitful myrtle tree of the new?   —H.G.B.

> Jesus, Rose of Sharon, bloom within my heart;
> Beauties of Thy truth and holiness impart,
> That where'er I go my life may shed abroad
> Fragrance of the knowledge of the love of God.
> — I. A. Guirey

"Grace makes the last first, and the unlovely beautiful!" — H.G.B.

KEEP YOUR MOUTH SHUT

SUGGESTED SCRIPTURE READING: Psalm 19

Let another man praise thee, and not thine own mouth.
Proverbs 27:2

If you want to lose your friends, just talk about "yourself." Nothing is more boring than to listen to a conceited and proud person telling all about how clever he is, where he has been, and how much he knows. Someone has said, "It doesn't matter how dumb you are, if you keep your mouth shut no one will catch on."

A frog was wondering how he could get away from the cold climate in which he found himself during the winter. Some wild geese suggested that he should migrate with them. The difficulty was, how it could be accomplished, seeing the frog had no wings. "You leave it to me," said the frog, "I've got a splendid brain." After due deliberation, he got two geese to pluck up a strong reed and then suggested that each of them hold one end of it. He in turn would hold on to the middle of the reed with his mouth. Thus in due time, the geese and the frog started on their migratory journey. Soon they were passing over a small town and the villagers turned out to see such an unusual sight as that of two geese with a reed to which a frog was clinging with his mouth. "Oh! how wonderful! Who could have invented such a device?" they cried. This remark made the frog so self-conscious, and puffed him up with such a sense of importance, that he could not help opening his mouth and exclaiming, "I did it!" His self-advertisement was his undoing, for the moment he opened his mouth he let go his hold and fell to his death. Pride will always meet with a fall; while the Lord always crowns the queen of graces—humility — with his blessing.

If we would talk more about HIM, we would have less time to talk about ourselves. Solomon said, "A fool's mouth is his destruction and his lips are the snare of his soul" (Prov. 18:7).   —M.R.D.

Guard well thy lips; none, none can know
What evils from the tongue may flow. — Anon.

"Humility is the Christian's loveliest virtue and his crowning grace."

THE POWER OF THE SMALL

SUGGESTED SCRIPTURE READING: James 3:1-5

Behold also the ships, which though they be so great, and are driven of fierce winds, yet are they turned about with a very small helm. James 3:4

We should pay attention to little things. The power they wield is tremendous. The energy in an atom can destroy a whole city, a comparatively small rudder can completely control the movements of a giant ocean liner, and a single life dedicated to God can move a multitude.

The story is told of a lady who was fixing a box for the missionaries in India. A child came to her door giving her a penny, all that she had, to be used for the Lord. With this copper the Christian lady bought a tract and put it into the box. Eventually this gospel leaflet came into the hands of a Burmese chief, and it was used of God to lead him to a saving knowledge of Christ. The chief in turn told the story of his conversion and his great happiness to his friends. Many of them also believed and cast away their idols. A church was built there, a missionary was sent, and at least fifteen hundred natives were converted from heathenism. All this, and probably more, was the result of one shiny penny given for Jesus with a heart full of love.

Someone has said, "The beginnings of faithfulness are always the little things that we think will make no difference." No one was ever called of God to a high position who did not lay the foundation of that call in courageous faithfulness to the small details of life. But whether our position be high or low, it is required of a steward that he be found faithful. He who is conscientious now about the little things will be made "ruler over many things." Some day the words of Jeremiah 30:19 will apply to all the faithful. "I will glorify them, and *they shall not be small.* —H.G.B.

> If for my hands there is no larger task,
> Then, precious Lord, for this I ask —
> That unto those who come my way
> I might impart a shining ray
> New light of hope by word, or just a smile,
> And thereby cheer some soul a while.
> — R. Magines

"He who is a Christian in small things is not a small Christian!"

THE PATH OF LEAST RESISTANCE

SUGGESTED SCRIPTURE READING: Romans 6:11-13

. . . . a child left to himself bringeth his mother to shame.
Proverbs 29:15

Did you ever see a straight river? I am sure you never did. You may have seen straight canals built by man but a straight river has never yet existed. They all twist and turn and wind and double back on their way to the sea. I remember years ago we fished a trout stream. We left our car at the bend in the river and fished a stretch of water over two miles long. It took us some five hours until we ended up within 100 feet of the place where we began. How many fish did I catch? That is an embarrassing question and has nothing to do at all with the subject! I am talking about crooked rivers. A much better question is: Why are rivers always crooked? That I can answer. It is because water always flows downhill and a river just follows the path of least resistance. When it comes to a hill or other firm obstruction it just goes around it. It follows the downward pull of gravity.

Now that is the reason the natural man is crooked — very, very crooked (See Rom. 3:9-18, Ps. 14). Until he is regenerated and made alive in Christ, he can only do "what comes naturally." The natural man cannot please God. Human depravity leads down, until overcome by the Power from above by being born again. But even in the believer the "old nature" still pulls down, and it takes spiritual effort to overcome it. This power depends on keeping in touch with God, by prayer, Bible study, testimony, fellowship and obedience to His will and Word. Then the river of your life will cease winding and run straight. Have you prayed today, read your Bible, sought strength to face the current of the world today? Remember, any dead fish can float downstream but it takes a live and healthy one to ascend the rapids to the fresh headwaters of spiritual victory. —M.R.D.

I want to scale the utmost height,
And catch a gleam of glory bright;
So, still I'll pray till Heav'n I've found,
"Lord, lead me on to higher ground."
— J. Oatman, Jr.

"In what direction are you moving? All growth that is not toward God, is growing to decay." — G. MAC DONALD

NOT FORSAKING THE ASSEMBLY

SUGGESTED SCRIPTURE READING: Hebrews 10:19-25

Not forsaking the assembling of ourselves together, as the manner of some is; but exhorting one another: and so much the more, as ye see the day approaching.

Hebrews 10:25

When we are born into the family of God we are spiritual "babies." There are at least four things that an infant requires. He needs food, fresh air, exercise and the help and fellowship of others. This is also true in the spiritual realm. We need *food* (the study of the Word of God), *fresh air* (communion and prayer — "that ye faint not"), *exercise* (service and witnessing), and *fellowship* with others (a good church home). Any child of God who neglects any of these four things cannot expect to be well-rounded in his Christian life and experience. Even though the visible church is imperfect, it is essential in order that we may experience the communion of saints, partake of the ordinances, unitedly advance the cause of missions, and receive thoughtful exhortations from the Word. Especially as we go toward the end of the age and see the Day of Christ approaching are we urged to join hands with other Christians.

All his life, Old Bill had never gone to church; no matter how much he was coaxed, he could never be persuaded to attend even on Christmas and Easter. "When it *freezes in June,*" he would say, "then I will go to church." One year it was unusually cold and stayed that way until late spring. The first part of June the mercury dipped to freezing for several nights. Everyone thought about Old Bill and what he had said. Perhaps this spell of cold weather would force him to attend church. It did! One Sunday Old Bill made his first appearance in the meeting house — while the organ played softly — *six men carried him in!* Don't be like Old Bill! —H.G.B.

I love Thy kingdom, Lord,
The house of Thine abode,
The Church our blest Redeemer saved
With His own precious blood. — T. Dwight

"The church is not a gallery for the exhibition of eminent Christians but a school for the education of imperfect ones, a nursery for the care of weak ones, and a hospital for the healing of those who need diligent care." — BEECHER

DOWN! DOWN! DOWN!

Suggested Scripture Reading: John 1:1-14

For I came down from heaven.   John 6:38

The coming down of Jesus to be our Saviour meant infinite humiliation for Him. He was the infinitely holy Son of God, yet was willing to humble Himself to become a man to save us. Jesus therefore said, "I came *DOWN*." From the infinite heights of glory, He went to the infinite gloom of Calvary. Out of the ivory palaces (Ps. 45:8) into this world of woe He came to redeem us. After He came down, He did three things:

1. He laid *DOWN* His life. (John 10:15)
2. He sat *DOWN* in heaven. (Heb. 1:3)
3. He will put *DOWN* His enemies. (I Cor. 15:24, 25)

Christ was not a victim, He was a willing substitute. He *laid down* His life. Jesus did not die of pain or agony or weakness or of a broken heart, but instead, when He had paid the price for sin, He dismissed His spirit (Luke 23:46). He could have hung on the Cross indefinitely, but when the work was done, He gave up the ghost.

And because the work was done, He therefore sat *DOWN* in heaven. He *SAT* down. It is our assurance that the work of redemption is completed. There is nothing we can add to it. We must simply accept and receive it (Rom. 4:5). Jesus is sitting down today, but will some day arise to put *DOWN* every enemy. For this glorious day every believer waits and longs.

In these three *"DOWNS"* we have Christ's complete redemption work.

1. The past — He laid *DOWN* His life to save us.
2. The present — He *SITS DOWN* in heaven to keep us.
3. The future — He will *COME DOWN* to take us to Himself and destroy His enemies.   —M.R.D.

> O listen to the wondrous story:
> Counted once among the lost,
> Yet, One came down from heaven's glory,
> Saving us at awful cost! — J. Gray

"We can only know God's estimate of sin by the sacrifice which He had to provide to atone for it."

WHEN THE SPIRIT IS OVERWHELMED

SUGGESTED SCRIPTURE READING: Psalm 143:1-10

When my spirit was overwhelmed within me, then thou knewest my path.   Psalm 142:3

Theodore Cuyler tells of a woman striving to find rest for her troubled and burdened soul. As she sat in her summerhouse, suddenly through an open window there flew a bird. Being greatly alarmed, it circled up toward the roof and tried to get out, hurling itself first against one window and then against another. Flying from side to side, it finally began to pant with fright and weariness. The woman said, "Poor bird, why do you not come down lower, then you would see this open door and you would fly out easily?" But the bird kept wounding itself against the closed windows trying to force its body through every small crevice it saw. At last its wings grew tired, and it flew lower and lower in its exhaustion until it was on a level with the open door. Then, seeing the way of escape, the little feathered creature suddenly found freedom. Soon its song was heard in the trees of the nearby churchyard. A new light dawned upon the mind of the woman. "I, like that poor bird, through my pride and self-sufficiency, have been flying too high to see the door which stands wide open," she said. Her heart was quieted and she realized, even as did the Psalmist, that though her spirit was now overwhelmed with difficulties, God still had an open door through which she could find freedom if she would but stop her struggling and humbly await His direction. Once she had yielded her will to God, she found the way of escape she was seeking, and her life became a symphony of harmony and praise.

Oh, troubled soul, cease your futile battering against the walls of circumstance; rest in the Lord, look for His way of deliverance, and you too will soon be singing songs of gladness and relief.

—H.G.B.

He giveth more grace when the burdens grow greater,
He sendeth more strength when the labours increase,
To added affliction He addeth His mercy,
To multiplied trials, His multiplied peace. — Anon.

"God often digs wells of joy with the spade of sorrow." — ANON

WATCH YOUR SPEED

SUGGESTED SCRIPTURE READING: John 8:3-11

. . . . I have lived in all good conscience before God.

Acts 23:1

Conscience should always be man's guide, even though it is not always a safe guide. To live conscientiously is to live honestly and follow what we believe to be the right way. Yet we may be all wrong in following our conscience. It is not doing what *WE* think is right, but what God *SAYS* is right. Unless conscience is in harmony with the will of God and the Bible, it may be all wrong. Paul in "all good conscience" persecuted the Church, he thought he was doing God a favor (I Tim. 1:13, Acts 26:9). He was zealous, sincere and honest, *but all wrong* till he met Jesus. Conscience, therefore, is only a safe guide when it is in harmony with the revelation of Jesus Christ. The Bible is the standard of conduct and until conscience is synchronized with the Word of God, it is not a safe guide.

I was driving a new car and noticed in my rear view mirror a policeman following me. I looked at my speedometer and it registered 25 miles. I kept it there for a half mile, feeling perfectly secure and at ease, but the policeman followed me and finally beckoned me to the side of the road. "What's your hurry?" he asked, and I answered, "I'm not in a hurry." Quick came the reply, "Then why do you speed?" He accused me of going 32 miles an hour. We argued for a few minutes for I knew I had not exceeded 25 miles. Finally, I said, "Do I look like a fool? I saw you following me from Wealthy street all the way to Hall. Can you imagine me deliberately speeding when I knew you were right behind?" This made him think and he finally said, "This is a brand new car. Maybe your speedometer is at fault." Sure enough, we checked it and found my speedometer in which I had securely trusted was "off." I was let "off" too with the warning, "Check your speedometer." Conscience is your speedometer but it will get you in trouble unless checked with the official standard — the Word of God. *DON'T NEGLECT THE BIBLE!*   —M.R.D.

Holy Bible, Book divine, precious treasure, thou art mine;
Mine to chide me when I rove, mine to show a Saviour's love;
Mine thou art to guide my feet, mine to judge, condemn, acquit.
— John Burton

"A good conscience is one conditioned by the Bible."

WHEN JESUS STANDS STILL

SUGGESTED SCRIPTURE READING: Matthew 20:25-34

*And Jesus stood still, and called them, and said, What
will ye that I shall do unto you? They say unto him,
Lord, that our eyes may be opened.*   Matthew 20:32, 33

Jesus came into the world to serve others and to save the lost
(Matt. 20:28). Because of this, the years of His public ministry
were especially crowded with action. He was ever on the move.
Constantly under pressure from the crowd, His enemies, and the
enormous responsibility of His earthly task, He wore Himself out
for others. He worked almost without rest until His body became
thin and emaciated from the strain. When nailed to the accursed
tree for our redemption, He was so gaunt that all of His bones
could be counted (Ps. 22:14-17). So swift was the pace that
Jesus set, so crowded was His schedule, that if all His activity
had been recorded, the Bible today would not be a single book,
but rather a library of tremendous size (John 21:25). Yet, with
all His heavy duties and vast activity, Jesus was never too busy
to help any individual who in faith claimed His attention. When
two blind beggars on the Jericho road cried out for help and
mercy, *Jesus stood still!* With a look of pity He turned, touched
their eyes, and restored to them the gift of sight. Having ministered to their need, He again immediately moves forward, for we
find that *to thank Him they had to "follow Him."*

Today, too, Jesus is never too busy to hear the individual cry of
those who seek help or desire spiritual sight. If you are in strait-
ened circumstances, feel free to call upon Him, for He will never
pass you by. He will stand still and minister to your need. If you
have received His blessing you no longer should sit by the side of
the Jericho road. *Show your gratitude by following Him!* —H.G.B.

Pass me not, oh gentle Saviour,
Hear my humble cry;
While on others Thou art calling,
Do not pass me by.   — F. J. Crosby

"No matter how weak their faith, or how feeble their call, Jesus is
never too busy to hear the cry of the needy." — G.W.

REDEEMED

SUGGESTED SCRIPTURE READING: Romans 6:14-19

Ye were not redeemed with corruptible things . . . but with the precious blood of Christ.   I Peter 1:18, 19

Among the many, many names by which our Lord is called in Scripture, there is one which has no peer. It is the name *Redeemer.* Literally the word "redeem" means to "buy back again." It suggests that something has been sold or forfeited in order to pay a debt. By paying the price of its redemption, this lost article can be repossessed. It suggests a shop where we "pawn" a watch or a piece of jewelry. To obtain it again it must be "redeemed" by paying the redemption price.

Man originally was created in God's image. Had he not sinned he would have lived forever. But he fell and sold out to the devil for a morsel of food from a forbidden tree. He now belongs to the devil, for the unconverted are children of the devil instead of God (John 8:44). To redeem these lost ones, the purchase price was the death and resurrection of the Son of God. His blood was accepted as a complete, satisfactory payment to meet the demands of God's justice and holiness. And now being set free, we willingly become the slaves of our Redeemer.

An Englishman visiting a slave market in Egypt kept bidding on a certain slave till no one was able to go higher. Upon payment of the price he took the bill of sale, duly receipted, and giving it to the slave said, "I have purchased you to set you free." But the slave, overcome with gratitude, refused to leave such a wonderful master and became for life his willing and devoted servant.—M.R.D.

My new life I owe to Thee,
Jesus, Lamb of Calvary;
Sin was cancelled on the tree,
Jesus, blessed Jesus. — H. P. Blanchard

"Too many spend time counting the cost of following Christ when they should consider the cost of not following Him."

CHOOSING THE BETTER PART

. . . Mary hath chosen that good part.   Luke 10:42

Life offers us a multitude of choices. Mary and Martha, the friends of Jesus, were both spiritual women, but Mary was praised by Jesus as being the wisest. She was not satisfied with God's second best but loved to sit at Jesus' feet, there to drink in His Words and seek the things of God which were of the highest good. We too as Christians are not only required to choose between right and wrong, but oftentimes we also have an opportunity to decide between what is good and what is better. It is then that true spirituality shows itself. If you would win the praise of God and live the "more abundant life," you must be satisfied with nothing less than God's best. There are many things which are not actually wrong in themselves but yet they should be rejected. The question is not where will we find the most pleasure, receive the greatest earthly honor, or enjoy the most ease and contentment, but rather will the decision I make today result in the highest good when viewed in the light of eternal values? Young person, if you must decide a life's course, ask yourself this question: "Where can I bring the most glory to God and render the most significant service?" Like Mary, be sure that you choose that "good part."

Wilbur Chapman tells of a visit he had with General Booth as follows: I said, "General Booth, tell me what has been the secret of your success?" He hesitated a second, and I saw the tears come into his eyes and steal down his cheeks, and then he said: "I will tell you the secret. *God has had all there was of me to have.* There may have been men with greater opportunities; but from the day I got the poor of London on my heart, and a vision of what Jesus Christ could do, I made up my mind that God would have all there was of William Booth. If there is anything of power in the Salvation Army today, it is because God has had all the adoration of my heart, all the power of my will, and all the influence of my life." Chapman said he learned from Booth that the greatness of a man's power is the measure of his surrender. — Don't be satisfied with God's second best.   —H.G.B.

Give of your best to the Master,
Give Him first place in your heart;
Give Him first place in your service;
Consecrate now every part. — H.B.G.

"Not is it wrong, but is it BEST?"

UNION OR UNITY

SUGGESTED SCRIPTURE READING: John 17:13-26

*That they all may be one; as thou, Father, art in me, and
I in thee, that they also may be one in us: that the world
may believe that thou hast sent me.*   John 17:21

The Body of Christ is a unity. It consists of members from every
people, tribe, and nation; of every color, nationality and denomination. The divisions into local assemblies are merely local repre-
sentatives of the one universal Body and Church. Denominations
and sects are artificial, manmade classifications. No matter how
the different sects, denominations and groups may fight one another, the true members of the Body of Christ are still one in Him.
They are united by the blood of Christ. Any other basis of union
is false and artificial. You may tie the tails of a dog and a cat
together and you will have a union, but you surely will not have
unity. True unity comes only when we realize that every born-
again believer walking in the light is a fellow-member in Christ.
The greater heights of spirituality we attain, the less the human
divisions and classifications mean to us. As we rise in our Christian
experience these human differences fade away and we see our
unity in Him.

It is like traveling in an airplane. As we climb higher and higher
the fences that divided the fields and farms fade out, until we see
only one beautiful landscape of forest, field, winding stream and
river, presenting one grand and beautiful picture. So it is as we
rise higher in love and faith. The fences that divide His Church
grow smaller and more insignificant. The divisions are still there
but we live above them, for Christian unity is not absolute una-
nimity. All men are different, nor would we want them all alike.
Each musical instrument has its own quality and tone, but when
perfectly tuned all these different sounds make one harmonious
concert to delight our hearts. The important question is: Are you
a member of His Body, the one True Church? Then other things
become unimportant.   —M.R.D.

I love Thy Church, O God, Her walls before Thee stand,
Dear as the apple of Thine eye, and graven on Thy hand.
                                              — T. Dwight

**"Those who love Christ the Head should also consistently love the mem-
bers of His Body."**

THE VALUE OF PAIN

SUGGESTED SCRIPTURE READING: I Peter 4:16-19

. . . thou hast enlarged me when I was in distress.

Psalm 4:1

When Adam fell, he died immediately in his spirit, progressively in his soul, and eventually in his body. Even though he had the sentence of death upon him he was allowed to bring forth children. Thus God made possible the Incarnation and the future redemption of the human race. In this same progressive order of spirit, soul and body, man is once again brought back to his original perfection. When we are saved, our spirit is immediately made perfect (see I John 3:9). Our soul, however, is progressively redeemed through the process of sanctification. This is not completed until we enter heaven, for it is only there that "just men (are) made perfect" (Heb. 12:23). Finally, our bodies will be touched by redemption when we are glorified in the Resurrection. A Christian in this life, therefore, is still subject to the same laws of sowing and reaping, pain and death, that govern the physical existence of other men. Pain is frequently God's purifying agent sent to produce greater holiness in His children. Like the Psalmist, our souls too are often "enlarged" in distress.

In Western Canada there is living a young woman who has never felt an ache or a pain in her life. By some strange twist of nature she was born without the sense of feeling. No one envies her, however, for they say that her body is a mass of scars and bruises and she has been repeatedly hospitalized for infections that the rest of us avoid. You see, she does not have the usual warning devices to alert her to danger. Pain has its values! With the sharp chisel of distress our Lord sculptures beautiful lives. If the knife of trial therefore is cutting you sore, submit your will to His, bow your head and say, "Thank You, Lord, for this pain; through it do Thy gracious work in my life." —H.G.B.

The cry of man's anguish went up unto God,
"Lord, take away pain!"
Then answered the Lord to the cry of His world:
"Shall I take away pain,
And with it the power of the soul to endure,
Made strong by the strain?" — Anon.

"Most of the grand truths of God have to burned into us with the hot iron of affliction, otherwise we shall not truly receive them."
— C. H. SPURGEON

THE THING

SUGGESTED SCRIPTURE READING: Luke 12:16-21

. . . whose shall those things be?   Luke 12:20

What is a *thing?* Do you know, and could you define a *"thing"?*
You say, "That's easy, a 'thing' is — well, a thing is — well, you see
a thing can be almost 'anything.'" Yes, but what is a "thing"?
Sounds foolish, doesn't it? You say a house is a thing — but a
thing is not necessarily a house. A chair is a thing — but all things
are not chairs. You just can't define a "thing" — it is something, but
what is it? This is a graphic picture of "what the world consists
of and all it has to offer." The world is full of "things," but all of
them are unstable, here today and gone tomorrow. Here is a
chunk of wood — it is a thing — it is something. But I place it in
the fire and in a half hour it is gone. Where did that *"thing"* go
anyway? All the things the world has to offer are like that — now
you've got it — now you haven't! Really exasperating, isn't it?
The only "things" which are permanent are "heavenly things."
Jesus despised earthly things, for Satan said, "All these *THINGS*
will I give thee" (Matt. 4:9). They were only things and Jesus
ignored them. Again Jesus said, "After all these *THINGS* do the
Gentiles seek" (Matt. 6:32).

All the things of earth are transient and perishable. Peter says,
"that all these *THINGS* shall be dissolved" (II Peter 3:11). The
rich man had built his bigger barns, but that night he was called
to leave all these "things" behind. Today may we learn to set our
affection on things above where Christ sitteth on the right hand
of God. Seek those things which are above, not the *"THINGS*
on the earth." Only the heavenly things will abide — all else must
perish. The writer of Hebrews makes the distinction clear. Concerning earthly things he speaks of the "removing of those things
that are shaken, as of things that are made, *THAT THOSE
THINGS WHICH CANNOT BE SHAKEN MAY REMAIN"*
(Heb. 12:27).   —M.R.D.

Worldly joy is fleeting — vanity itself;
Vain the dazzling brightness, vain the stores of wealth;
Vain the pomp and glory; only Thou canst give
Peace and satisfaction whilst on earth we live. — Anon.

**"The more of heaven there is in our lives, the less of earth we shall
covet."**

OUR GREAT SAVIOUR

SUGGESTED SCRIPTURE READING: I Corinthians 2:7-9

Howbeit I believed not the words, until I came, and mine eyes had seen it: and, behold, the half was not told me.
I Kings 10:7

These words spoken by the Queen of Sheba concerning the glory, honor, and majesty of Solomon are pregnant with symbolic meaning far beyond their mere literal significance. Happily amazed at the things she saw in this marvelous kingdom, overcome by the blessing and beauty of the scene, she exclaims in awe and wonder: " . . . the one half of the greatness of thy wisdom was not told me; for thou exceedest the fame that I heard" (See II Chron. 9:6). In a larger sense all of this is typical of One who is "greater than Solomon" (Matt. 12:42), the Lord Jesus Christ Himself!

Before we were saved, we heard others speak of the Saviour. They exulted over His blessing, His sweetness, His joy, His glory; but we did not fully appreciate their testimony. Not until our eyes were opened and we were brought into His presence by the new birth did we actually begin to realize His beauty. Then we saw that He was "altogether lovely" and "the fairest among ten thousands." Truly those who had witnessed to us of Jesus had, with all their glowing terms, underestimated Him.

A new Christian spoke to a saint of God, who had long been walking with his Saviour, as follows: "My, isn't it a grand thing to be saved?" "Yes," said the other, "but I know something better than that." "Better than being saved?" "Yes, I know *the companionship of the Man who saves me,* and believe me, the half has never yet been told."

One day we shall experience the fullness of joy in the presence of our Heavenly Solomon. What a wonder of surprises awaits us on those blissful shores of eternity. Then in awe and adoration we will exclaim anew with the Queen of Sheba, *"The half was not told me!"*
—H.G.B.

And oh, what rapture it will be with all the hosts above
To sing through all eternity, the wonders of His love,
The half was never told, the half was never told,
Of grace divine, so wonderful, the half was never told.
— P. P. Bliss

"In time we can but read the title page of our inheritance; but in eternity we shall find a never ending volume of joy and blessing." — G.W.

THE TALKING ASS

Answer not a fool.   Proverbs 26:4
Answer a fool.   Proverbs 26:5

Here indeed is a seeming contradiction in the Word of God, for Solomon tells us to "Answer not a fool according to his folly," and in the next breath he tells us the very opposite, "Answer a fool according to his folly." But there is no contradiction if we read the last phrase in each verse. In Proverbs 26:4 we are *NOT* to answer a fool like a fool, lest we "also be like unto him." But in verse 5 we should answer him lest he take it for granted that he is so smart, that you are unable to answer him. There is, therefore, a time when we should ignore foolish questions, and at other times they should be answered "according to their folly." We receive many, many letters from "fools, nuts, and crackpots." Some of them we ignore, others we answer.

But when we answer the fool it must be with the purpose of showing him his own foolishness, or as Solomon puts it, according to his foolishness. A scoffing, mocking blaspheming infidel once made fun of a sincere believer. Ridiculing the miracles of the Bible, he sneeringly said, "And do you really believe that an ass ever spoke to Balaam?" (Numbers 22:30). Quick as a flash the Christian replied, "My friend, I cannot possibly doubt the truth of that story for I have been spoken to in the same way myself." The infidel was given something to meditate upon.

The world is full of "talking asses." You will probably meet up with some of them today. There will be occasions when silence will be the best answer to those who scoff and laugh at your faith. At other times you will have to speak up and rebuke the fool according to his foolishness. Oh, for the wisdom and discernment to know when to speak and when to be silent. "Oh God, give us wisdom today, so that we may know how to meet the enemies of the Gospel. Teach us when to speak and when to be silent, in Jesus' Name, Amen."   —M.R.D.

Fools to talking ever prone,
Are sure to make their follies known;
Wise men by God's wisdom true,
Weigh their words, or make them few! — Gay

"Knowledge is folly unless grace guides it."

PARDON FOR THE PENITENT

SUGGESTED SCRIPTURE READING: Luke 7:37-50

And he said unto her, Thy sins are forgiven.   Luke 7:48

This benediction of pardon was lavished upon an evil woman of the streets who manifested all the marks of repentance and faith when she came face to face with Jesus. We find here a tender and beautiful revelation of the heart of God. This poor harlot, conscious of her deep need, had left her earthly lovers and found the "Lover of her soul." Her many tears and incessant kisses showed her impassioned earnestness. She was not ashamed to kneel and admit her need before the assembled guests at the huge banquet. Her flowing tresses and her costly ointment, once employed as enticements in her lustful trade, are deflected from their former evil use and lavished upon the feet of the Saviour. Her all is laid in complete surrender upon the altar of repentance. She cares not for the reproachful stare and the hypocritical smirk of the self-righteous Pharisee who sits near by. She is interested only in a look of forgiveness from the Master — and her faith is not disappointed. Jesus said, " . . . him that cometh to me I will in no wise cast out" (John 6:37), and He keeps His word. A penitent never fails to obtain a blessed reception from Him. The weeping harlot, who before had seen only lust in the eyes of men, never forgot the warm, pure, soulful look of tender compassion that flooded the face of the Son of God as He breathed that gracious word of salvation and comfort: "Thy faith hath saved thee; go in peace."

A hardened criminal in a Japanese prison once picked up a copy of the Bible and began to read the story of the trial of Jesus. He was unmoved until he came to the words of our Lord, "Father, forgive them; for they know not what they do." He was stabbed to the heart. Later he said, "Through this simple sentence of gracious pardon, I was led into the truth of Christianity." "Yes, there is peace — eternal peace — waiting for the penitent who comes in faith seeking forgiveness.   —H.G.B.

> She heard but the Saviour: she spoke but with sighs;
> She dared not glance up to the Heaven of His eyes;
> He looked on the lost one: her sins were forgiven,
> And the sinner went forth in the beauty of Heaven!
> — Anon.

"The wages of sin is death, but by receiving Christ you can leave before Payday."

THE LOVE OF GOD

<small>SUGGESTED SCRIPTURE READING: John 17:1-15</small>

Christ died for the ungodly.   Romans 5:6

We can understand the love of a Mother for her child, the love of a husband for his wife, the love of a friend. Jesus said, "Greater love hath no man than this, that a man lay down his life for his friends" (John 15:13).

This is the acme of human love, to die for a *FRIEND*. Mere human love is not able to go beyond this. We love our friends; we love the lovable and the lovely. We may be willing to die for such, but to die for our enemies requires a higher love than human. And so Paul says, "But God commendeth his love toward us, in that, while we were yet sinners, Christ died for us" (Rom. 5:8).

Christ died for the "ungodly." We can hardly understand this. We can understand a love which loves those who also love, but how can we fathom the depth of love of a Holy God who was willing to give His Son to save His Son's murderers? Oh, the forbearance, the longsuffering, the patience of God!

An atheist, blaspheming God at a street meeting, turned to the crowd and said, "If there is a God I challenge him to strike me dead in five minutes." Breathless silence reigned as the seconds ticked off and after five minutes the scoffer said sneeringly, "See, there is no God or He would have killed me. The five minutes are up." An old lady stepped up and said, "Have you children?" "Yes, I have a son." "Well" she said, "If your son gave you a knife and asked you to kill him would you do it?" "Why no," he said. "And why not?" "Because I love him too much." The old lady turned away with the remark, "God loves you too much to accept your foolish challenge. He wants you to be saved — not lost." —M.R.D.

> Though I forget Him and wander away,
> Still He doth love me wherever I stray;
> Back to His dear loving arms would I flee,
> When I remember that Jesus loves me. — P. P. Bliss

"Oh, the love of Christ, . . . the love of Christ, we can never understand it, but what a beautiful study for eternity it will be."—JUDSON OF BURMA

"WINDOWS IN HEAVEN!"

SUGGESTED SCRIPTURE READING: Psalm 28

> *. . . Behold, if the* LORD *would make windows in heaven, might this thing be?*   II Kings 7:2

In the days of Elisha there was a great famine in Samaria and they were being beseiged by the hosts of the Syrians. The situation was desperate (II Kings 6:25). Mothers in their frantic hunger were boiling their own children and eating them (II Kings 6:29). The wicked king Jehoram had determined to behead the prophet of God, whom he unjustly blamed for the catastrophe. Elisha, however, was spared when he made a remarkable prophecy of astounding plenty which, he said, would be their portion on the following day. The king's most illustrious courtier, realizing that this would require an incredible miracle, sneered and scoffed "Why," said he, "if the Lord would make windows in Heaven, might this thing be?" He not only disparaged the prophet, but in effect, his scoffing infidelity was directed against God Himself. His unbelief later cost him his life (II Kings 7:20), but the word of Elisha was marvelously fulfilled. There came a supernatural manifestation of sound to the ears of the beseiging hosts which made them flee in fear, leaving behind a great spoil and an abundance of food for the starving inhabitants of Samaria (II Kings 7:16).

God is as mighty to deliver His own today. He can, if necessary, still carve windows in heaven and pour out unexpected blessings on those who fervently and expectantly trust in Him. Some years ago a Nova Scotia town was on fire. An old retired minister entered the church and kneeled to pray for its safety, for it was their only place of worship. The oncoming sea of fire drew perilously close. His friends entreated him to leave, but he prayed on. Then a strange thing happened the flames divided into two streams and by-passed the church completely. God was glorified by all, for so great a deliverance.

Are you walled in by circumstances? Then pray and wait for God to carve a window.   —H.G.B.

> So shall we not trustfully tell Him
> When things seem straitened and black —
> "Lord, thou canst make windows in heaven
> And we nothing good shall lack." — J. D. Smith

"Faith has never yet outstripped the power of God."

IT SPOILED MY COFFEE

SUGGESTED SCRIPTURE READING: Mark 4:1-9

> *. . . prepare your hearts unto the* LORD, *and serve him only.* I Samuel 7:3

So you didn't enjoy your pastor's sermon? I heard you say, "That was surely a poor message, I didn't get a thing out of it. I don't think our pastor spends enough time *preparing* his sermon." Now just a minute, brother, here is a strange thing; I thought it was one of the best sermons I ever heard and I just heard three others tell how they were blessed. And you are finding fault with the message that greatly blessed others, but somehow missed you. Could it be possible that the fault lies with *you?* How much time did you spend *preparing yourself* for the message? It takes just as much preparation to *receive* the blessing of a sermon as it does to *deliver* it. Did you arise early enough on the Lord's Day to spend a little quiet time in prayer with the Word? Or did you sit up till twelve Saturday night looking at television? Did you oversleep and then, because of a hurried breakfast, become irritated and excited? First the children got on your nerves, then the coffee boiled over, and finally the baby threw his plate on the floor. At last you were off to church but you got there all out of breath just as they sang the first number. And then you blame the poor preacher for lack of preparation! Shame on you! Come to church prepared for a blessing by prayer and the Word and even a mighty poor sermon will satisfy you.

A few mornings ago I awoke early and prepared my usual cup of coffee. Eagerly I took a swallow and — ugh! Bah! It nauseated me. I said, "Who bought this awful coffee, it isn't fit to drink!" Then suddenly I remembered. The night before I had gargled with strong salt water for a sore throat and left some of the brine in the cup. In the dusk I hadn't seen it and so poured the coffee into it. I blamed the coffee when I was at fault. Next time before you criticize your pastor, "Look in your own cup." —M.R.D.

> Before you criticize another,
> Be sure that YOU are right, my brother!
> For oft the faults you in others see,
> Are not as bad as the ones in thee! — Anon.

"Beware of trying to gloss over your own inadequacy by criticizing others!" — G.W.

WHAT THEY SING IN HEAVEN

SUGGESTED SCRIPTURE READING: Revelation 21:5-21

And they sung a new song, saying, Thou art worthy to take the book, and to open the seals thereof: for thou wast slain, and hast redeemed us to God by thy blood out of every kindred, and tongue, and people, and nation.

Revelation 5:9

Moody in his anecdotes tells about a Wesleyan preacher in England by the name of Peter McKinsey. Although a godly man he was still full of native humor. He was once preaching from the text, "And they sung a new song," and he said: "Yes, there will be singing in heaven, and when I get there I want to have David with his harp, and Paul, and Peter, and other saints gathered around for a sing. And I will announce a hymn from the Wesleyan Hymnal; I will say let us sing hymn number 749 —

'My God my Father, while I stray —'

"But someone will say, 'That won't do, You are in heaven, Peter; and there is no straying there.' And I will say, Yes, that's so. We had better sing number 651 —

'Though waves and storms go o'er my head,
Though friends be gone and hopes be dead —'

"But another saint will interrupt, 'Peter, you forget you are in heaven now; there are no storms there.' Well, I will try again — How about singing number 536 —

'Into a world of ruffians sent —'

"Peter! Peter! someone will say, 'We will put you out unless you stop giving out inappropriate hymns.' And I will say, 'What can we sing?' And they will say: 'Sing the New Song, the Song of Moses and the Lamb.'"

Yes, things will all be so different and wonderful there that we will need a new theme for our joyous praises. Let us hymn our way to heaven with a singing heart, so that we shall not find it strange to join the great "New Song!"   —H.G.B.

We shall sing on that beautiful shore,
The melodious songs of the blest,
And our spirits shall sorrow no more,
Not a sigh for the blessing of rest! — S. F. Bennett

"Praise is the dress of saints in Heaven, it is meet they should fit it on below!" — SPURGEON

DOING YOUR BEST

SUGGESTED SCRIPTURE READING: Titus 3:1-8

Not by works of righteousness . . . but according to his mercy he saved us. Titus 3:5

Everyone is expected to do his best. No one has a right to do anything less than the best he is able. But doing our best may not be enough, because of our limitations. I may do my best in trying to save a drowning man but if I am unable to swim myself my best will not be good enough. This is universally true also in the matter of salvation. Here all human effort and work fails. No one can, ever has, or ever will be saved by doing "one's best." Man's highest achievements and most noble endeavors fall infinitely short of God's lowest demands. Yet, in spite of the clear revelation of God that "all our righteousnesses are as filthy rags" in His sight, the most common excuse men give is, "I'm doing my best." In most cases it is an outright lie, for they are not doing their best at all. But suppose they are trying their best, it still is not enough to save them. A man may be honest, sincere, zealous, earnest and religious in trying to earn favor with God, but it cannot avail. Paul tried it and failed. Nicodemus tried it and failed. Man's best is not good enough for God.

A certain evangelist, burdened for the souls of men, was sitting in a barber's chair waiting for a shave. While the barber was stropping his razor the evangelist asked, "Sir, are you saved?" and the barber gave the stock answer, "I am doing my best and that's enough, isn't it?" The evangelist was silent until after he was shaved and the next customer was in the chair for a shave. Then the evangelist arose, grabbed a razor and said, "Let me shave this customer." "Oh, no," said the barber, "not you." "But," said the man, "I would do my very best, my very utmost best." "But," said the barber, "your best would not be good enough for this customer." The evangelist laid down the razor and as he left said, "Neither is your best good enough for God." Salvation is receiving God's best, not offering Him your filthy rags. —M.R.D.

Not the labors of my hands can fulfill thy law's demands;
Could my zeal no respite know, could my tears forever flow,
All for sin could not atone; Thou must save, and Thou alone.
— A. M. Toplady

"You can't 'work your way' into the family of God; you have to be 'born' into it!" (See John 3:3)

FIRST THANKSGIVING

In every thing give thanks: for this is the will of God in Christ Jesus concerning you. I Thessalonians 5:18

In Richardson's *American School Reader* printed in 1810 we have the following account written by Benjamin Franklin:

> There is a tradition that in the planting of New England, the first settlers met with many difficulties and hardships, as is generally the case when a civilized people attempt to establish themselves in a wilderness country. Being piously disposed, they sought relief from Heaven by laying their *wants and distresses* before the Lord, in frequent set days of fasting and prayer. Constant meditation and discourse on these subjects kept their minds gloomy and discontented. . . . At length, when it was proposed in the Assembly to proclaim another fast, a farmer of plain sense arose and remarked that the inconveniences they had suffered, and concerning which they had so often wearied heaven with their complaints, were not so great as they might have expected, and were diminishing every day, as the Colony strengthened; as the earth began to reward their labor and to furnish liberally for their substance; and above all, that they were there in the full enjoyment of liberty, civil and religious. He therefore thought that it would be more becoming the gratitude they owed the Divine Being, if, instead of a fast, they should proclaim a Thanksgiving. His advice was taken, and from that day to this they have, in every year, observed circumstances of public felicity sufficient to furnish employment for a Thanksgiving Day which is, therefore, constantly ordered and religiously observed.

God does not want us to be continually dwelling upon our sorrows and trials, but rather to be meditating upon our blessings. Thanksgiving is one of the most delightful blossoms in the garden of sanctification. Few recognize that ingratitude is a grievous sin in the sight of heaven.

If our words of complaint and bitterness of the past year were placed alongside of our expressions of gratitude, how truly thankful would we appear? —H.G.B.

Count your many blessings, name them one by one;
Count your many blessings, see what God hath done.
— J. Oatman, Jr.

"Pride slays thanksgiving. A proud man never thinks he gets as much as he deserves." — H. W. BEECHER

THE LIVING WORD

SUGGESTED SCRIPTURE READING: Hebrews 1:1-12

In the beginning was the Word, and the Word was with God, and THE WORD WAS GOD. John 1:1

Jesus is called the *word*. Words are wonderful things and we could not do without them. Words are the only means whereby we can communicate one with another. For the interchange of thoughts and ideas we use words, constructing them into sentences and thus are able to transmit our thoughts to others. The usual method is the spoken word. In the case of the deaf we use printed or written words or signs; but we must use words. In the case of blindness we use the Braille system of raised characters, which are words to the blind. Whether through the ear, the eye, or the sense of touch, we are limited to the use of words in expressing ourselves. Now Jesus is called the Word of God. He is God's means of communicating with His creatures. Whether in the natural or spiritual, God speaks through His Son the Word. In nature we learn something *about* God, but it is still through the Word, for by the Word of God the heavens were made. All things were made by *Him*. In the spiritual sense Jesus is pre-eminently the Word, God's only means of communicating Himself to us. Jesus said, "I am the way, the truth, and the life, no man cometh unto the Father but by me" (John 14:6). John said, "No man hath seen God at any time, the only begotten Son which is in the bosom of the Father, he hath declared (revealed) him" (John 1:18). Jesus is our Mediator, our Saviour, and our new and living way to God.

May we this day avail ourselves of Him as revealed in His written Word.

—M.R.D.

Oh send Thy Spirit, Lord, now unto me,
That He may touch my eyes, and make me see:
Show me the truth concealed within Thy Word,
And in Thy book revealed, I see the Lord!
— M. A. Lathbury

"Other books were given for our information, the Bible for our transformation. Read it to be WISE, believe it to be SAFE!"

WHEN LITTLE IS MUCH

SUGGESTED SCRIPTURE READING: Mark 6:32-44

There is a lad here, which hath five barley loaves, and two small fishes: but what are they among so many? . . . (And) they . . . filled twelve baskets with the fragments of the five barley loaves, which remained over and above unto them that had eaten. John 6:9, 13

Frederick Hall has written an imaginative story about the little lad who brought Jesus the five barley loaves and the two small fishes. He relates how the boy ran home and reported the whole exciting incident to his mother. His eyes were big with the wonder of it all as he poured out the amazing story about the miraculous increase of the loaves and the fishes in the Master's hand. He told his mother how the vast crowd ate their fill, and of the twelve baskets of fragments that were gathered up afterward. Then Frederick Hall has the boy saying, "I wonder, Mother, if it would be that way with *everything you gave Him?*" This, of course, is but the fiction of one man's imagination, but it points up a spiritual lesson which we often overlook. If we unreservedly give our best, yea, our all to the Saviour, His hand of blessing will multiply our meager resources. The hungry hearts of others will then be fed, and someday we will surely be amazed at the "twelve-basket harvest" that will be gathered as the result of our meager but consecrated sowing.

God has not called many great or many noble to His service. Most of those whom He has seen fit to use have been "men of like passions" with us who have simply given their all over into the hand of God. Give your *best talent* in full surrender to the Saviour this day. In eternity you will be as surprised at what God has accomplished through you, as was this wide-eyed youngster when he saw his small lunch feed five thousand! When Jesus' hand of power touches us, the blessing is always multiplied. —H.G.B.

Go, then, earthly fame and treasure!
Come, disaster, scorn and pain!
In thy service, pain is pleasure;
WITH THY FAVOR LOSS IS GAIN! — H. F. Lyte

"Little is much when God is in it."

GOD OR MONKEY?

SUGGESTED SCRIPTURE READING: Genesis 1:26-31

> *So God created man in his own image, in the image of*
> *God created he him.*   Genesis 1:27

The natural man is a contradiction, a paradox, a puzzle which defies reason and understanding. While his Creator tells man he was originally created in the very image of God, man will turn heaven and earth upside down to prove that he evolved from a bit of green slime on a tepid pond and by gradual stages evolved into a monkey. We frankly admit that people who believe this theory are surely "making monkeys of themselves," but the pointed poem which follows will prove that monkeys have more sense than those who accept the "monkey story."   —M.R.D.

> Three monkeys sat in a coconut tree
> Discussing things as they're said to be.
> Said one to the other, "Now listen, you,
> There's a certain rumor that can't be true —
> That man descended from our noble race —
> The very idea is a disgrace!
>
> No monkey ever deserted his wife,
> Starved her babies and ruined her life,
> And you've never known a mother monk
> To leave her babies with others to bunk,
> Or pass them on from one to another
> Till they scarcely know who is their mother.
>
> And another thing you'll never see,
> A monk build a fence 'round a coconut tree
> And let the coconuts go to waste,
> Forbidding all other monks a taste.
> Why, if I'd put a fence around the tree,
> Starvation would force you to steal from me.
>
> Here's another thing a monk won't do,
> Go out at night and get on a stew,
> Or use a gun or club or knife
> To take some other monkey's life.
> Yes, man descended, the ornery cuss,
> But, brother, he didn't descend from us!" — Anon.

"Concerning those who claim their forefathers sprang from apes, some might conclude that their ancestors were apparently very poor jumpers!" — G.W.

ROLL IT ON HIM!

SUGGESTED SCRIPTURE READING: Psalm 37:1-11

Commit thy way unto the Lord. Psalm 37:5

A Christian must set his sights high! Time must be evaluated in the light of eternity; present difficulties must be judged in relation to heaven's gain. In Psalm 37, therefore, David justifies God's present "frowning providence" in the light of His eventual smiling benediction. Although God's ways may distress us at the moment, yet they are supremely right and gracious. Rather than "fretting" about the things that come our way (Ps. 37:1), we ought to "trust." Final vindication and blessing will be ours when He shall bring forth our "righteousness as the light." Yes, God's way is best and the end is glorious.

The word "commit" in our text means literally "to roll upon." How blessed it is to take all our cares concerning life's dark circumstances and with faith's abandon *roll them upon the Lord.* We shall find Him to be the great Burden Bearer who is abundantly able to carry the load. As He treads the unseen maze before us with certain step, we may trustingly follow knowing that all will be well.

The story is told of a mother who was holding on her lap her tired and fretful little daughter. Her loving embrace and her tender caresses soon quieted the four year old's uneasiness. However, the mother herself was feeling sad and weary, for she had just laid to rest her own dear mother, who had been her daily companion and spiritual helper. Little Mabel saw a tear trickle down her mother's face and she asked sympathetically, "Mama, do you want to be 'holded,' too?" In spite of herself the tears came in a torrent then, and the little one, patting her cheek, whispered, "Mama, God will hold you, won't He?" The mother was both rebuked and comforted, and she found grace to roll her care upon the Lord.

Oh, troubled one, commit your *"way"* (Ps. 37:5), your *"works"* (Prov. 16:3), and your *"care"* (I Pet. 5:7) to the Lord, and you, too, will find "peace of mind." Stop carrying the load, *roll it on Him!* —H.G.B.

I will commit my way, O Lord, to Thee,
Nor doubt Thy love, though dark the way may be,
Nor murmur, for the sorrow is from God,
And there is comfort also in Thy rod. — Anon.

"There are no accidents in God's purposes."

PETER'S POOR AIM

SUGGESTED SCRIPTURE READING: Romans 8:1-13

Then Simon Peter having a sword drew it, and smote the high priests' servant, and cut off his right ear.

John 18:10

Peter's aim was poor, for we are convinced Peter aimed to split the servant's head right in two. The servant must have ducked just in time to avoid being killed, but not without losing his right ear. This incident is of tremendous importance, for it is recorded by all four gospel writers (Matt. 26:51, Mark 14:47, Luke 22:50, John 18:10). Three of the writers do not mention Simon Peter's name. They only mention that it was one of the disciples; but John tells us who it was, although we might have guessed it was Peter.

Dr. Luke is the only one of the four who mentions the miraculous incident of the healing of the ear by our Lord Jesus. Why did the others fail to tell us this most important of all details? Simply because the Holy Spirit who inspired men to write the record knew it was a doctor's job to put back an amputated member. And so Dr. Luke tells us:

And he (Jesus) touched his ear, and healed him.

Luke 22:51

What infinite compassion! In the midst of His arrest He stops to consider the plight of His enemy. What a picture of compassion! But there is a deeper reason. He was protecting Peter, who in a few hours would deny Him with cursing. It would have gone hard with Peter for wounding this servant of the high priest had not Jesus come to the rescue. This is His mission: to step between us and judgment and let us go free. Oh how we adore Him! Wonderful, Wonderful Saviour!

—M.R.D.

My yesterdays, so dark with shame,
He has forgiven. Oh praise His Name!
My sins are gone; thank God for peace at last;
The blood of Jesus covers all the past!

— A. R. Ackley

"Alas, to think how many people's CREEDS are contradicted by their DEEDS!"

"MANSIONS" OR "PLACES"?

SUGGESTED SCRIPTURE READING: Psalm 16

*In my Father's house are many mansions. . . . I go to
prepare a place for you.*   John 14:2

I used to think that Jesus was preparing a *mansion* for me, until
one day I noticed for the first time the word "are" in John 14:2.
The mansions are eternal; they were already made when Jesus
spoke these words. What He is doing now, therefore, is preparing
"a *place*," a special apartment, in these sparkling mansions which
will just be suited to my needs and spiritual stature. How big an
apartment will be needed for me depends on how I enlarge my
spiritual capacities here by prayer, Bible study, personal holiness,
and Christian service. While it is true that all of the saved will
experience "fullness of joy" in heaven, some will have greater
ability to contain, because they have "stretched themselves out
for God" while here on earth. Others, having little heavenly
treasures, will need only small accommodations. Thanks to God's
grace, however, despite our failures, each apartment, large or
small, will still be supremely glorious and desirable.

An old preacher was once strangely comforted by a little
personal incident that befell him. He had always secretly feared
death and was consequently powerless to comfort others who
were facing it. One day toward the end of his life, he moved to
another house. Yet when the furniture had all gone, the old
preacher lingered in the home where his children had been born
and where his sermons had been prepared. At last his servant
came to him and said, "Sir, everything's gone, and *the new house
is better than this one.* Come away." It preached to him a lesson
that he never forgot. God, too, has prepared for His children a
home, and it is much better than our present earthly tabernacle.

—H.G.B.

"In my Father's House are many mansions,"
The blessed Master said,
And to prepare this blessed place —
He travelled on ahead.
Your loved one, too, has journeyed on
And free from every care
Within God's many mansions
Is waiting for you there! — Anon.

**"As the compass needle trembles until it stands at the north, so the soul
once united to Christ, cannot be at rest until it arrives at the Heavenly
Home."**

IT CAME TO PASS

Suggested Scripture Reading: II Corinthians 4:8-18

And it came to pass.   Genesis 29:10

I am going to take this familiar phrase, occuring over and over again in the Bible, for an application of a precious and comforting truth. We shall pay no attention to the context, and our treatment of the text will not be according to the strict rules of homiletics. The application is suggested by a story about a simple but devout colored preacher. He said, "This is my favorite text — 'It came to pass.' Whenever I am in pain I say 'cheer up; it came to pass.' When I am in trouble I just say, 'It came to pass,' and it always helps me to carry through."

The humble philosophy of the colored preacher is good medicine for all of us. Nothing comes upon us except by the permission of our loving Father. He knows what we need, but He also knows how much we can bear. With every trial He supplies sufficient grace and assures us that "It came to pass." He has promised to send us no greater temptation (trial) than we are able to bear, but He will with the "trial" also make a way of escape that we may be able to bear it. (I Cor. 10:13) Remember this today as you are confronted with trials and troubles along the way, and don't forget, "It came to pass."   —M.R.D.

Tremble not, though darkly gather,
Clouds and tempests o'er the sky;
Still believe, thy Heavenly Father
Loves thee best when storms are nigh.
See! At length the clouds are breaking,
Tempests have not passed in vain;
For the soul, revived, awakening,
Bears its fruits and flowers again.
Love Divine has seen and counted,
Every tear it caused to fall,
And the storm which love appointed
Was its choicest gift of all!
— Anon.

"Never bear more than one trouble at a time. Some people make the mistake of bearing three kinds: All they have ever had, all they have now, and all they expect to have." — E. E. HALE

THE REWARD OF HUMILITY

SUGGESTED SCRIPTURE READING: Psalm 138:1-6

. . . for God resisteth the proud, and giveth grace to the humble.   I Peter 5:5

Dwight L. Moody once said, "A man can counterfeit love, he can counterfeit faith, he can counterfeit hope, and all the other graces, but it is very difficult to counterfeit humility. You soon detect mock humility. They have a saying among the Arabs that as the tares and the wheat grow they come to show which God has blessed. The ears that God has blessed bow their heads and acknowledge every grain. The more fruitful they are, the lower their heads are bowed. The tares on the other hand, lift their heads erect, high above the wheat, but they are only fruitful of evil. The lesson is clear: If we only get down low enough, God will use us to His glory." Remember, Jesus said, "Learn of me, for I am meek and lowly in heart."

Francis Xavier, a truly humble servant of the Lord, was one day preaching in one of the cities of Japan. As he was speaking a man arose in the audience and came up to him as if to say something to him privately. The missionary leaned his head to one side to hear what he thought was to be communicated to him. Suddenly, instead of whispering, the unbeliever used the occasion to spit upon the face of the devoted missionary. Xavier, without a word or the least sign of annoyance, took out his pocket handkerchief, wiped his face, and went on with his Gospel message. The disinterest and scorn which his audience had been showing up to that point, immediately turned to admiration. A learned doctor in that city who happened to be present thought to himself that a religion which taught men such virtue, inspired them with such courage, and gave them such complete mastery over themselves, could not be other than from God Himself. He investigated the claims of Christ and afterward became a Christian.

If you let pride enter into your heart as you do the Saviour's work, you cannot expect His blessing; for His promised grace goes only to "the humble."   —H.G.B.

Humbly at Thy Cross I'd stay,
Jesus, keep me there, I pray;
Teach me more of Thee, each day,
Jesus, blessed Jesus. — H. P. Blanchard

"Whatsoever humbles me, helps me."

BEAR AND FORBEAR

SUGGESTED SCRIPTURE READING: Colossians 3:12-17

We then that are strong ought to bear the infirmities of the weak, and not to please ourselves.   Romans 15:1

A little girl was sent by her sick mother to go to church and to listen carefully so she could tell mother what the preacher talked about. When she came back, she gleefully reported that the minister had preached on The Three Bears: the *fruit* bear, the *cross* bear, and the *image* bear. That was all she could remember. Three bears! When we turn to the Bible we find many other bears. We mention some of them. There is first the papa bear, whom we shall call *Forbear*. Paul refers to him in Ephesians 4:2 and says, "*Forbearing* one another in love." Again in Colossians 3:13, "*Forbearing* one another, and forgiving one another." This is the big bear in the family of bears. If we can learn to "forbear" in love, all the little bears will follow. Here are a few members of the Bible family of bears.

1. The *Yoke* Bear (Lam. 3:27).
2. The *Fruit* Bear (John 15:8).
3. The *Cross* Bear (Luke 14:27).
4. The *Witness* Bear (John 15:27).
5. The *Weak* Bear (Rom. 15:1).
6. The *Burden* Bear (Gal. 6:2).
7. The *Image* Bear (I Cor. 15:49).

The "image bear" is the last bear which began with the big bear, "*Forbear*." Paul tells us in I Corinthians 15:49, "And as we have borne the image of the earthly, we shall also bear the image of the heavenly." Paul is looking forward to the resurrection and the end of the road, when in the perfect resurrection body we shall *Bear* the perfect image of the Lord Jesus. With this glorious prospect before us we can be *Love Bears* while we travel home. The "love bear" is found in I Corinthians 13:7 — "(Love) beareth all things."   —M.R.D.

Learn to forbear, in thy conduct be true,
Strive for the right, for the Lord is with you;
Bear all things sweetly, in His might be strong,
Live for His glory, fear only what's wrong — Anon.

"There is a great difference between patient forbearance and mere sullen endurance; one is a flower of grace, the other the bitter fruit of fatalism." — H.G.B.

BRIGHT CLOUD

SUGGESTED SCRIPTURE READING: Job 37:5-15

. . . behold, a bright cloud.   Matthew 17:5

All sunshine makes a desert. Clouds in life are both necessary and desirable. The torrential showers of trial may beat hard upon the flower of our existence, but they will nourish and strengthen the roots of our spirituality if we are exercised by them to a new appreciation and understanding of God and His blessed promises. If we let the light of God shine upon our clouds we will ever find His cheering rainbow. If we "stand still, and consider the wondrous works of God," then the Lord will cause "the light of His cloud to shine" (Job 37:14, 15).

Dr. Robert Collyer, of Yorkshire, England, came to America as a blacksmith and settled in a little town in the State of Pennsylvania. He became known not only for his excellent workmanship in iron but also for his constant Christian cheerfulness. When asked the secret of his optimism, he said, "A dear, good old lady taught me to look for the silver lining. Although she was very poor and overwhelmed with troubles, she was still supremely cheerful. One day I said to her: 'Mary, you must have some very dark days; they must overcome you with clouds.' 'Yes,' she replied, 'but then I often find there's comfort in a cloud.' 'Comfort in a cloud, Mary?' 'Yes,' she said, 'When I am very low, I go to the window, and if I see a heavy cloud, I think: *a cloud received Him out of their sight.* I look up and see the cloud sure enough, and then I think — well *that may be the cloud that hides Him;* and so you see, *there is comfort in a cloud.*'"

By the eye of faith have you seen Christ in your cloud? Christ is coming back upon a literal cloud — it may be soon; but in the meantime He often loves to come to us upon the billows of distress. For the Christian, every cloud comes provided with its proper and sufficient supply of comfort. Where is your spiritual eye focused? Are you looking down in discouragement? Then probably you are only seeing the "mud" of your distress. Oh, look up instead, and you will see that your cloud is bright with God's rainbow.   —H.G.B.

> Sorrow can never last, darkness must fly,
> Where saith the Light of light —
> "Peace! It is I!"   — Anon.

"God sometimes puts us in the dark to prove to us that He alone is the Light."

WHERE IS YOUR TREASURE?

SUGGESTED SCRIPTURE READING: James 1:9-12

Lay not up for yourselves treasures upon earth . . . .
But lay up for yourselves treasures in heaven.
Matthew 6:19, 20

All ready to go to work are you? What are you going to work for today? Just to make a living and keep the wolf from the door? Then it will be a dreary day and the time will drag along wearily. Or are you going to work today to make a lot of money, so you can buy everything your heart desires and retire at an early age and enjoy yourself? What a disappointment awaits you. Of course we are to work to make a living, and there is no evil in saving something for the "rainy day," but in addition to these legitimate motives, this day is also given to you that you may lay up spiritual treasures for eternity. So while you work and faithfully perform your task, don't forget to witness for Him, to tell others about Him, and work a little harder so you may have something extra for the work of the Lord. It is good to make "money," if it is used with a sense of responsibility to God. When you "get" wealth, be sure your wealth doesn't "get" you.

A very poor countrywoman was handing to an agent of the Bible Society her "mite," kept in a jug. More than $20.00 had been gathered in her poverty, chiefly in pennies and nickels. Not liking to take the money, the agent said: "Are you sure, Mary, that you gave this out of your heart?" "No sir; indeed, it is out of the jug." "Yes, but did it first come out of your heart?" "Nay, nay, sir for it was never there." If Christ can keep the heart free from the love of money, He can keep it free from any other sin.

There are some things which should not be in the heart, namely: Impurity (Eph. 5:3); Love of money (I Tim. 6:10); Unbelief (Heb. 3:12); Pride (Ps. 101:5); Love of the world (I John 2:15); Envy (James 3:14); Doubting thoughts (Luke 24:38).   —M.R.D.

The "treasures" of earth are as dross,
No matter how brightly they glow;
The favor of Christ maketh rich
Eternal His blessings shall flow. — G.W.

"Money is a universal provider for everything but happiness, and a passport everywhere but to heaven!"

ALONE WITH GOD

SUGGESTED SCRIPTURE READING: Psalm 5:1-3

> *But thou, when thou prayest, enter into thy closet, and*
> *when thou hast shut thy door, pray to thy Father which*
> *is in secret.* Matthew 6:6

All Christians pray, but few have a "quiet time" when they can be alone with God and not only speak to Him, but reverently await His holy impress upon their soul. All of us need a place for undisturbed, private devotions.

In our text Jesus teaches the value of intimate fellowship with heaven that can be attained only in the sacred solitude of our prayer closet. He is not condemning public prayer as such, but He does warn against the evil of seeking notoriety and attention by "parading in prayer" and attempting to impress others with our piety.

We all have "private business" with God, which can only be transacted in secret. How long since you have "shut the door" upon the distractions of life and poured out your heart before the Father's Throne? The "pure oxygen" of the inner chamber would revive many Christians who in the clouded atmosphere of life are about "to faint" (Luke 18:1b).

A committee was once assigned to tour a great factory to judge of its efficiency. They were shown the various departments where many large machines were whirring and making a great deal of noise. Then, they were led to a much smaller room. Here everything was very quiet. One of the men said, "This isn't very important; nothing doing here." The guide smiled, "Oh, but you misunderstand, sir. *This is the most important room of all.* This is where all the *power* comes from to run the rest of the factory." . . . So, too, in the Christian life . . . the "Quiet Room" is the "Power Room." —H.G.B.

> Alone with God — the doors all shut —
> I see His face;
> I feel His love, so strong and true;
> I know His grace.
> His comfort comes in strengthening power
> To fill my heart.
> Alone with God — how blest it is
> To come apart!" — S. R. Lockwood

"A lot of kneeling keeps you in good standing with God."

"WHERE ART THOU?"

SUGGESTED SCRIPTURE READING: Genesis 3:6-19

. . . God called unto Adam . . . Where art thou?
Genesis 3:9

The third chapter in Genesis contains the first two questions in the Bible. The first question was asked by the devil, the second was asked by God. The first question raised a "doubt" about the Word of God, the second question created "fear" of the judgment of God. If our first parents had not listened to Satan they would not have doubted God. And if they had not doubted God they would never have been "afraid" of Him. When God called Adam, "Where art thou?" he fearfully answered, "I was afraid, because I was naked; and I hid myself" (Gen. 3:10). Nothing will cause "fear" like doubt, and nothing will banish fear like "faith." If Adam had not doubted he would not have been afraid.

Are you afraid of God? Then it is because you do not believe God's Word and promises. The sinner can be delivered from fear by believing God's Word of salvation (John 3:16, Romans 10:9, Romans 10:13, and I John 5:1). The saint who lives in fear can be delivered by "believing" such promises as are found in Romans 8:28, Hebrews 13:5, 6, and I Peter 5:7. Maybe someone reading these words is a "doubter" and a "trembling saint," because you do not know the promises of God. You have a Bible full of them but they must be believed. Adam, where art thou? Living in the cave of "doubts and fears," or walking in the light of His Word?

A negro preacher discoursing on the text "Adam . . . Where art thou?" said, "I have three divisions to my text. Firstly, every man must be somewhere. Secondly, some people is where they got no business to be, and thirdly, they that am where they shouldn't be, is going to find themselves where they don't want to be." Where art thou, Adam? Come out of hiding, claim the promises of forgiveness, and find the blessing. —M.R.D.

God calling yet! I cannot stay;
My heart I yield without delay:
Vain world, farewell! from thee I part;
The voice of God hath reached my heart.
— G. Tersteegen

"Doubt is the father of fear; but peace is the offspring of faith."

CARRIED BY GOD

SUGGESTED SCRIPTURE READING: Isaiah 46:1-4

. . . I will carry and . . . deliver you.   Isaiah 46:4

Henry Moorhouse was once occupied with work that seemed to demand more than the usual exercise of his faith. Soon he was much burdened. Then it was that the Lord gave him a most tender revelation concerning the fact that His everlasting arms were underneath, bearing him up. It seems that his little daughter, who was a paralytic, was one day sitting in her wheelchair as he entered the house with a package in his hand for his wife. Going up to the child and kissing her, he asked, "Where is mother?" "Mother is upstairs." "Well, I have a package for her," said Henry Moorhouse. "Oh, let me carry the package to mother." "Why, Minnie, dear, how can you possibly carry the package? You cannot even carry yourself." With a smile on her face, Minnie said, "I know, Papa; but if you will give me the package, I will hold it, while you carry me." "Taking her up in his arms he bore her tenderly upstairs. Little Minnie was indeed holding the parcel, but he was holding Minnie. Then it came to him very suddenly that this was just his position in the trying work in which he was engaged. He too was carrying a heavy burden, but praise God, he could proceed with confidence knowing that the Lord was in turn carrying him.

Yes, God promises to support His own even though they in a sense must still bear their own burdens. They may be sure that He will not only bring them through their difficulties, but will also comfort them, and still their fears at the same time, if they will but trustingly recline in His everlasting arms. Because of His kindness and ever available support, it is unreasonable and unbecoming for any saint to sink beneath his burdens and afflictions. "Ask the Saviour to help you . . . He will carry you through."

—H.G.B.

Nothing is too small for Him to carry
Take your burdens to Jesus:
Nothing is too great, why longer tarry?
Take your burdens to Him.
Take your burdens to Jesus, take your burdens to Jesus,
All your load Jesus will carry, take your burdens to Him!
R. J. Oliver

"Burdens grow lighter as we lean them upon the Everlasting Arms.
— H.G.B.

INSPECTING YOUR HOUSE

What have they seen in thine house? Isaiah 39:4

Hezekiah was a God-fearing king of Judah. He was taken sick with a deadly "boil" and was told by the prophet Isaiah, "Set thine house in order: for thou shalt die, and not live" (Isa. 38:1). In answer to Hezekiah's desperate petition the Lord healed him and added 15 years to his life (verse 5). The news of Hezekiah's recovery reaches the king of Babylon who sends a delegation to Jerusalem to congratulate him. What an opportunity for Hezekiah to witness to these ungodly men and tell them of Irsael's God. But instead Hezekiah proudly shows them his wealth, his power, his possessions — the vessels of gold and of silver, his army and armaments. But we do not read that he spoke one word about the Lord and His faithfulness.

God sends Isaiah to the palace and faces the king with the question, "What have they seen in thine house?" and Hezekiah had no answer except that they had seen nothing of the Lord, but only the things which he had accumulated. The men left as ignorant of Israel's God as they had come. What an opportunity! But he lost it, and as a result the prophet pronounces judgment. He declares that this very Babylon will soon come and spoil the city, carry away the treasures and raze the house of God.

What do men see in your house when they visit you? Is there anything to indicate that you are a believer? What would they discover on your magazine table? What would they see on your piano and music rack? What would they find you listening to on the radio, or watching on television? What would be the main topic of conversation? Do people come to visit you and leave again without seeing anything to suggest you are a Christian? Soon you, your treasures, and ultimately even your house will be gone — but the spiritual impact of your life will remain. Tell me, "What have they seen in thine house?" —M.R.D.

So I'm praying each day,
Just to live Jesus' way,
That my Lord in my home may abide. — C. R. Piety

"Home should be the ground floor of heaven, a seminary for the soul."

BROKEN VOWS!

SUGGESTED SCRIPTURE READING: Numbers 30

> *Better is it that thou shouldest not vow, than that thou shouldest vow and not pay.*   Ecclesiastes 5:5

I recently received a letter from one who had made solemn vows to God while in distress, but who had failed to pay that vow. The anguish she is suffering has prompted me to cite the following as a warning to all others who have failed to keep their solemn promises to the God who "is not mocked"!

A certain man was once very much under conviction concerning the needs of his soul and the urgency of acknowledging Christ as his Saviour. His only child became very sick and finally was at the point of death. He prayed God earnestly to restore her to health, promising at the same time that he would confess Christ and serve the Lord for the rest of his life if the child was spared. His daughter recovered, but *the man forgot the promise he had made* and did not seek the Lord. Now listen to the tragic end of this true incident. Shortly afterward the child was suddenly made violently ill by an unknown disease and almost before they knew what had happened their little daughter was taken from them by the icy hand of death. The father was prostrated with grief and realized that God had justly punished him for his careless, hardened unbelief and his broken vow.

Let us not be like the Israelites who also forgot their vows and lusted exceedingly in the wilderness and tempted God! For like them, we too may then be permitted for a time to enjoy our blind and carnal desires only to later experience God's judgment and a terrible "leanness" in our soul! (Ps. 106:14, 15)

> Oh let us be faithful to Jesus,
> The vows that we've made, let's renew.
> And prayerfully ask Him each morning:
> "Lord, what wilt Thou have me to do?"
> —J. Tangborn

"As a serious wound leaves a scar — so too a gross sin though it be forgiven, still in this life may leave a grievous mark."

COMPLAINING OR PRAISING?

SUGGESTED SCRIPTURE READING: Psalm 142

And when the people complained, it displeased the LORD.
Numbers 11:1

I heard once about a certain old lady who "enjoyed very poor health." There are some people who would be greatly disappointed if they did not have something to "gripe" or "grumble" about. Some people are so occupied with their little troubles that they lose sight of all their big blessings. In my practice of medicine I had a number of these folks who "enjoyed" their "complaints." I could not find a thing wrong with them, yet all they did was whine and complain. Pains here, aches there, and as one expressed it, "I just feel no good all over." Yet it was all imaginary. If they would only count all their blessings they would soon forget their troubles. Said the patient to the doctor, "I am never well — I don't know why. I get a sort of pain — I don't know exactly where, and it leaves me in a kind of — oh, I don't know how." The doctor replied, "Here is a prescription for I don't know what; take it I don't know how many times a day for I don't know how long, and maybe you'll feel better, I don't know when!"

How different the case of the very, very old lady, penniless and weak who was asked by a missionary, "Auntie, how is your health?" "Oh, I have so much to be thankful for," she replied. "I's only got two teeth left, but thank God, *they are opposite each other!*"

Before you begin this day, why not stop to count your blessings, instead of dwelling on your troubles all the time? In our text we are told that Israel's complaining "displeased the Lord." If you are saved — *praise Him!* You have the greatest blessing of all. A saloonkeeper met a converted drunkard and said, "I heard you gave the preacher your last nickel, now you'll have to walk home." "Yes," answered the man, "and many a time I've given *you* my last nickel and *couldn't* walk home." —M.R.D.

I will praise Him! I will praise Him!
Praise the Lamb for sinners slain;
Give Him glory, all ye people,
For His blood can wash away each stain. — M. J. Harris

"If you can't see the bright side, then polish the dull side; stop living on GRUMBLE CORNER, move to THANKSGIVING STREET!"

DON'T "CAVE IN"

... men ought always to pray, and not to faint.   Luke 18:1

Hierocles, a fifth century philosopher of Alexandria, compiled a book of humorous stories which were meant to teach a lesson. One of these was about a man who made a ridiculous vow that he would never go into the water until he had first learned to swim! Of course, he never got anywhere! It is equally foolish to postpone praying until we have mastered the art of eloquence and beauty in public speech. We can learn to swim only by getting into the water and making an attempt; so too, we can learn to pray publicly only if we make it a point to begin, even if at first our words are stumbling and halting. Prayer, after all, is talking to God and communing with heaven. This is much more important than "saying something beautiful for other people to hear." While all of us can pray silently, it must be admitted that praying publicly is something that often has to be "learned."

Our text, however, is not speaking so much of audible, formal prayer, but rather of that inward attitude of devotion and supplication which ever looks expectantly toward God. A missionary writes: "My concordance shows *the root meaning of the word 'faint' is to 'cave in.'* What causes a 'cave-in'? It is weakness on one hand, and pressure on the other. What causes a 'cave-in" in our prayer life? Is it not often pressure either from things of secondary importance, or else from the powers of darkness?" Are we holding on in prayer, yea, persisting in prayer, at all seasons, whether we feel led to or not? Let us all be reminded that Scripture exhorts us to pray: 1. *"Always"* (Luke 18:1; Eph. 6:18); 2. *"Everywhere"* — (I Tim. 2:8); 3. *"For all men"* — (I Tim. 2:1); and 4. For *"everything"* — (Phil. 4:6).

When the going gets rough don't lose heart and "cave in"; just pray, trust, and move forward!   —H.G.B.

I shall pray on. Though distant as it seems
The answer may be almost at my door,
Or just around the corner on its way,
But whether near or far, yes, I shall pray —
I shall PRAY ON!   — E. Mapes

"He stands best who kneels most."

AFTER ME, PLEASE — THEN YOU

Suggested Scripture Reading: Philippians 2:1-11

. . . let each esteem other better than themselves.
Philippians 2:3
Submitting yourselves one to another in the fear of God.
Ephesians 5:21

So you are not speaking to each other this morning? You had a little spat, a trivial misunderstanding yesterday and you went to bed last night letting the "sun go down upon your wrath"? (Eph. 4:26) Does it make you happy to carry your petty grudge? Will your stubbornness help your testimony today? How foolish can you be anyway? Listen to the Word of God for the solution of your petty squabble. I guarantee your selfish insistence upon your point of view will vanish if you will prayerfully read the Scripture, especially verses 5 to 11 of Philippians 2. If we could only learn the great lesson of Ephesians 5:21, "Submitting yourselves one to another."

Take a look at the other side, instead of just your own. No court of law will render a verdict or judgment until it carefully hears the witnesses on both sides of an argument. Yet we Christians refuse to hear both sides but consider only one side — *our own.* How much better to submit ourselves — be the least — be like Christ who was sinless, yet took our guilt upon Himself. In every test we face, we should ask: How will this affect *others?* Will it help or hinder others? One little act of "consideration for others" will bring its own reward. A king once had a rock placed in a footpath. One after another, coming to the stone, turned out and made a new crooked path. The king had hidden himself so he could watch. One after another avoided the rock, leaving it for some traveler to stumble over in the dark. Then a humble peasant came, saw the stone, realized its danger to others, and stooping he removed the stone — and found hidden beneath it a purse of 1000 dollars. Doing things for others brings blessing to self.

—M.R.D.

Clamor, and wrath, and strife begone;
Envy and spite forever cease;
Let bitter words no more be known
Amongst the saints, the sons of peace. — Anon.

"We pardon as long as we love." — ROCHEFOUCAULD

SELF-PITY IN SORROW

SUGGESTED SCRIPTURE READING: Lamentations 3:1-18

I am the man that hath seen affliction.

Lamentations 3:1

Lamentations 3 in the original is arranged in the form of an acrostic using each of the letters of the Hebrew alphabet. We would say that the prophet's lament, therefore, covers everything "from a to z." Much of what Jeremiah prophesied in this chapter can be applied to the Messiah who as the sin-bearer would indeed be a "man of sorrows and acquainted with grief." By application, however, Jeremiah's words seem accurately to characterize much of our own feelings of self-pity when circumstances for us become adverse. Beecher says: "Every man feels . . . there never was such an experience in life as his own . . . No sorrow was ever like our sorrow. Indeed, there is a kind of indignation excited in us when one likens our grief to his own . . . for though we know that the world groans and travails in pain and has done so for ages, yet *a groan heard by our ears is a very different thing from a groan uttered by our mouth.* Sorrows of other men seem to us like clouds of rain which empty themselves in the distance, and whose long traveling thunder comes to us mellowed and subdued; but our own troubles are like a storm bursting right overhead."

When we find ourselves occupied with thoughts of self-pity, we may be sure that we have not gotten our eyes sufficiently upon the Lord and the lesson He is teaching us through our sorrows.

A man once met a little fellow on the road carrying a basket full of blackberries. "Sammy," he said, "where did you get such lovely berries?" "Over there, sir, in the briars!" "In the briars! oh, they must have scratched you painfully." "Yes, sir, they did, but mother is so pleased when I bring home the lovely fruit, and praises me so, that I forget all about the briars in my feet."

Let us follow Sammy's example, forget our self-pity and complaining, and think only of the bright smile and the words of commendation which will flow from the lips of the Saviour when we bring Him the ripe fruit of our sanctification induced by our trials.

—H.G.B.

It will be worth it all when we see Jesus,
Life's trials will seem so small when we see Christ;
One glimpse of His dear face all sorrow will erase,
So bravely run the race, till we see Christ.
— E. K. Rusthoi

"Joy during times of testing is the most powerful witness that the Christian can render."

OFF AND ON

SUGGESTED SCRIPTURE READING: Jude 1:20-25

Are ye so foolish? having begun in the Spirit, are ye now made perfect by the flesh?   Galatians 3:3

The Bible gives the answer to three great errors among men concerning the plan of salvation. The first error is legalism, which teaches that man is saved by keeping the law. One whole book — Romans — is devoted to a refutation of this damning error. The second error is the exact opposite. It teaches that we are saved by grace and so works are unnecessary and we can live as we please. This error is dealt with in James. But there is a third more subtle error called theologically, "Galatianism." It teaches that we are saved by grace and then *KEPT* saved by our works. This is dealt with in Galatians. The believers in Galatia were taught by Paul that they were saved by grace, and then certain legal teachers had come telling them they would lose their salvation unless they kept the law of God perfectly. They were disturbed, as anyone honest enough to admit his daily shortcomings would be; they wavered and faltered, happy one moment and discouraged the next, because they had failed and imagined all was lost.

The Bible has made provision for all who are saved by grace. When we sin (which we should not — but do) He does not cast us off but promises to forgive when we confess and repent (I John 1:9). Are you worried about your salvation? Then go to Him, confess your sin, and receive His forgiveness. A man was asked how long he had been saved and he replied, "Thirty years off and on." How sad!

Don't be an "off and on believer."   —M.R.D.

Come, thou weary, Jesus calls thee
To His wounded side;
"Come to me," saith He,
"And ever safe abide!" — Rev. S. Morgan

"When we abhor ourselves, and look alone to the free grace of God in Jesus Christ for pardon and salvation, we then have a hope that maketh not ashamed!" — L. KLOPSCH

"OUR FATHER"

SUGGESTED SCRIPTURE READING: Psalm 68:1-5

After this manner therefore pray ye: Our Father which art in heaven. Matthew 6:9

It is said that the Mohammedans have 99 names for the Supreme Being, but among them all there is none that resembles the intimacy of the Christian's "Our Father." The tender love of God for His children is only revealed in the Bible. Heathen religions present their deities as gods who should be feared, but do not conceive of them as gracious, compassionate beings filled with concern for suffering humanity. The Christian alone is able to look up with intimacy of a child stretching forth his arms to his affectionate parent and exclaim, "Abba, Father!" (Gal. 4:6) The term "abba," which we are allowed to reverently lisp as "babes in Christ," literally means "papa." This tender relationship exists between us and God because of His grace whereby He has once again *adopted* us as His children (Rom. 8:15). Sin had separated us from our original relationship to the family of heaven, but through the reconciliation provided by Jesus Christ we now have the right once again to call God "Our Father."

A ship sailing between Liverpool and New York was at one time caught in a sudden squall of wind that arose at sea. The boat was instantly thrown on her side by the force of the gale, crashing everything that was movable and awakening the passengers to the consciousness of their great danger. Everybody on board was alarmed with the exception of the little eight-year-old daughter of the captain. "What's the matter?" asked the child, rubbing her eyes as she was thrown out of her bed. Her mother told her of the imminent peril. "Isn't Papa on deck?" asked the child. Informed that he was, she trustfully commented, "Then I'm going back to bed." So saying, she dropped herself on the pillow without a fear and in a few moments was fast asleep.

We, too, as God's children are in His keeping. In His Father-care we are not only safe, but secure. — H.G.B.

Fear not the windy tempest wild,
Thy bark they shall not wreck.
Lie down and sleep, oh, helpless child!
Thy Father's on the deck. — Anon.

"Some people who say 'Our Father' on Sunday go around the rest of the week acting like orphans." — KOBER

AUTOMATION

Suggested Scripture Reading: Psalm 139:1-16

I will praise thee; for I am fearfully and wonderfully made.
                                                        Psalm 139:14

The crowning achievement in the creation of the universe was the creation of man in the image of God. There is nothing more wonderful in creation than the body of man. It is the most perfect machine for the expression of the soul, and though subjected to the greatest abuses, manages to keep on going for 70, 80, 90, sometimes even 100 years. And most of its activity is autonomous — without an act of the will. The word "automation" has suddenly become prominent in this industrial age of assembly lines and automatic machinery. Crude material is dumped into a machine and in a few minutes an intricate, finished product emerges at the other end, without the aid of a human hand. But think of automation in terms of the human body. All the vital functions are automatic, without conscious act of the will. Breathing, heart action, circulation, digestion, secretion, temperature control, elimination, blood pressure, chemical balance, specific gravity, these and countless other functions are maintained *AUTOMATICALLY*, awake or sleep. Surely we are wonderfully and fearfully made.

A normal man at middle age performs among many others, the following automatic functions: In each 24 hours your heart beats 103,680 times, your blood circulates every 23 seconds, and travels 43 million miles, you breathe 23 thousand times and inhale 438 cubic feet of air. You digest 3¼ pounds of food, assimilate over a half gallon of liquid. You evaporate 2 pounds of water by perspiration, you generate 98.6 degrees heat, and generate 450 tons of energy. You use 750 muscles, your hair grows 1/100 of an inch and your nails 1/200 inch, and you will use 7 million brain cells. And all automatically! Say — who keeps all this going? What unseen hand maintains the machinery? Don't forget *Him* but with David say, "*I will praise Him,* for I am fearfully and wonderfully made." Take care of that body today.   —M.R.D.

In Your blessed image we are wonderfully made,
Every part essential and in perfect balance laid,
Functioning in union — 'tis a mystery supreme;
What will be the glory when this body You redeem?
                                                        — G.W.

"Despite scientific investigation, man's being is still full of eternal mystery which attests to the greatness of his Creator." — H.G.B.

SLUMBERING SEEDS

Suggested Scripture Reading: Ecclesiastes 11:1-6

Cast thy bread upon the waters: for thou shalt find it after many days. Ecclesiastes 11:1

I was reminded of this verse of Scripture recently when I ran across a little item, by an unknown author, which I had filed away among my clippings many years ago. It was the story of a gentleman who tore down an old building that had stood for many years in his yard. He smoothed over the ground and left it. The warm spring rains fell upon it, and the sunshine flooded it. Soon there sprang up multitudes of flowers, unlike any growing in the neighborhood. The explanation was simple; there had once been a garden on that spot, and the seeds had lain in the soil without moisture, light, or warmth all through the years. However, as soon as the sunshine and rain touched them, they sprang up into life and beauty.

So, often times, the seeds of truth lie long in the human heart, growing not, because the light and the warmth of the Holy Spirit are shut away from them by sin and unbelief; but after long years the heart is opened in some way to the Heavenly influences, and the seeds, living still, shoot up into beauty. The instructions of a pious mother may lie in a heart, fruitless, from childhood to old age, and yet at last be the means of saving the soul.

Christian, keep on casting the precious Seed around you as you journey! If the sowing is constant, the harvest is certain. Although it sometimes seems delayed, yet the tide of blessing will roll back in God's own season and the fruits of victory will then be both glorious and abundant! —H.G.B.

> Tho' sown in tears through weary years,
> The Seed will surely live;
> Tho' great the cost, it is not lost,
> For God will fruitage give.
> — J. H. Brown

"Be earnest in sowing the Seed, remember the Bible promises no loaves to the loafer!"

SHEEP OR PIGS

SUGGESTED SCRIPTURE READING: I Corinthians 1:18-24

> *. . . ye do always resist the Holy Ghost.*   Acts 7:51
> *My sheep hear my voice . . . and they follow me.*
>   John 10:27

What do you know about pigs? Most of you know that bacon, pork chops, and ham come from pigs, and that is about all. Swine are set in contrast to sheep, at opposite ends of the list of domestic animals. A hog in the ceremonial economy of Israel was an unclean beast — while a sheep was a clean animal. But it is in the nature of the two animals where we find the sharpest contrast. Their appetites are not only different but their dispositions are entirely at odds. A sheep is tractable and will follow; but a pig is obstinate and must be driven. Unclean animals represent sinners (II Pet. 2:22), while sheep represent believers (Ps. 23, John 10:11). The hog resists its master — the sheep obeys (John 10:27). The spirit of stubborn opposition in the pig is so well-known that man turns it to his own advantage. When a pig driver wishes to make a pig advance in a certain direction against its will, he drags it with all his force by the tail in the opposite direction. As the beast supposes that it is required to go backwards, it precipitates itself ahead.

It may not be complimentary to liken an obstinate man to a pig, but the analogy is only too palpable. The obstinate man refuses simply because he is requested. The sinner is stiff-necked and obstinate in his treatment of the Holy Ghost. Stephen charged the members of the council thus: "Ye stiff-necked and uncircumcised in heart and ears, ye do always resist the Holy Ghost: as your fathers do so do ye" (Acts 7:51). You cannot change a pig into a sheep. It is a matter of birth. So too with the sinner, he cannot be made a saint by training, education, environment, or feeding him vitamins and antibiotics. Only a new birth — not a rebirth — can effect the change. Jesus said, "That which is born of the flesh is flesh . . . Ye must be born again."   —M.R.D.

> Perverse and foolish oft I strayed,
> But yet in love He sought me,
> And on His shoulder gently laid,
> And home, rejoicing, brought me. — H. W. Baker

"Be a sheep ever so dirty, it is still a 'clean animal'; on the other hand, a scoured and dressed-up pig remains 'unclean.' Ye must be born again!"

APRONS, NAPKINS AND ANOINTING!

SUGGESTED SCRIPTURE READING: John 12:1-8

And Martha served: but Lazarus was one of them that sat at the table with them. Then took Mary a pound of ointment of spikenard, very costly, and anointed the feet of Jesus, and wiped his feet with her hair: and the house was filled with the odour of the ointment.   John 12:2, 3

In Martha, Lazarus, and Mary we have pictured three important aspects of the Christian witness. Martha is the epitomy of *service,* Lazarus of *fellowship and partaking of the Word,* and Mary of *adoration and prayer!* All are necessary to the well-rounded life of spiritual victory, but it is remarkable to note where the Holy Spirit puts the emphasis. Two words are devoted to Martha, twelve to Lazarus, but a full thirty-five to Mary! How accurately our Lord puts his finger upon the lack in our lives. We are all so busy and troubled about serving! Ninety per cent of our Christian experience seems bound up with doing something; but all of our action becomes pretty empty and futile without Bible study and prayer. How much are we occupied in communing with God and reading and digesting His Holy Word? And most neglected of all, how much time do we spend in adoring God for what He is, what He means to us, and in agonizing prayer and supplication coupled with thanksgiving? Do you see why we are such lop-sided Christians, such spiritual dwarfs? The perfume of the Christ-adoring life will be wafted to all within the house with heaven-sent blessings only if we spend much more time kneeling at Jesus' feet. This will not receive the adulation of men, but it will bring down the favor of heaven. Yes, a life of prayer and adoration is efficacious, but *very costly!*

Aprons, napkins and *anointing* — which is your chief concern? If God would judge your spiritual life today, how many words would He need to describe it: two, twelve, or thirty-five? —H.G.B.

> Let me hold fast, Lord, things of the skies,
> Quicken my vision, open my eyes.
> Show me Thy riches, glory and grace,
> Boundless as time is, endless as space!
> — Anon.

"Praying is to the soul what breathing is to the body!"

FEAR NOT

SUGGESTED SCRIPTURE READING: I John 4:11-18

I will fear no evil: for thou art with me. Psalm 23:4

How many Christians profess to know Christ and yet are living in fear and doubt! The joy of the Lord depends on our knowledge of the absolute certainty of the promises of God. If we fully know the faithfulness of God we shall not fear. If we doubt Him we shall be filled with fear. The story is told of a western traveler in the pioneer days who came one winter night to the banks of a wide river. He had to get across but there was no bridge. The river was coated with a sheet of ice but he knew not how safe it was. After much hesitation he gingerly tested it with one foot and it held. Night was coming on and he must get across. With many fears and with care he crept out on his hands and knees, hoping to distribute his weight on the uncertain ice. When he had gone some distance painfully and slowly, he heard the sound of horse's hoofs and joyful singing. There in the dusk was a happy Negro driving a team of horses and a load of coal across the ice and happily singing as he went. He knew the ice was safe.

Christians do you know that you can rest the whole weight of your salvation on Christ? He has been tested by millions and the "ice will hold." Have you come to Him in faith? Then believe His promise, "Him that cometh unto me I will in no wise cast out." Praise Him, believer – and trust yourself fully to His promise.

"Trust in the Lord with all thine heart and lean not unto thine own understanding" (Prov. 3:5). —M.R.D.

Thou dost my soul restore, strengthened with might,
In paths of righteousness guiding aright!
E'en though death's darkling vale should bar my way,
Thou wilt my steps attend, my fears allay! — H.G.B.

"Today He knows 'why'; tomorrow so shall we! 'Be not afraid, only believe!' " — P. L. BERMAN

HARBOR LIGHT!

SUGGESTED SCRIPTURE READING: Revelation 7:15-17

So he bringeth them unto their desired haven.

Psalm 107:30

All of us are afloat upon the sea of life. If we seek to be the captain of our own fate, we shall experience shipwreck and go over the Niagara of death to our eternal doom. However, if Jesus is our Pilot, we may be sure that we will anchor after the storms are past in the "desired haven."

Those who have watched at the deathbeds of saints and sinners alike tell us that there is a marked difference between them. Some Christians who were conscious in their last few earthly moments have even been privileged to view the Celestial City and the angel escort sent to bear their soul to heaven. Among those so blessed were Dwight L. Moody, the great evangelist; Augustus M. Toplady, the hymn writer; Baudicon Oguier, when being burned at the stake in 1556, and hundreds of others.

Miss Frances Ridley Havergal, who wrote so many beautiful gospel songs, including "I Gave My Life For Thee," had such a glorious departure. After singing a song of victory and heaven, she looked up steadfastly as if she saw the Lord. Such a heavenly glory lit her face; such ecstasy shown from her eyes for a full ten minutes that her relatives were amazed. "We knew she was having an invisible meeting with her King, for her countenance was so glad, as if she had already talked to Him. Then she tried to sing again; but after one sweet, high note her voice failed, and as her brother commended her soul into the Redeemer's hand, she passed away."

Heaven is real; the angels are our friends; and Jesus loves us! Our departure for Home and Heaven is a sacred and treasured delight to our Saviour who earnestly desires that we shall come to dwell with Him and bask in His glory (John 17:24). In this blessed confidence of faith let us sail on without fear until we receive a joyous welcome in the homeland of the blessed! "Precious in the sight of the LORD is the death of his saints" (Ps. 116:15). —H.G.B.

Now in heaven's peaceful harbor
They have anchored from life's gale,
They are singing with the angels
Waiting till our barque shall sail! — G. Woods

"The Great Lighthouse sheds its beams most brightly upon the voyagers nearest the Celestial Harbor." — G.W.

TOO POOR TO PAY

SUGGESTED SCRIPTURE READING: Matthew 5:17-24

And when they had nothing to pay, he frankly forgave them both.   Luke 7:42

Two men were indebted to the same creditor, but were absolutely penniless and could not pay. One man owed 500 pence, while the other owed only 50 pence. One was in debt for ten times more than the other but it made no difference at all, for neither one had a penny to pay. If the one had owed 5000 pence instead of 500, it would have been no worse. If the other had owed only one pence instead of 50, it would not have made it any easier, for he had *nothing* to pay. This is the picture of every sinner. Some are guilty of more open, overt sins than others. Some people live fine, moral, ethical, religious lives but without Christ they are as surely lost as the most blatant sinner. As long as a man is "broke," it does not matter how much he owes, as far as payment is concerned.

There was a great difference in the amount these two men owed, but the Scripture says both "had nothing to pay." Their only hope was the mercy of the creditor. And both were equally forgiven, for "he frankly forgave them both." This is God's message to the sinner. No matter how moral, religious or cultured he may be, he cannot pay. No matter how low, wicked and filthy the sinner may be, God offers to forgive all, for the Son of God Himself assumed his debts.

There lived in a little village a doctor noted for his kindness and charity. After his death they found written across many of his accounts the notation: "Forgiven — too poor to pay." The widow objected and sued the people for payment. But the judge asked, "Is this your husband's signature?" "Yes," she replied. "Then," said the judge, "there is not a court in the land who can order a collection of the accounts where the doctor has written 'Forgiven.'" Jesus offers to forgive and receipt your debt in full if you will but admit that you are "too poor to pay!"   —M.R.D.

Jesus paid it all, All to Him I owe;
Sin had left a crimson stain,
He washed it white as snow. — Mrs. H. Hall

"It is both impossible and insulting to try to pay for God's great GIFT of salvation with our own poor works." — G.W.

THE LIGHT IN A STABLE

SUGGESTED SCRIPTURE READING: John 12:35-46

I am come a light into the world, that whosoever believeth on me should not abide in darkness. John 12:46

For over 400 years the heavens had been sealed and no new revelation had come to brighten the landscape of man's sinful night. Then, suddenly, the silence is broken. The excellent glory is revealed, and Jesus Christ steps from the Ivory Palaces of eternity into the evil-smelling stable of this world. In self-sacrificing love He comes to shed His warming beams of grace into the cold hearts of men. You would think that the world would rejoice, and bask in the sunlight of the love of God, but instead they cling to the clammy darkness of their own depravity and the icy chill of death. With wicked hands they crucify the Prince of Life and seek to snuff out the Light of Heaven. No wonder we read: *"This is the condemnation,* that light is come into the world, and *men loved darkness rather than light,* because their deeds were evil"* (John 3:19).

Although others, such as John the Baptist (John 5:35a), were designated as luminaries, Christ was the only "True Light!" The Holy Spirit indicated this by using a word which in the original meant *"radiance"* when He spoke of our Lord, while He employed the word *"lamp"* or *"lantern"* when referring to those who were mere men. Jesus was Himself the *essence* of light, while the others were only *"light bearers";* they had no illumination of their own.

An artist once drew a picture of a dreary, wintry twilight. The trees were heavily laden with snow, and a dark house, lonely and desolate, stood bleakly in the midst of the storm. It was a sad picture. Then, with a quick stroke of yellow crayon, the artist put a light in one window. The effect was magical. The entire scene was transformed into a vision of comfort and cheer. The birth of Christ brought similar illumination to this dark world. Have you come to the Light? —H.G.B.

No darkness have we who in Jesus abide,
The Light of the world is Jesus;
We walk in the Light when we follow our Guide,
The Light of the world is Jesus. — P. P. Bliss

"The Light of Christ transforms the 'stable' of men's hearts into a 'temple' for the Holy Spirit." — G.W.

WORSHIP HIM

Suggested Scripture Reading: Luke 2:8-20

And they came with haste, and found Mary, and Joseph, and the babe lying in a manger. Luke 2:16

And when they were come into the house, they saw the young child with Mary his mother, and fell down, and worshipped him. Matthew 2:11

The first ones to arrive after the birth of our Saviour were the shepherds. They found Him in a manger. The magi came much later and discovered that the baby had grown to be a "young child" lodging now in a "house." The Jewish shepherds led the procession to the manger, for salvation is first to be offered to Israel. Later the Gentile wisemen arrive to also worship the newborn King. The order of these events is prophetic. Although Israel was first to receive the proffered blessings of salvation, their rejection of the Messiah resulted in the gift of grace being extended to all men. For Israel's fall was "the riches of the world, and the diminishing of them the riches of the Gentiles" (Rom. 11:12).

Another important fact to notice in the story of the nativity is that we have in these scenes no "MARIOLATRY" nor any adoration of "Saint Joseph." The attention of all is focused upon the Christchild, and we read, they *"Worshipped Him!"*

In Rembrandt's famous painting of the nativity all the light is made to fall upon the Babe in the manger. The other figures he shrouds in shadows. He seems to have had the spiritual discernment to realize that to concentrate upon Mary, Joseph, the wisemen, the gifts, or the shining star, is to miss the real import of the momentous scene of God "manifested in the flesh." This Baby who is born in Bethlehem is none other than the God-man, the Messiah, who left heaven to rescue fallen mankind; for Jesus came not just to be a great Teacher but to "save his people from their sins." With shepherds and wisemen then, let us worship and bow down, let us kneel before the Lord — our Maker, and our Redeemer!

—H.G.B.

You glorified a manger
When You chose it for Your own.
O, Saviour, come into my heart
And take it for Your own! — M. Martin

"Though Christ a thousand times in Bethlehem be born, it shall avail thee naught save He be born in thee."

ANSWER YOUR OWN PRAYERS

. . . ye ask amiss, that ye may consume it upon your lusts.
                                                          James 4:3

God does not answer all our prayers, but completely ignores many of them. Selfish prayers are not heard by God, and He will not do for us the things He expects us to do for ourselves. James gives a striking illustration of this. "If a brother or sister be naked, and destitute of daily food, And one of you say unto them, Depart in peace, be ye warmed and filled; notwithstanding ye give them not those things which are needful to the body; what doth it profit? Even so faith, if it hath not works, is dead, being alone" (James 2:15-17).

God expects us to do our part in accordance to His Word, and then we have a right to ask God to do that which we are unable to do ourselves. If you come upon a wounded man, it will do little good to kneel beside him and pray, unless you also provide whatever "first aid" you are able to give. If a house is on fire, it will avail very little to pray for the people upstairs unless you set up the ladder for them to escape, and turn on the water from the faucet. Our prayers must be accompanied by works. It is useless to ask God to answer our prayers when we have the wherewithal to answer them ourselves.

A farmer whose barns were full of grain which he was holding for a rise in prices, was accustomed to pray for the poor and needy, and constantly repeated his petition, "Oh God, remember the poor and needy and supply their wants and needs." But he never offered them any help himself. He expected God to do it all. One day after hearing his father pray, his little son said to him, "Daddy, may I have half of your corn in the barns?" Astonished, the father replied, "Why my son, what would *you* do with all that corn?" The boy replied, "I would answer your prayers!"

—M.R.D.

I knelt to pray when day was done,
And prayed: "O Lord, bless everyone."
But — as I prayed, into my ear
There came a voice that whispered clear:
"Pause, hypocrite, before you pray:
Whom have you tried to bless today?
God's sweetest blessings always go
By hands that serve Him here below." — Anon.

"Prayer and consecrated effort belong together." — G.W.

GOD'S LAST PROMISE

SUGGESTED SCRIPTURE READING: I Peter 4:1-7

He which testifieth these things saith, Surely I come quickly. Amen. Revelation 22:20

This is God's last promise and our Lord's last message to His waiting Bride. It was the thing which was heaviest upon His heart as He closed the canon of Scripture. For 1900 years there has been no additional word from heaven.

If you knew you had only five minutes to live and spend with your family, what would *you* talk about? I am sure you would not spend those last few moments in idle talk about things of little consequence. You would seek to pack into those final moments the things which seemed most important and of greatest profit. You would carefully phrase the sentences which you would want remembered as your "last words."

Last words are precious words. They carry the most weight. So it must have been with Jesus. As He spoke this last promise by the Holy Spirit through John He knew it was His final message. And what was the message? "Surely I come quickly. Amen." Only five words, the number of grace, but they tell us five things. "Surely" speaks of the certainty of His coming. "I" speaks of the personality of His coming. "Come" tells us that it is not death (which is our going to Him) we are to look for, but His personal return. "Quickly" speaks of the time of His return. Since a thousand years are as one day with the Lord it is less than two days ago (in God's reckoning of time) since He left this promise. He will come quickly. And then the promise ends with 'Amen' — the response of every child of God to His last promise. If Jesus should come today would He find you ready with an "Amen — even, so, come Lord Jesus?" Precious promise! —M.R.D.

Our longing hearts His promise claim,
And, blest with hope, repeat His Name! — Anon.

"Every Divine promise is built upon four pillars: God's holiness, which will not suffer Him to deceive; His goodness, which will not suffer Him to forget; His truth, which will not suffer Him to change; and His power, which makes Him able to accomplish!" — SALTER

STONES FOR A CROWN

SUGGESTED SCRIPTURE READING: Isaiah 62:1-3

For they shall be as the stones of a crown!
Zechariah 9:16

It is a blessed thought that God's own are so extremely precious to Him that He guards them "as the apple of His eye" (Deut. 32:10) and considers them the future jewels of His eternal crown! The world affords the righteous no such gracious reception, but rather labels them "the filth . . . and offscouring of all things!" (I Cor. 4:13)

Jesus, however, has given in these words His eternal verdict of those who obtain a good report through faith: "they shall walk with Me in white: for they are *worthy!*" This worthiness of course is not in ourselves, but is due to what we have become by His grace! Let us beware then if all men speak well of us, for many who are first here, shall be last over there. We are beveled, shaped, and polished by the crude abrasive of trials in this world so that we will fit the better and shine the brighter in the Saviour's crown by and by!

Someone has compared us to poor little colorless drops of water, hanging weakly on the fragile blade of time. We are not beautiful at all in our unregenerated self. But look again after the "Sun of Righteousness" has arisen upon us. Behold, now we sparkle like a diamond! . . . A change in the winds of adversity and we glow like a ruby; . . . and presently when the Sun is more fully upon us . . . like a precious emerald! If we were to slip out of the sunshine we would be only dirty bits of water; but now, bright with His eternal brightness and grace, we are precious drops destined to be crystalized and fitted into the heavenly diadem.' . . . "And they shall be mine, saith the Lord of hosts, in that day when I make up my jewels!" (Mal. 3:17)   —H.G.B.

Thy Saviour is coming in tenderest love,
To make up His jewels and bear them above:
Oh, child, in thine anguish, despairing or dumb,
Remember the message, "Hold fast till I come"!
— E. W. Griswold

"The more we suffer for Christ here, the brighter we shall shine over there!"

THE HIGH PRIEST WHO "SAT DOWN"!

Suggested Scripture Reading: Hebrews 10:9-14

But this man, after He had offered one sacrifice for sin for ever, sat down on the right hand of God; From henceforth expecting till His enemies be made His footstool.
Hebrews 10:12, 13

The priest in the Tabernacle in the wilderness never sat down. When Moses gave instructions to Israel for the building of the Tabernacle in the wilderness he made provision for all of its utensils and furniture, but one thing was strikingly lacking. *There was not a chair* in the Tabernacle. There was an altar, a laver, a table, and a lamp, censers and an ark, and all its implements and tools, but *no place to sit down.* They were always on their feet. Now this lack of chairs was not an oversight, but one of the most significant and illuminating truths concerning the work of the Lord Jesus Christ in salvation. The work of the priest was never done. He could not sit down at any time. It was work, work, work, work, work, without ever being finished. When the Lord Jesus Christ, the *great* High Priest, came, He made but one offering, never to be repeated — and when it was completed He cried, "It is finished!" Because it was finished He arose from the grave and ascended into heaven and *sat down* — the first priest who could *sit down!* That, my friend, is the meaning of the words "It is finished," as explained by Hebrews 10:11-14. —M.R.D.

Once my hands were always trying,
Trying hard to do my best;
Now my heart is sweetly trusting,
And my soul is all at rest!
Once my life was full of effort,
Now 'tis full of joy and zest;
Since I took His yoke upon me
Jesus gives to me His rest!
— A. B. Simpson

"If you cannot come to Christ WITH faith and repentance, come to Christ FOR faith and repentance, for He can give them to you!"

LIGHT IN THE FATHER'S HOUSE!

Suggested Scripture Reading: I Corinthians 15:51-58

And there shall be no night there; and they need no candle, neither light of the sun; for the Lord God giveth them light: and they shall reign for ever and ever.

Revelation 22:5

"And there shall be no night there"! What a glorious promise! It assures us that earth's shadows will not always last, that there is a terminus to our pilgrimage which is as bright as it is beautiful! In that land of unending day we shall neither need nor desire the rest and anesthesia of sleep. Nothing shall weary us, nothing shall tax our boundless energy! Someone has said: "Night is nature's growing time," and that is true. Here in this unhealthy state of imperfection we need the sorrows of affliction and the darkness of trouble to make us develop; but not in heaven! There the natural man will have been done away for ever, for from the ugly chrysalis of death we shall have emerged with glorious, spiritual bodies — complete in Him!

Here night blinds our eyes and erases color; there with perfect sight we shall see and know "even as we are known." The tapestry of God's perfect providence will be unrolled before our enraptured gaze, and we shall recognize in His leading all the prismatic colors of His unmatched love and unplumbed wisdom. After the fearful night of sin will come God's morning! After the drab existence of earth, the rainbow glory of His presence! After all the trouble and darkness of this fleeting, turbulent state, the joyous tranquillity of heaven and the beatific vision!

What is the source of all this light and blessing? None other than the Person of our lovely Lord! As we anticipate with eager longing the fulfillment of His promise, our eyes shine with tears of gratitude. With swelling hearts we would sing with fresh ardor: "Jesus is the Light in my Father's House; There is joy, . . . joy, . . . Joy"!

—H.G.B.

There is a land of pure delight,
Where saints immortal reign;
Eternal day excludes the night,
And pleasures banish pain! — Isaac Watts

"Light after darkness, gain after loss; strength after weakness, crown after cross!" — F. HAVERGAL

THE IRREVOCABLE PAST

Suggested Scripture Reading: I John 1

Ye shall henceforth return no more that way. Deut. 17:16

These words are part of the instructions to Israel by Moses their emancipator. They had been led out of Egypt by a strong arm, and Moses warns them they shall never return again that way. Leaving the primary interpretation and its warning to Israel never again to seek help from Egypt, we want to make a seasonable application. This is the last day of the year. It is a solemn day of reflection. The things which lie behind are irrevocable. They are a matter of record. And we seem to hear God say to us, "Ye shall henceforth return no more that way." As we look back over this past year it is with mingled emotions. There is joy and also sorrow. There is assurance, but also regrets. There is rejoicing and praise as we contemplate God's long-suffering, patience, and faithfulness in bringing us this far; but there is also shame for our failures. Our mistakes and sins make us hang our heads in repentance and shame, knowing we cannot undo the wrongs of yesterday, "for we shall henceforth return no more that way." The book of the year is closed and sealed and we cannot go back.

What shall we do? There is only one thing to do. Confess our sins and failures and receive His full cleansing and forgiveness before the year closes (I John 1:9). Our blessed Lord has made provision for just such a time as this.

O Lord, we confess we have so often failed. We repent of our sins, and now accept Thy forgiveness according to the promise, "If we confess our sins, He is faithful and just to forgive us our sins, and to cleanse us from all unrighteousness." Read Proverbs 28:13, 14. —M.R.D.

Yesterday He helped me,
Today I'll praise His name.
Because I know tomorrow,
He'll help me just the same! — Anon.

"Life is a one way street! Live in the consciousness that you shall not pass this way again!"

TOPICAL INDEX

TOPICAL INDEX

TOPICAL INDEX

SCRIPTURAL INDEX